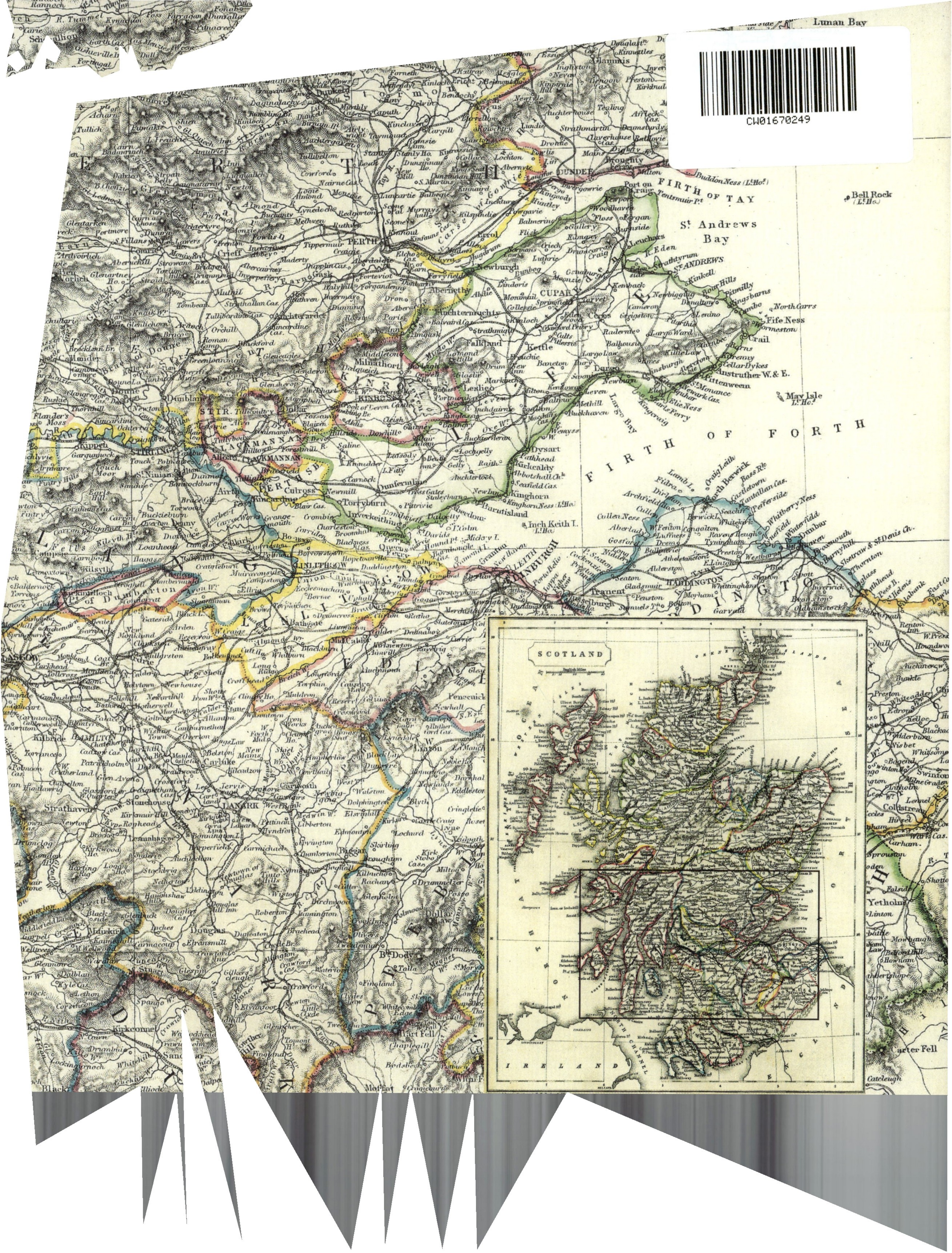
Lunan Bay
FIRTH OF TAY
Bell Rock (Lt. Ho.)
St. Andrews Bay
ST. ANDREWS
PERTH
DUNDEE
CUPAR
North Carrs
Fife Ness
Crail
May Isle (Lt. Ho.)
FIRTH OF FORTH
Inch Keith I. (Lt. Ho.)
LEITH
EDINBURGH
HADDINGTON
Dunbar
STIRLING
LINLITHGOW
LANARK
Glasgow
Kinghorn
Dunfermline
Kirkcaldy
Tweedsmuir
Hart Fell
Carter Fell
Yetholm
Moffat
SCOTLAND
IRELAND

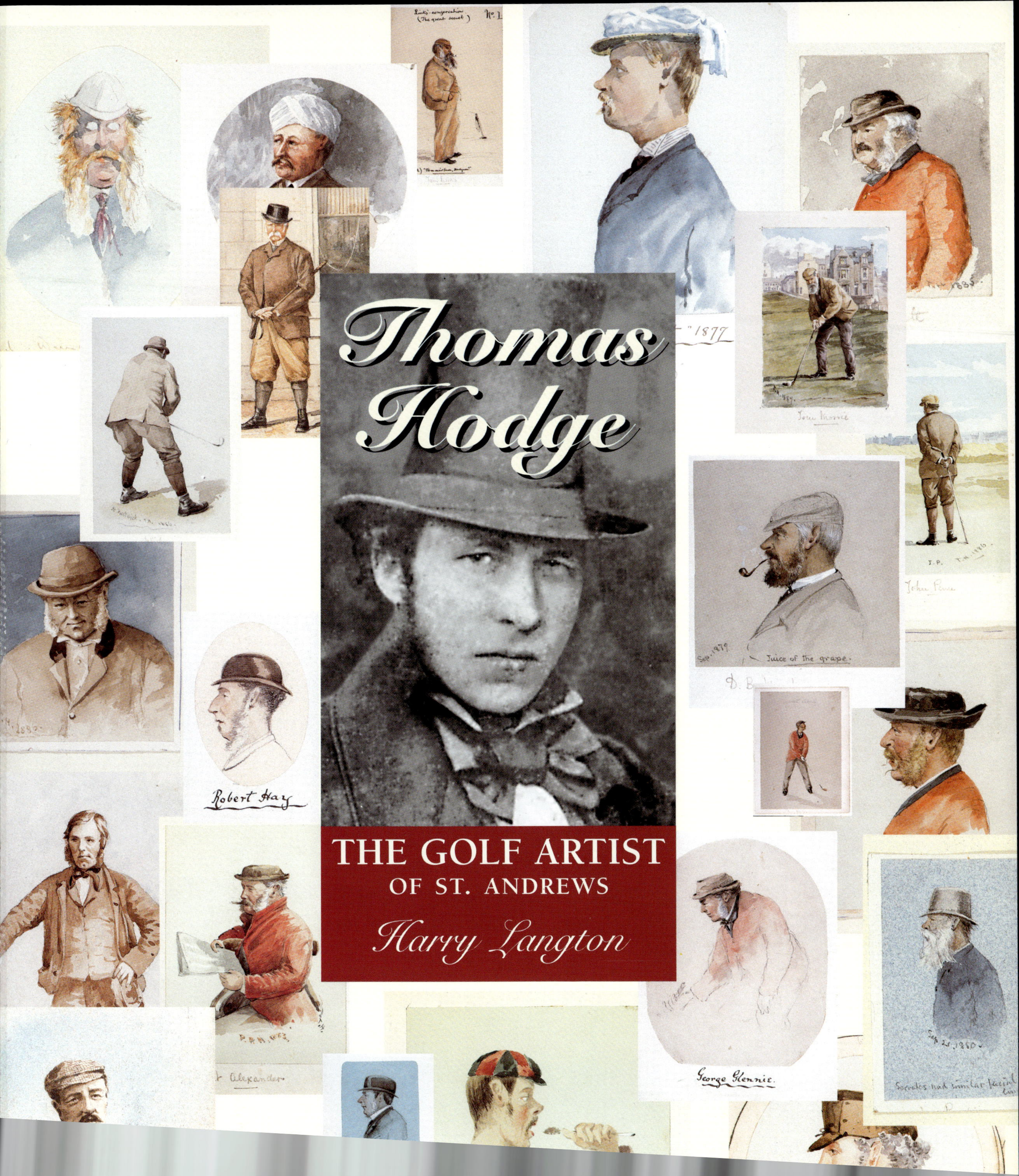

Thomas Hodge

THE GOLF ARTIST
OF ST. ANDREWS

Harry Langton

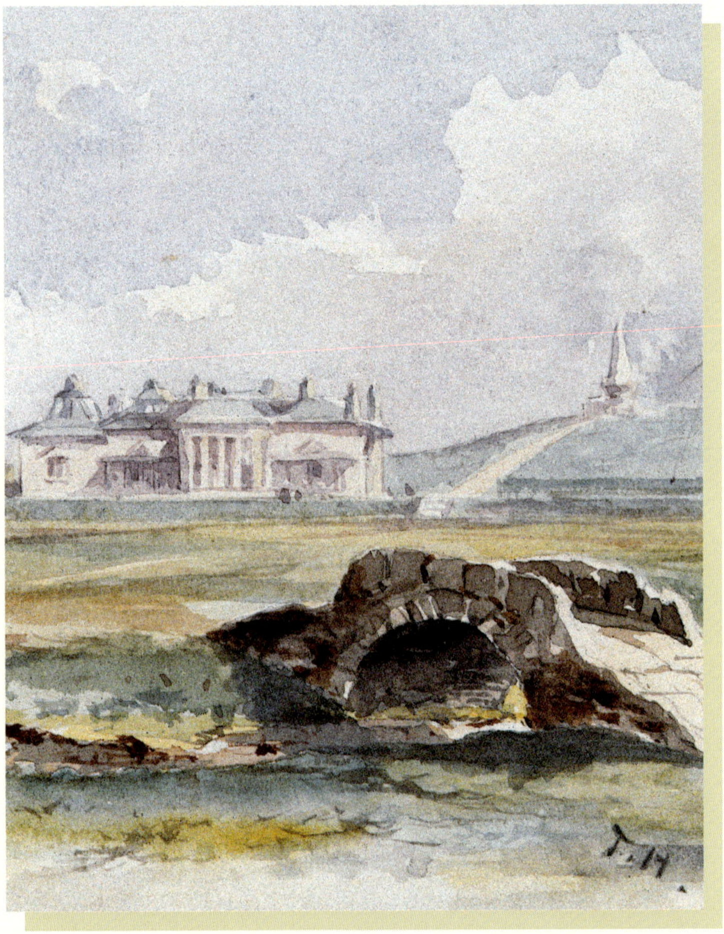

For Ann

Thomas Hodge, The Golf Artist of St. Andrews

THANKS

Thanks are not merely due, but gratefully proffered, sometimes I regret to say posthumously, to: Chad Sansean and Trevor Quartermaine, without whose sharp eyes and quick action Hodge's story might still be buried; Miss Norah Sheward; Sir Michael Bonallack; the Royal & Ancient Golf Club; Robert N. Smart, University of St. Andrews picture library; Mathew Jarron, St. Andrews Preservation Society Museum; Morton Olman of Old Golf, U.S.A.; British Library staff at Colindale; H. L. Douch, Royal Institution of Cornwall; Ben and Matthew Weinreb, Peter Crabtree, Robbie Burnett, Hilary Kay of Sotheby's for the first Hodge exhibition in the 1980s, and countless other charmers of the antique world who have "stood" fearlessly in fields and palaces and never felt the pain.

Special thanks to Elizabeth, Caroline, Hannah, Alex and Sam.

First Published in the United Kingdom in 2000 by
Sports Design International
London N6 6JD

Designed and produced for Sports Design International by
Open Door Limited
80 High Street, Colsterworth,
Lincolnshire NG33 5JA

Design and production: Open Door Limited
Production Director: Robin Burgess
Design Director: Rachel Rush
Editor: Mary Morton
Colour separation: G.A. Graphics Limited, Stamford
Printed and bound in Italy by L.E.G.O.

British Library Cataloguing-in-publication Data.
A catalogue record for this book is available from the British Library

Title: THOMAS HODGE, The Golf Artist of St. Andrews

ISBN: 0-9538556-0-0

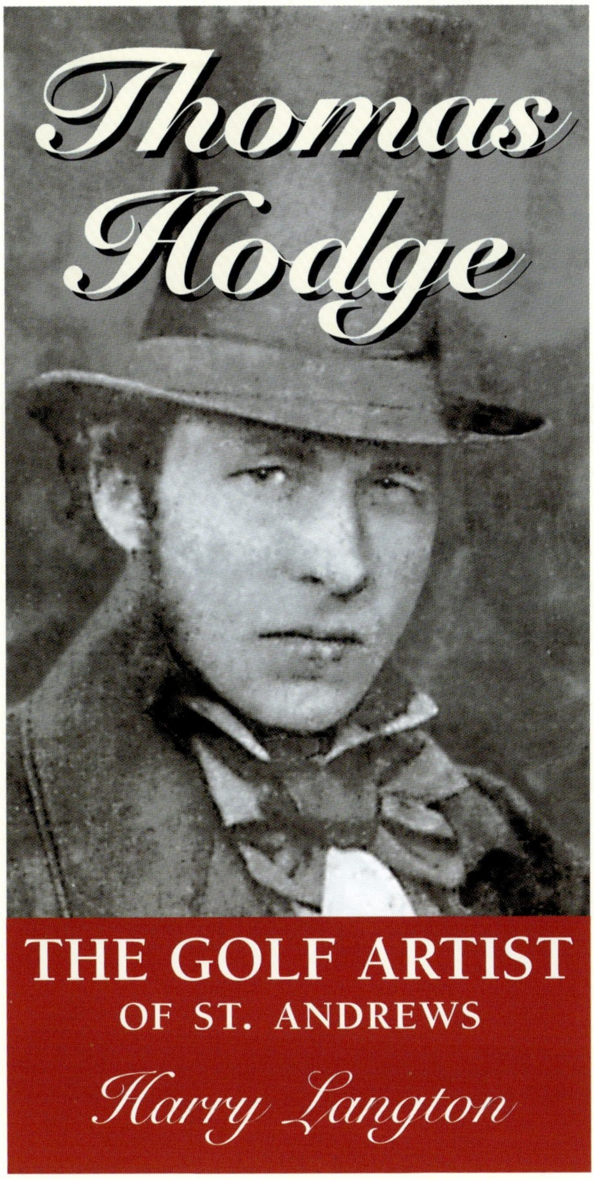

THE GOLF ARTIST
OF ST. ANDREWS

Harry Langton

SD
SPORTS DESIGN
INTERNATIONAL

For a period of 13 years my desk in my office, as Secretary of the Royal & Ancient Golf Club, faced a now disused fireplace, above which hangs a beautiful and colourful water painting of the 1862 Autumn Meeting of the club. The club house is smaller than today but, otherwise, apart from the dress styles of the numerous men and women portrayed, one would immediately recognise the scene, should one have happened to have been here in September of this year. The artist who captured this nostalgic picture was Thomas Hodge, a member of the R&A, who was to record for posterity, through a wonderful collection of small sketches and paintings, the well known St. Andrian characters of the day, including many of his fellow members.

Thanks to the generosity of his granddaughter, Miss Norah Sheward, almost 200 of these paintings are now back in St. Andrews. The dining room in the club, in particular, has benefited from this gesture, as the walls are hung with portraits of ghosts from the past, to remind us that the spirit of the club, St. Andrews and golf is very much the same today as it was 100 years ago, when Thomas Hodge so painstakingly used his artistic skills to such good effect.

Until now he has been something of a mystery man, and for that reason I look forward to finding out more about this gifted artist whose talent has only recently been recognised. However, one thing is certain: his paintings will continue to give pleasure to, and be appreciated by, generations to come. We should all be thankful for men like Thomas Hodge.

MICHAEL BONALLACK
Captain
Royal & Ancient Golf Club

September 1999

Contents

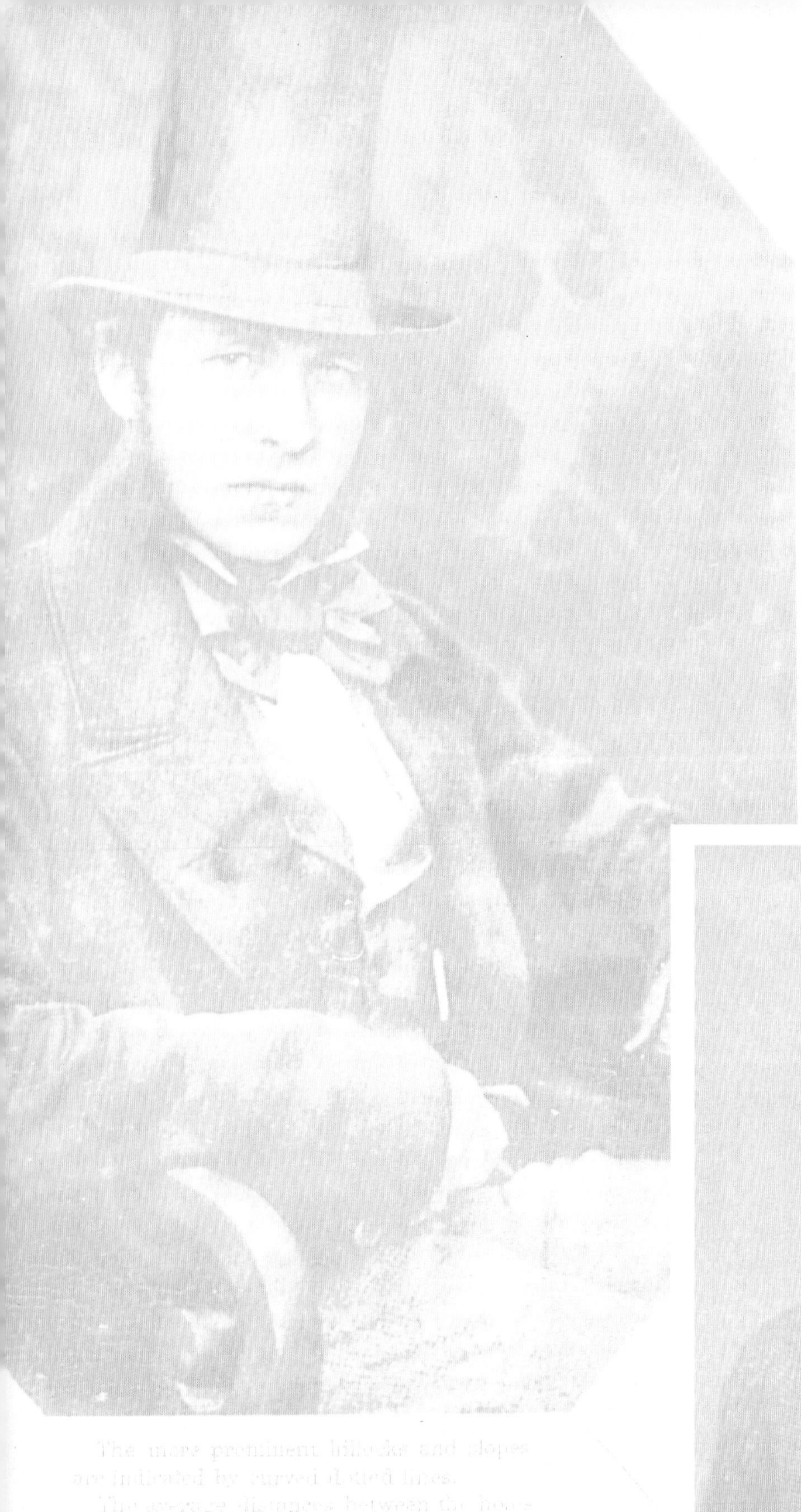

The more prominent hillocks and slopes are indicated by curved dotted lines.

The average distances between the holes are as follows:—

		Yds.
From	Home Hole to Burn Hole . . .	390
,,	Burn Hole to Dyke Hole . . .	430
,,	Dyke Hole to Third Hole . . .	288
,,	Third Hole to Gingerbeer Hole	375
,,	Gingerbeer Hole to Hole o' Cross	470
,,	Hole o' Cross to Heathery Hole	432
,,	Heathery Hole to High Hole .	340
,,	High Hole to Short Hole . .	155

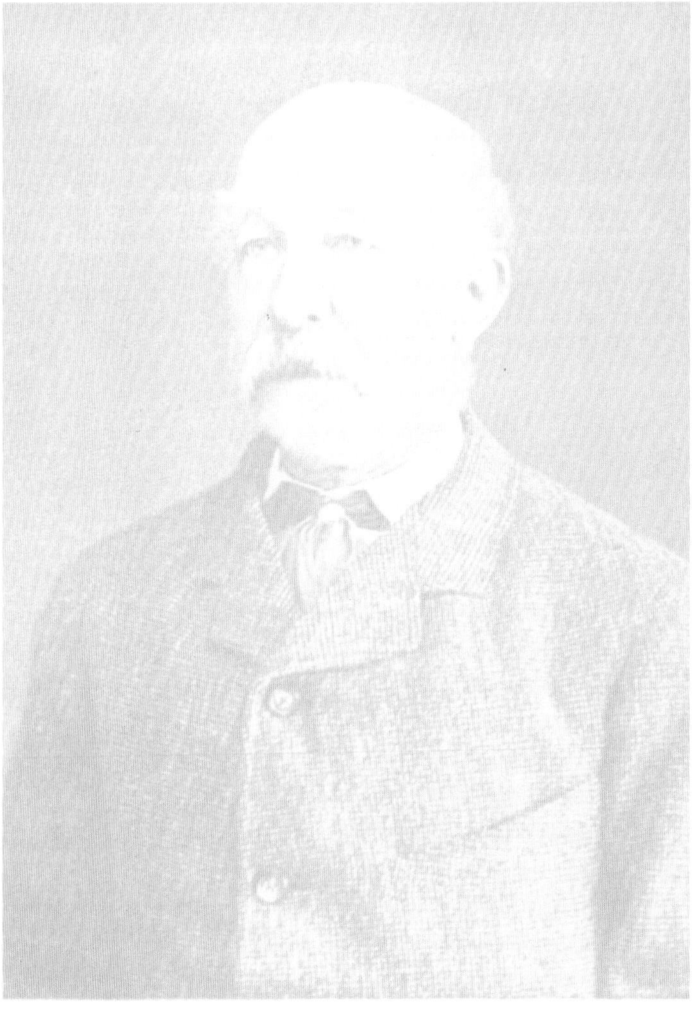

Hello Mr. Hodge

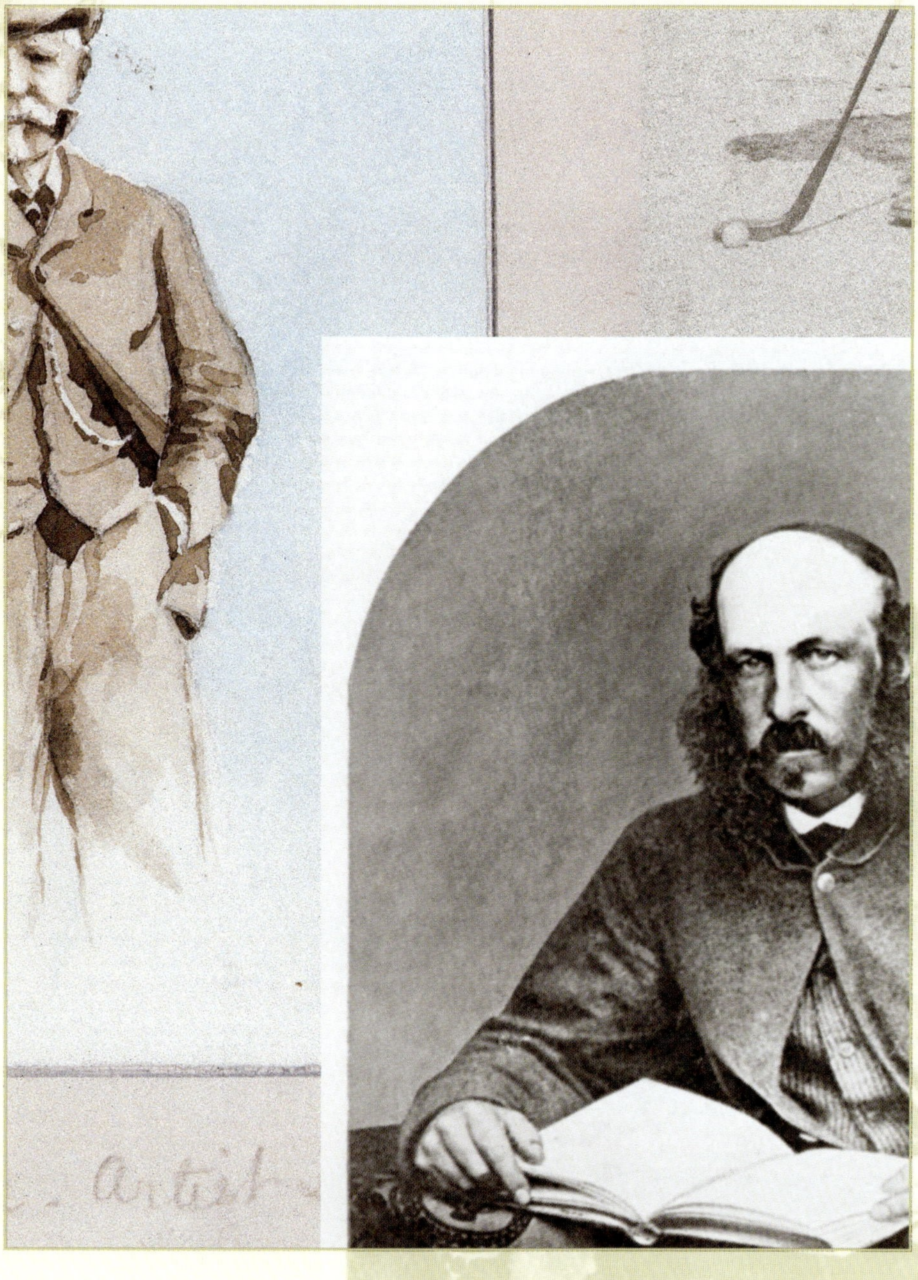

Hello Mr. Hodge!

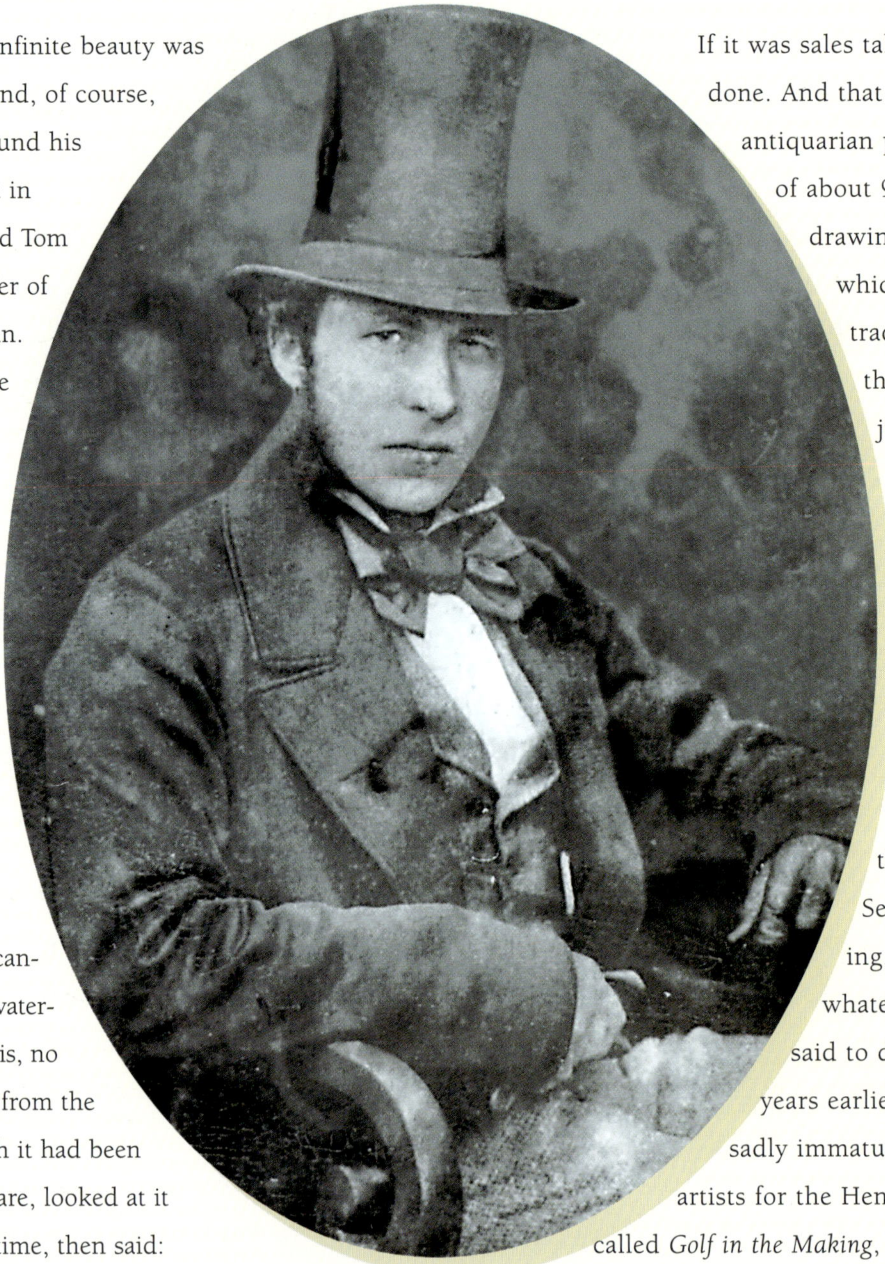

A black cherub of infinite beauty was dancing naked, and, of course, totally unashamed, around his parents' tiny apartment in North London when Old Tom Morris, the noblest golfer of them all, was brought in. No doubt Thomas Hodge would have managed a dry chuckle at the improbable scene.

The baby's father, a dealer in antiquarian books and prints who was locked, barred and chained into his premises to protect his family and his goods against the local thugs and thieves, was quite candid. He took the little watercolour of Old Tom Morris, no bigger than a postcard, from the acid-free tissue in which it had been sheltered while in his care, looked at it intently for some little time, then said:

There is something very unusual about this. I feel it though knowing nothing about the man or the game he is playing. Reluctantly I will sell it to you even though I don't even know who the artist is. I think something good will come from this transaction.

If it was sales talk, it was disarmingly done. And that was how an African antiquarian parted with the last of about 90 watercolours and drawings by Thomas Hodge which he and other small traders had bought at the Camden Lock junk-to-antiques market, also in North London, a few months earlier in 1983. By immense good fortune, one of these cheerful punter-gamblers had alerted me to the sale of the hoard. Serendipity was smiling, or striking, or whatever happy chance is said to do, because only two years earlier when compiling a sadly immature listing of golf artists for the Henderson-Stirk tome called *Golf in the Making*, I had suggested Thomas Hodge as a key, but shadowy, figure in the game's artistic history.

Above: Hodge in the 1850s, complete with dogskin gloves.

Right: Hodge in his early 40s.

Where the newly discovered pictures had surfaced from in 1983 remains a puzzle, but possibly from the collection of a famous 19th-century amateur golfer called Gilbert Mitchell-Innes, a friend of Thomas Hodge. Yet again, though no-one knew it at the time, Camden Lock market is only two miles from Hodge's last London home in Quex Road just off Kilburn High Road.

Hodge was completely unknown to the sporting art world in 1983. The Camden Lock collection, then housed in a battered red album, had been shown by the dealer into whose hands it had somehow drifted to a famous London auction house. They had rejected it totally as of hardly any interest or value. Incensed, the dealer split the album up and began to sell its pages individually to all comers from his small boutique in the crumbling railway warehouse on the edge of the Grand Union Canal.

When these pages were mostly back together again later that year, after many weeks of chasing round England pursuing examples which sometimes had been sold three or four times in as many days, it became a certainty that here was a remarkable archive of immense importance to the story of golf.

As a direct result of the publicity generated by the sale of this 'Camden Lock' material at Sotheby's in 1985, an even more extensive group of paintings, drawings and photographs was donated to the Royal & Ancient Golf Club at St. Andrews by Hodge's only grandchild, Miss Norah Sheward. Together, about 200 pictures of all kinds now illuminate the story of golf's development in the 19th century, for some people the golden age of the game and certainly the era when it expanded from a minor pastime into a worldwide wonder.

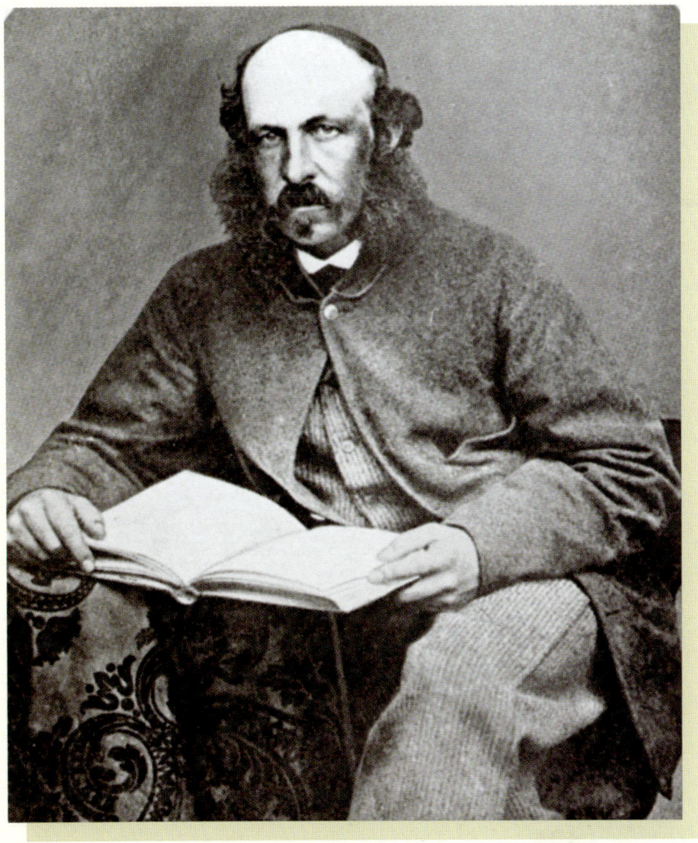

Many of Hodge's works are tiny portraits or caricatures of members of the Royal & Ancient over a period of 40 years when Hodge lived in St. Andrews. These are golf's legendary early characters, and they are shown warts and all.

Events both dramatic and woeful come to life in Mr. Hodge's visual diary of the golfing times. All this is a belated gift from a man who became known during his lifetime, and in what was then an esoteric exercise, as "The Golf Artist of St. Andrews". With understandable enthusiasm over Mr Hodge's rediscovery, he was billed as "Artist to the Royal & Ancient Golf Club" by the R & A when an exhibition of some of the pictures given by his granddaughter was staged by them at the University of St. Andrews art gallery in April 1986.

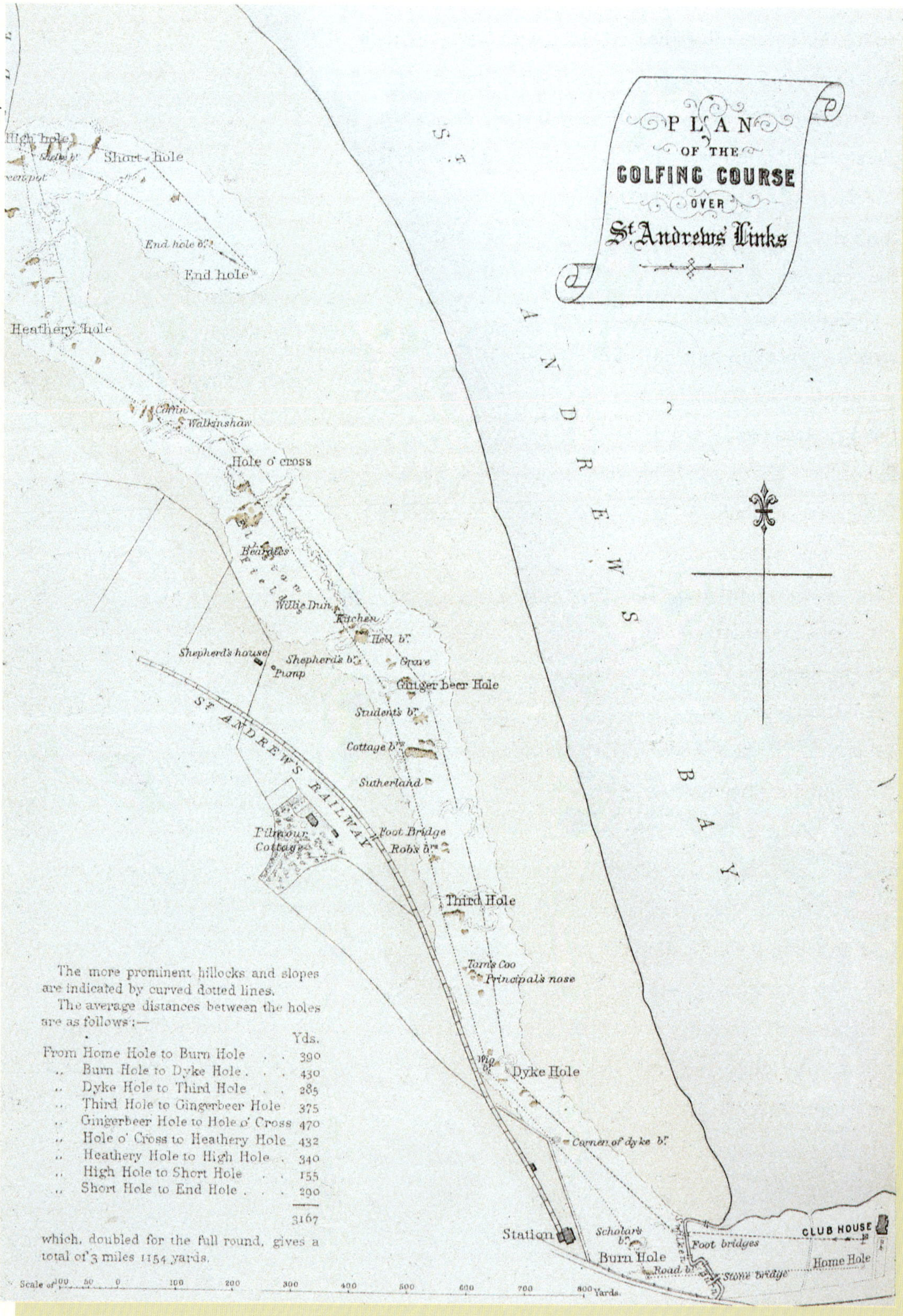

Such a grand title was never sought by or given to Hodge in his lifetime of amateur limning for his own and his friends' pleasure. That the friends and acquaintances he sketched with pen and brush were also lions of golf is the game's present good fortune.

The story of how Hodge, a penniless Cornish schoolmaster, bumped into the home of golf, is told in the following pages. It may aid an understanding of the era of the game he illustrated, from about 1855 to the 1890s, by placing the period in statistical context.

In the late 1850s, roughly matching Hodge's early days at St. Andrews, there were no more than 18 golf clubs in Britain, which in those distant days meant practically the sum for the entire world.

By 1866, this British total had doubled and by the

1880s there were more than 60 clubs with a total membership of about 5,000 players, some of whom belonged to several clubs. By 1890, when Hodge helped illustrate the classic "Golf" volume of the famous series of books called *The Badminton Library*, over 300 more clubs had been formed in Britain. This total soared to 2,330 by the end of the century.

Organised golf took off in the 1890s in the U.S.A., largely influenced by Charles B. Macdonald, who learned the game while a student at St. Andrews University from the age of 16. As he lived with his St. Andrews grandfather from about 1872, he must have known Thomas Hodge and his family. Macdonald also knew "Young Tom" Morris briefly before this peerless champion son of "Old Tom" died on Christmas Day 1875 aged 24.

In Canada, other Scottish exiles formed clubs: Montreal (1873), Quebec (1874), Toronto (1876) and Niagara (1882). Thomas Hodge's sons, Thomas Kenwyn and Donald "Dod", also played golf in North America, where "Dod" died a citizen of the U.S.A.

Many of the golfers Hodge painted as young men lived to take the game powerfully into the 20th century. John Ball and Horace Hutchinson, brilliant amateur golfers, and, in Hutchinson's case, a prolific writer on sport, are only two examples. Another was that ear-blistering custodian of the St. Andrews links, Andra' (Andrew) Kirkaldy, painted by Hodge as a boy caddie and much later as a successful professional.

Left: a plan, said to be by Hodge, of the links at St. Andrews, as it was in 1879.

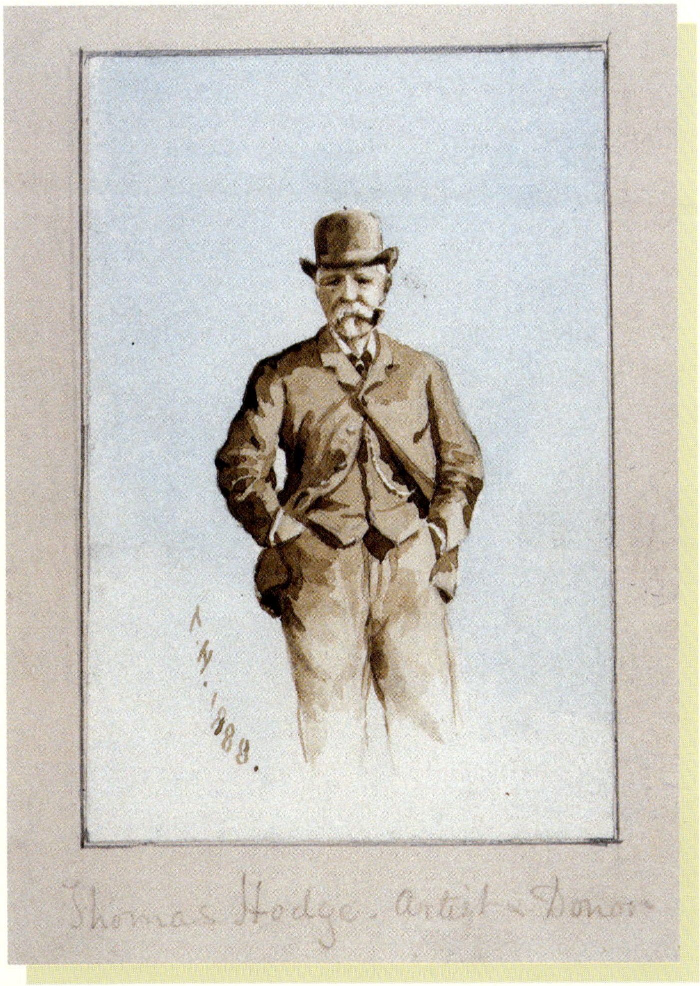

Above: a self-portrait of Hodge found at Camden Lock in 1983.

Unearthing the life story of Thomas Hodge was a frustrating business for a long time. Frequently it seemed as if it were deliberately buried with him. Even finding his grave, a humble and timeworn memorial in a North London cemetery a mile or so from his last home, somehow became infuriatingly difficult. In the end it proved scarcely more than walking distance from our own London house. I like to consider that as just one more of Thomas Hodge's sardonic little jests.

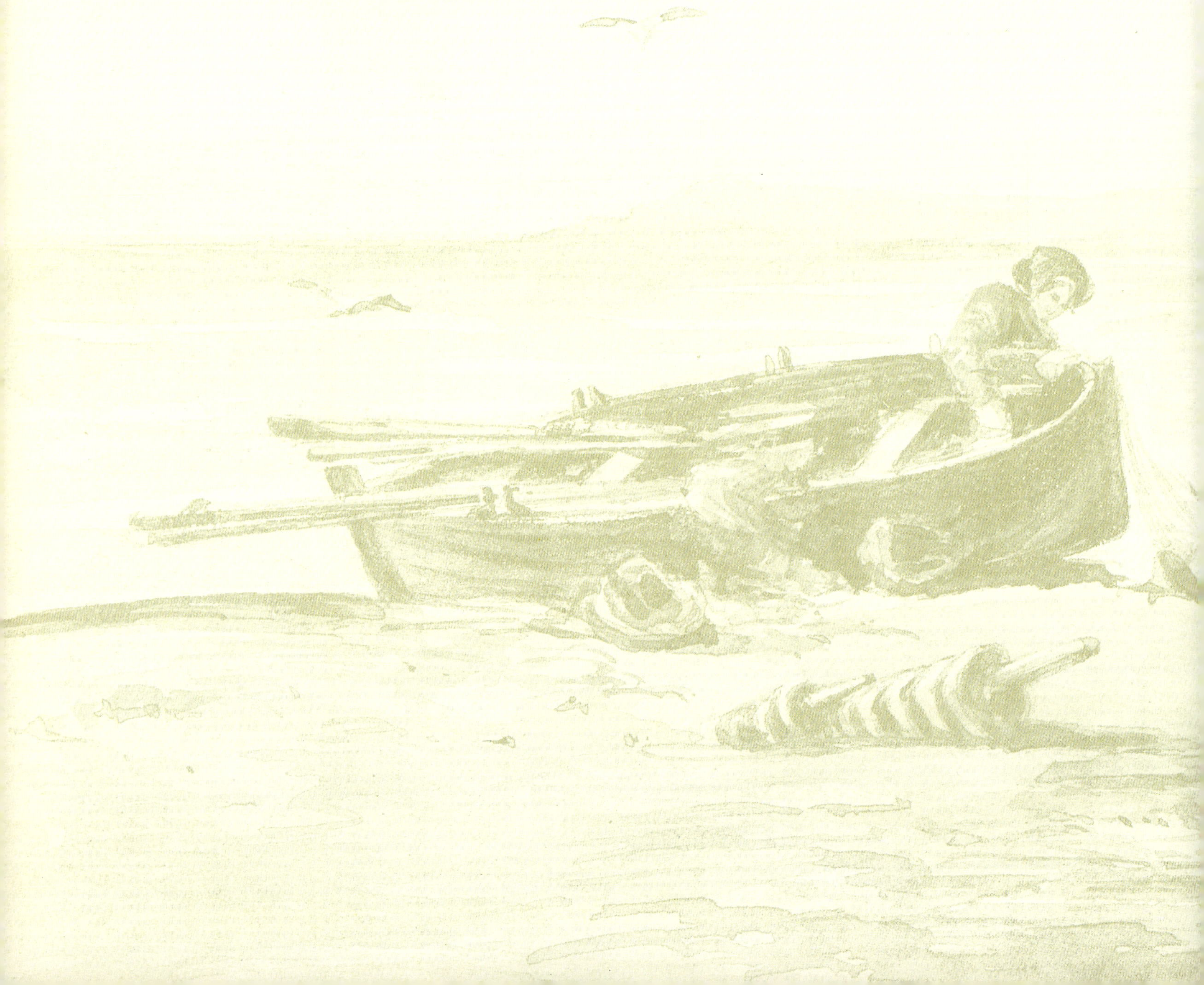

Life at St. Andrews

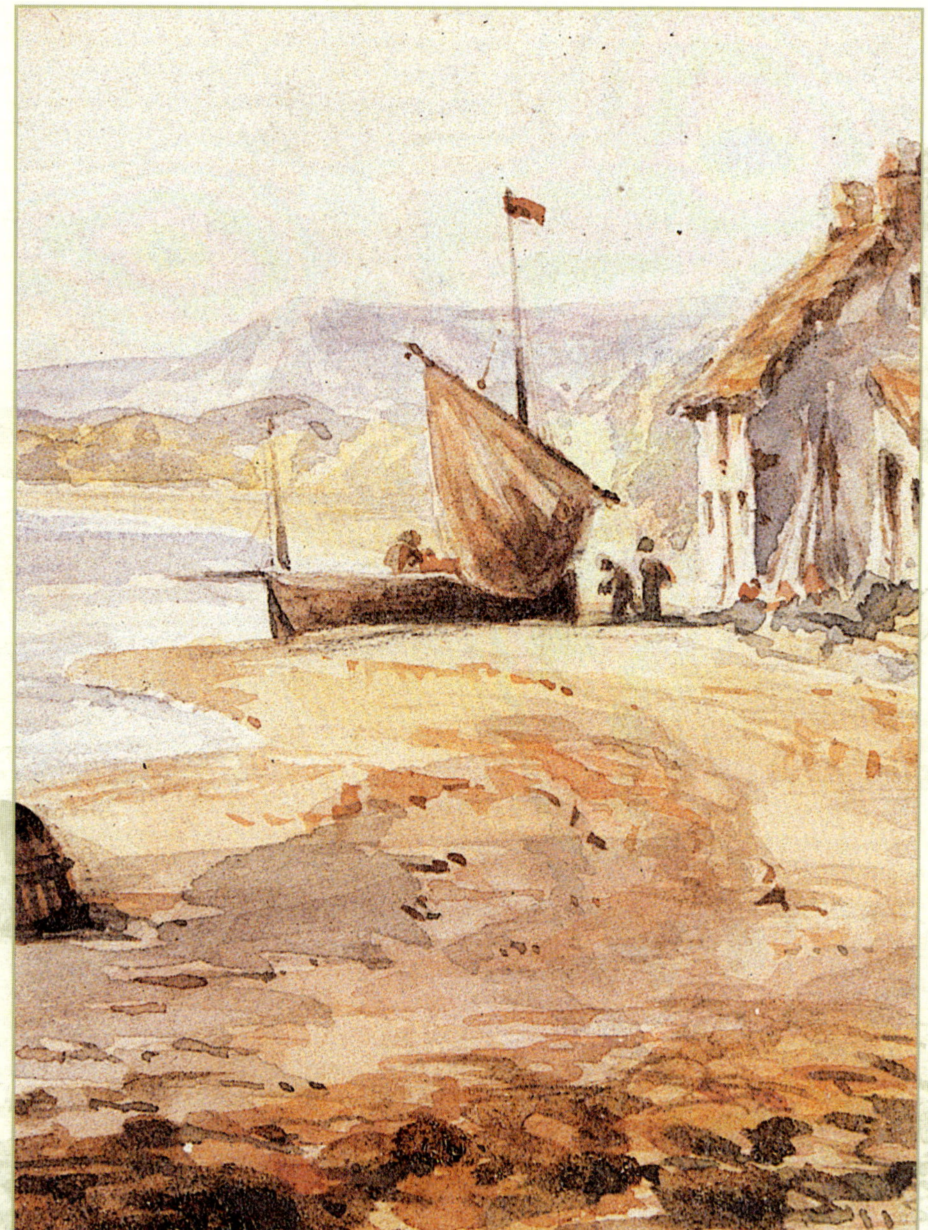

Life at St. Andrews

Golfer, stand humbly and gratefully on the rising ground behind the Royal & Ancient Golf Club at St. Andrews, Kingdom of Fife, Scotland! Pay homage in whatever way suits you, but pay it generously, to the birthplace of the links game.

Behind you, masked from view by stone-faced hotels and university buildings, are the jagged ruins of this ancient city. Their hidden presence can be felt with the suspicion of a shiver if you are of a highly sensitive nature and have glanced at the ancient histories of the place.

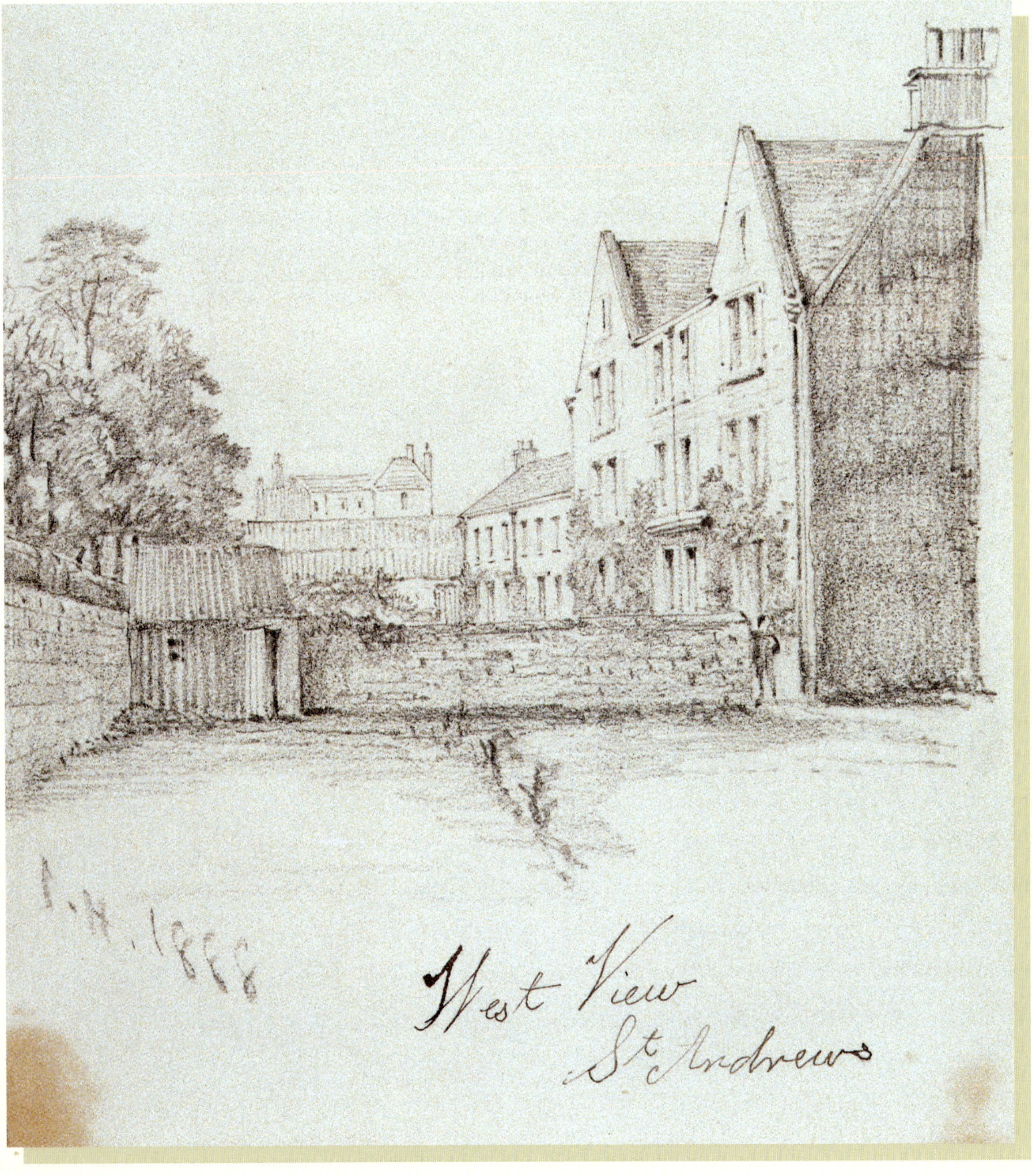

Nearby is the club house, a living, breathing antique which outshines the adjoining block containing a newish golf museum. Next to them is a stark monument to martyrs which was erected in the middle of the 19th century as a long-overdue apology to a group of people burned alive on St. Andrews‘ streets when religious fiends ruled there in an era unsurpassed for grisly horror anywhere.

Austere beauty must be acknowledged in the long, thin lines of surf rolling constantly to the beach alongside the links. That very cradle of modern golf stretches into a distance fringed by low hills and Tentsmuir Forest, where the spirits of golfers centuries dead are said to gambol, happy spectres at their play.

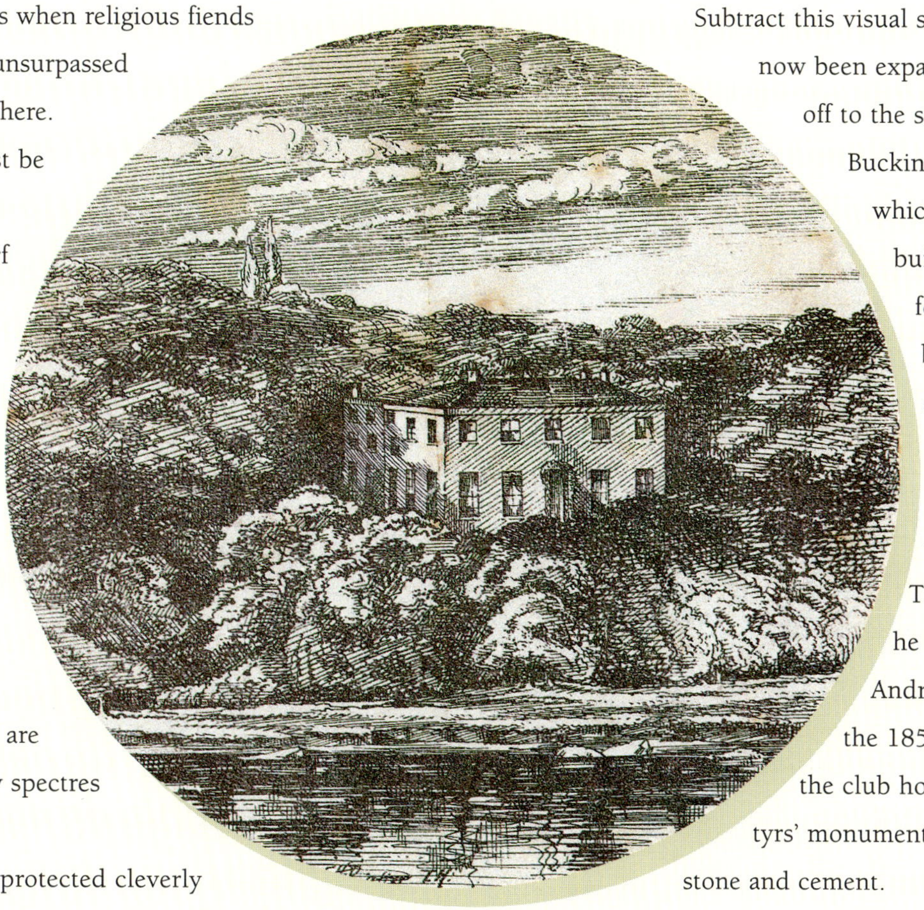

These fragile acres, protected cleverly from the eroding North Sea over a century ago by stone-filled sunken boats, should be inviolable terrain for the world's golfing millions and for Scotland.

The presence of a vast modern hotel, which had the profile of an abandoned battleship when it was opened by Princess Anne in 1983, at the hub of this sacred panorama is nowadays accepted as just one more example of St. Andrews' incurable eccentricity.

To old conservationists it still remains quite unbelievable, but this monumental incursion has happened and the Scots live with it and make a virtue of it. Well they might, as in the 1990s the hotel had countless thousands of paying guests from all round the globe every year.

Subtract this visual stunner, which has now been expanded and rounded off to the size and majesty of Buckingham Palace (and which serves the best buffet lunch in Europe for affordable bawbees, it must be allowed), and the view would be more or less that which greeted Thomas Hodge when he first arrived at St. Andrews. This was in the 1850s, a time when the club house and the martyrs' monument were fresh-cut stone and cement.

Above: An etching signed "F. H. after T.H." of the Hodge family home at Truro, Cornwall, in the 1840s before the financial crash. F. H. was almost certainly Hodge's sister Sarah Frances, or "Fan".

Left: Hodge's drawing of his school and attached houses at West View, St. Andrews in 1888.

The university city's sound level then would have been less oppressive, lacking the whine of jet aircraft landing and taking off just a couple of miles ahead and the buzz of motor traffic. A far cry from the days when old golfers used to complain about the noise the larks made overhead when they were putting. There were also smells from rotten sewers to put them off their stroke.

It is tempting to imagine that Thomas Hodge's first sketch of a golfer, then the rarest breed of sportsman in the world, only a few hundred strong, could have been from this viewpoint when he first idled away an hour there in the early years of Queen Victoria's reign.

Did he become curious about that poor fellow leaning on his stick and glaring at the ground, his fixed posture suggesting a sudden stab of back pain? Or did Hodge know already that this was one attitude of the golfer golfing? (It is more than possible that he had glimpsed golfers in action at Blackheath in England when he was an army officer cadet at nearby Woolwich)

He was immediately attracted to the game, but hardly ready to play it seriously. His absolute priority and long-term duty in life was to make his new school prosper in a strange little community which had, and still has, more ghost stories and semi-believers in the paranormal than the followers of television's wildest fantasies. The ugly phantom of poverty was the only wraith Hodge feared.

Thomas was born the fourth and youngest son of Joseph A. Hodge, near Truro in Cornwall in 1827. He was gifted. His talent included a nimble mind and an unusually powerful physique, athletic though strongly set; a formidable middleweight.

His hands and thick wrists spoke of this power, almost matching those of the legendary long-hitter of early 19th-century golf, whose portrait hangs in the Royal & Ancient Golf Club, the French university professor, Samuel Messieux. With big hands and monumental calf muscles. Thomas joked in letters to his five sisters about his "ugly" appearance. His blunt fingers were the kind that sometimes play musical instruments with delicacy. In his case, the unexpected deftness was reserved for paintbrush and pencil.

Hodge's most notable feature was his eyes, possibly green like those of his granddaughter, Norah Sheward, who looks much like him facially, the hooded top lids curving downwards strongly. Their keenness enabled him to draw acutely observed miniature portraits, the best of them almost as if done with the aid of a magnifying glass. The famous eyesight was also responsible for much of his easy success at any sport he cared to take up.

In his youth he became a fine cricketer, a formidable sprinter, and an accomplished boxer and wrestler in the Cornish and West Country traditions. Later he was equally good as a racquets player, as a swordsman and one of the best rifle shots in Britain. In the gentlemen's clubs, impregnable sanctuaries of the Victorian male ego, he proved almost unbeatable at billiards.

His prospering banker father adopted a fairly obvious course and aimed son Thomas towards a career as a military officer in a country which had at least ten young gentlemen pursuing each suitable salaried vacancy. So many manly skills surely must have earned this prodigy a glittering army record. However, the prospect of patrolling the Empire for a lifetime was to vanish overnight.

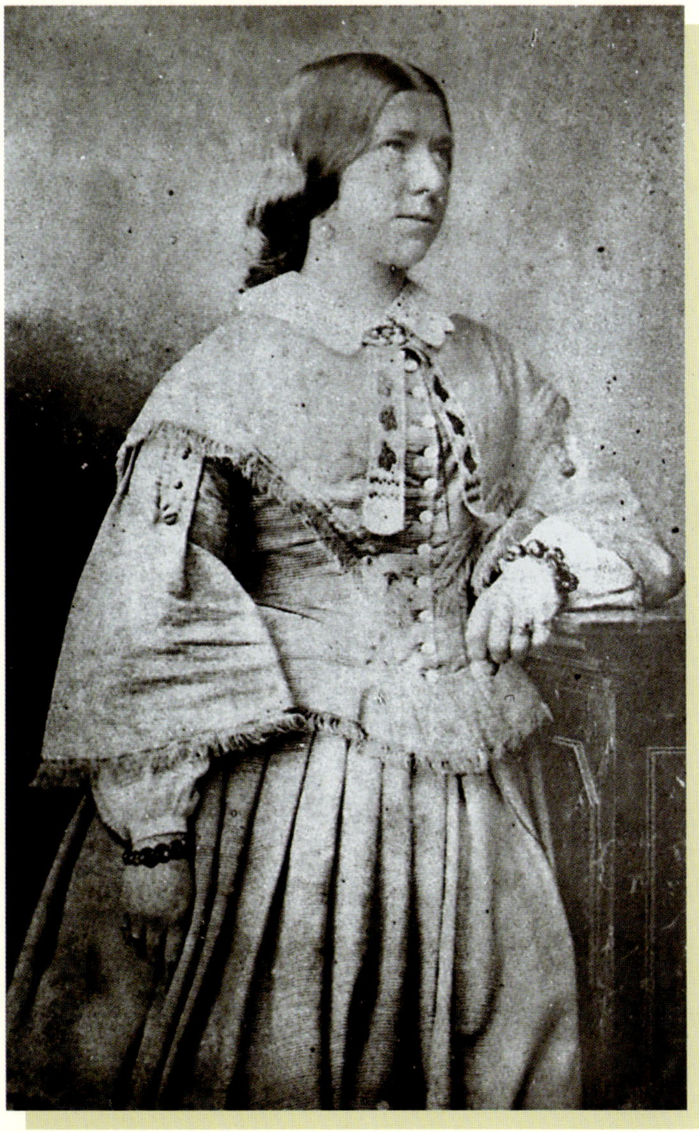

Above: Sarah Frances "Fan" Hodge, one of the sisters who gave immense help in creating her brother's school at St. Andrews. Their plain appearance was a disadvantage in the Victorian marriage market. Thomas Hodge tried always to insinuate lightly that to value good looks highly was a superficial nonsense.

Young Hodge's character included a moody, romantic streak to conflict with his up-front Kiplingesque patriotism. Like his three brothers, he was ready to sing chauvinistic ballads until dawn after their Cornish cricket club dinners. Later, he would make long speeches to the other ranks as a part-time officer at Edinburgh Volunteer feasts, stuffed with ringing phrases about brotherhood and goodwill making men better soldiers.

If, during the first half of his 80 years, he became depressed and vindictive on rare occasions, the contradictory elements in his nature and the shock arrival of poverty when a boy could be blamed as well as his long bachelordom.

In his early maturity, Thomas Hodge may have looked rather like a dark descendant of Cornish sea pirates, whereas he was in fact simply a born observer of the passing scene with the artistic knack to record it. He may have played the warrior, but as far as is known never fired a shot in anger.

He also made himself into a diligent teacher, at first through dire necessity and later by inclination. His unquestioned asset called charm, all his friends spoke of it, offset his forbidding exterior.

Hodge's father Joseph was the son of a tin and copper miner whose mild success enabled him to live the desirable life of a country gentleman in Cornwall. As a man nearing 80, Thomas wrote to one of his sisters, May, from his home in London:

My earliest dawn of recollection goes as far as Trevarth. Grandfather Hodge lived there: a walled garden, fruit trees, box-edged flower beds, standard apple trees and so on. Aunts Betsy and Harriet. I was their pet. I was very small and stood between grandfather's knees, could scarcely see over them. He was old and kind, breeches, buckles and black tight stockings with all befitting a country gentleman.

This god-fearing haven (Thomas Hodge's maternal grandmother had been among John Wesley's first ardent supporters) was in Gesennap Parish, about eight miles from Truro.

Joseph Hodge, Thomas's father, wasn't as lucky as Grandfather Hodge. Joseph became manager of the Miners' Bank in Truro, where his partner Humphry Willyams was said to have ruined him through a deeply concealed financial scandal in 1846. Thomas Hodge's sister May wrote to her brother once when he was an elderly man:

Father lost his money in mining speculations of his partner, Mr Humphry Williams (sic). Father paid up with his own money rather than others should suffer loss.

Humphry Willyams, Truro born, was a dashing mining "adventurer" and speculator in the railway-building mania which gripped Britain in the mid-19th century. A man who expressed boldly radical political ideas, he was "magistrate, merchant and banker" as well. One who at first violently opposed Willyams was George Wilkinson Kneebone, publisher of the local newspaper, the *Royal Cornwall Gazette*. In 1849, Willyams was elected a Member of Parliament for Truro by a margin of 14 votes. Kneebone wrote that Willyams was a liar who used unscrupulous arts to win.

A clue to the disaster which ruined Joseph Hodge is that, in 1845, he and Willyams were on the committee of a proposed Cornwall and Devon Railway which never saw a rail laid nor a wheel turn. They were the bankers for what was only one of 23 ambitious schemes jostling for permission to open up the South West tip of England. When its ill-prepared plans based on "three million pounds capital" collapsed, there were claims that up to £30,000 of preliminary public subscriptions, then a huge sum, had gone adrift.

How Hodge had managed to pass three-quarters of his life without unravelling the story of the family's disaster says a great deal about the secrecy and the "shame" surrounding the crash. Apparently, Tom had lived for decades with the idea that one of his shiftless relatives had been given £6.000 to save him from some sort of disgrace.

The trappings of fine living enjoyed by the lucky in England of the 1840s had to be sold by Joseph, including a spacious mansion on the banks of the inner reaches of Falmouth Bay, near Truro. Thomas was withdrawn from the Royal Military Academy at Woolwich near London, where it was impossible for his father to meet even the basic fee of £80 a year for board and tuition.

However much of a shock this withdrawal from the military life may have been, Thomas claimed he was scarcely heartbroken. Long afterwards he said his reaction to the news that he had to leave was "Thank God!". He had been sent to Woolwich on the banks of the River Thames at the age of 15 years and six months on August l, 1842. Thus, he was still barely 19 when discharged 16 days after his birthday on March 6, 1846, the diplomatic reason entered in the record book as: "At the request of his friends".

Thomas knew immediately that he had to find his own salvation. His father had five worthy, home-loving, but devastatingly plain daughters on his hands. There were three other sons, all older than Thomas, all encouraged to think of themselves as country gentlemen, excellent members of the Cornish Cricket Club, but unfitted for the realities of scrimp-and-scrape poverty.

It was a cruel world if you were poor, as Thomas could see all around him without being told. There were scores of crippled and blinded miners, plus women and children, in the Truro workhouse. Judges and magistrates, men of Christian faith all, savagely punished the desperate petty crimes of the West Country's starving, sentencing men, women and children to transportation to places like Australia for offences such as stealing bread and meat. "Don't make the excuse you were hungry.", one judge would caution defendants before hearing evidence.

Diseases like cholera and smallpox scythed through a population whose homes had primitive sanitation. At Mevagissy, a picturesque fishing village on the Cornish coast, up to 30 people a week died in one cholera epidemic. Survivors through these good old days had to be immensely resolute and above all born healthy, harder than the hardships. Thomas Hodge was blessed with that leathery constitution.

At first, on leaving Woolwich, he went to live with his brother Ned at Camborne in Cornwall, and one of his letters written from there to his oldest sister Catherine when she was about to visit them by boat, indicates the role of leader of the family he would soon assume. He wrote in July 1846:

Ned says he thinks there is no occasion to take berths before you get on board. The first thing you do when you get on board is to call for the stewardess and say how many berths you want. She will show them to you and you must there throw some of your wearing apparel or any kind of property such as an old bonnet, gown, or even a bustle. If you neglect to do this, it is very probable that some old stager who has travelled the briny wave from her youth will deprive you of a night's rest.

From being a young gentleman with most avenues open, Thomas found himself virtually penniless and quickly turned to the only source of income available: his military training.

He took appointments with small private schools in the South of England over the next few years; a useful, willing junior member of the staff with that valuable extra knowledge of military discipline, excellent at health-promoting sports. He also possessed the formal training in landscape drawing given to most officer cadets of the era.

(N.B.: A photograph stuck into one of Hodge's albums shows boy cadets c. 1850 at the Addiscombe military academy close to Woolwich. Addiscombe was noted for a series of famous art teachers and also introduced a special unit on the construction of forts. Its cadets were mainly intended for the East India Company's army engineers. Whether Hodge visited there or briefly worked there is not known. But clearly there was a strong link of some kind.)

He was especially suited for "cramming" boys wishing or being obliged to enter the British military academies. He wrote and had published in London in 1851 an instructional booklet called *A Catechism of Fortification*, in which he described himself as "First-class prizeman in fortification at the Royal Military Academy, Woolwich, and tutor for the Army".

When Hodge's father Joseph died in 1854, "widely respected" and taking the secrets of his financial ruin to the grave, the youngest son took upon himself the family problems. One of their friends, a woman called by the family "Grannie" Blair, suggested the answer to the predicament of the spinster girls together with a possible future for her favourite godson.

Thomas had shown such talent for the teaching profession, especially in educating boys for officer careers, she said, why not go to Scotland, to St. Andrews in particular. and set up a boarding school. A number of children belonging to the Scottish gentry away working or fighting for the East India Company needed both a home and an education. St. Andrews, close to Edinburgh, was a reviving centre for education where such a boarding establishment would fill a need then neglected.

"The Golf Artist of St. Andrews" was on his way, though that was the last thing in the world he could have known on the long and tedious journey, partly by sea, to the area of Scotland known as the Kingdom of Fife.

Premises had been obtained, West View in Lade Braes Lane, just alongside Madras College and a short walk from the legendary golf links. The help and advice of "Grannie" Blair had been crucial. With him, or shortly to join him, Thomas had his sisters May (Mary) and Fan (Sarah Frances), both in their early 20s, and his oldest sister Catherine ("Kit"), in those days very much an old maid at 37.

The sisters had eaten their ample portion of humble pie during the financial struggle in Cornwall, and tackled the day-to-day running of the new establishment while brother Thomas mustered pupils from his Scottish friends and acquaintances. Kit later had her own annex at 1, Pilmour Place, looking after the smaller children of the Empire exiles.

The success of the venture seemed remarkable. Others were to make fortunes through the same method, as the Rev. A. K. H. Boyd, prolific author and parish minister of St. Andrews, revealed in one of his books. One man found the financial rewards so great he couldn't bear to retire and killed himself through overwork.

Hodge owed a great deal to his energetic and intelligent sisters, but he also possessed shrewd business acumen. And he got results. He belted the boys if it was felt they needed punishment, yet he was far from harsh by the standards of the age. He had a notable regard for victuals so that the children had plenty of old-fashioned food to keep out the notorious winter rheums brought on by the chill of the North East coast of Britain.

Educationally, Hodge's school did not merely produce toy soldiers for Empire service so much as boys with a well-rounded start which could gain them entrance to senior schools. (Subjects: geography, arithmetic, Latin grammar, Euclid, French, English and ancient Greek history, etc.)

To build Christian muscularity, it was cricket in season, where Thomas also made his mark as an all-rounder with Scottish teams as well as coaching the boys. In winter, the school played a Rugby School style of football, and year-round nothing could prevent an involvement with golf – not with grand matches and grand players to watch a few hundred yards away.

No doubt Hodge's charges had the same experience on the Old Course as one of the next-door Madras College boys when the student reminisced:

> *In those days* (mid-19th century) *we could start when and where we liked, and unless we dawdled unduly, played execrably or indulged in horseplay, sometimes laughing until we were fit to greet, we were seldom in the way of the players.*

One of Hodge's ex-pupils, Edwin Ludgrove, wrote a series of letters to a friend, George Forbes, in 1861, sentences from which read:

You say you are surprised at Mr. Hodge giving you another book besides your prize. I am not. Has Mr. Hodge won the medal this time? Does he still play golf as much as ever? It appears Mr. Clint's death was owing to his drinking a quantity of cold water when he was hot. I suppose by now Mr. Hodge has someone to fill his place? (Luckless Clint was obviously one of the masters.)

How is the old college getting on? How I should love to be able to attend it. Give my compliments to Mr. and Misses Hodge. Is poor Skinner, the shoe black, still alive?

Skinner may have been the shoe repairer Hodge kept at West View, whose cobbling was added to the tuition bill of £35 per annum. Hodge had about 30 day boarders, plus full-time boarders. Often several classes of 17 to 20 pupils were in progress.

St. Andrews had not long begun to emerge from its sourest period,decay and ruin all round, portrayed in this eye-witness description of the town in 1830:

Filth and squalor abounded unchecked; cows and pigs grazed in front of the colleges; the venerable ruins were fast going to decay, and were littered with rubbish; there were few visitors of any distinction even to the splendid links, which lay with all its vast capabilities almost untrodden; and generally St. Andrews was at the lowest pitch of miserable neglect and decay.

"The Golf" was just a pastime for a few gentlemen and academics and the local artisans. It also supported a cottage industry for the handful of club and ball makers.

In 1851, the population was 6,716. Ten years later, it had risen to 7,041, and by 1891 the head count was still only 8,755 – scarcely the figures for a boom town.

Hodge and his sister Kit had entries among the 14 Boarding Establishments listed in the local directory of 1861, and under Miscellaneous Educational Establishments, Professors and Teachers, etc, "Hodge, Thomas (and boarding), West View, St. Andrews", was one of nine entries.

The Gentry had 103 entries in 1861, including many who would become friends of Hodge even though he never graduated to their list: the two gallant Majors, Robert Bethune and Robert Boothby, the Blackwood brother publishers of Strathtyrum House, D. L. Burn Esq, John Inglis and Robert Balfour.

Four golf club and ball manufacturers were listed: Robert Forgan, Robert Kirk and Thomas Morris ("Old Tom"), all with addresses in Pilmour Links, and James Wilson of Golf Place.

Famous surnames in golf's history also appeared among the 12 Boat Owners and Skippers (James Fenton, David and James Gourlay), and among the 23 Boot and Shoe Makers (Auchterlonie, Gourlay).

A woefully faded photograph of Hodge taken at St. Andrews in 1857, wearing a truly wondrous stove-pipe top-hat, shows him to be a youthful 30 at about the time he was sufficiently secure in his new background to plunge into the golf "madness" seriously.

With his natural dexterity and strength, it was obvious that before long he would be among the top flight of players in Scotland. He had the respect and sometimes friendship of enough members of the Royal & Ancient Golf Club for his membership to be accepted without question in 1861.

W. W. Tulloch, a son of the learned Principal Tulloch of St. Andrews University, who knew the Hodges well, summed up the impact of Hodge the golfer when he interviewed Thomas just before his death in 1907.

W. W., author of the life story of Old Tom Morris, wrote:

It was almost as a middle-aged (sic) man that Mr Hodge took to golf and joined the Royal & Ancient Club. He very soon developed into a first-class player. In 1861 he won the first prize, the silver cross, at the Spring Meeting, with a score of 92, a record at that time. Next year he was second and won the silver medal with 97, and eleven years later, in 1873, occupied the same position with 99.

At the Autumn Meeting in 1866 and 1867, he won the King William the Fourth gold medal in 97 and 96 and again won it in 1869 with a score of 89, which had only been surpassed by Mr George Glennie's 88 in 1855.

From another quarter, the Rev. John Gordon McPherson, an outspoken, some thought opinionated and self-promoting golf pundit and cleric of the 1880s and 1890s, there was a much more acid view of Hodge the golfer.

Writing about "Style in Golf" for the *Edinburgh Gazette* in 1889, in an article later incorporated into his book *Golf and Golfers*, he said:

The fine eye and hand of Thomas Hodge were carried from the billiards table and curling pond and cricket field to the Links of St Andrews. He was on the whole a successful player, but O what a style!

By some accident he fell into it when commencing, and he was bound to continue. Though he carried off the highest honours, he could not be trusted in a challenge match, when a critical stroke was needed. No-one imitated him, and fortunately his style will die out.

Hodge was tickled evidently by this criticism, for he cut out the article and stuck it into one of his scrapbooks. It was strikingly at odds with the view of Harry Everard, another of golf's many fine writers, who lived at St. Andrews and whose turbulent love story is told alongside his portrait in this book. Everard wrote that Hodge taught his pupils to play golf so well that if anyone learned the game at his school it was the same as saying he was a good player.

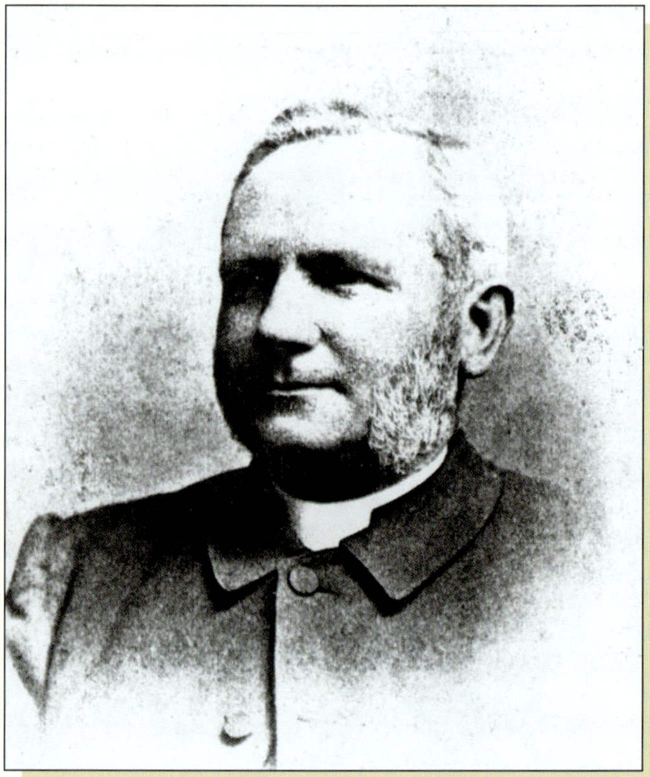

Above: the Rev. John G. McPherson, who publicised himself without recourse to modesty as being in the top rank both as a golfer and as a golfing critic.

Throughout the 1860s, Hodge was eager always to break from St. Andrews for annual summer tours abroad by himself. His bachelor status, in view of his lack of funds from 1846 to the late 1850s, is hardly surprising.

No really fine "catches" would have been steered his way by watchful Victorian mammas, rather the opposite, while Thomas was also intent on underpinning his financial future.

This was the age of the jealously chaperoned young woman, and Hodge wrote of encountering battleaxes aplenty on his holidays, all defending their charges from the "threat" of over-familiar young men seeking a diverting flirtation.

Such obvious behaviour was unlikely from Thomas, who was wary of official entanglement before he could afford it, though there remain strong suggestions in St. Andrews even nearly a century after his death that he was more than a discreet admirer of the ladies, home and abroad.

His great affair with golf and his diverting artistic production provided some solace for Hodge as he lived through a decade when his end of the family's fortune and position was restored.

He was ready for marriage towards the close of the 1860s, by now more of a prospect in the marriage circus, though "middle-aged" and bald on top. The girl proved to be Jane Frances Mackinnon, an orphan of the "Indian Mutiny" of 1857. Her father was Captain Donald William Mackinnon of the East India Company's armed forces. His first wife died in India leaving six children and his second wife was left with three more children when the Captain died of wounds at Jhansi in 1859.

His first wife's children, among them daughter Jane Frances, were sent home to Britain on a voyage reputed to have lasted six months through endless gales, in the care of the captain. Jane Frances was six years old.

As a Mackinnon of Kyle, Jane Frances was well aware of her Highland blood. She was also particularly tough, through the circumstances of her childhood, and a long way ahead of her time in her impatience with the predestined role of the voteless 19th-century woman. She arrived on a visit to Hodge's school to see one of her orphan brothers, and, so to speak, married the headmaster. The wedding took place on July 27, 1870 at Killearnan, Ross and Cromarty. The bride was 20, the groom 43.

Jane Frances was not so much a ray of sunshine as a flash of lightning in Hodge's settled and predictable life. It is instructive to examine photographs of him before and after marriage.

In the portrait used in W. W. Tulloch's *Life of Tom Morris*, he is a ponderous man of letters aged about 40. Soberly dressed, he looks very heavy going, presenting the facade of a bachelor set in his ways.

After marriage, with bairns arriving regularly, and with the irresistible influence of his young wife on his lifestyle, Thomas Hodge appears a transformed man. From being moody and almost sullen, his expression in his portraits is invariably lighter and more cheerful. He looks slimmer, and his natty suits and cravats are youthful and fashionable. The engulfing muttonchop whiskers are shaved off.

There is no doubting the romantic nature of the marriage from the idyllic watercolours Hodge painted of their honeymoon at Lake Windermere.

One of the liveliest watercolours by Hodge that has survived shows a dramatised incident on a later family holiday. Three of his small children are with him in a rowing boat while their pet dog cleverly rescues a lost hat from the foaming briny. The rowing boat bears the title "T. Hodge. Pilot". He's the happiest man alive.

The young Mrs. Hodge was fiercely protective towards her brood and nursed them all through the dangerous childhood illnesses which decimated so many huge Victorian families. Her health service was the medical dictionary always at hand. She invariably accompanied her husband on trips to London, occasionally by boat despite her fear of sea travel. On one trip, in the early 1880s, the family set off from nearby Dundee, Mrs. Hodge taking with her a bottle of chloroform. This was to put the children and herself to sleep in the event of the dreaded shipwreck. During the voyage, the coaster caught fire, and Mrs. Hodge, true to her word, went to her cabin with the children and got out the chloroform. Fortunately, the fire was extinguished and they reached the Thames safely.

The indomitable spirit of this lady can be gauged by her surviving the catastrophic emotional impact of the Indian Mutiny which engulfed her parents and consumed all previous notions of Empire for the British in 1857.

Below: Hodge's painting of a boat outing with his children.

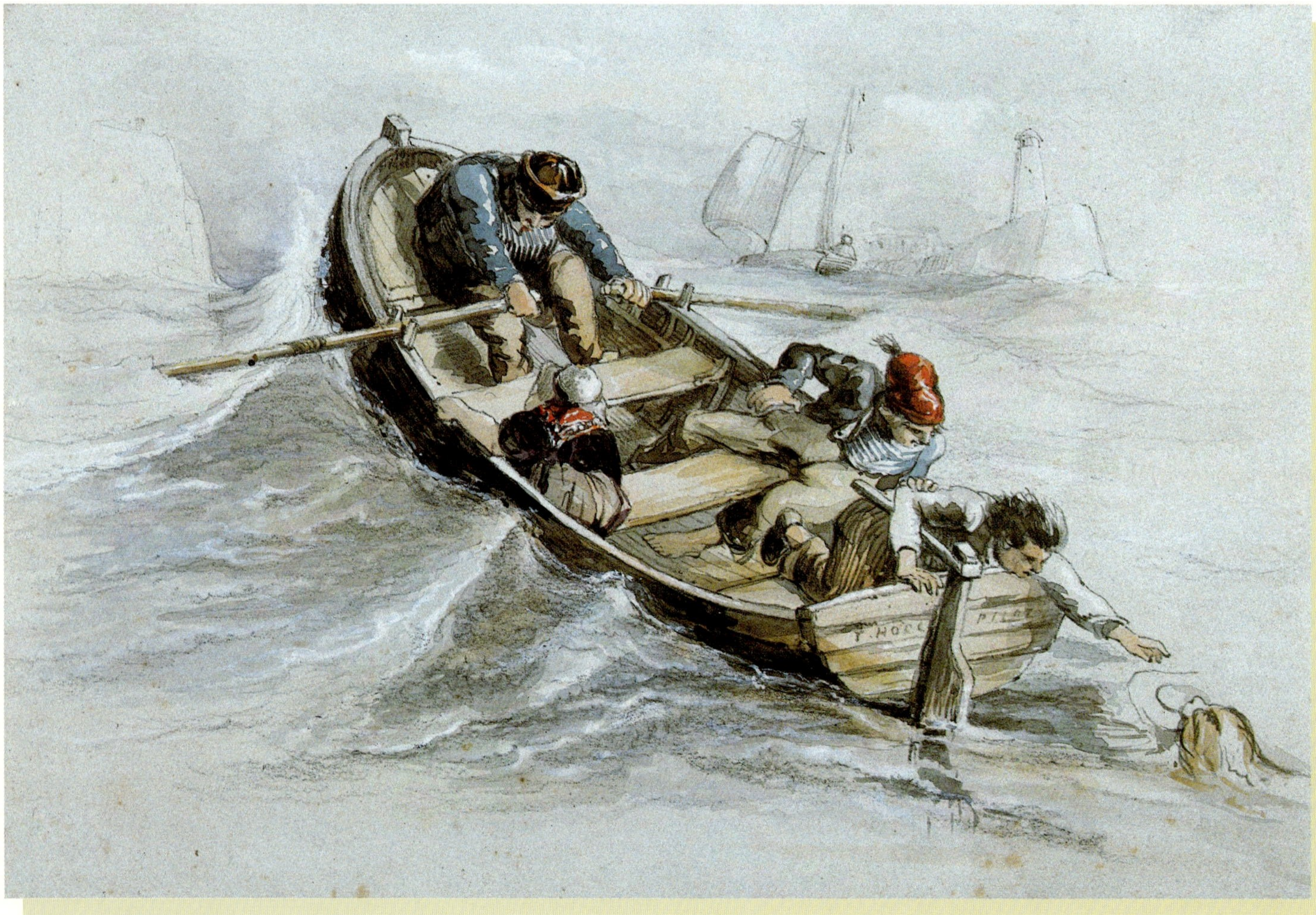

Hodge had lived with the fury of the sea as a boy in Cornwall, going to the shore after storms to watch upturned craft bobbing in to land. St. Andrews Bay continued this love-hate attachment, a constant supply of wrecks hitting the sandy beach as the cargo and passenger coasters lost their battles with the gales. He painted and drew many of the hulks, grim souvenirs as relevant to the travel of the day and just as chilling as modern air, motorway and rail disasters.

The Hodges wound up with seven children, three boys and four girls, the last girl, Emma Mary ("Dickie") born when her father was almost 60, and a source of much masculine pride.

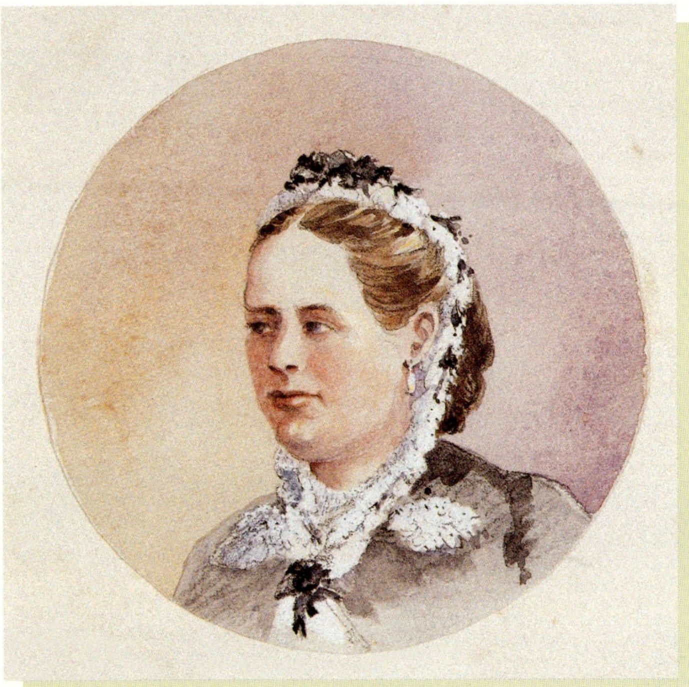

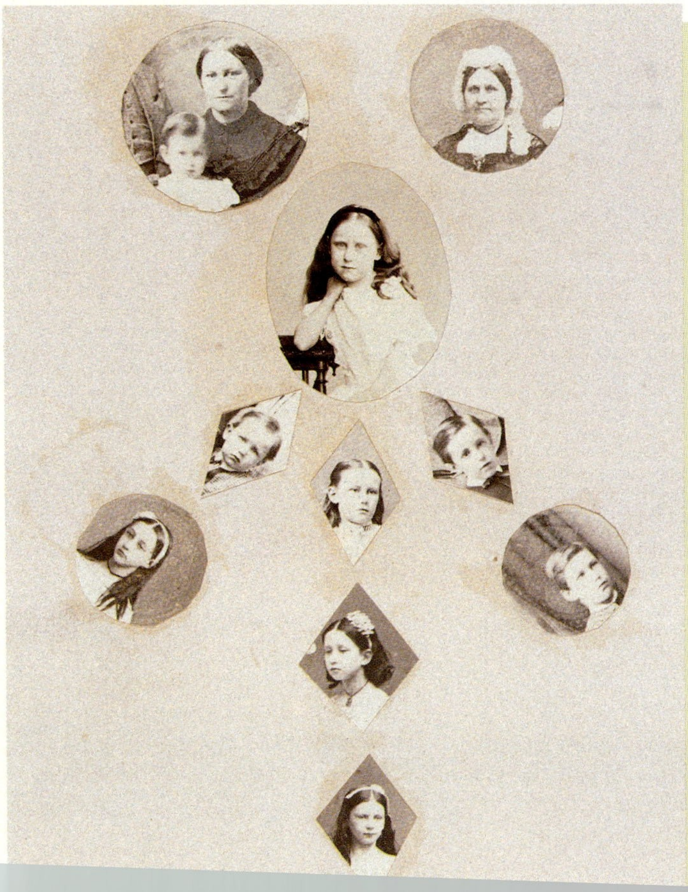

Above: Mrs. Hodge as a sturdy young matron.

Left: a page from a Hodge scrapbook of Thomas's young family with Mamma featured twice.

He decided to educate the children himself, one of the reasons for closing the West View school in the mid-1880s. It had made him, as the Rev. Boyd would have confirmed, a tolerable fortune. Inevitably he came up against the problem that his sons, Edward Hamilton ("Ned"), Donald William Mackinnon ("Dod") and Thomas Kenwyn, had inherited a great deal of their mother's fiery Highland temperament. They were also in very lively company for some of the year, when the young Freddie Tait, soon to be a charismatic Scottish golf hero, was also in residence at St. Andrews.

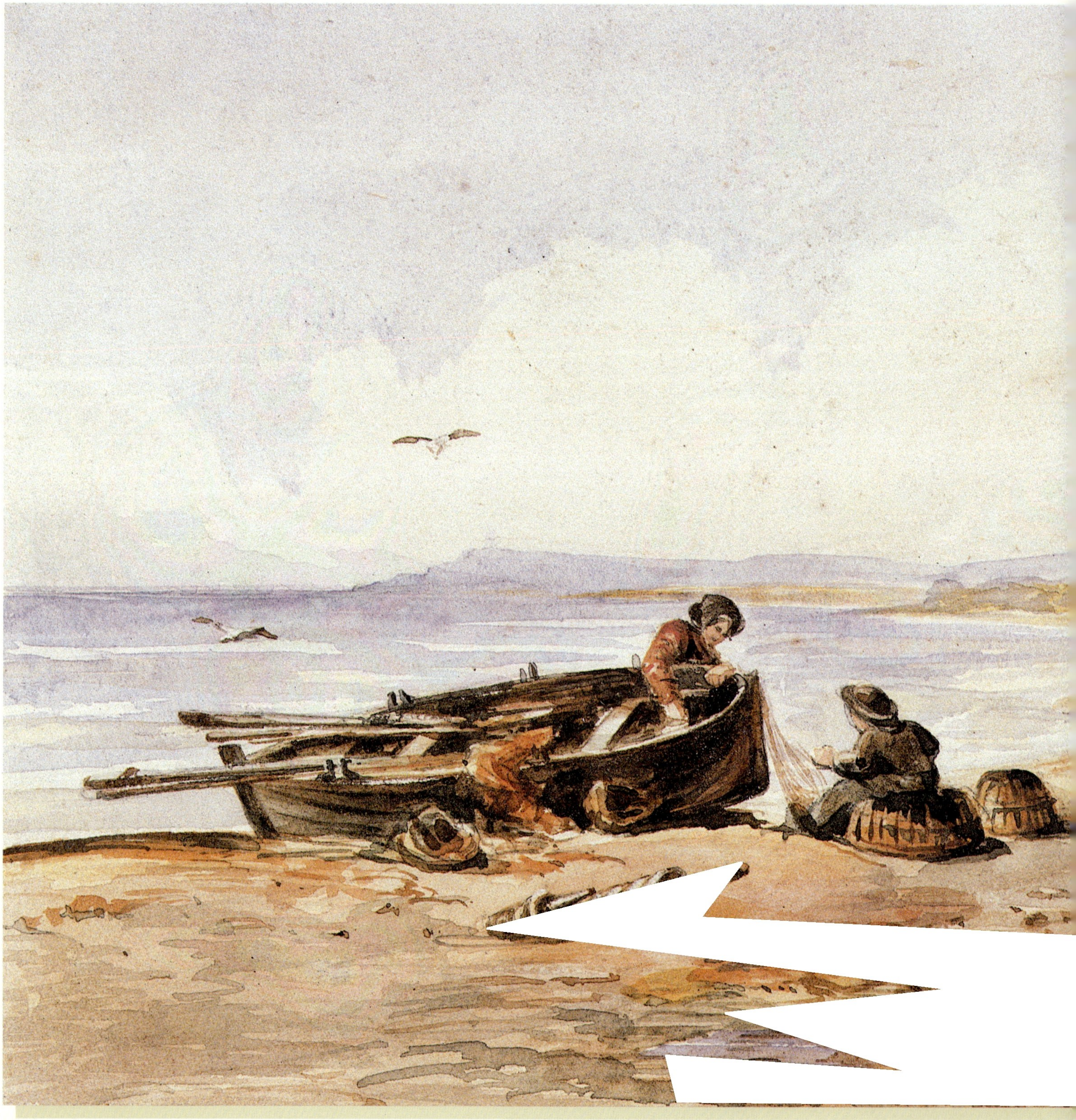

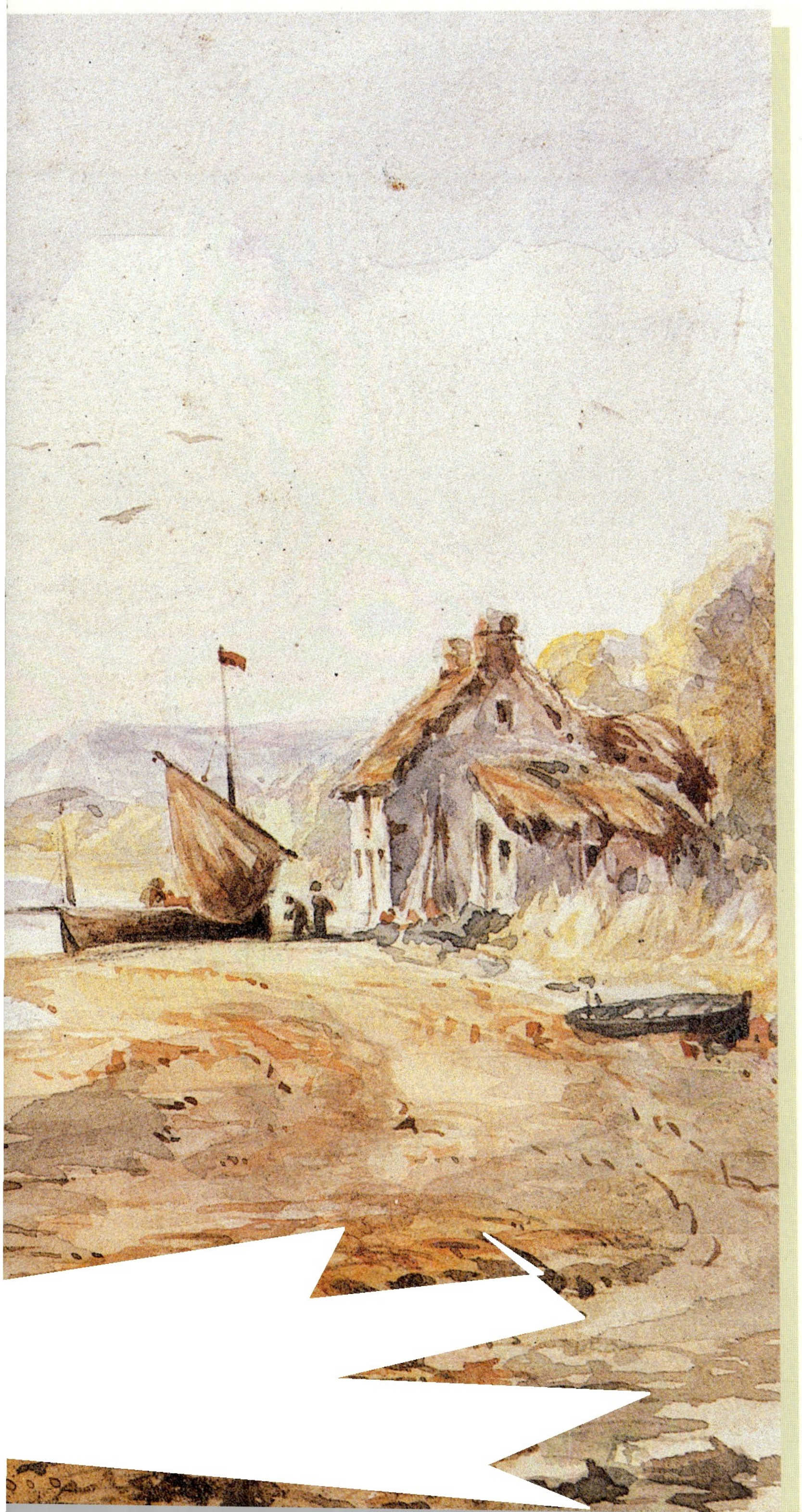

Left: life on the edge of the sea could seem idyllic. Except that the children Hodge shows apparently playing round the boat are in fact mending the fishing nets.

Together, they were a notable quartet for the local populace, endlessly inventive in the cause of a practical joke. Hodge looked out the old school taws that had whacked many a boy's backside at West View, but his wife stepped between him and his targets and denied him the right to administer corporal punishment to their children. He gave in, but said that although he would never chastise the children ,Jane Frances must be responsible in future for their discipline, whatever the problems.

Hodge did keep an eye out for them, though, once diving into the sea fully clothed to rescue a son in difficulties.

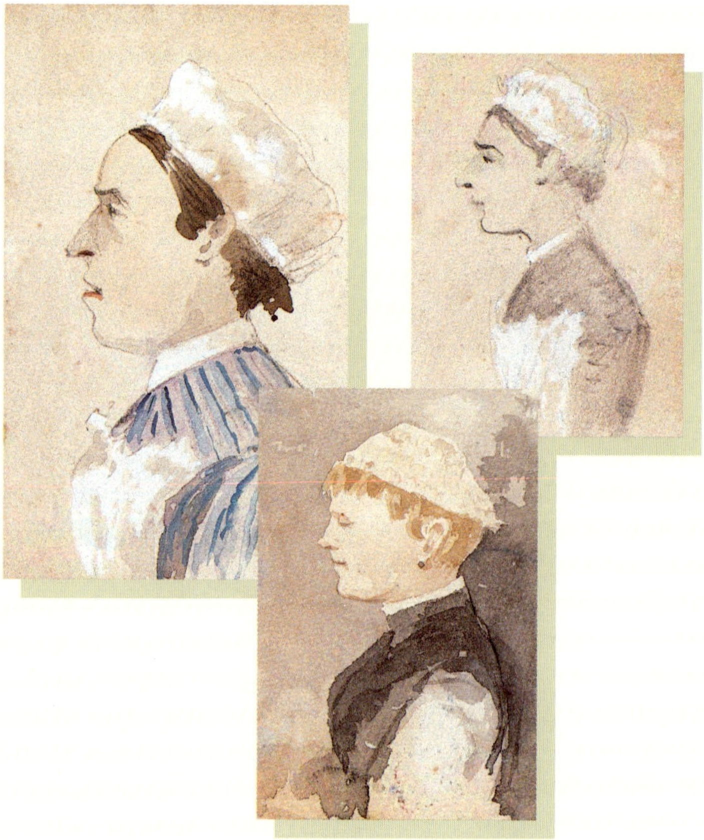

Above: servants at West View.

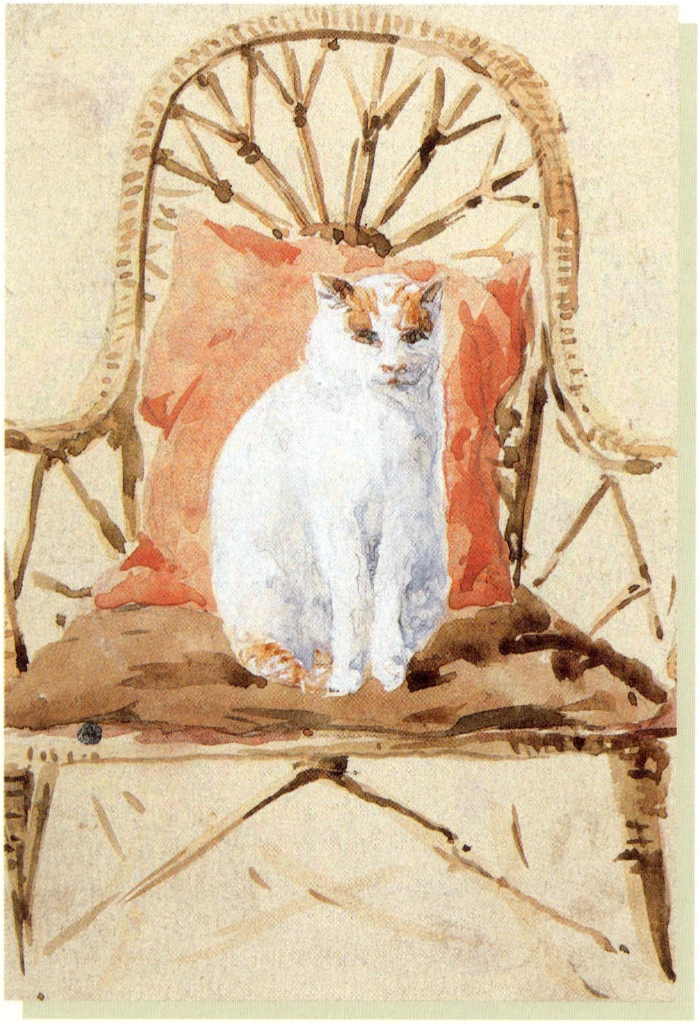

Left: a pet cat. This and the above may be by Thomas Hodge Jr., who also liked to paint.

As the children grew, the indomitable Mrs. Hodge became increasingly restless in St. Andrews, which had developed a close social pecking order founded on academic or literary status, university or church position.

There was also a degree of intolerance which a century later would have made even men in Victorian days considered moderate and good citizens appear gross chauvinists. The contempt for other nations and races now seems bizarre. The parish priest, the Rev. Boyd had a quantity of peculiar attitudes. He burned books when he had finished with them. "Have a very hot, clear fire", he instructed. "Drop the book in solid, like a brick. Then it disappears, leaving no traces." He burned hundreds.

Proud Highlanders were not immune from local bigots, and there was one ludicrous incident when a member of Hodge's household, either family or one of the servants, endured reproving sniffs and glares when she walked round the centre of the town in a petticoat that actually rustled. This arousal of St. Andrews sensibilities extracted from Thomas a poem entitled "A Ballad from Dreary Town", in which he criticised the locals for being "So saintly, so very goody good; so very pious and proper".

Hodge was increasingly disenchanted with the direction he felt golf was taking. In fact, ever since the arrival of the railway in 1852, soon literally forming the boundary of the links, a rapid growth in the popular appeal of the game had been inevitable. This was especially so as the new "gutta percha" golf ball had ousted the expensive "feathery", a thing of superlative craftsmanship and a joy to behold, but terribly slow in the making. Playing the game was becoming cheaper and easier for the novice masses.

The journey to St. Andrews remained complicated until the completion of the Forth Bridge in 1890, when Hodge and his club cronies saw the encroaching hordes of new enthusiasts pretty well as a barbarian assault on their paradise.

It was ironic that just as his reputation as the artist of the home of golf was evolving, so the game and its players he was recording was slipping from what he considered to be the highest standards. Some of the anonymous letters and articles appearing in the nearby Edinburgh newspapers probably came from his pen. He stuck the following extract from the *Daily News* of April 30, 1890, into his personal copy of the *Badminton Golf* volume:

Everywhere and every day of play, are medals, shields, silver cleeks and other prizes for competition. Everywhere the arithmetician is at work, and the competitors proudly assume privileges above the decent people who play their singles and foursomes in the quiet old way, umambitious of prizes.

These competitions, again, produce wild and extravagant handicaps. Beginners, or noted incompetents, receive about 50 'strokes', not as one could wish, applied firmly in the proper place, and so win prizes. The competitive tendence, too, is actually tampering with the ancient law which never allowed a ball to be moved or lifted. Where it fell, there it lay, and if it lay in an impossible place, the hole had to be given up.

The sport is becoming as artificial as fasting, or pheasant shooting, and without any compensating advantages. All this is produced by the eternal counting of strokes, nobody wishing to expend ten strokes in forcing a way out of a furze bush or a sand hole. Such are the results of playing for fame, or publicity, instead of playing for amusement.

Hodge's inclination at "The Club" was to associate with the scribes and poets flourishing by now around golf and the Royal & Ancient: Horace Hutchinson, Andrew Lang, Harry Everard, Pat Alexander and the like. He could match quip for quip in dead or living language in heavy Victorian style, or insert quantities of his droll "gentle sarcasm" into St. Andrews gossip. But an Englishman's jests were not always a laughing matter for the local establishment.

Hutchinson turned to him for the bulk of the illustrations in *Badminton Golf*. Andrew Lang, who had seen the enormous range of Hodge's work in the albums kept at West View, announced that he was thus inspired to use Hodge to illustrate a book he was going to write on the history of St. Andrews. There is so much ancient history in St. Andrews and the Kingdom of Fife, and so many zealous custodians of it, this is not a task to be undertaken lightly, which is what Andrew Lang may have done.

Lang did the words, Hodge did the pictures. The book, published by Longman, Green and Co., was on sale towards the end of 1893. Waiting in ambush for it was a native of St. Andrews, who wrote long historical columns for the *St. Andrews Citizen*, David Hay Fleming. The son of a local ironmonger, Hay Fleming won his final academic eminence through relentless research. Married to Scotland's dusty records, this Calvinist bachelor by nature resisted interlopers. His brain was a computer loaded with irrefutable facts on Scotland's yesteryear. Later, in a life of accepted professional academic standing, he permitted himself the scholarly badges of silk cap and a full-length grey beard. And a voluminous fur-trimmed cloak. Those who laughed, laughed at their peril.

Highly respected by his own folk and infinitely, fanatically painstaking, for Hay Fleming any careless mistake was a little death. He did not spare Lang or Hodge, writing:

> *To most readers his (Lang's) book will prove extremely disappointing. Mr. Lang speaks modestly of his work as 'a little sketch of the history of St. Andrews, the writing of which was suggested by the drawings of Mr. Hodge'. Some of these drawings are very good. Some are rather poor. Even a somewhat cursory reader will perceive errors enough to make him dubious as to accepting any of the book's statements....*
>
> *Perhaps Mr. Lang does not wish his readers to accept his work as a piece of serious history. In his own estimation it is probably only a hasty essay – smart and superficial.*

Thus boomed the voice of David Hay Fleming, author of *Historical Notes and Extracts concerning the Links of St. Andrews*, also published in 1893.

Lang wrote a brief letter to the *St. Andrews Citizen* about proof corrections overlooked. From Hodge there was nothing. He and his wife and children had left St. Andrews, in spirit if not in actual fact, the precise date of their departure not being known.

A brief news paragraph had appeared in the *St. Andrews Citizen* of October 29, 1892:

> SALE OF PROPERTY,· *We are informed that Provost Paterson has purchased from Thomas Hodge, at the price of £2,800, his property of West View, consisting of five houses and a large piece of eligible feuing ground near Madras College, in order that parties wishing to come to St. Andrews for educational purposes may have houses at moderate rentals.*

No other comment surrounding the Hodge family's departure has been traced.

Right: Nemesis! The St. Andrews historian Hay Fleming in his ostentatious academic costume. His savage attack on Hodge and Andrew Lang for their indifferent history of his beloved home town may have contributed to Hodge's departure from Fife.

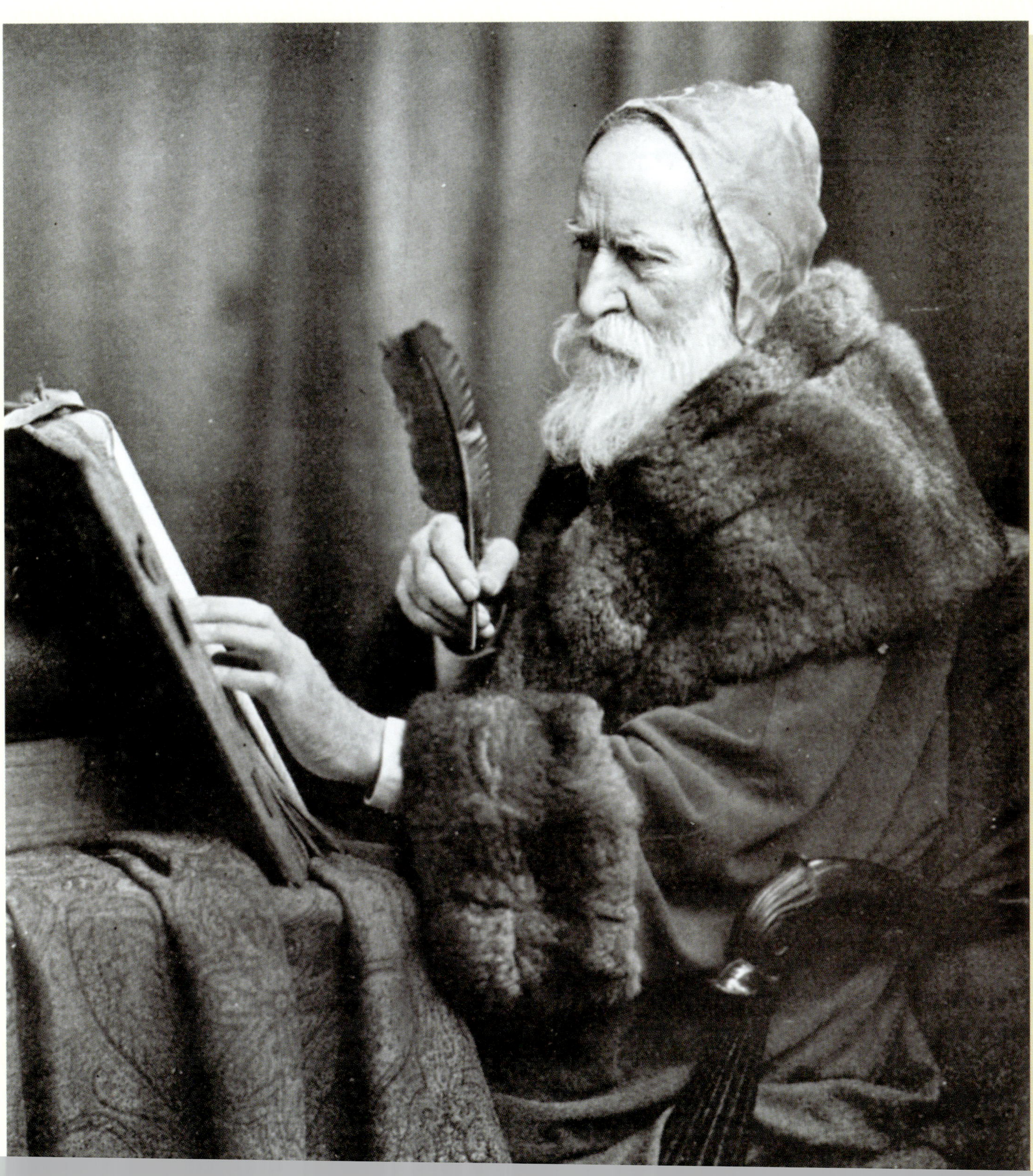

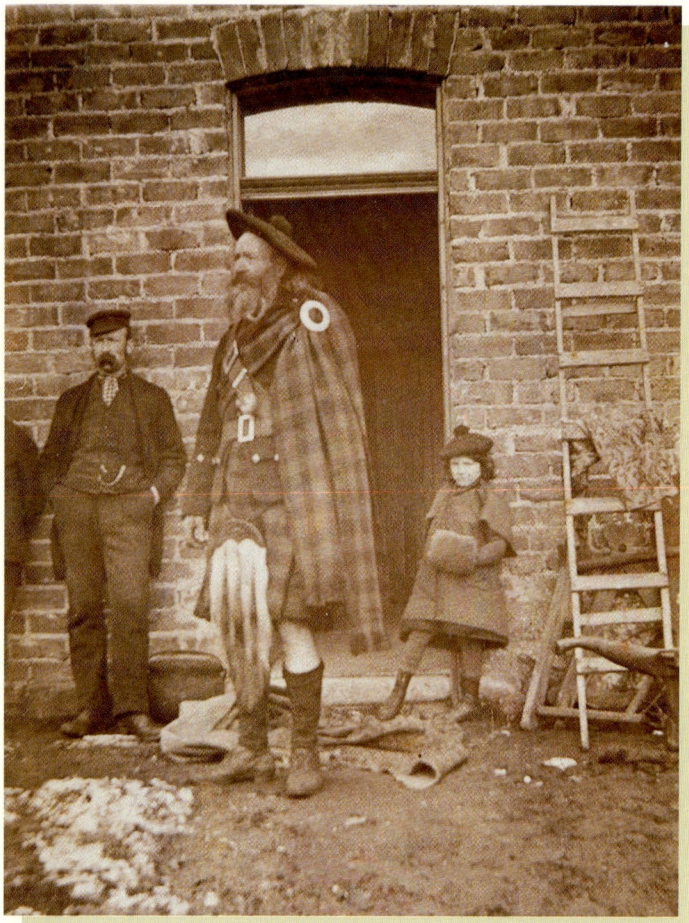

Above: Hodge and his sons used the new-fangled camera widely. Here a monumental Highland visitor to St. Andrews was a sight not to be missed. No-one has yet identified the giant.

The hold of St. Andrews on Hodge's affections may have been further strained at this period by a protracted squabble over the custodianship of the famous links. The detail of this endless dispute has been sweetened to a degree by some interpreters of golf history over the years (the Royal & Ancient on one side of a triangle completed by the local council and the owner, a Mr Cheape), but at the time it was poisonous.

Hodge was quite certainly on the side of the Royal & Ancient faction which, with paternalistic good faith, some thought arrogance, wanted the club to buy the links without the involvement of St. Andrews. Later they intended to give the local people all those rights of access held "from time immemorial". This would not have endeared him to St. Andrews people, championed successfully by the tenacious historian Hay Fleming, whose wrath in leading the locals' counter-proposals to buy the links for themselves sprang largely from a foolish lack of candour shown by one or two of the negotiators.

According to their granddaughter, the actual decision to leave St. Andrews was taken by Mr. and Mrs. Hodge through the imminent departure of Jane Frances's youngest and dearest son, Thomas Kenwyn, to take up articles with a Glasgow accountant.

Any suggestion that Hodge had scandalous contact with one of the district's young females was even in the 1990s just part of the St. Andrews whispering circuit, although straying from the marital fairway is not unknown in R & A circles.

Whatever the final straw, Hodge was not in the mood to argue when his wife insisted on a permanent change of address after his stay of almost 40 years in Fife.

Provokingly for the rumour-mongers, Hodge is not included in a remarkable "montage" oil painting which now hangs in the Royal & Ancient, showing 191 members and staff and entitled "Medal Day at St. Andrews – 1894", with the captain of the club, the Right Hon. A. J. Balfour M.P., driving off assisted by Old Tom Morris.

The absence of Hodge, by now a member for well over 30 years, might have been at his request, or it might have

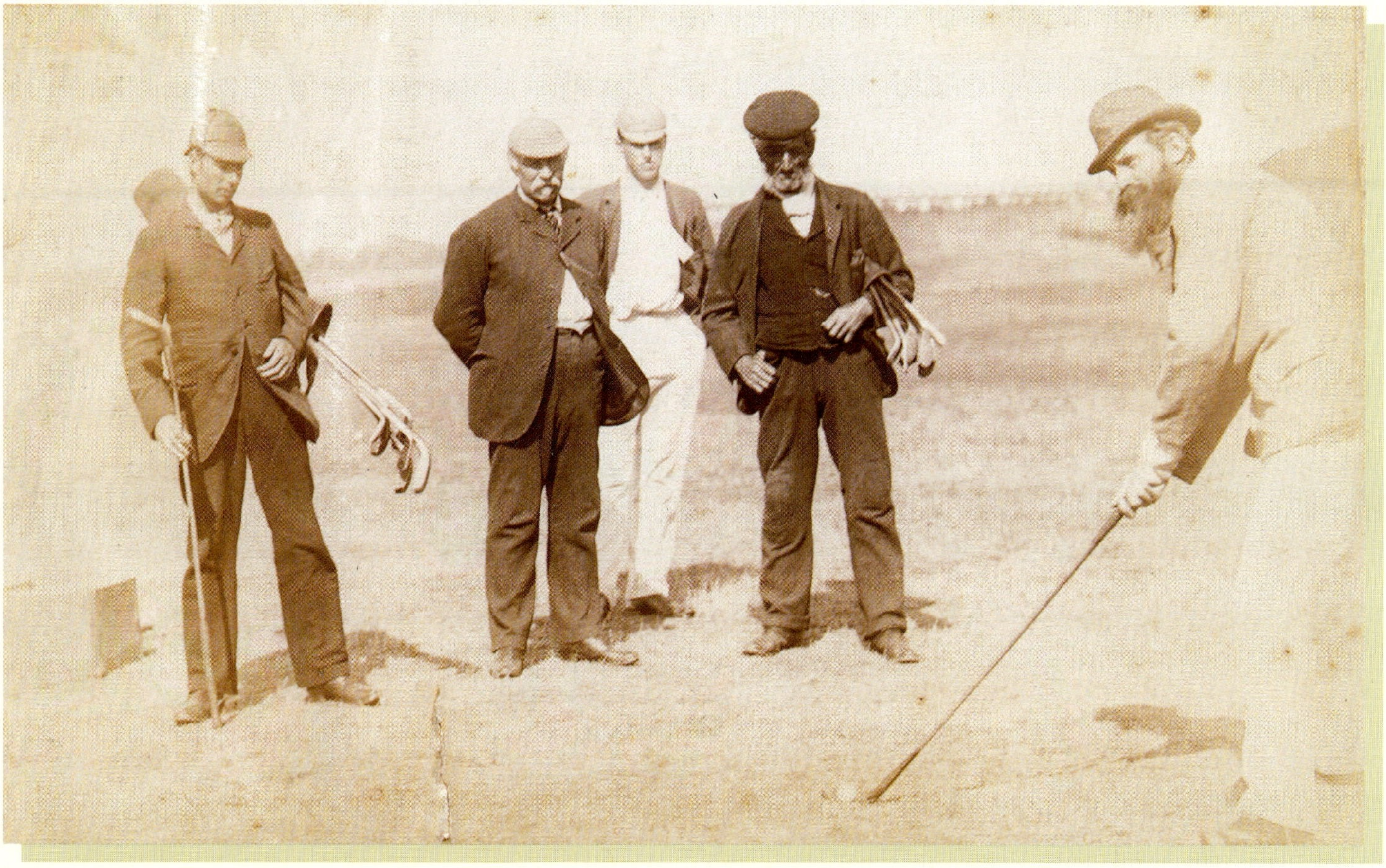

Above: An ample Thomas Hodge (second left) watches his bounteously bearded opponent attack the hole in a St. Andrews match. The caddy on Hodge's left is Skipper Fenton.

been one of those dreadful oversights which are glaringly obvious too late. Or it might have been deliberate.

However, Hodge clearly had not left the Royal & Ancient itself in a huff, as there is a brief handwritten note in the Royal & Ancient archives written from 7 Great Kelvin Terrace, Hillhead, Glasgow, in March 1894, which says:

Mr Hodge with apologies for delay begs to enclose his subscription to Golf club.

He was still a member in 1895. Furthermore, he was almost certainly present in person at the 1894 meeting.

When son Thomas Kenwyn qualified as an accountant and moved to London to work, the family went too, close to the turn of the century. Hodge bought a house in Quex Road, Kilburn, on the very outer fringe of fashionable Hampstead. He was engrossed in the doings of his lively and much-travelled family as an old man in his late 70s. A daughter, Sine, possessed a splendid contralto voice, training abroad and giving London concerts; another son, Edward Hamilton ("Ned"), at first worked on an indigo plantation in India for his uncle Farquhar Mackinnon.

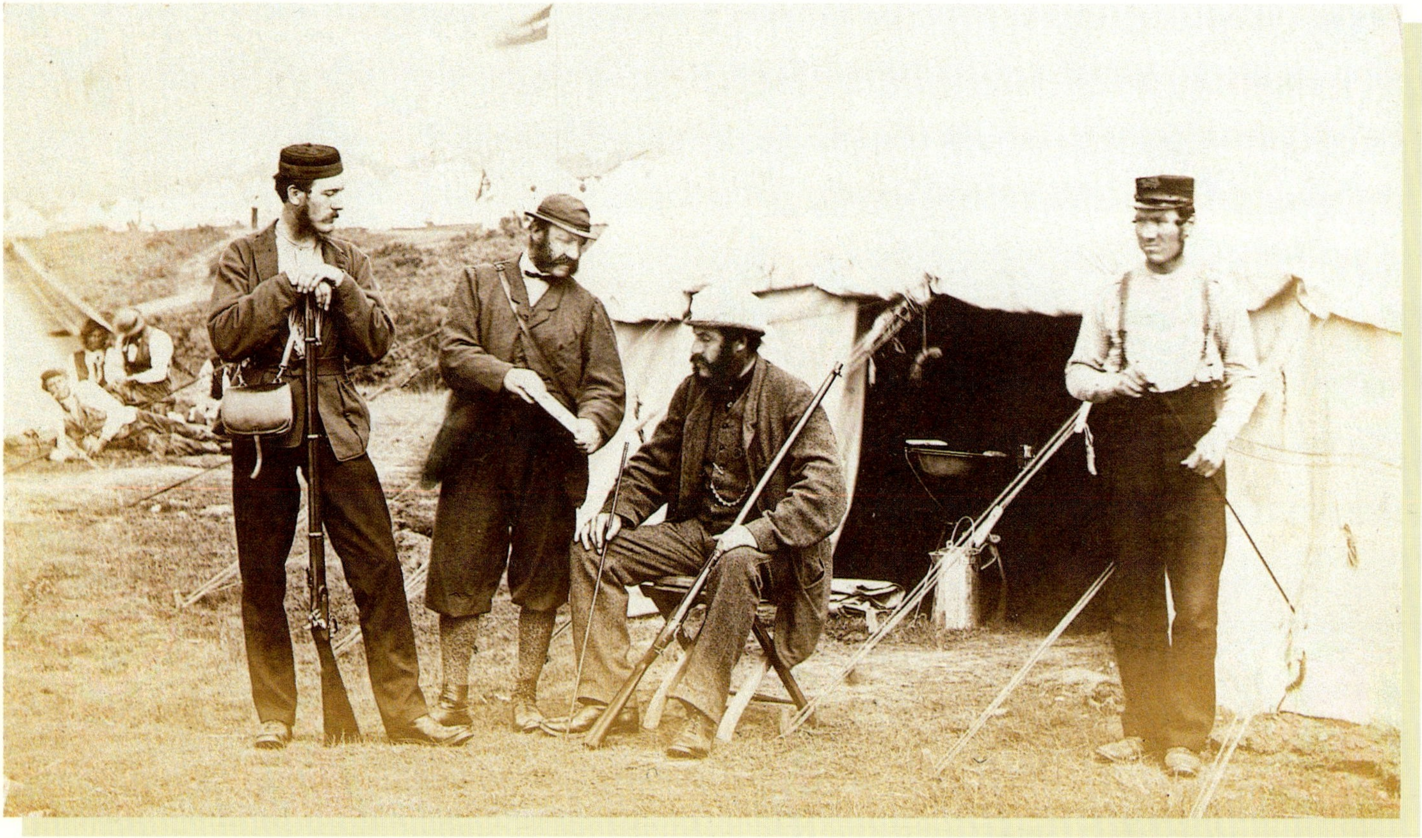

Above: Hodge shows his friend Major Boothby a scorecard at the Wimbledon rifle-shooting tournament they attended each summer.

Then there was Donald William Mackinnon Hodge ("Dod"), who fought in South Africa in the Boer War and later went to the U.S.A., where he became a citizen and was reputed to have married his girlfriend "Cody" in a circus-ring ceremony. He died in San Francisco. Thomas Kenwyn had a spell in Canada, where he was secretary of a Vancouver golf club.

Another daughter, Charlotte, became Mrs Sheward and gave birth to Hodge's only known grandchild, Norah Sheward, in 1903. Norah was largely responsible for rescuing quantities of his dispersed work in later years, which she donated with great generosity to the Royal & Ancient in 1986.

Hodge had earned the lasting affection of many of his old West View pupils, some of whom visited him in London.

His final, brief moment of visibility in the now surging world of golf, occurred in 1907, shortly before his death, when he was visited by W. W. Tulloch, the golf historian, who wrote a pleasant, full-page article on the old man for the magazine *Golf Illustrated*.

Hodge, as Tulloch said, was ready to have "a crack" about the old St. Andrews days, but refused to discuss modern golf, which he didn't believe in. "There is no golf played nowadays" he told Tulloch, "with the pleasant sarcasm at which he is such an adept", pushing away golf magazines offered by his visitor.

When he died on May 20, 1907, leaving an estate valued at £4,886 after over 20 years in retirement, he was so far forgotten and so little recognised in London that not a line, paid or unpaid, appeared to record his passing in any newspaper.

Golf Illustrated gave him a small but fulsome obituary notice:

It is with sincere regret we record the death of this wilom, very well-known and popular golfer, clever illustrator of the Badminton, in his day admirable coach and very charming man. He was laid to rest in Hampstead Cemetery and it is pleasing to think that though he died far away from St. Andrews which he had made peculiarly his own, several dear ones who held him in lifelong respect and esteem were present at his funeral.

Old golfers will regret his death and will long cherish the memory of his golfing achievements, his brilliant prowess as a sketcher and caricaturist, and his great personal charm of manner and disposition.

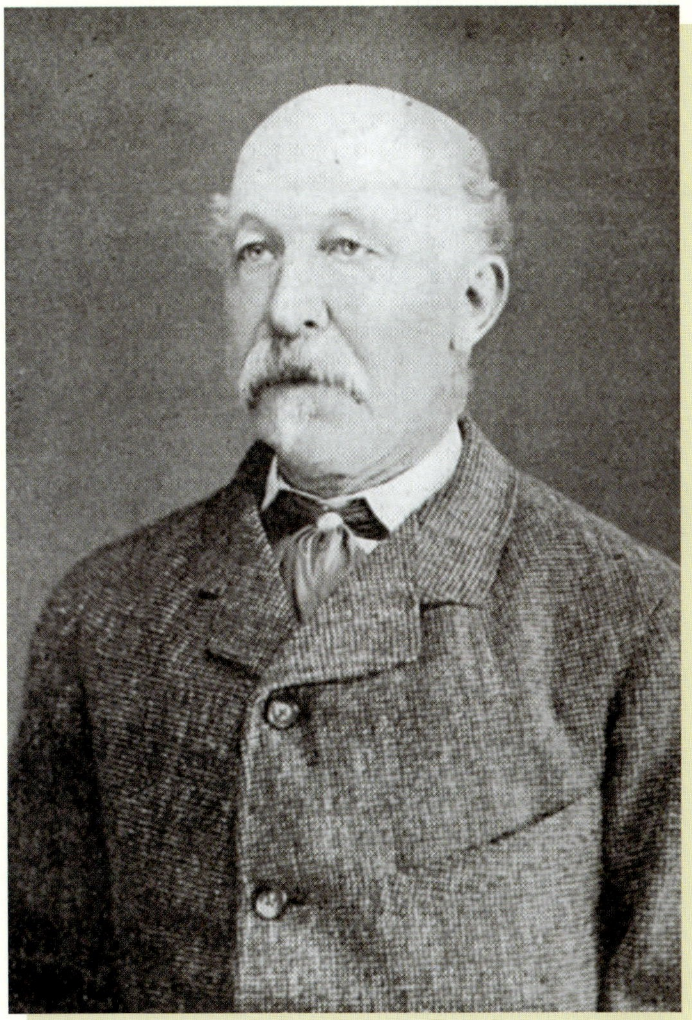

Above: T.H., as he signed his work, photographed in his retirement years.

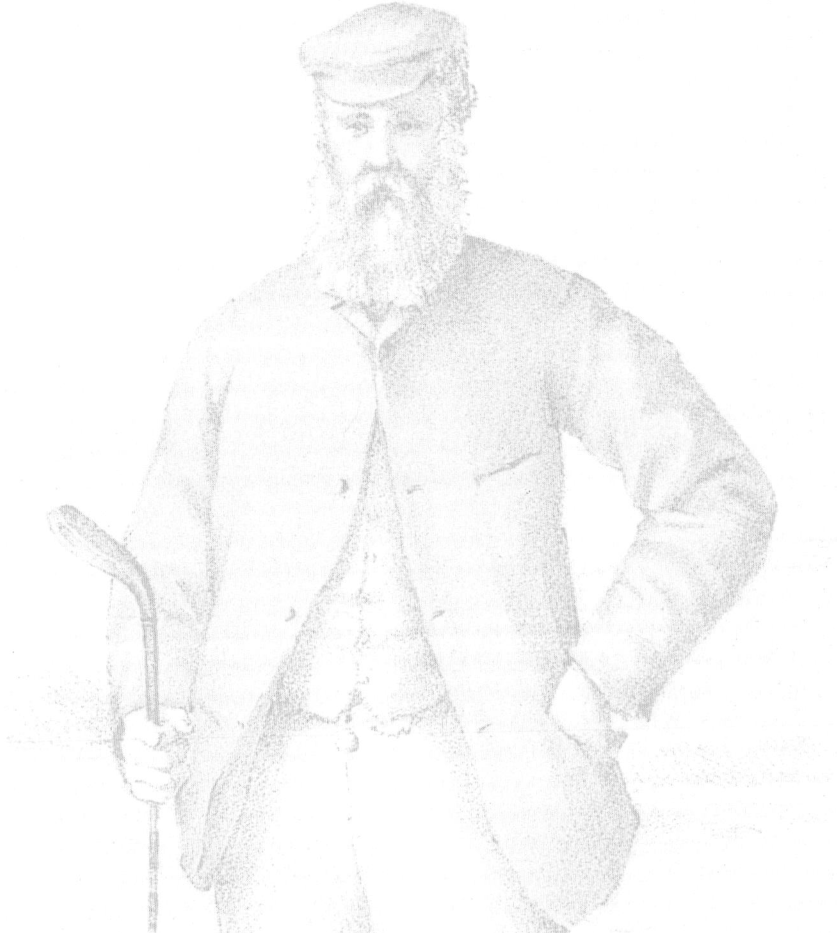

A Golfer's

The game of
Does it
Have
Have
I
Have
Peacock
U
Have
Y
Have
O
Who pl
Y
Have
A
Wishe
Y

Status of Hodge

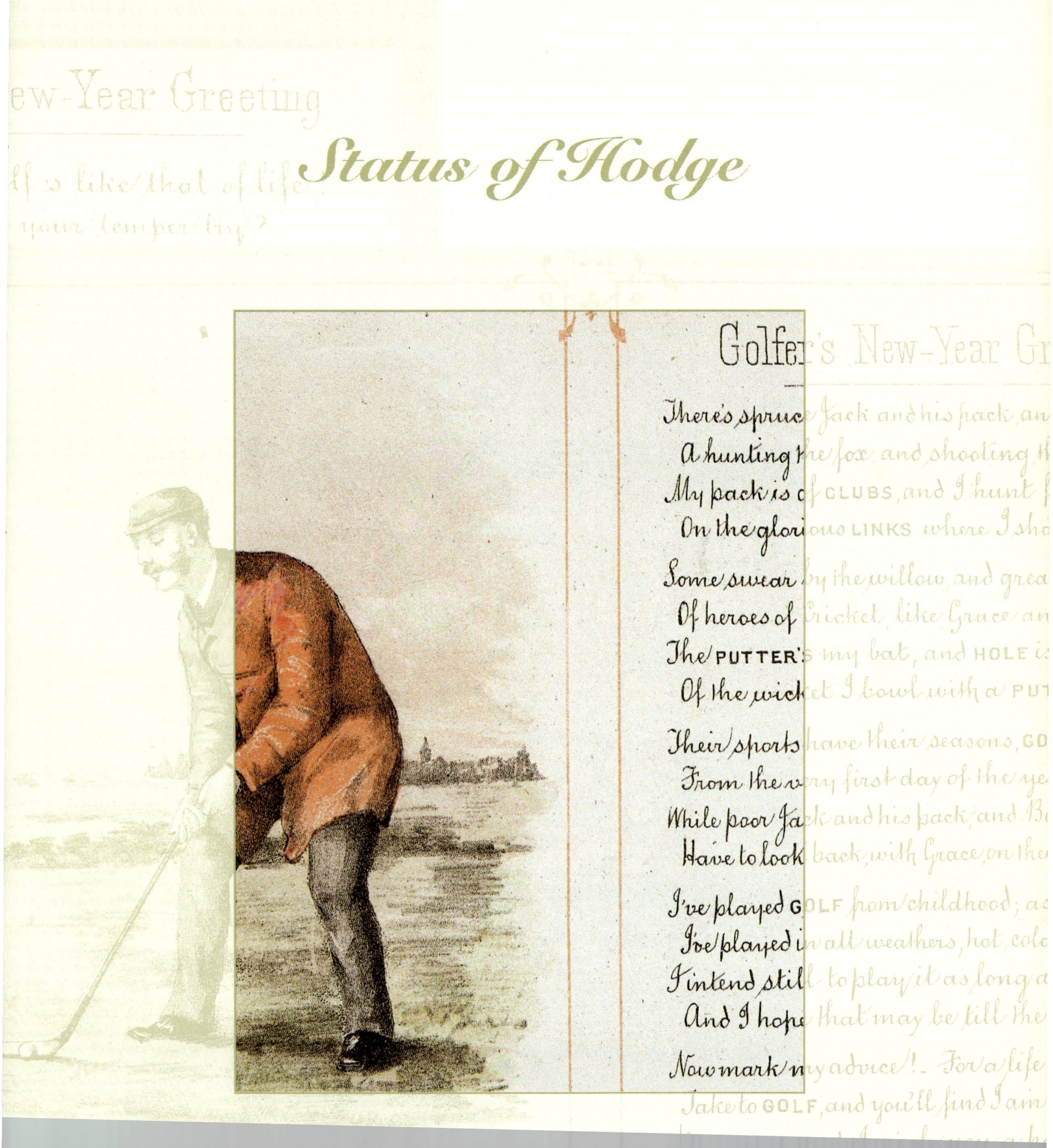

Status of Hodge

No-one could pretend that Thomas Hodge is a "great" English artist. His status in the world of golf stems simply from being the right man in the right place at the right time.

The image he cherished of golf, as an honourable pastime for men of good spirit, may now help the curious activity of knocking a small white ball into a hole by means of a stick to keep what's left of its ancient charisma and dignity.

If some of today's veteran sporting pundits preach despair for the future, it is worth recalling that over 100 years ago Hodge and his chums thought the game was out of control and would not survive much longer. Once more leaning on the contents of Hodge's personal scrapbooks, another plaintive cutting inserted there by him, from *Blackwood's* magazine of 1890, reads:

The golfer of olden days had something far more potent than written rule to guide him. He was imbued with the spirit of the game. Oh, for the wish-wash of the sea, and the laird and the doctor and the major, and the old caddy – the humourous, keen, wicked wastrel – and the clubmaker's shop with its smell of pitch and shavings, and the old play-club with its third shaft and sixth new head, and – The Old Golf!.

Was Hodge the author of this fogeyish whinge? Perhaps.

The world's millions of golfers now spread throughout scores of nations should be aware that Thomas Hodge and a tiny band of golfing reactionaries, stubbornly and, although they were not to know it, successfully defended much of their game's unwritten code of conduct. They also defended traditions like forbidding women (except charming menials!) to enter the male sanctum of the Royal & Ancient Golf Club. This absurdity meant that in 1986, Norah Sheward, Hodge's granddaughter who had just given the club perhaps half a million pounds' worth of her grandfather's paintings, wasn't allowed through the door. "Quite right!" said she at the time. "The men need a rest from us sometimes." Which just goes to show something or other....

Far grander artists than Hodge, knights of oil and canvas, studio and international standing, were employed to paint the massive portraits which adorn British club houses, notably the Royal & Ancient. But it is well appreciated, especially by the club members, that some of these canvas prairies, splendid though they seem, don't exactly reflect the models. The portrait of John Whyte-Melville by Sir Francis Grant, no less, is a delight as propaganda for the glories of old golf. Unfortunately, Melville has been flattered out of all recognition, and the background has been fiddled around to show every golfing landmark at once.

The portrait of Freddie Tait by J. H. Lorimer RSA would be comic if it were not commemorating such a tragic waste of a brilliant life.

On the other hand, Hodge's tiny portraits, especially his earlier works, are above all accurate, accurate in the sense that, no matter how small and slight, they reveal the inner man. They also frequently mirror the nature of a remote, careworn and in many ways peculiar community which thought of itself in terms of a noble city though long reduced to little more than a village. Crabby, jealous isolationism seems to have bitten into the features of many heroes, or is it sometimes just a reflection of 19th-century dental agonies?

Often, out of sheer absorption in the character he was drawing, Hodge's hand and eye created an acute portrait, far more than simply a clever likeness. It was this subtle gift that caused men like Harry Everard to christen Hodge "The Golf Artist" and irritated some of the slicker limners who began to flutter round the suddenly fashionable game for their livings from the 1880s onwards.

Who would dare to thwart the iron will of Scotland's Lord Chief Justice as profiled by Hodge? See the glint in the eye of Old Tom Morris in Hodge's only known oil painting. Not much of the "lovely old man" there. Another cunning "eyenote" concerns George Honeyman, the St. Andrews links worker, in a series of sketches on the conservation of the course. Two little dabs of Hodge's brush reveal all, capturing the sly glance of a knowing time-server whose speciality was convincing gullible visitors to dig up St. Andrews alleyways for tunnels and hidden treasures.

When golf began to expand into a national sport in the mid-1880s, Hodge found himself in demand from every quarter. He was in his late fifties, he had a young, headstrong wife and a large family, a busy, successful school which had brought him prosperity, and his golf and his art. The sudden, wider interest in golf meant that book publishers, popular magazines and newspapers needed writers and illustrators who actually knew something about the strange new hobby described as "that damned Scotch croquet" by one Sassenach. Hodge began to create pictures by a formula to meet the needs of the publishers. He took old and new photographs, sometimes from Rodger of St. Andrews, sometimes his own, or, later, those by his son Donald, and used them as basic reference.

Also, he would use his own close knowledge of the characters observed, so that the end products sent to the publishers were satisfactory as originals even if they did not always translate on the page so well in monotone and on cheap paper.

Hodge was born 20 years too soon for the "magic" of mass printing in colour so that his older watercolours on golf remained virtually unknown for a century except to the circle immediately around him. The innate quality of his work, and the acute shortage of artistic material on early golf, is illustrated by the way in which ambitious publishers of recent histories of the game have pounced greedily on his work for their pages. It fills otherwise yawning gaps.

Hodge did make a stab at the blossoming greetings cards industry which had begun to flourish around 1890 throughout Europe and North America. Here, slower, more painstaking colour printing enabled a tiny series of his New Year cards and larger postcards on golf to be published in Edinburgh by F. Huth and Co. The postcards were of famous golfers like Old Tom Morris and George Glennie, sometimes signed T. H. and dated. The New Year cards were from splendid little watercolours of golfers in action, looking very similar but not exactly like Old Tom and Harry Everard.

He also composed and wrote out as artwork in his finest script the sentimental verses linking golf and life which went with the cards. In some way these may have caused him embarrassment. Most of the cards do not bear the usual T. H. signature. Perhaps Hodge had a mild commercial deal with Huth, and the players pictured didn't like it. Two of the original pieces of artwork, very tiny, of "Old Tom" and "Everard" were sold for £7,500 each in London

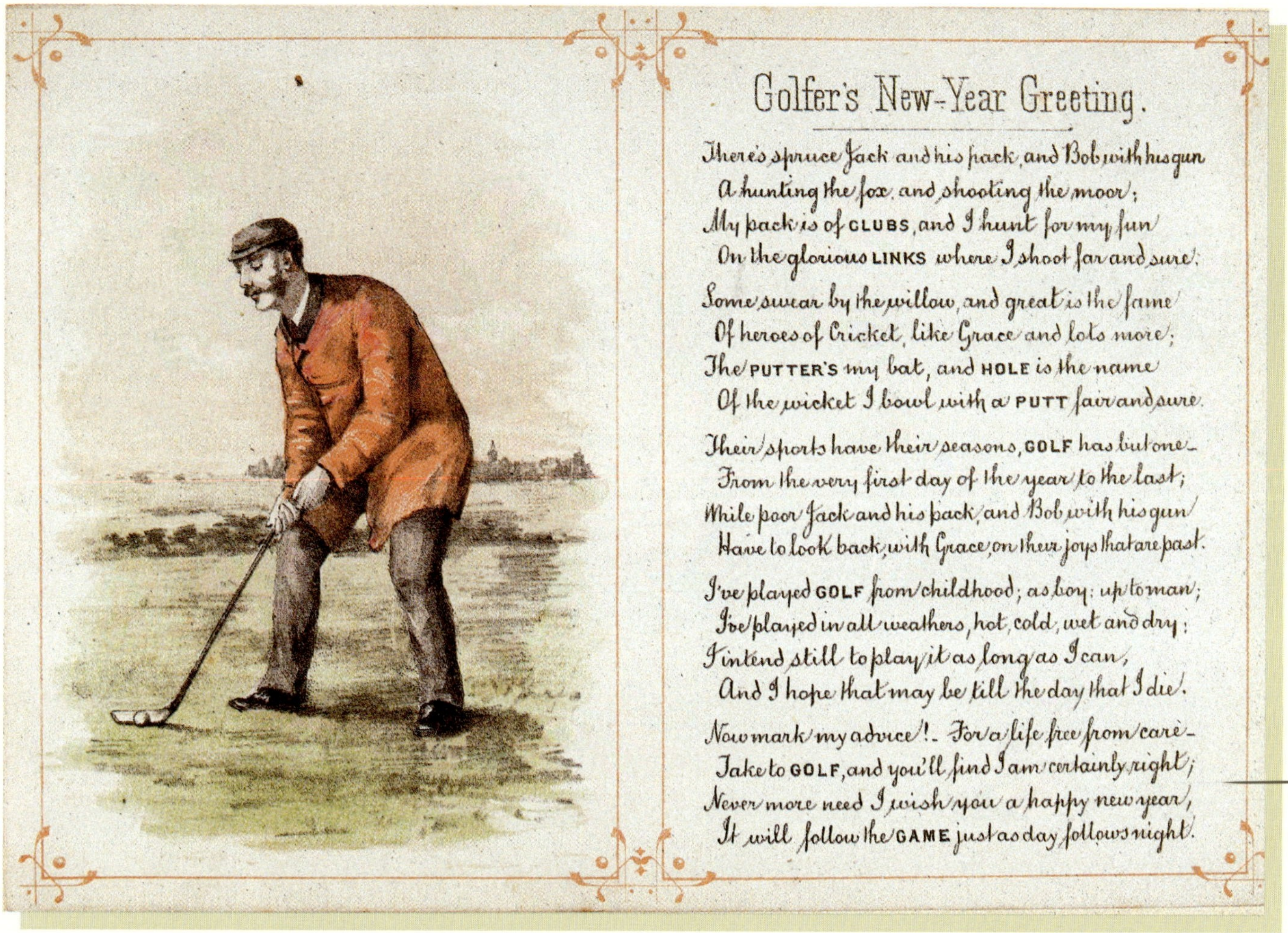

Above and right: Hodge's rare greetings cards. Similar watercolour paintings sold for £7,500 each in London in 1998. The golfers pictured are close to being portraits of Old Tom Morris and Harry Everard. The differing verses attached to the 1998 paintings indicates that the publicity for Hodge in the late 20th century is starting to unearth more of his missing work.

in July 1998. Nevertheless, family tradition insisted that Hodge himself, defending his important gentlemanly status, never painted or drew for vulgar pay.

A guide to recognising Hodge's unsigned work is that he is one of the very few artists supplying commercial printers in the 1880s where the golfers pictured actually look as if they know what they are doing. The playing clubs are invariably well drawn. Miniature scenes appear transfer-printed, then hand-coloured, on souvenir ceramics of the period many of which are almost certainly after Hodge originals. Dalziel of Edinburgh published a colourful golfing song-sheet with vignettes of players that are probably by Hodge. There are also several sets of rare "scraps" which appear to be from his designs, although again never signed.

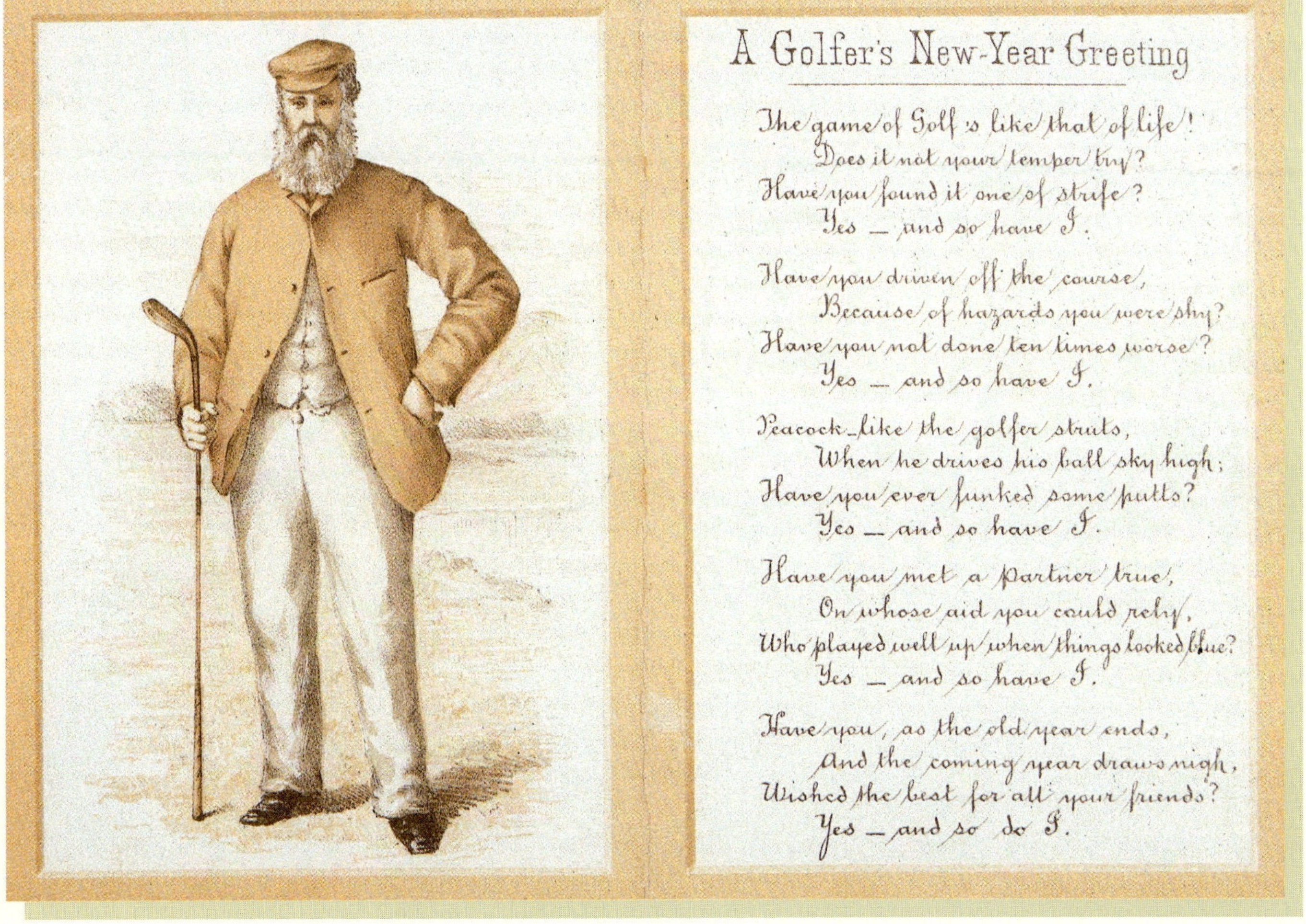

Many other commercial designs on golf at this early time, although often nice to look at, betray the artists' ignorance of the subject in some way. No wonder. They had probably never even seen the game.

Everyone close to him always maintained that Hodge remained an amateur. He is not thought to have received payment even for his contribution to the *Badminton* golf volume in 1890. He was living in the days when amateurs were regarded as a superior class to professionals on virtually every level of British life, especially sport. In fact, golf was one of the few areas where long experience of the skills of artisan players like Allan Robertson and Old Tom and Young Tom Morris, to name but three, had shown that those who had to earn money from their abilities could behave in a decent manner as well as picking up a few gold sovereigns. The point was not so much missed by Hodge and his contemporaries as deliberately and sometimes brutally ignored because of the wider implications which would have turned upside down the "natural order" of 19th-century society.

The New Year cards and postcards from Hodge designs have become such rarities that it is possible he had them printed solely for himself and Royal & Ancient members at the appropriate season. Huth and Co. may have sold a few in Scotland in return for Hodge having quantities at lower cost.

His technique of recalling veteran golfers by the use of his large collection of golfing photographs, possibly the best that existed in the 1880s, was copied by other artists. These included the astounding Michael Brown, born in Fife in 1853, whose hyper-realistic groups of famous late Victorian and Edwardian golfers produced annually as calendars for the Life Association of Scotland fetched anything up to £48,000 apiece when 18 of them were sold in London in 1995. Then there was Francis Powell Hopkins (1830–1913) who signed himself Major S. or "Shortspoon", a jokey title which suited his pretty watercolours and illustrations. Hopkins' pleasant compositions were commerce-friendly and remain so, original watercolours reaching five figures at auction.

Hopkins also used photographic images to ease his workload. But there is nothing new in this. Vastly more eminent artists worthy of international galleries and prices in millions have used "photographic" devices to help them over the centuries.

Hodge believed that a man's back view could sometimes reveal as much about him as his front, especially at golf. He was not above asking his son Donald to take snapshots which fitted in with his notions. Hence, for instance, the rhinoceros bulk of H. J. Whigham, American Amateur winner in 1896–97, in one sketch – a ludicrous pose made successful because somehow it says as much about Whigham as a normal portrait.

The pinnacle of Hodge's late artistic "career" came when author Horace Hutchinson asked him to illustrate the *Golf* volume of the *Badminton* series of sporting books. Hodge was proud of his contribution and pasted into the front of his own copy the following comment from *The Speaker* of 1890:

> *For many years this brilliant amateur has devoted his humourous genius to the sketching of golf celebrities. Fifty of those sketches are here very creditably reproduced. What golfer cannot recognise the enthusiastic devotion to the game in the face of Mr. Sutherland, the Bohemian ease of Mr. Pat Alexander, the manly dignity of Sir Robert Hay, the unruffled tranquillity of Mr. Wolf Murray on his pony, the dogged determination of Mr. George Glennie, or the characteristic calm of the veteran golfer Mr. Whyte Melville?*

Hodge had helped also to illustrate Robert Clark's magnificent *Golf: A Royal and Ancient Game*, published 15 years earlier. He drew a delicate map of the course at St. Andrews published on page 181. He illustrated the famous poem "The Nine Holes of St. Andrews" with what must have been refined vignettes before the engraver diminished them with a fairly cavalier interpretation. Hodge's minuscule landscapes appear in Clark's book to be studded with lumpish golfers.

The originals, certainly watercolours, would have been ideal for reproduction in lithographic colour. In the book they are attacked vigorously by an engraver who awarded himself a large signature on several and missed out the tiny "T. H." altogether. Nevertheless, the refinement of the still-missing originals shines through. They may have been among Hodge's finest paintings, a lost delight. Hodge seems to have been saving his collected golf paintings and drawings in the hope that a history of the game in the 19th century could be embroidered round them by one of his writer friends. Harry Everard, the golf historian, said:

A collection of his many sketches would afford an interesting history of golf so long as he has been acquainted with it.

John Kerr, the editor of the classic *Golf Book of East Lothian*, said in its pages:

Mr Thomas Hodge, the artist whose illustrations of golf and golfers at St. Andrews are by far the best artistic productions in connection with the game.

Gilbert Mitchell-Innes and John Penn M.P., Royal & Ancient Club members, each formed extensive collections. If they, or anyone else for that matter, admired a particular portrait, Hodge might repeat it as a gift. Thus he created duplicates which can cause questions about authenticity now that his clever doodles can be bought and sold for thousands of dollars or pounds.

How many works on golf did he create? Simple arithmetic says it was several thousand over a period of nearly 40 years. How many were known in the late 20th century? Two to three hundred.

Of the missing pictures, those that may have survived, there could be many unrecognised for what they are in the possession of descendants of Hodge's relatives and friends. Others may have gone to America, Canada and India through members of the family. At one stage there may have been as many as 40 albums of Hodge's sketches and photographs, "No.40" in his handwriting being the title of one battered book that has been rescued.

The summits of many a golfing year between 1858 and 1890 must have been his large, busy scenes of the spring and autumn meetings at St. Andrews. Where are they now, beg the golf historians? Well, we know of two, one saved by his granddaughter Norah Sheward and now gracing the office of the R & A.secretary after restoration. And the ghost of another, turned into an engraving for the *Badminton* volume on golf in 1890.

Thomas Hodge's virtual disappearance from the centre of the golfing world, a vanishing act so complete that his role in recording the game's historic personalities was almost totally forgotten after his death, was hastened by a new school of commercial artists. Professionals like John Hassall, Cecil Aldin, Charles Crombie, Tom Browne, Lance Thackeray, John Wallace ("George Pipeshank" of Cope's tobacco fame) and Harry Rountree (or is it Rowntree?) and many others were giving the new world of popular publishing the stuff that sold the millions.

Plenty of strong design, plenty of strong colour, plenty of belly laughs. A pity such brilliant talent sometimes sold itself so cheaply.

By 1910, Thomas Hodge, who had died three years earlier, was scarcely more than a shadowy name from the past.

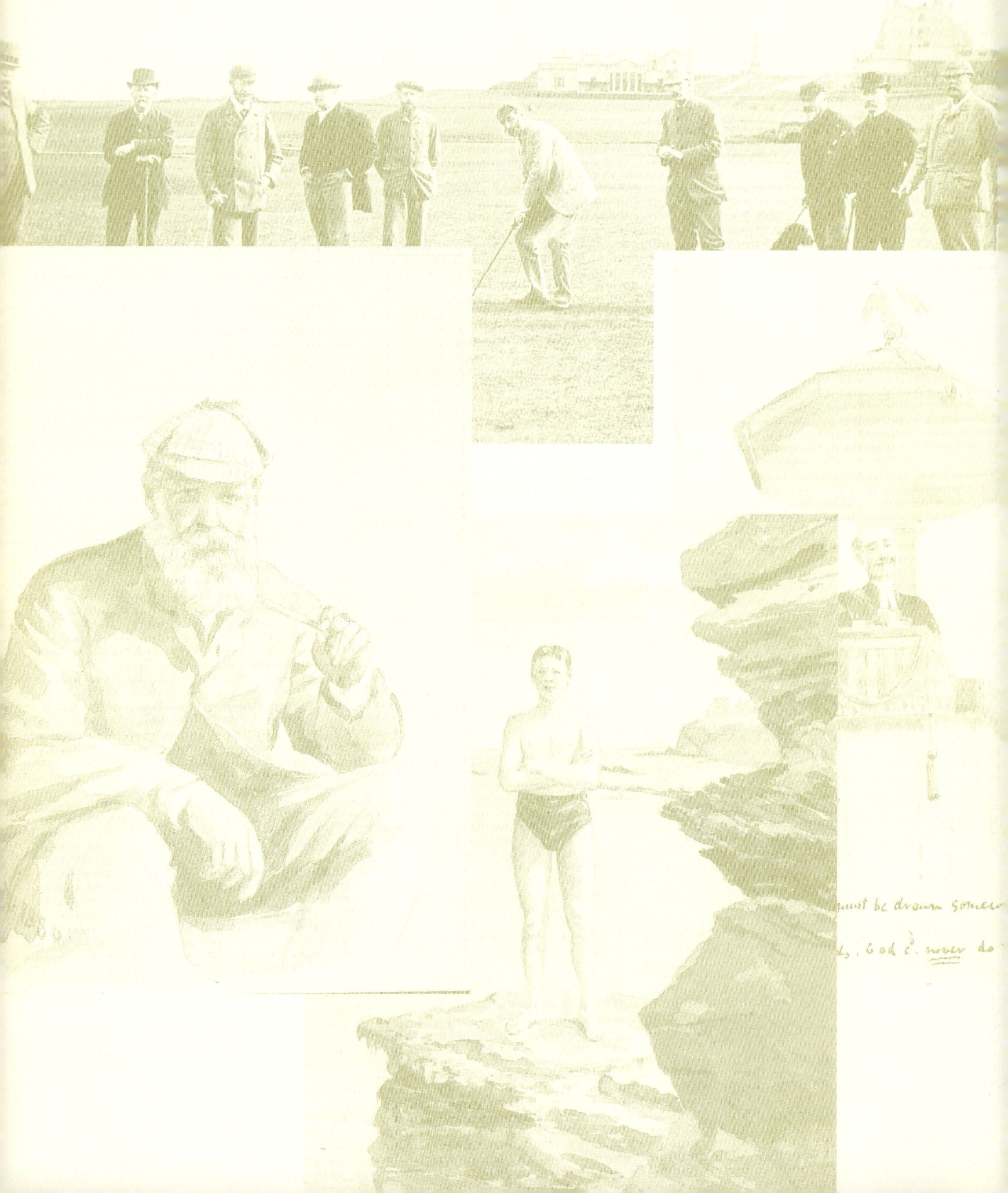

The Legendary Golfers

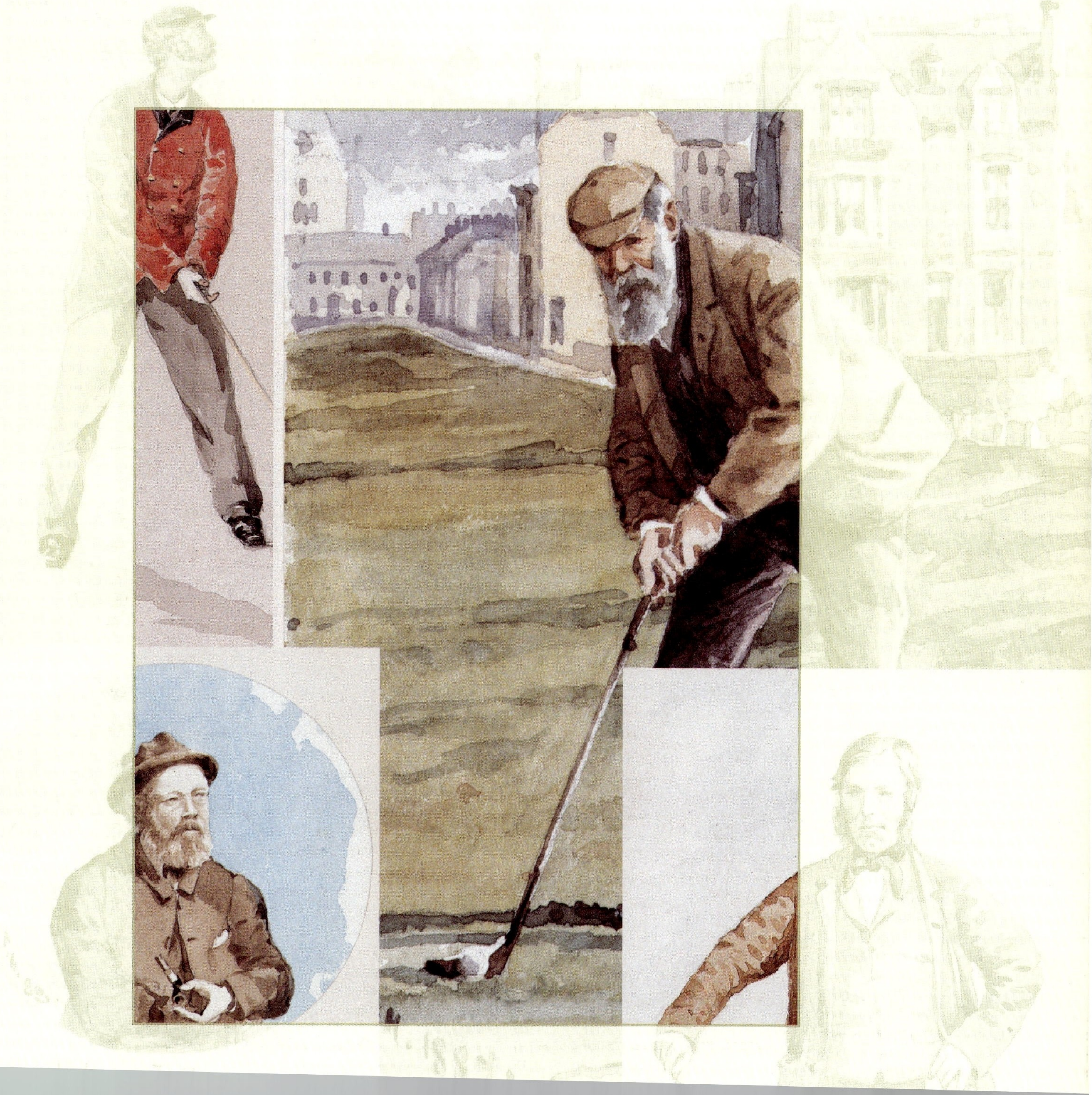

The Legendary Golfers

From the mid-1850s to the early 1890s, Thomas Hodge painted and sketched the members of the Royal & Ancient Golf Club and the local heroes of Fife. His miniature gallery of the game only started to be revealed almost a century after the artist's death. Old Tom Morris was by far his favourite subject.

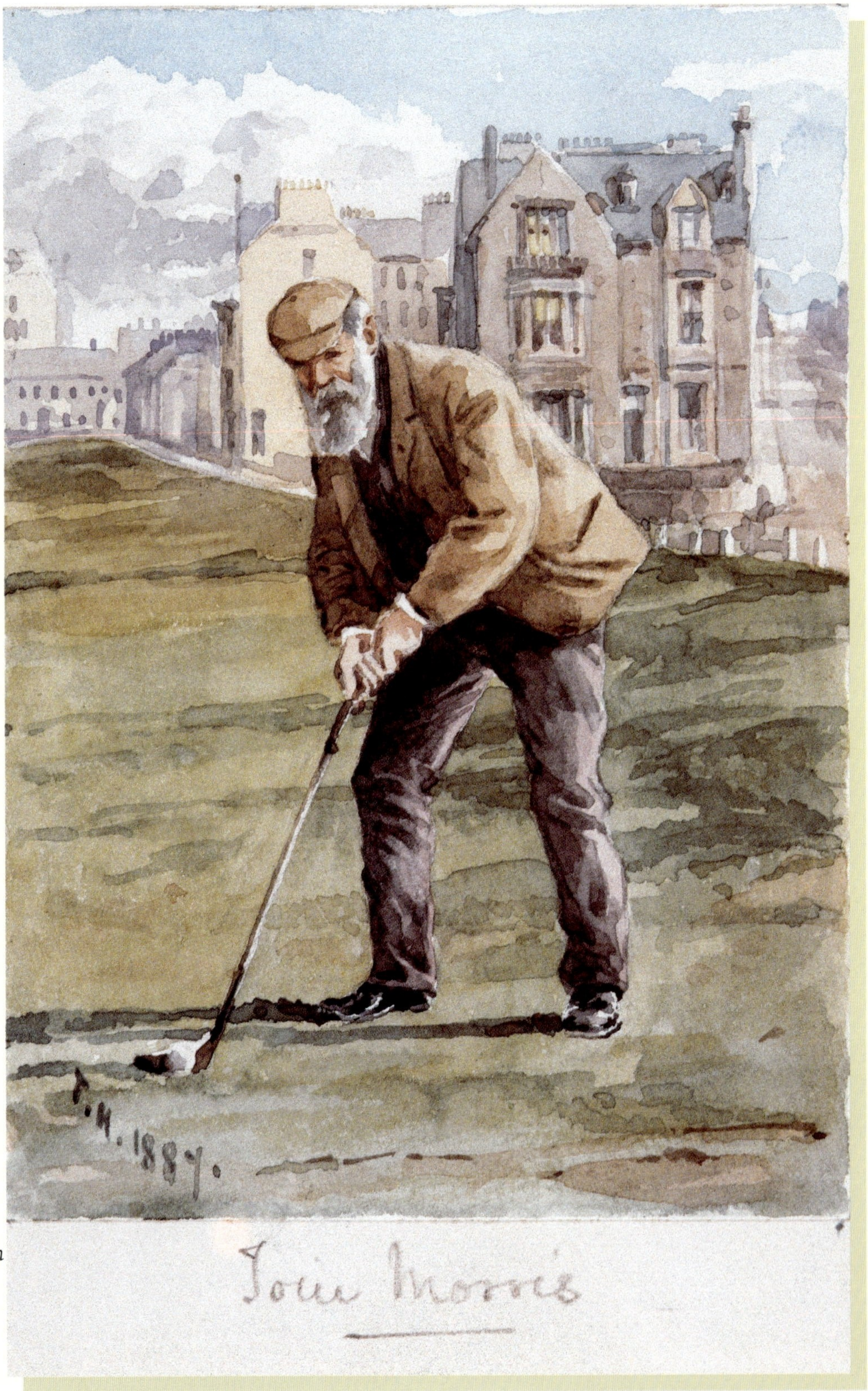

Right: Hodge's favourite subject Old Tom Morris, drawn here in 1887 on the edge of the links.

"A.K.H.B."

A slightly comical portrait of a minister in his St. Andrews pulpit may seem a perverse introduction to the Thomas Hodge gallery of legendary golfers.

However, Andrew Kennedy Hutcheson Boyd, thanks to his prolific diaries of St. Andrews life, has provided a vast amount of background to the Thomas Hodge era which roughly matched "A.K.H.B.'s" own stay of 34 years in Fife.

What is more, the social environment in which the Royal & Ancient Golf Club was set in the 19th century, and also Hodge's portraits, may be better appreciated after digesting Boyd's attitudes.

He believed in Right and Wrong, Heaven and Hell, God and The Devil. He said he believed that if a parishioner walked the 242 steps round the great parish church of St. Andrews three times, "withershins" (the opposite of the way the sun goes) at midnight on Hallow E'en, he might come face to face with Old Nick.

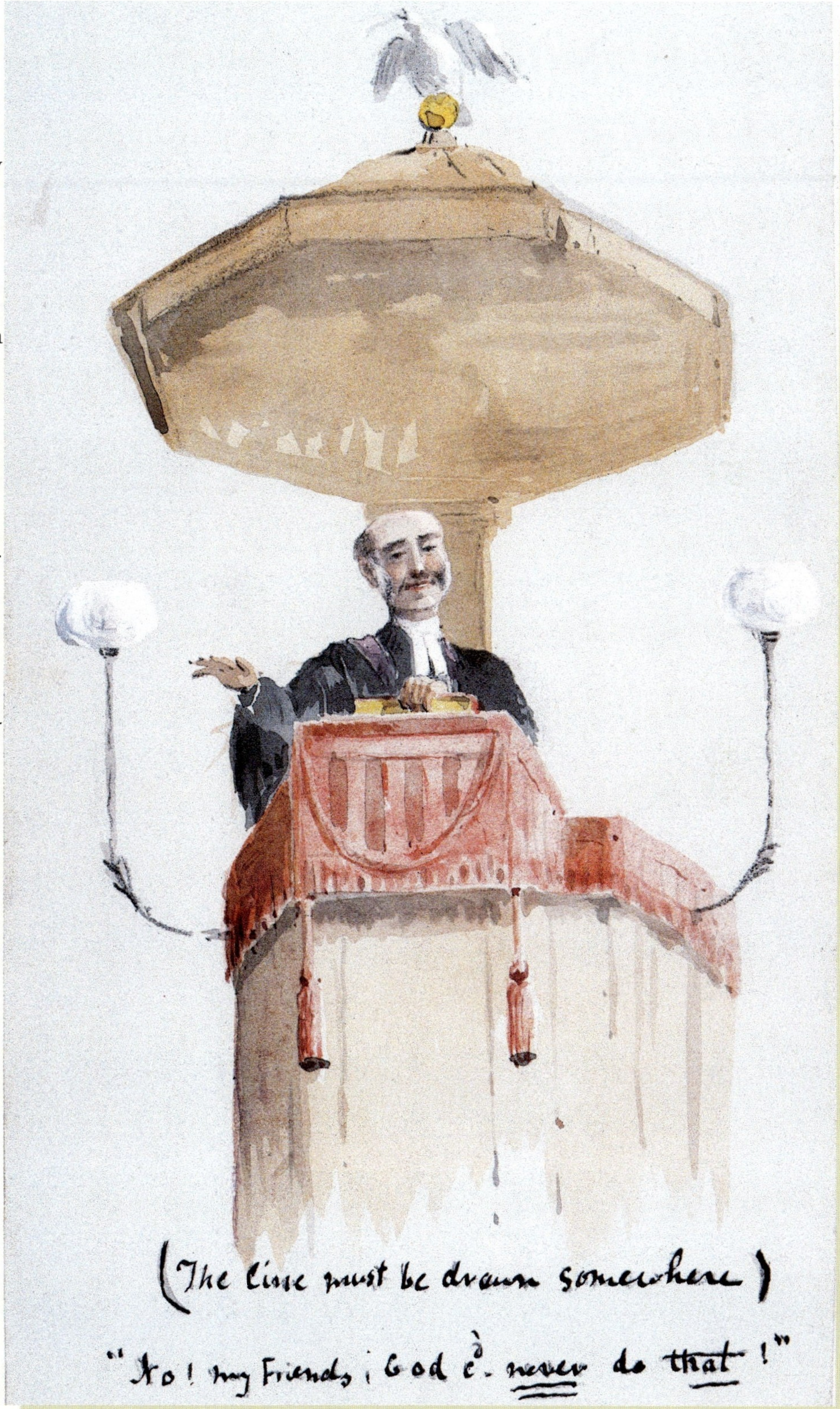

Right: Andrew Kennedy Hutcheson Boyd.

The overwhelming majority of Boyd's congregation would have agreed with him in superstitious fear and trembling, even if many of the wordly gentlemen golfers, including his neighbour Thomas Hodge, would have waited until they got home from the parish kirk before having a good laugh.

Hodge often must have been among the massive congregations of several thousand people which the charismatic Dr. Boyd attracted to his church services. The artist has inscribed this watercolour:

The line has to be drawn somewhere. No. My friends, God could NEVER do THAT.

Hodge also commented on Boyd:

Always known as A.K.H.B. A station porter once translated these well-known initials as meaning 'A Kind 'o Haverin' Body'. He was wrong.

The railway servant may have been from Perth, which Boyd castigated as the place where service to the railway traveller was at its nadir. Boyd was a hardened rail traveller long before the 1890s, steaming thousands of miles between bishops' palaces throughout Britain, hob-nobbing with great men of religion, literature and government.

The reason why this "modest son of the manse", as he called himself, could afford to enjoy the height of modern living at 50 miles an hour was simple – he was an immensely successful diarist and sermoniser. His volumes could sell over 100,000 copies apiece. Among the 30 or more of his books was a three-volume summary called *Twenty Five Years of St. Andrews* and *Last Years of St. Andrews*.

In the snippets of gossip he revealed about his friends and enemies – he didn't dislike a bit of hate, saying "I'm a good hater" – there were a few on golf. (Golf was still poor relation to the Ruins, the History and the University of St. Andrews when a new edition of the local guide book was published by W. C. Henderson, the University Press, near to 1900. Only three of its 150 pages discussed golfing facilities. Critics of this imbalance were sharply rebuked by the editor.)

One of Boyd's golf notes was in October 1866:

In that year, the third of October was the day of the great Golf meeting; and that afternoon, amid a crowd of 200, I walked round the Links to see the decisive match between two crack players, Mr. Hodge and Mr. Lamb. Mr. Hodge won, by the narrowest possible advantage.

Charles Kingsley, author of *The Water-babies*, stayed a week with Boyd in 1867, and wrote to him later:

Golf is the Queen of games, if cricket is the King; and the golfing gentlemen as fine fellows as ever I saw.

That year, Boyd recorded the death of a schoolboy at the local Madras College while playing golf.

In half an hour he was carried back, stone-dead. A ball had struck him behind the ear; and he never stirred.

The only time Boyd walked the links with a foursome – he doesn't record ever trying to play though visiting the R & A for half an hour every day, possibly for a dram and a chat – the match ended in uproar. In his own words: "It was extraordinary how peppery the golfers became."

The Very Rev. Principal Tulloch, chaplain to the Royal & Ancient, revered head of the University who had been a member of the golf club for 30 years at his death in 1886, was then one of the players.

Tulloch, seeing his partner doing something he felt was incorrect, made some suggestion to him. On which, his irate friend brandished his club in the air and literally screamed out: "No directions! I'll take no directions!."

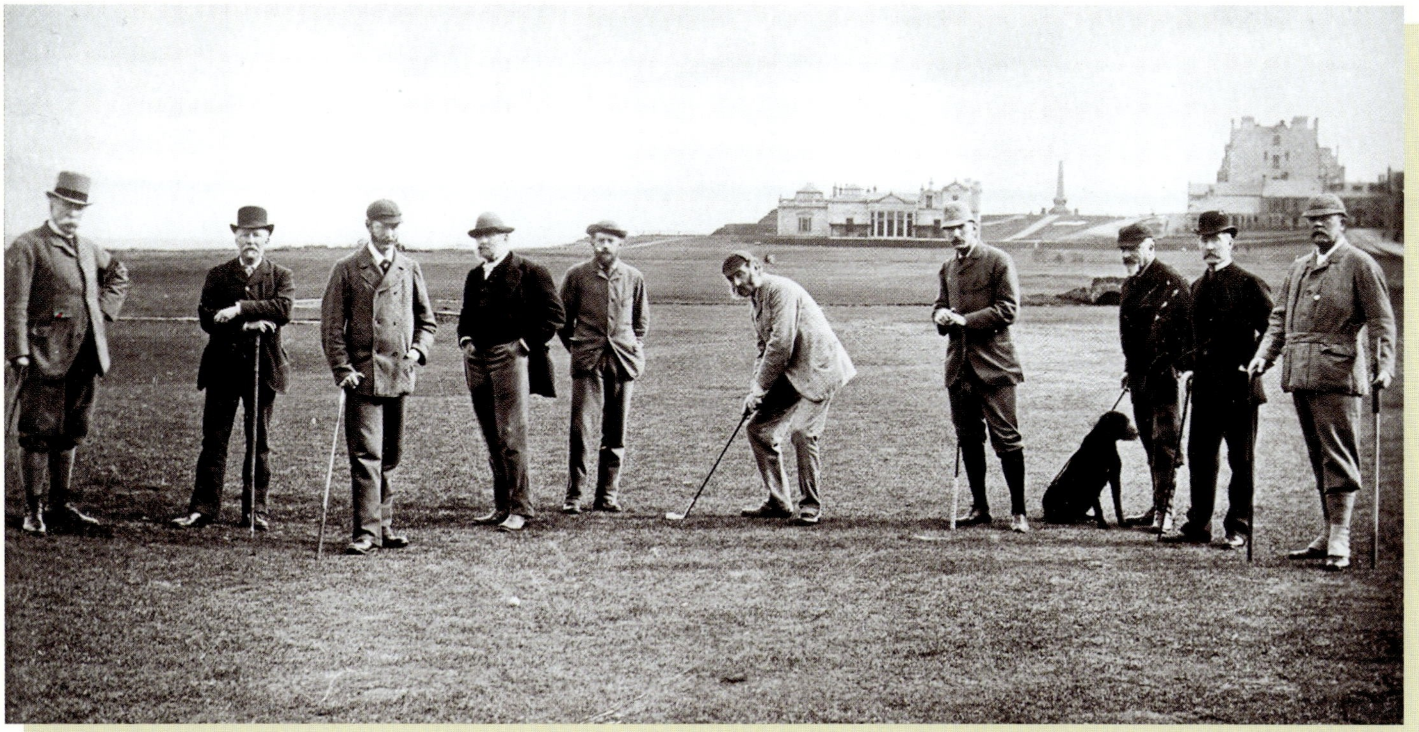

Above: the Rev. A. K. H. Boyd, with the Royal & Ancient clubhouse in the background. Left to right: Mr. Blackwell, Thomas Hodge, Harry Everard, Patrick Alexander, Mr. Hull, Robert Boothby, Mr. Oliphant, Bob Bethune with dog, the Rev. Boyd, Mr. White.

It was Boyd who had the task of trying to comfort the Morris family during their terrible grief at Christmas 1875.

After his young wife and new-born baby died in the September, Young Tom Morris "lived as if in a trance". Unfortunately, Captain Molesworth and his three golfing sons (gambling men who it was said would bet on anything, any time) came up to Scotland from Westward Ho!, playing all the amateurs and winning their matches. Arthur Molesworth, particularly good, and particularly insensitive with it, challenged any professional with receipt of "a third". Against his will, Young Tom was induced to play, probably by the gambling fraternity. He won the first match on November 30. The next three days, the snow and frost was so thick, the referee wanted to postpone the match. The Molesworths wouldn't agree.

Tommy won, but it was obvious he was in bad health and his mind was distraught. He wanted to give up and said so, but continued "for the sake of his friends". He left home for a few days, sick and depressed, returning on Christmas Eve, possibly the worse for drink. He talked with his mother, went to bed, and died in the night from a ruptured artery in his right lung.

W. W. Tulloch described how the revered parish minister, the genial and able A.K.H.B. said the prayers at Young Tom's grave-side, finishing with the phrase:

A better golfer never played a further or a surer ball.

Old Tom Morris

The Father Figure, the Grand Patriarch of golf, is Old Tom Morris. His voluptuously bearded image, superficially the twin of his counterpart and contemporary in cricket, Dr. W. G. Grace, adorns scores of books on the game. And whenever golf's publicists and "spin doctors" need a noble image to add a measure of gravitas to their latest outpourings, they reach first for a head and shoulders portrait of Old Tom.

Old Tom was born in North Street, St. Andrews, in 1821, six years older than Thomas Hodge, who was always known as "Mr. H" to Morris though their relationship was as friendly as it was possible to be between an aspiring gentleman and an artisan.

Their mutual passion, the golf, meant that Hodge and Old Tom met daily on or near the links for months on end. Hodge was endlessly fascinated by Old Tom's character and never tired of drawing and painting him.

Opposite is reproduced what is reputedly the only oil painting Hodge ever attempted, a portrait of Old Tom in the mid-1880s, still in the original frame where the painting was put carelessly when tacky for hanging in a place of honour at Hodge's home. Thus, the picture, on a paper base, became stuck perhaps irrevocably to the fronting glass when it dried. Nothing could better exemplify the cavalier treatment Hodge and his family accorded his hobby even though he was proud enough of the end results.

The oil painting gives an intense insight into Old Tom's character, not surpassed even by the large oil portrait hanging in the Royal & Ancient clubhouse and painted by Sir George Reid in 1903.

Hodge's portrait may be only a few inches square, but there is a strength and depth in the subject's appraising eyes which reveals exactly why he was held in a respect sometimes close to fear and reverence by lords and locals.

Companion with this oil there is a watercolour of the same period again showing Old Tom in his beloved deerstalker hat. This is another of Hodge's outstanding works. Both these paintings come from his granddaughter Norah Sheward's collection given to the Royal & Ancient in 1985. Similar paintings were used in now rare golf books of the 1880s–90s, one at least published by G. Stewart and Co. of Edinburgh, a delicate masterpiece.

A good example of Hodge's use of photographic reference as a foundation for his own skill and knowledge places Old Tom in front of his shop in Links Road, adjoining the St. Andrews course itself. Old Tom is clearly in good form, bursting for a long chat in his broad Fifeshire dialect. Perhaps like the conversation he held with Horace Hutchinson on New Year's Day 1886 (published in the *Badminton Golf* volume in 1890), which, slightly edited, went like this:

I was born on June 16, 1821, sir, born and bred in St. Andrews, an' a gowfer a' ma days. The very first time I hae mind o' mysel' I was toddlin' aboot at the short holes wi a putter.

I was made 'prentice to Allan Robertson as a ba'-macker at eighteen and wrocht wi' him elivin years. We played Allan and me thegither, some geyan big mautches – ane in parteecler wi' the twa Dunns, Willie and Jamie, graund players baith, nane better. It was a 'through a braw fecht, but we snoddit 'em bonnie ere the end o't.

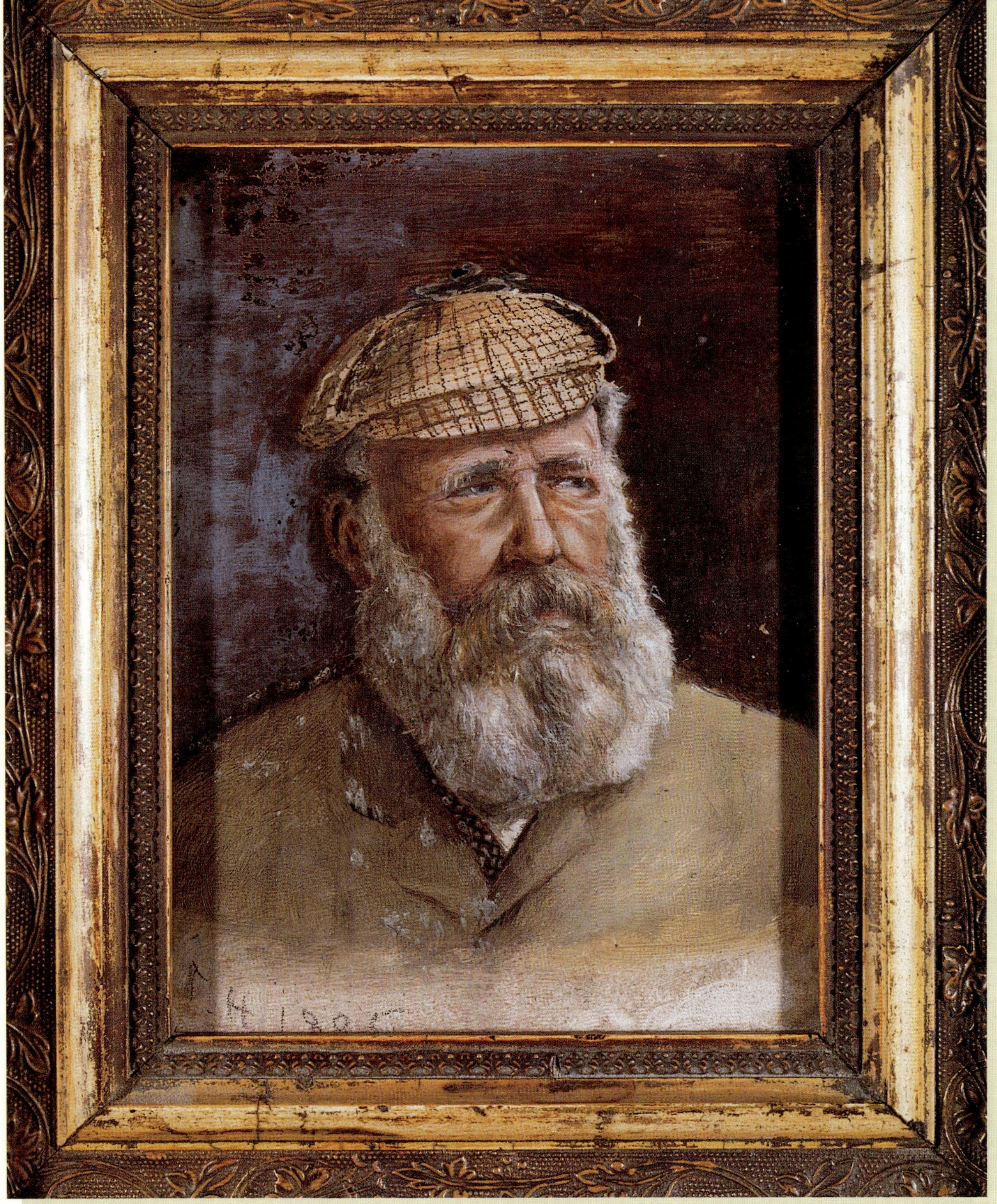

An awfu' player, puir Allan! The cunningest bit body o' a player, I dae think, that iver haundled cleek an' putter. A kindly body tae, as it weel fits me to say, sir, an' wi a walth o' slee pawky fun aboot him.

Three years after Allan deed, I cam fra Prestwick to keep the green at St. Awndrews; here I hae been sin syne. I think I can play aboot as weel yet as I did in ma prime. No, maybe, drive jist sae lang a ba'; but there's no muckle odds e'en in that yet. Jist the day I was sixty-four, I gaed round wi Mr. H. in 81.

(Hodge records this feat in another portrait.)

No that ill for the "Auld Horse" as they ca'me.

An it had na' been for gowff, I'm no sure that at this day, sir, I wad hae been a leevin' man. I've had ma troubles an' ma trials, sae that I thocht to "lay me doun an' dee" as the song says, lookit aboot a' that was left in life for Puir Tam.

(This refers to the death of his famous son Young Tom Morris on Christmas Day 1875, only a few weeks after Young Tom's wife and baby died.)

It was like as if ma very sowle was a'thegether gane oot 'o me. But wi' the help of ma God' an' o' gowff, I've aye gotten warsled through some-how or ither. The tae thing ta'en wi'the tither, I hae nae had an ill time on't. I dinna mind that iver I had an unpleasant ward frae ony 'o the many gentlemen I've played wi'. I've aye tried – as my business was,sir – to mak masel' pleesant to them; an they've aye been awfu' pleesant to me.

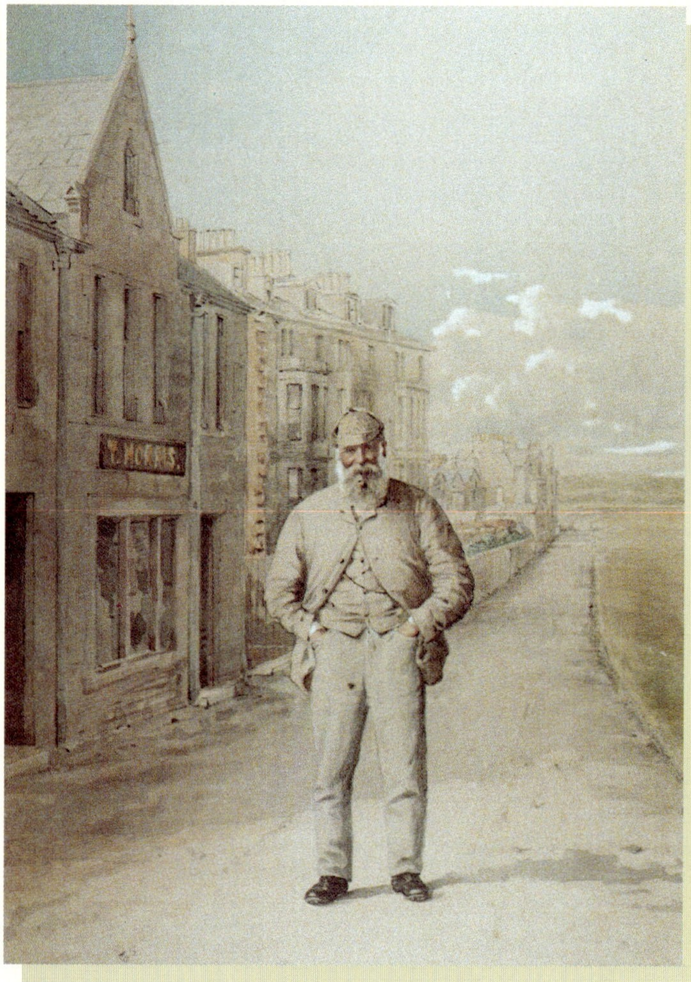

Above: a benevolent Old Tom outside his shop in the battle-scarred Links Road.

Hodge used a similar Old Tom Morris-ish portrait in another setting in front of the Royal & Ancient clubhouse and the martyrs' monument for one of the rare small litho-graphic prints produced by Huth of Edinburgh.

Two more full-length watercolour portraits of Old Tom which were discovered in 1983 complete a formidable visual record of one of the strongest, most influential characters in the history of world sport.

The first, signed T. H. and dated 1887 (size 12.6cm x 8.8cm), shows Morris about to putt with a long-nosed club on the St. Andrews course not far from the old station-master's cottage.

The latter records him, through Hodge's inscription: "On the day, the 64th anniversary of his birth, he holed the links at 81." Dated '85 (image size 9.2cm x 3.7cm).

Hodge must have composed this charming, modest portrait of Old Tom immediately after the outstanding golfing feat, and then no doubt stood his old friend his customary pint of "black strap" ale in celebration.

Below: two of Hodge's superior works, portraits of Old Tom Morris which were used in several rare books.

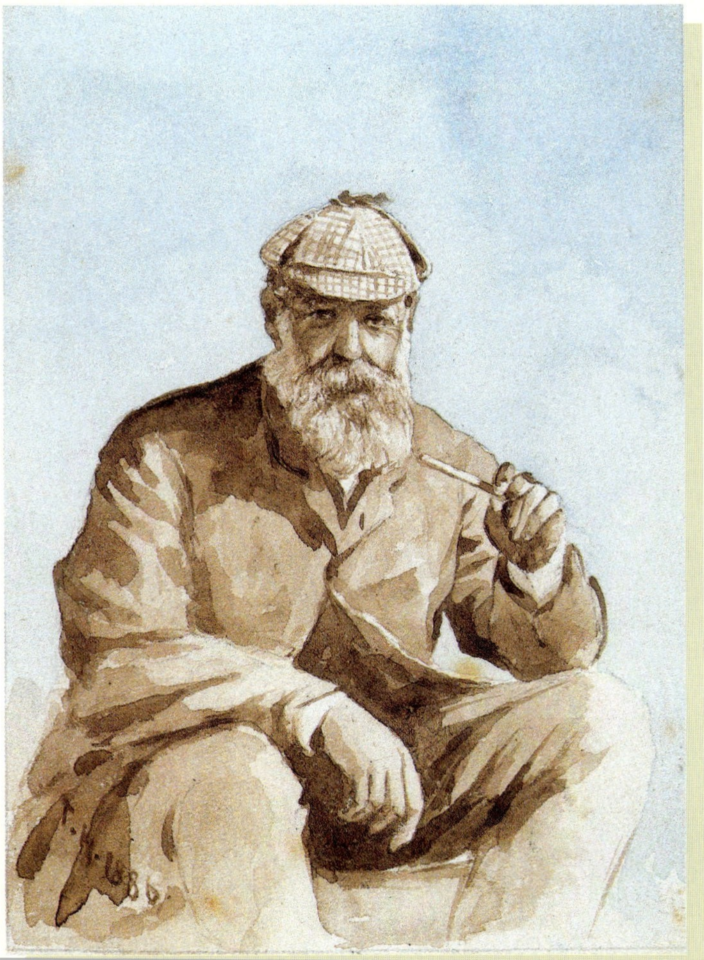

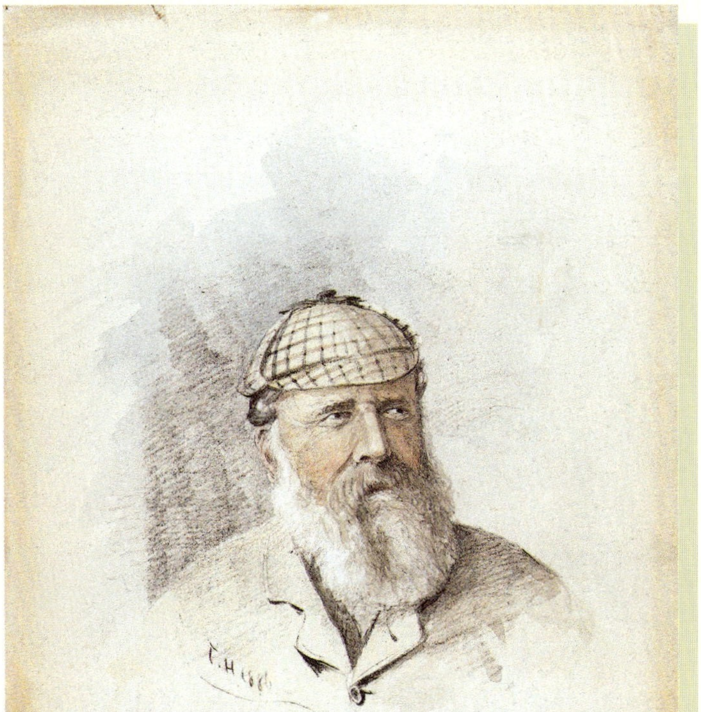

Old Tom Morris was the Open Champion in 1861, 1862, 1864 and 1867. His putting sometimes betrayed him, so that there may have been greater golfers in the mid-19th century; his son Young Tom (Open Champion 1868, 1869, 1870, 1872) and the "immortal" Allan Robertson for instance. In 1863 he was appointed "as a servant of the Royal & Ancient Club in charge of the entire course" at a salary of £50 a year plus £20 for the upkeep of the links.

Over the years he kept a canny foot in the camps of his own folk and "the gentlemen", becoming revered universally for his dignity and nobility of character. Search where you will, rattle the old skeletons of golf till they crumble, there's never a sour word about "Old Tom", a devout Christian and pillar of the local church.

His father had been a letter carrier in Edinburgh, turning to caddying at St. Andrews. (In Edinburgh the word "caddie" originally meant errand porter).

Old Tom died in sad circumstances at the age of 87 in 1908. Now absent-minded, he visited the New Club next to the links one day and mistook the wine cellar door for that of the adjoining lavatory, falling down the steep steps to his death.

Never could there be met with a more perfect specimen of what is called Nature's Gentleman than Old Tom

wrote Harry Everard.

The day after Old Tom's funeral, the *Glasgow Herald* printed the poem :

Thou King o' Men,
High Priest o' Gowff,
Thou'rt sadly ta'en
To thy last howff.

Thou play'dst wi Allan
Lang years ago;
But wha's this callan
Has laid thee low?

Thou's taen on Death
Wha plays unseen;
Thou's held him faith,
To his last green.

Right: Old Tom at 64 in 1885. Another Hodge gem which also indicates his close friendship with the master golfer.

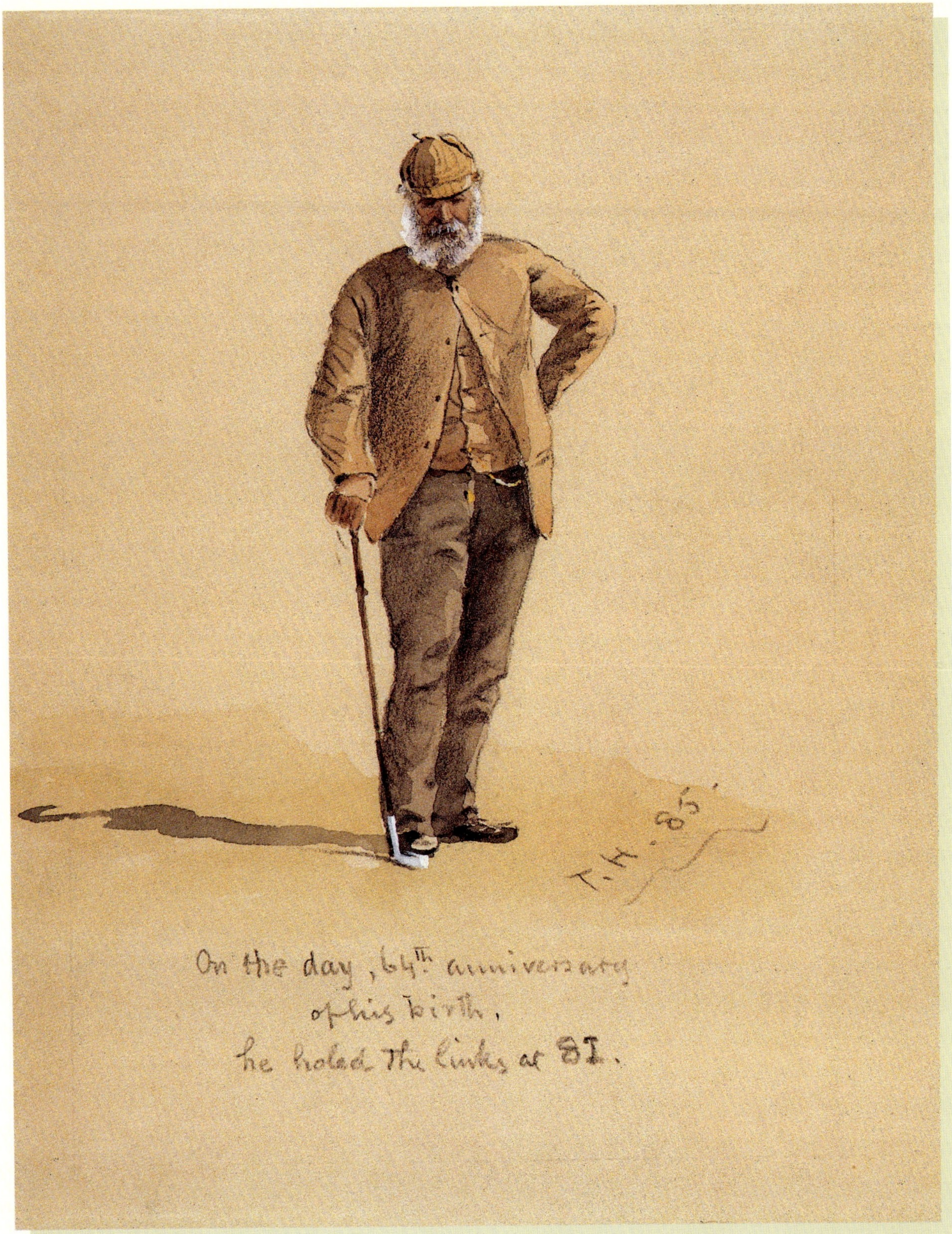
T.H. 85.
On the day, 64th anniversary
of his birth,
he holed the links at 81.

The Incurable Romantic H. S. C. Everard

Harry Stirling Crawfurd Everard is the kind of name that might have been created for a fictional saga. His real-life story might have been dreamed up by Barbara Cartland for one of her novels. Except that it is absolutely true.

H. S. C. Everard (1848–1909) is shown to be a dashing, dramatic golfer by Thomas Hodge. His full-length watercolour of Everard in dark blue cap and red golfing jacket is inscribed by the artist "The correct address".

A member of the Royal & Ancient Golf Club for 45 years, Everard was elected as a boy of 16. He was an outstanding player of golf, lawn tennis and cricket, keeping wicket for the Warwickshire County Club. Nearly a century after his death at the age of 61 in 1909, an event which plunged the whole of Fife into mourning, he is mostly remembered as a brilliant golf historian and writer.

He contributed a priceless mass of detail on players of the 19th century as his section of the *Badminton Golf* volume in 1890 and his fluent magazine and newspaper articles were always superior reading. His triumph was *A History of the Royal & Ancient Golf Club, St. Andrews, from 1754–1900*, published by William Blackwood in Edinburgh, 1907. As this was the year of Hodge's death in London, he most likely didn't have the pleasure of reading his friend Everard's giant work, described by the the American golf book expert Joseph Murdoch as "Another of the great books of the game and a monumental effort of original research".

Obituary notices a century ago often told a superficial story. John Low's notice in *Golf Illustrated* of May 21, 1909 was slightly more revealing. After noting that Everard started golf as a schoolboy at St. Andrews and Westward Ho!, Low commented that after 1880 when Everard settled in St. Andrews:

He probably played more golf than anyone else in the society As a golfer he had ways and methods of his own and has had no imitators. He worked out his own postures and practices.

Sitting down, as it were, very much to his stroke, he swung his club backwards with a scythe-like motion, while in the downward swing the right shoulder and even the right leg were moved forward into the work.

Though not an impressive player to watch, few could give such long odds and win so many matches.

Mr. Everard was not possessed of those gifts which make a man quickly popular, and his manner seemed to many to carry too much reserve. But this was a surface thing, caused by a highly-strung and nervous disposition. Underneath the man was all tenderness and full of love and sentiment. He was one who loved his books and his house and his family. A fine linguist, he loved the romantic of all nations and the weird mediaeval stories of things occult....

Right: Harry Everard, by Hodge, an image he has inscribed "The correct address", a subtle admonishment for Rev. McPherson, the wordy golf critic, and others who disliked Everard's playing methods.

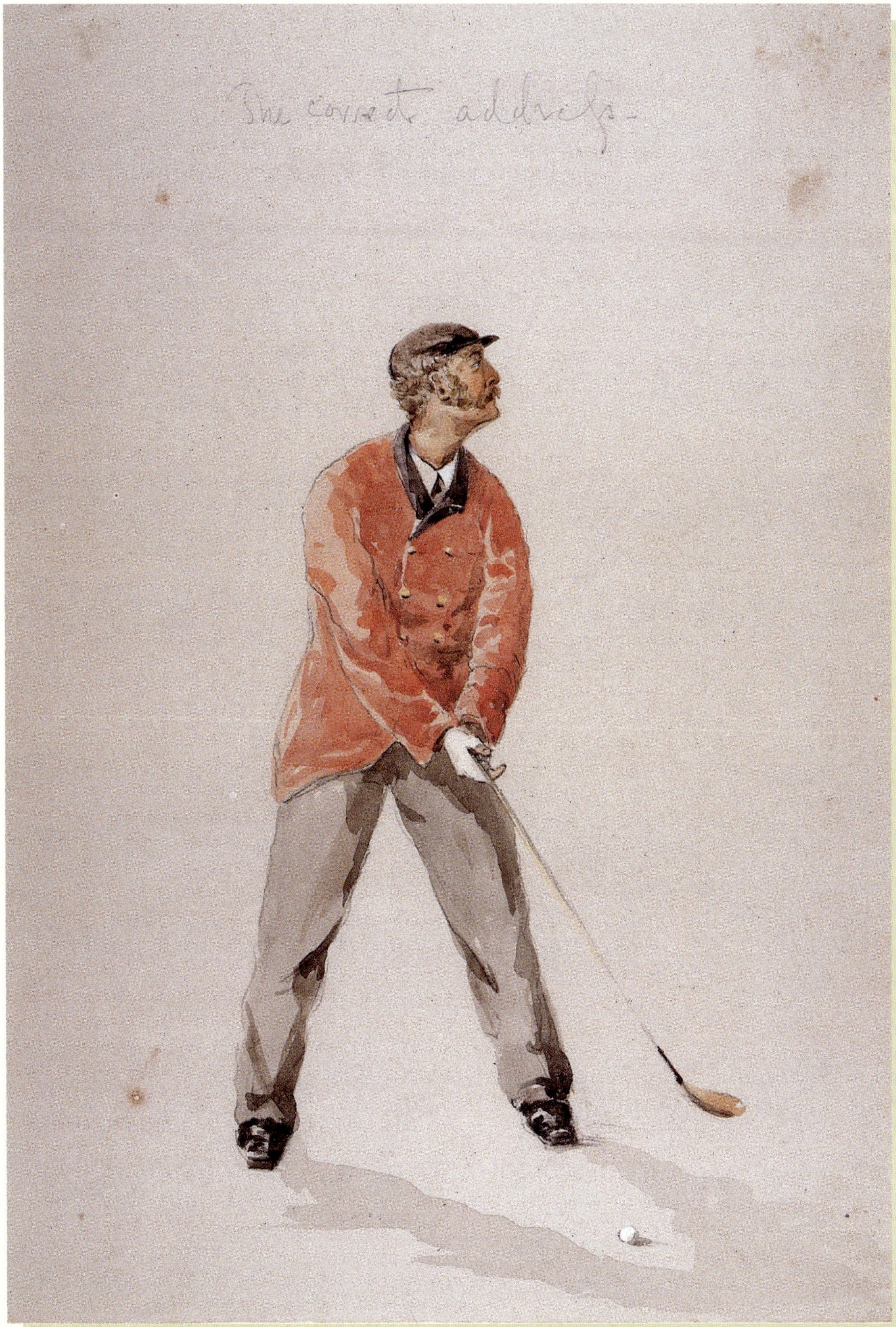
The correct address-

Everard's "highly-strung and nervous disposition" sprang largely from his agonising conflict with his father over a period of 12 to 15 years. The cause of the unforgiving schism was Harry's love of a St. Andrews girl called Annie Boothby.

Harry Everard was the heir to a vast fortune. He was born at Claybrook, north of Rugby, in the rich English midlands, into the Everard family which inherited assets difficult to quantify in present day terms of hard cash. His father was Henry Everard of Gosberton in Lincolnshire who was, like many others of his class, apt to take holidays in a Scotland, made fashionable by Queen Victoria. It was on visits to St. Andrews that the infant Harry Everard became a golf fanatic, his enthusiasm and precocious skill so compelling that he was elected a member of the Royal & Ancient as a boy of 16. This may have amused his father, but what didn't amuse him was Harry's other enslavement by a girl seven years his junior.

Sky-larking on holiday with a lass whose family Everard senior found impossible to like was one thing. But when Harry maintained his fierce bond of affection with Annie through his career at Oxford University and into his mid-20s, that incensed his father.

When Annie was 20, in December 1874, after she had been Harry's soul-mate for at least ten years, Harry proposed marriage. His father, on being told, said he would disinherit his son rather than give his approval. And he did. The Hodges, married only four years earlier and with Thomas a close friend of Annie's father, must have been well aware of the emotional melodrama.

Harry Everard plunged off on the Grand Tour of Italy to soothe his badly bruised feelings. He was away from Scotland for several months, writing almost daily letters to Annie. When he returned he visited Annie at her family's summer home at Tillywhally near Stirling, where he was in camp as an officer in the volunteers as were a great many patriotic gentlemen including Hodge and Annie's father.

At this point, Harry gave Annie what amounted to an engagement symbol, a gold bracelet he had bought for her in Rome. Annie described it years later as:

Roman mosaics on one side – two butterflies and in the centre two white doves, the other half of the circle being gold with ROMA in raised letters. I prized it very much and wore it almost constantly.

In a curious, dry document, hand-written by Annie, she summed up the continuing heartbreak and family fury like this:

Well, after various ups and downs, I think it would be the end of September 1876, I had to return all Harry's letters to him, and among other things my bracelet.... he had begged I would not return it, whatever else I sent back to him, but keep it for friendship's sake. He said if I did he'd throw it into the sea. Well, it had to go, and for some time after that we had no communication whatever. Then we met again as friends but I never dared ask what had become of my bracelet tho' I often wondered – and often prayed to God it might be returned to me some day.

Annie's testament, entitled "The History of My Bracelet", continues that in September 1879 (although she may have confused the date a little), while at Edinburgh, her mother pointed out a paragraph in *The Scotsman* about a fishing boat called the "Valiant" hauling an ancient bracelet covered in shells from the sea among its catch in the River Forth estuary.

The description caused Annie to cry out "That's my bracelet!". Her brother found the skipper of the "Valiant", a man called French who thought he had netted an ancient jewel. He had sold it already to a jeweller called Crighton in Edinburgh who bought it "as a curiosity for his wife". Annie's brother recovered the bracelet and she recorded:

One evening I again found my dear bracelet in my own possession. Harry was at St. Andrews at the time. Someone told him about the bracelet and we met shortly afterwards as friends. Whether this incident gave him fresh courage and me more faith, I cannot say, but the end of it was before another year had passed we were man and wife.

When Annie met skipper French, he told her the bracelet had been almost covered by barnacles. After nearly three years in salt water, the mosaic was badly damaged. Annie filled in the gaps with black sealing wax. The bracelet was still in the possession of members of the Everard family in the late 1990s at their home in Cambridge, a fearfully battered but much-cherished souvenir of golf's most dramatic love story. Annie wrote her unvarnished record in January 1888 to end a quantity of highly embellished accounts of the discovery, including one widely believed yarn which said that the bracelet had been cut out of the stomach of a monster fish.

Harry Everard himself explained that on receiving the bracelet from Annie in 1876 in despair he threw it into the sea from the steamer crossing the Forth estuary.

Harry and Annie lived out their married lives in St. Andrews, Harry always playing 18 holes of golf before lunch, and 18 holes of golf after lunch. Annie watched his progress round the links from home through binoculars to make sure the midday meal was perfect on his return. He never missed his father's millions.

Annie and golf were his life.

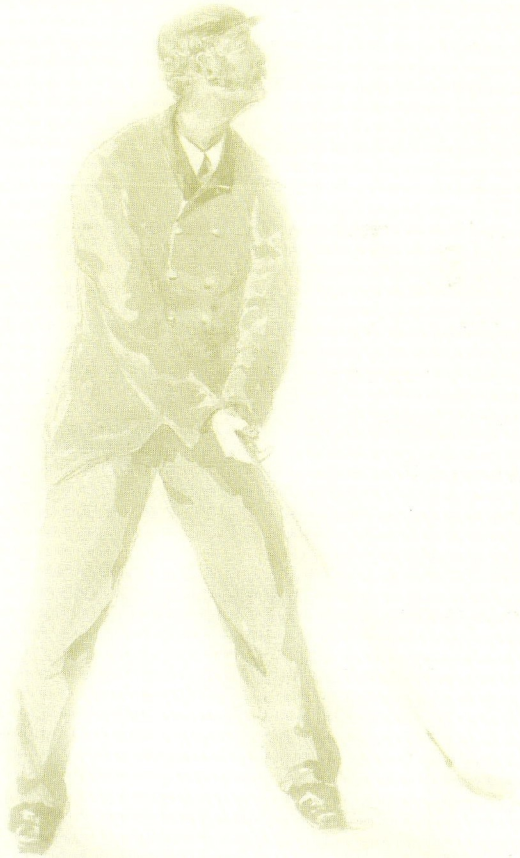

Allan The Emperor

When Thomas Hodge arrived at St. Andrews in the middle of the 1850s, the King of Golf, no The Emperor, was not Old Tom Morris, but a man who looked rather like his slightly roguish older brother – ALLAN ROBERTSON. The name is in capital letters for a reason.

Robertson was a member of a large Robertson clan which had been making feathery golf balls at St. Andrews for a century. Rediscovered in the 1980s, Hodge's portrait of him, based on a well-known photograph as reference, indicates a complicated individual. Then again, the sketch of Robertson and Morris together on the putting green, which is one of the game's best-known and most plagiarised images, is also extracted from a group photograph that had been taken by the era's notable cameraman Thomas Rodger.

Records show that Robertson was a peerless golfer, beyond most experts' question the finest of the 19th century. Certainly he impressed the young Cornishman as a player beyond compare. In Hodge's scrapbooks, early groups of most of the best golfers in Scotland are all captioned in his neat hand. Robertson is simply identified as ALLAN in capital letters, the same five-letter royal title Robertson stamped or penned on his feathery golf balls.

Hodge even contradicted Harry Everard, when that hallowed authority wrote an article suggesting some sort of parity as golfers between Old Tom and Robertson. "Tom was never the player that Allan was", Hodge commented sharply.

Allan's life was short enough, born 1815, died 1859 aged 44, so that he and Hodge knew each other perhaps five or six years. Allan's warmest years with Old Tom Morris, during which they won many famous challenge matches together, cooled to freezing point in moments when Tom almost accidentally played with the new gutta percha ball (then described as solidified Malayan tree fluid) in the late 1840s.

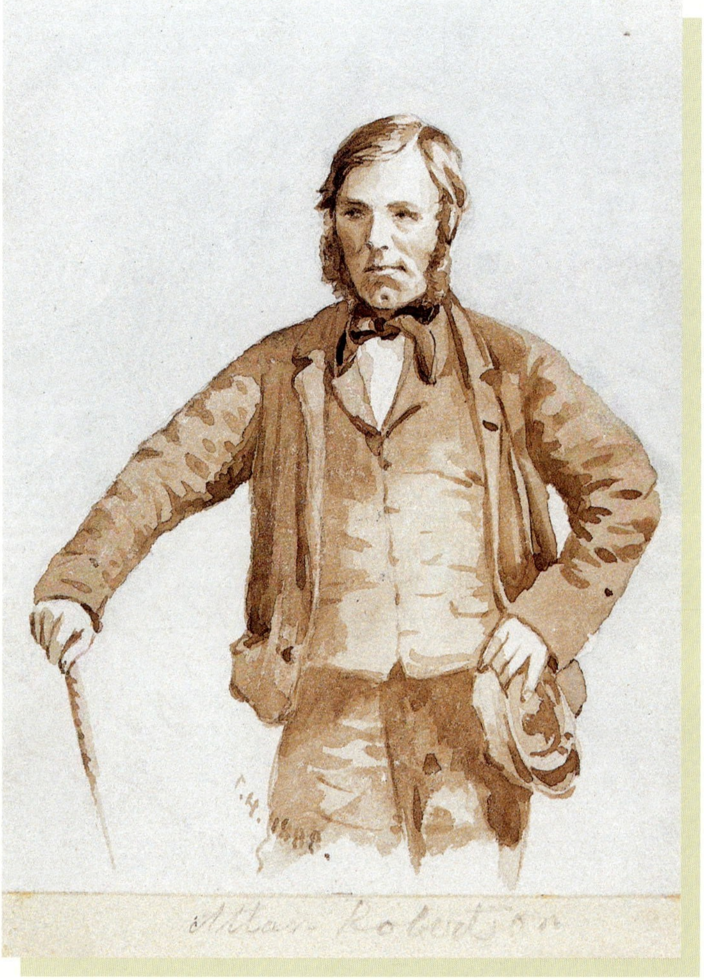

Above: Allan Robertson, by Hodge; from a photograph.

Right: Hodge's drawing of Robertson (bending) and Old Tom Morris which was plagiarised endlessly in prints throughout the 20th century.

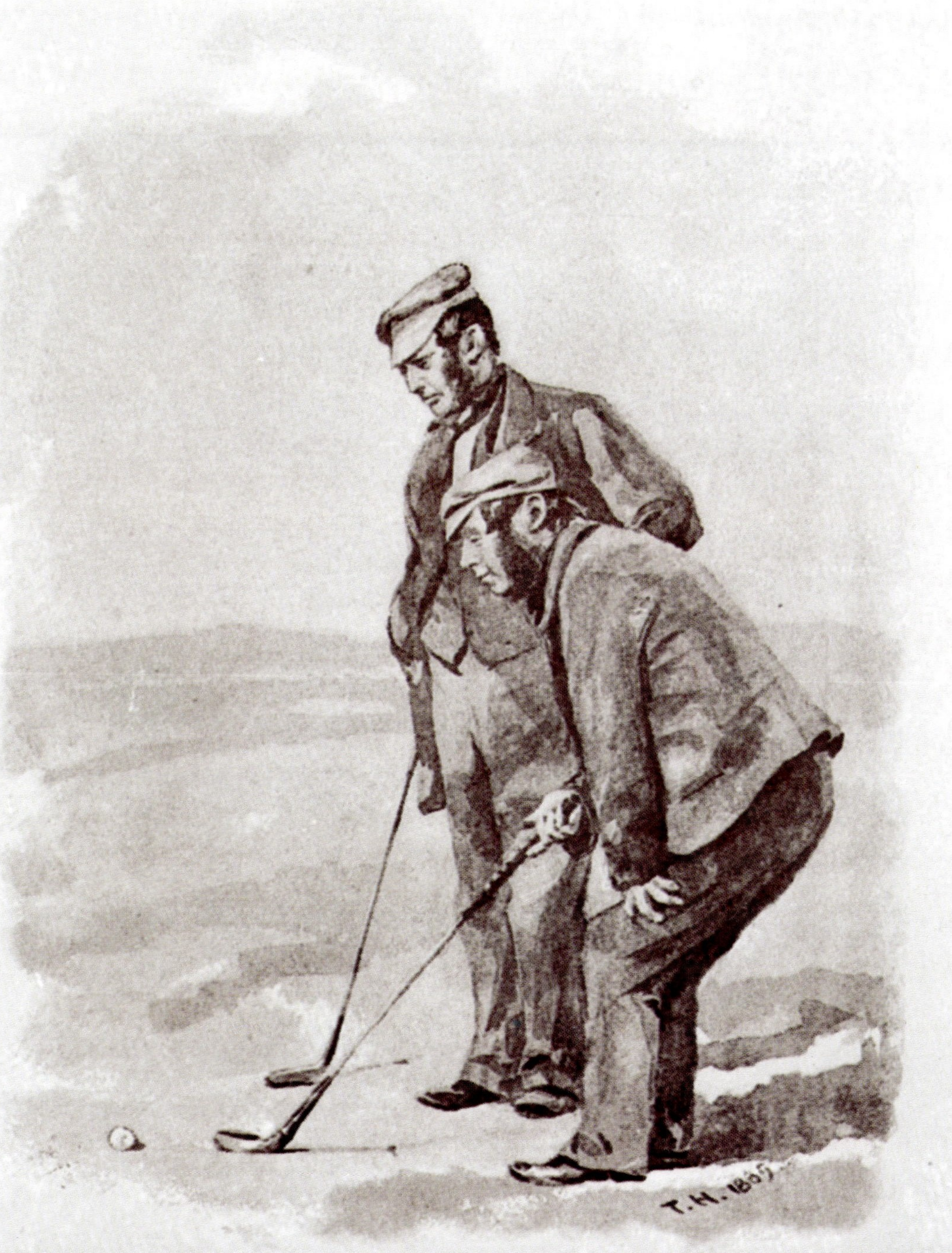

ALLAN ROBERTSON AND TOM MORRIS

Firstly as an apprentice feathery ball maker, Old Tom had been in Allan's employment for about nine years. One day he was partnering a Mr. Campbell of Sadell on a round of golf at St. Andrews when his last feathery ball burst three holes from home. "Try that", said Mr. Campbell, and gave Tom one of the new guttas. Unfortunately, Allan arrived on the scene, when Mr. Campbell told him innocently what a fine game Tom had been playing with the new type of ball. Allan immediately attacked Tom for "destroying St. Andrews' ancient livelihood". This blazing tantrum ended their working partnership although Old Tom claimed later they never ceased to be friends.

Allan was already in a state verging on paranoia about the new gutta percha ball at this time. Because he could see the gutta wiping out the traditional "feathery" ball, the manufacture of which created so much treasured local employment, Allan's reaction to its introduction was at first hysterical as the gutta was much cheaper and (eventually) gave a superior performance. His answer was to buy up all the guttas on offer and burn them!

St. Andrews was then selling over 10,000 feathery balls annually, producing a much-needed income of up to £4,000 a year.

Robertson's panic was soon over. The revolutionary gutta ball quite quickly brought its rewards from higher sales to the rapidly expanding army of golfers.

An insight into life with the Robertson family can be gained from the poetry of George Fullerton Carnegie, "laureate of golf", when discussing Allan's father David, also a famous ball-maker and golfer:

He has a statesman's elements,' tis plain,
Cheat, flatter, humbug – anything for gain;
And had he trod the world's wide field, methinks,
As long as he has trod St. Andrews Links,
He must have been prime minister or priest,
My Lord, or plain Sir David, at the least.

Carnegie rated Allan a far greater golfer than his father though inferior as a manipulator of people.

Some histories of golf credit Allan Robertson with the development of approach play with iron clubs, thus making a powerful contribution to the expansion of the game and its playing equipment.

Hodge, and it has to be born in mind that he was one of Allan's unstinting admirers, would have none of this. In the margin of his own *Badminton Golf* volume of 1890, where Harry Everard said:

To Allan was due in great measure the introduction of irons and cleeks for the approach to the hole, these shots having previously been played by baffy spoons,

Hodge wrote:

Not correct.

A little earlier, his margin note was:

Quite incorrect. Allan never played an iron through the green.

N.B: Writing about the manufacture of feathery golf balls in the "Delineations of St. Andrews" in 1807, James Grierson said:

Balls are used of about five quarters of an inch diameter and weighing from 26 to 30 drams avoirdupois. They are made of strong, alumed (treated) leather and stuffed with feathers.

The feathers are forced in at a small hole left in the covering by a blunt-pointed iron instrument, which the maker applies to his shoulder, and the operation is continued till the ball acquires a degree of hardness and elasticity scarcely credible to those who have not seen it. The balls are afterwards boiled, and then dry painted with white oil paint to exclude the water and render them easily seen.

The manufacture of golf balls at St. Andrews affords employment to about ten or twelve men, constantly at work; and besides the consumption of the place, which is about three hundred dozen annually, they export every year to Edinburgh, Glasgow, Aberdeen, Perth, and other places, upwards of 60 gross, or 8,640 balls. A good workman makes about 9 balls a day.

The employment is accounted unhealthy and many of the ball-makers have been observed to fall sacrifices to consumption; whether it be that the flue arising from the musty feathers they use being inhaled by the breath communicates a taint to the lungs, or that the mode of forcing in these feathers confines and injures the chest. It is likely, however, that at present the employment is not so injurious to health as formerly; for at one time their practice was to place the instrument by which they force the feathers directly against the breast, but they now apply it to the shoulder.

These persons are generally great judges of the game of golf, and expert at playing it; and are ready, for a trifling consideration, under the name of "cadies" to attend any gentlemen who chuses to take up the amusement.

A wealthy collector of old golf equipment might have paid £15,000 sterling or $20,000 for one authentic and perfect feathery ball bearing the magic stamp of ALLAN at the end of the 20th century, enough to buy about 60,000 featheries when new.

Below: ALLAN was the imperious title Robertson stamped on the golf balls, featheries and gutties, which came from his workshop.

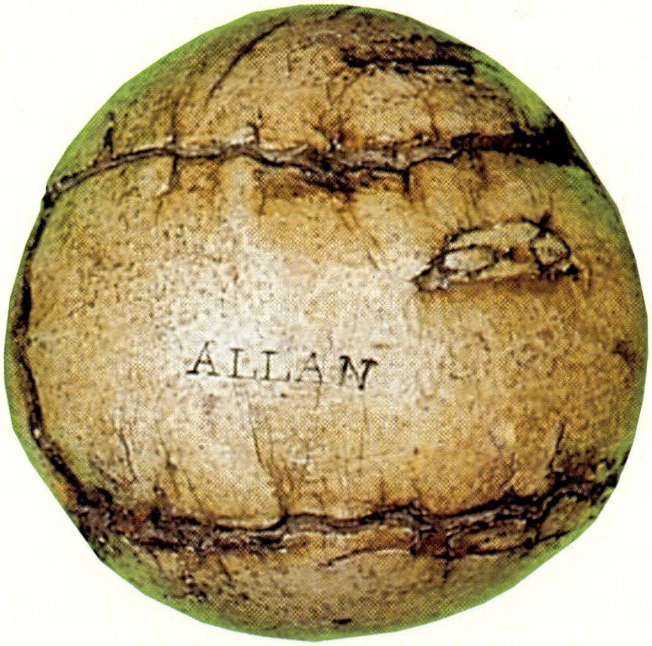

The Taits; Triumph and Tragedy, the Prof and Freddie

Thomas Hodge helped Professor Peter Guthrie Tait, for 41 years the holder of the Chair of Natural Philosophy at Edinburgh University and renowned throughout the academic world during a brilliant career, set up golf's first scientific experiments at St. Andrews.

Hodge was also one of the few players with the stamina to join Tait on the links at dawn for the first of his five rounds a day, a golfing marathon which lasted for some years after the professor first began taking his holidays at St. Andrews in 1868.

Tait was a remarkable man. Fluent in several European languages, he delighted in singing German ballads to his companions as he went round the course.

He wrote one of his jaunty poems set to Scottish airs about this morning bracer, entitling it "The Morning Round (6–8am)". The last of nine verses went like this:

Beautiful Round! I think of thee
Through months of labour and misery;
Round thee the strings of my heart are wound,
Round of the morning. Beautiful Round.

"The Prof", as Hodge has captioned him in one revealing, jaunty caricature of a portrait, was ever on the look-out for new experiences. On one occasion he convinced his guests that a round of golf might be played better with phosphorescent balls.

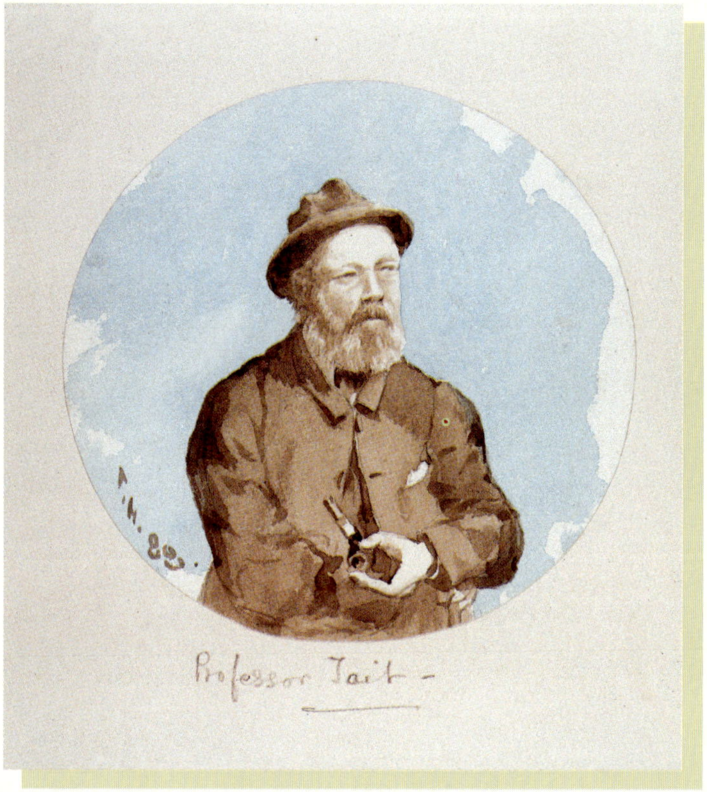

Above: Professor Tait in his heyday at St. Andrews.

The idea seemed plausible. The balls were easier to follow and find as they shone in the rough. The players were inspired to make fine shots until on passing the burn it was discovered that the gloved hand of one of the players, Professor Crum Brown, was on fire from the phosphor paint. His flaming glove was torn off and he was rushed back to his lodgings for medical attention.

Tait's experiments with golf balls, to discover why they often travelled much further than the force of the golfer's drives merited, were the source of a great deal of unfair but predictable hilarity.

They became a national joke when his famous golfing son, Freddie Tait, appeared to demolish his father's published

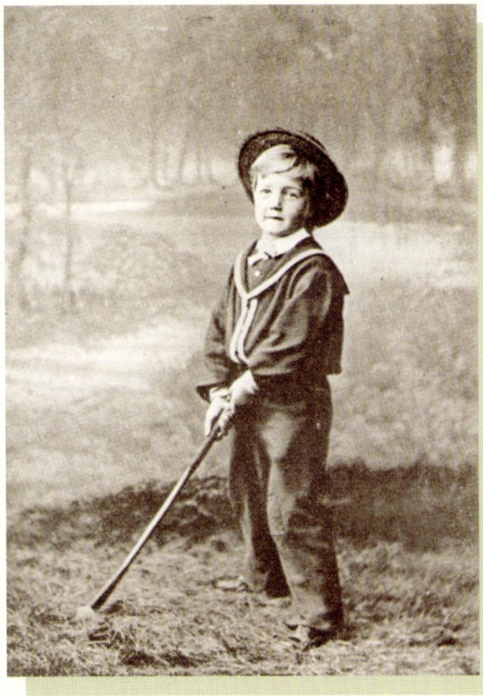

Above: Freddie Tait as a golfing toddler.

Right: Freddie Tait as a powerful teenaged swimmer about to dive off the Step Rock at St. Andrews.

scientific paper in the magazine *Golf* of December 1890, strictly defining the limits that the gutty ball could be driven. Freddie then hit the ball a huge distance further, following up with a deal of ribald comment. Andrew Lang embellished the joke in his newspaper columns, leaving the professor to respond on the lines of "Bah! Humbug!".

What the professor really wrote was woven round with careful reservations about playing conditions and lack of spin on the ball. Freddie, in a family notorious for its practical jokes and general levity, had probably never read the treatise and enjoyed putting one over The Guvnor, who in fact adored Freddie and thrilled to his golfing wizardry.

Freddie Tait, the professor's third son, was born on 11th January 1870. When his father started holidaying at St. Andrews, Freddie found golf. As a toddler he thought golf balls grew like potatoes and buried them in rows. By the age of seven he was a prodigy. He was also a powerful swimmer, his favourite diving place being the Step Rock at St. Andrews where Hodge painted him at about the age of 17. He was also a dynamic rugby forward, good enough many critics said to play for Scotland though he was never selected. Hodge painted him kicking for goal, the ball held by one of his sons.

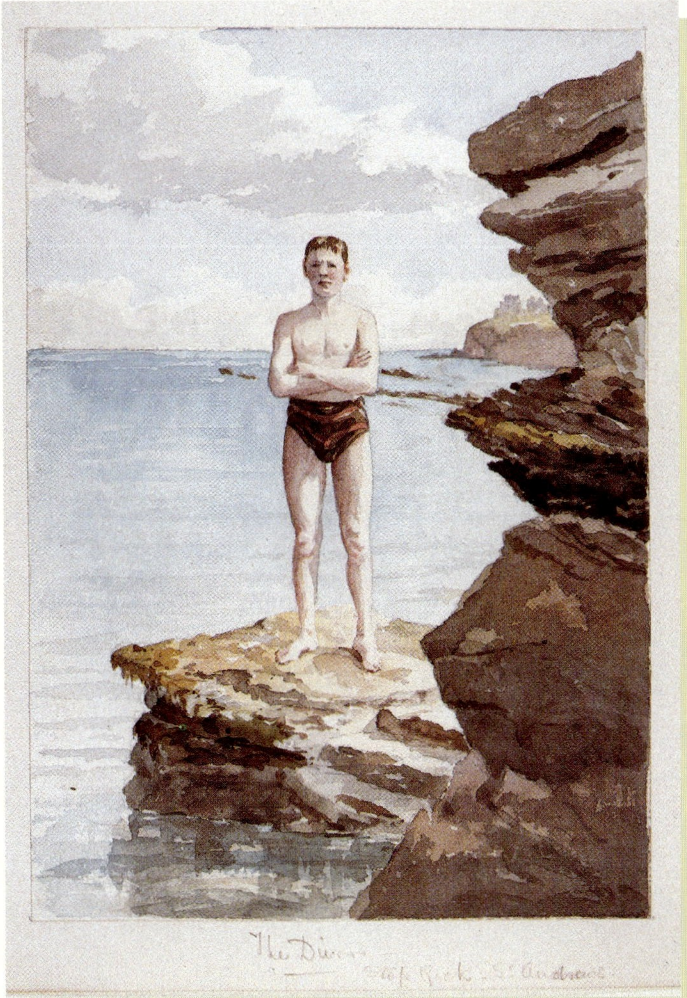

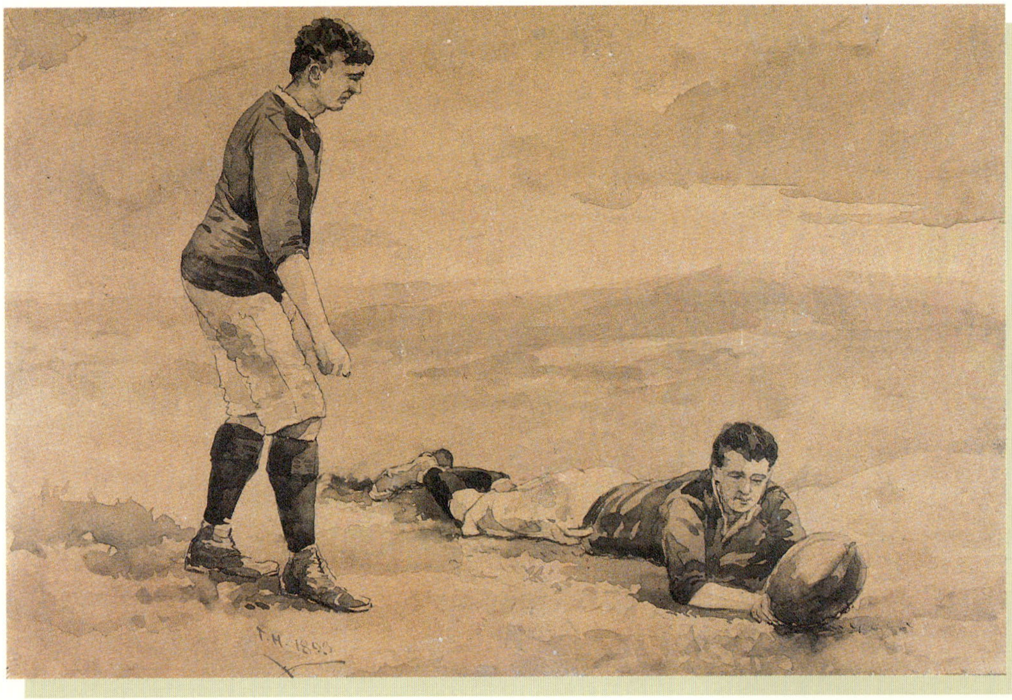

Left: *Freddie Tait, a fine rugby player, drawn by Hodge kicking for goal in 1895.*

Below: *Freddie Tait the champion golfer before he left to fight the Boers.*

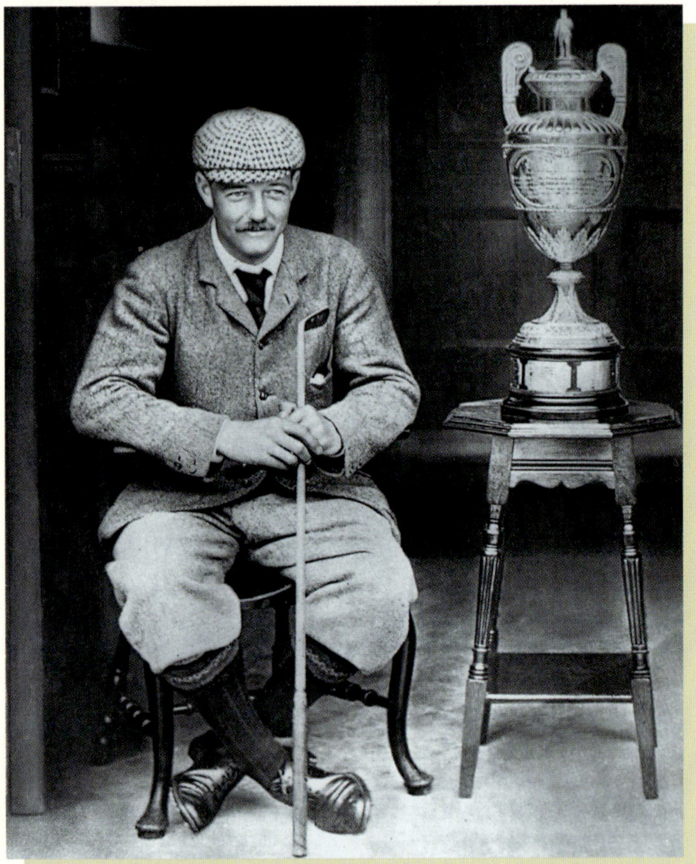

Freddie's ambition was to be a soldier. He went to Sandhurst in 1880 after a summer playing golf at St. Andrews. In spare time from army duties, he set record amateur scores at St. Andrews, Deal, Folkestone, Ascot and in Northern Ireland. In 1893 he hit a record drive 341 yards, with a carry of about 250 yards. This was the hit which caused such mirth, as his father had written that it was virtually impossible, without the addition of spin, to make the ball carry more than 190 yards.

From 1894 to 1899, Freddie's golf story is told in records for competitions and courses. His place as the most glamorous golfer of the late 19th century was enhanced by thrilling British Amateur finals against giants like John Ball Jr.. and Harold Hilton. He won at Sandwich in 1896, defeating Hilton 8 and 7. He won at Hoylake in 1898, beating Samuel Mure Ferguson 7 and 5. He was losing finalist to John Ball Jr. at Prestwick in 1899, defeated at the 37th.

His *Boys' Own Paper* personality and his ability to produce staggering recovery shots at moments of crisis made him Scotland's national hero. Once, when he was trouncing Harold Hilton, a spectator shouted:

It's no gowff at a'; it's jist miracles.

Unfortunately, as an officer in the Black Watch, Freddie yearned for a greater glory. There were gentlemen ready and willing to ship Freddie and his kind to the battlefields of Empire, where they could follow the bagpipes and march on the foe.

In South Africa on December 11, 1899, a lunatic sent the Black Watch in a column 50 yards wide and 300 yards long towards the hidden Boer sharpshooters. The slaughter was terrible. Freddie, shot badly in the leg, wrote home:

Our brigade was simply thrown away; hundreds of splendid fellows killed and wounded.

Quickly recovered because of his marvellous fitness, brave Freddie Tait was shot dead by a Boer marksman eight weeks later. A private soldier, writing home, said:

Lieutenant Tait's servant came up with his dinner. He gave me and another man half of his dinner between us. Little did I think when we were joking, that we were helping him to eat his last dinner.

Freddie, leading his men forward, was shot through the heart. A sergeant wrote home:

He treated men as men and not as dogs.

Another Black Watch soldier wrote:

When we carried him over the rocks at night there were a good many tears shed. He was buried at Koodoosberg Drift, and we made a little cross for his head.

Professor Tait, who died in 1901, never recovered from the blow.

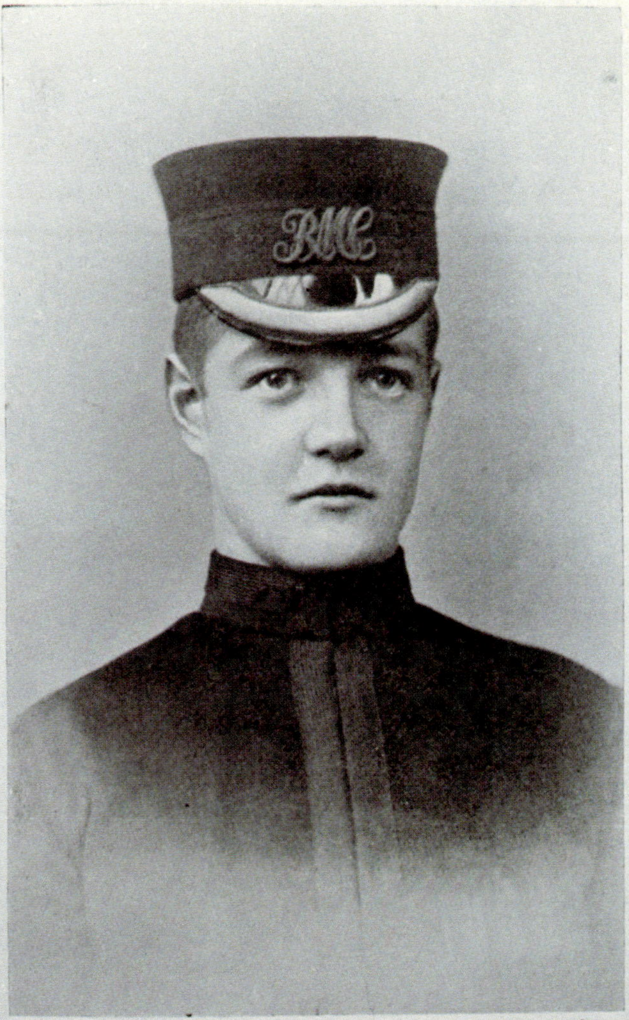

[Photo by Hill & Saunders.

F. G. TAIT AS A SANDHURST CADET.

Above: Freddie Tait as a Sandhurst cadet.

Tait sources: Life and Scientific Work of Peter Guthrie Tait, by C. G. Knott, Cambridge University Press 1911.

F .G. Tait, A Record, by John L. Low, J. Nisbet 1900.

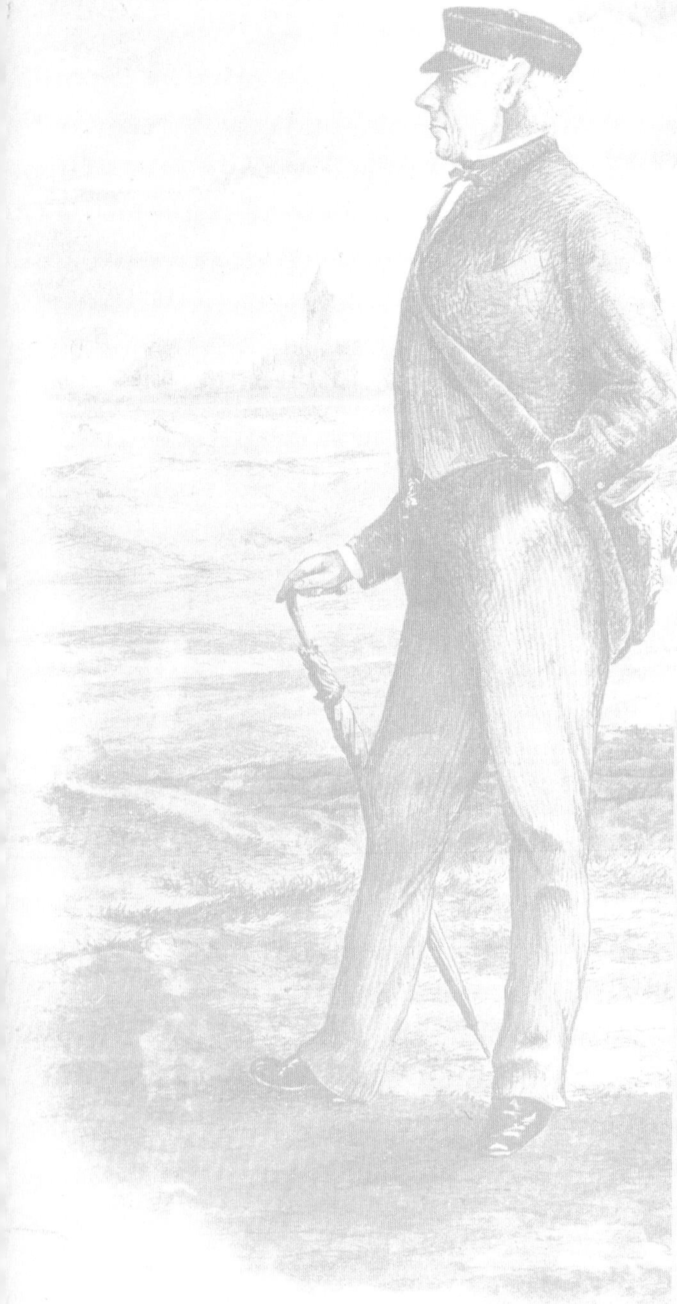

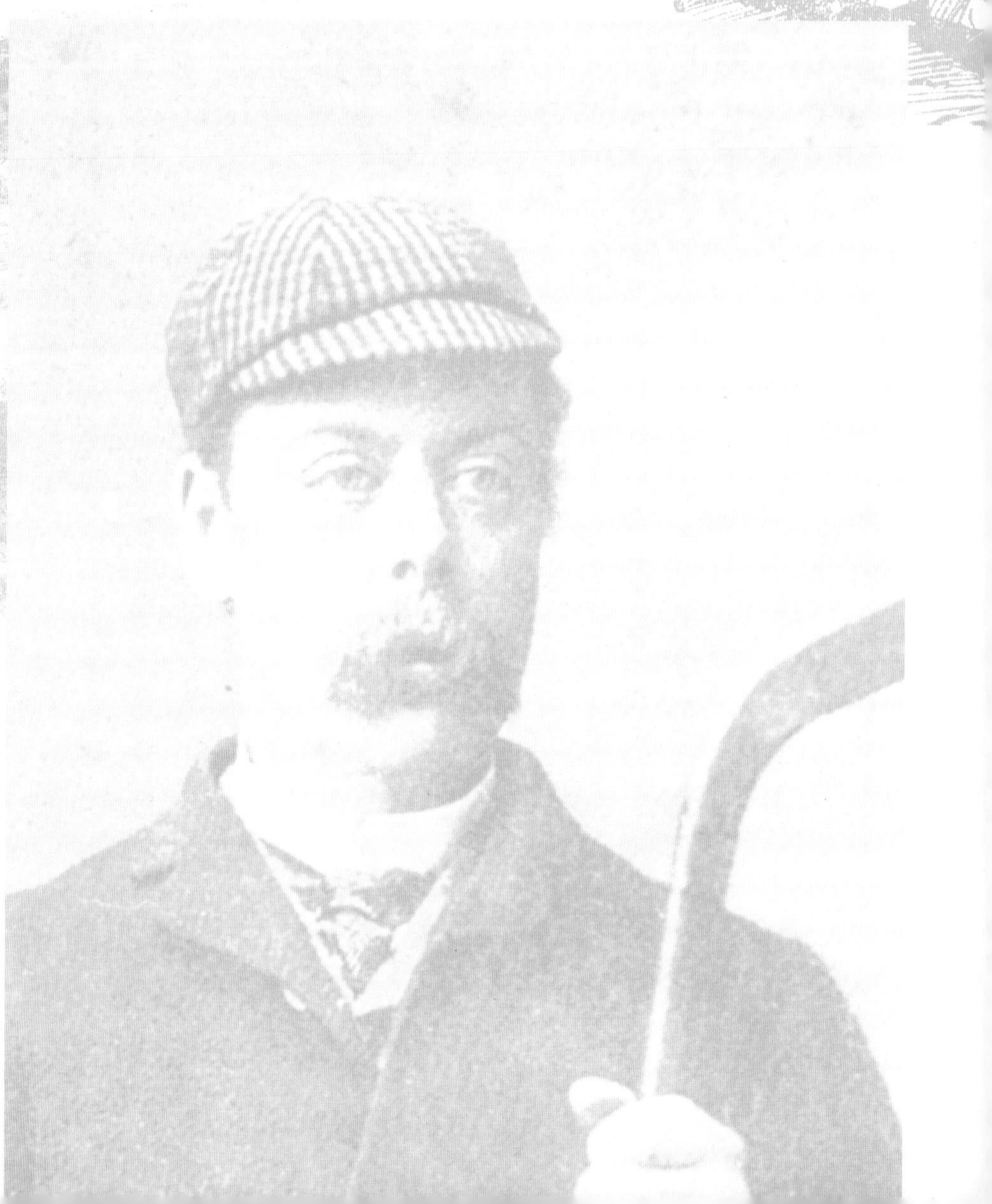

The Eccentrics

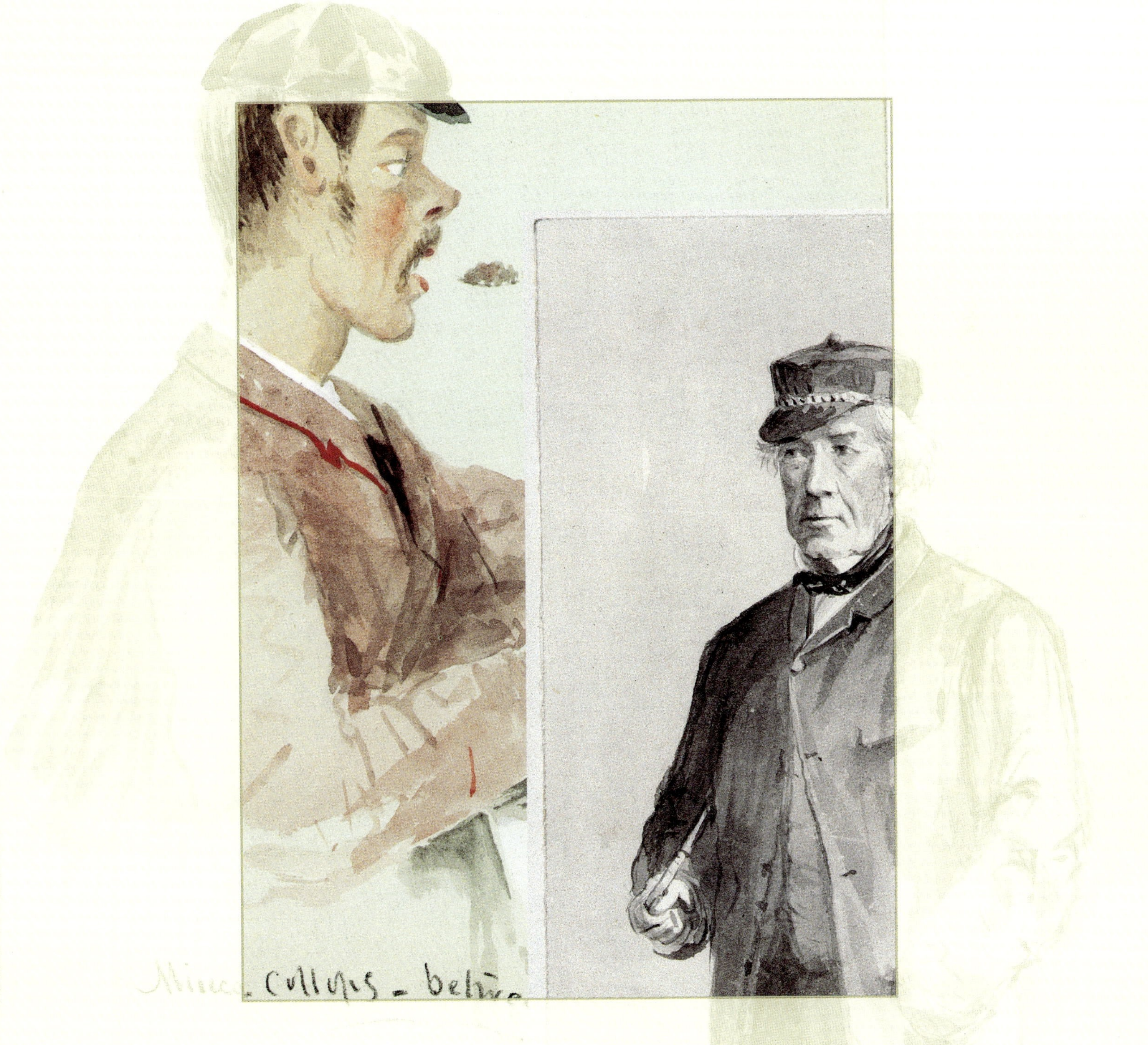

The Eccentrics

William T. Linskill

"Mince Collops. Between the rounds", is Hodge's inscription on his 1880s portrait of an Englishman whose passion for St. Andrews, golf and ghosts was almost as great as his appetite. Mr. and Mrs. Hodge loved a good trencher, and Linskill never let them or any one else down in this direction.

He drooled in particular over eel pie and was supplied with the slithery creatures by local fishermen who never ate eels themselves because of their reputation as scavengers in unsavoury places.

As a child, Linskill, son of the Mayor of Teignmouth, came to St. Andrews on his holidays and was taught to play golf by Old Tom Morris. Later he formed the Cambridge University Golf Club and aged 20 was elected a member of the Royal & Ancient in 1875. He claimed to have toured Britain for nine years with an opera company and to have lived "among the darkies on the Swanee River" in America, absorbing their music and culture.

Linskill's lugubrious expression with his bulging eyes and walrus moustache gave him a head start when he displayed his comic talents in pantomime and as a guest in the St. Andrews seafront pierrot shows. He used his fog-horn voice to staggering effect, singing music hall songs he had composed himself. His favourite was entitled "Have you ever seen an oyster walk upstairs?".

Linskill, as soon as he grew up, if he ever did, made his home in St. Andrews, where he plunged into local government and into the ruins of the ancient city with equal abandon. He was a member of the local council for almost 25 years and earned great respect for his tireless civic work.

Fascinated by the possibility that there was a network of secret passages underneath St. Andrews, he was the source of many a quick gold sovereign for local workmen like William Honeyman, the golf links groundsman who showed Linskill "the best places" to dig.

In 1879 an underground passage was discovered, but both it and the dreams of buried treasure proved empty.

Right: Linskill portrayed by Hodge enjoying his food.

Below: Linskill, as he was caricatured in a Scottish newspaper for his treasure and ghost-hunting exploits.

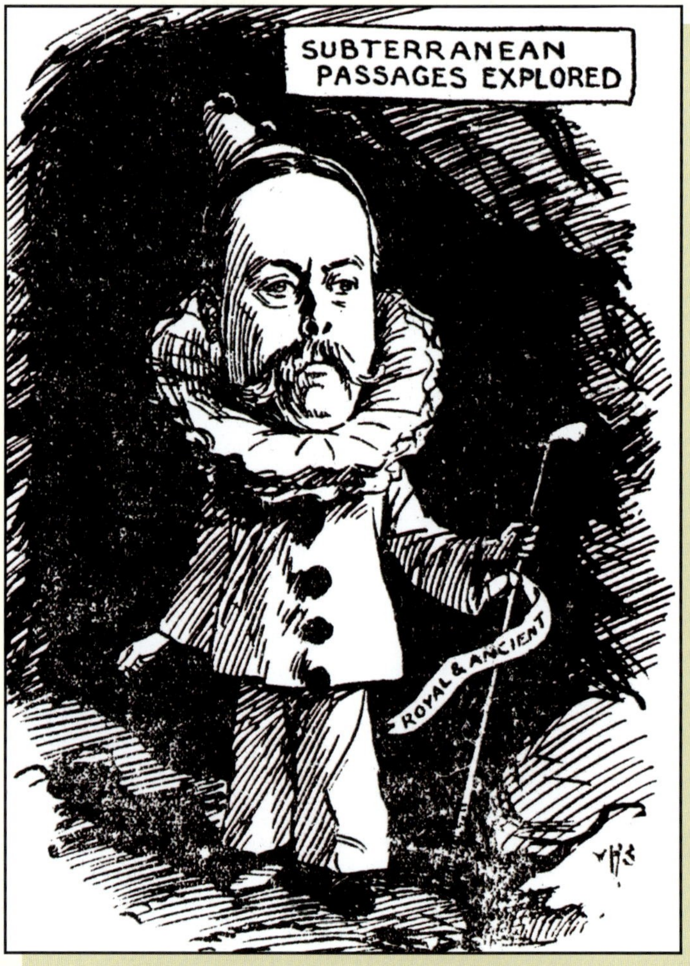

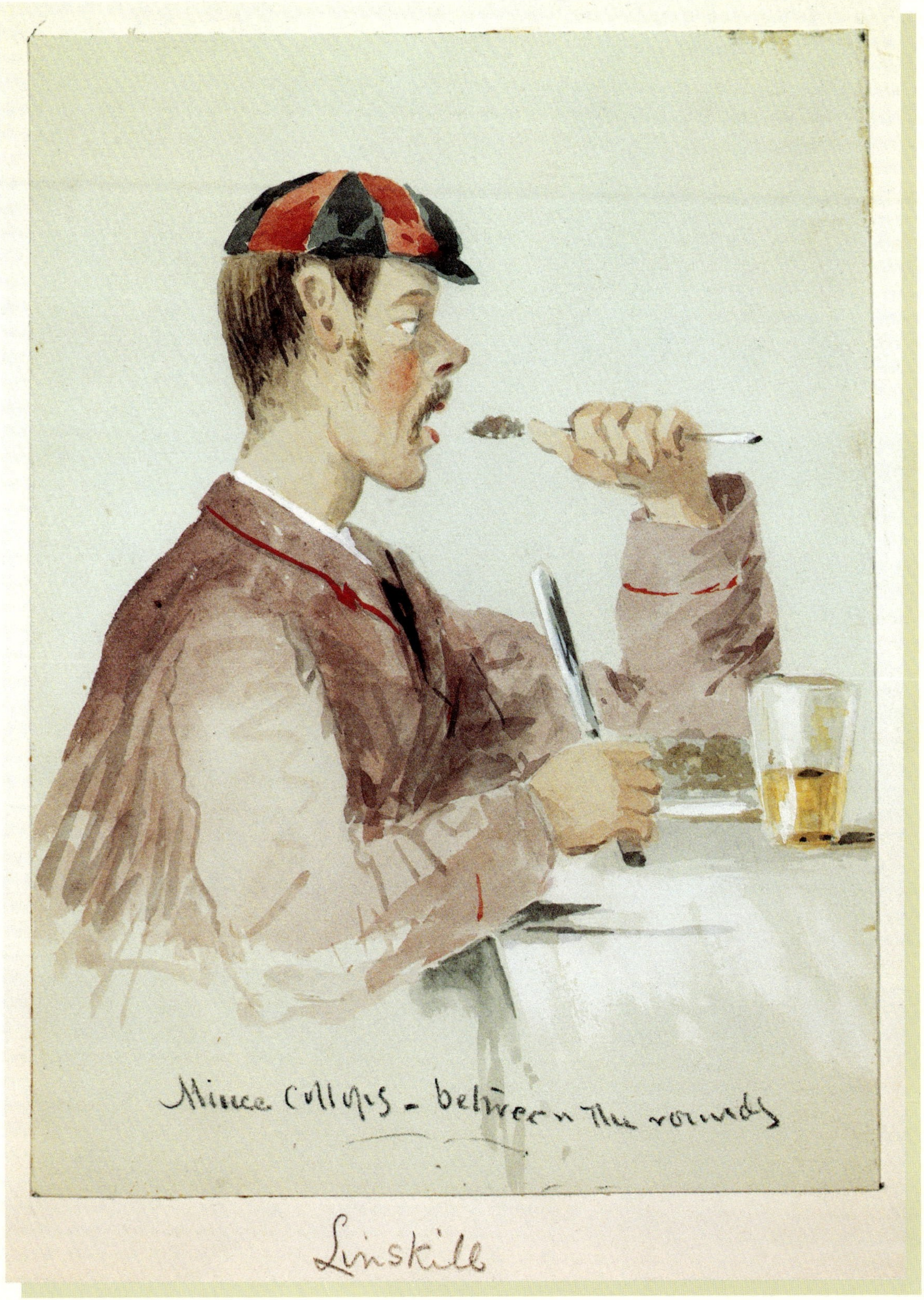
Mince collops - between the rounds
Linskill

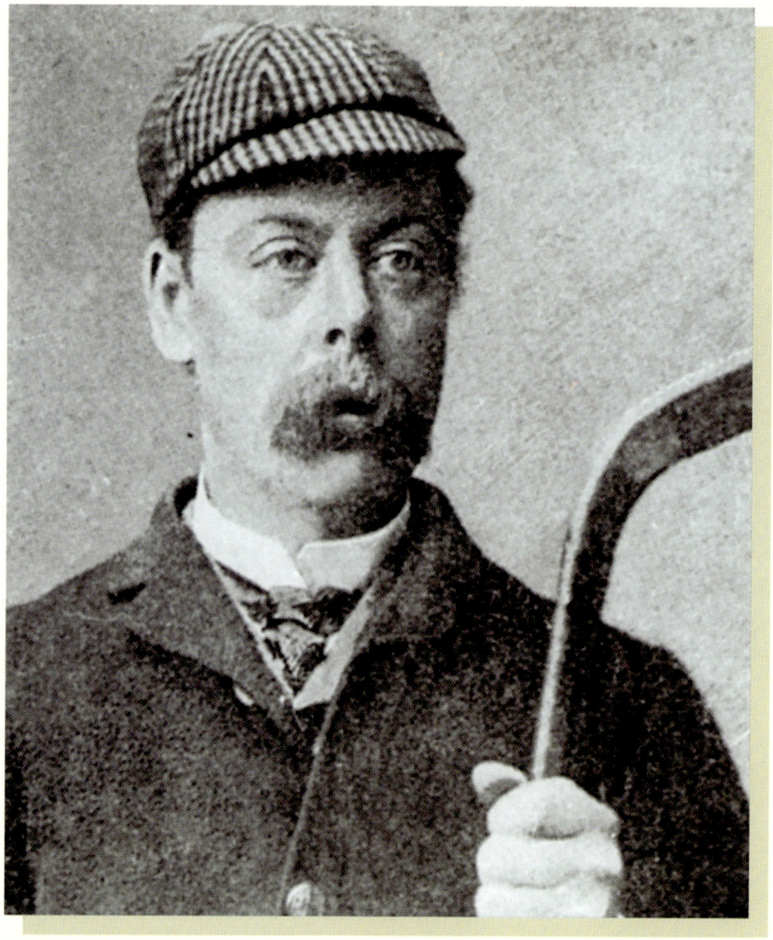

Above: Linskill, as he appeared on the links.

Later that year, Linskill had a miraculous escape from the Tay Bridge railway disaster in which all died. Travelling from Edinburgh, passengers for St. Andrews had to alight at Leuchars and then find transport for the few miles home. The train went on across the River Tay to nearby Dundee.

That gale-torn December night, Linskill, a passenger on the train, decided to go on to lodge at Dundee for the night as the cab to St. Andrews was missing. Just as the train moved from the Leuchars platform, the station master shouted that the cab was in sight. Linskill and a boy passenger leapt off. A few minutes later all 100 left on the train were dead in the river as the Tay Bridge collapsed.

Fife creaks and groans under hundreds of ghost stories. Linskill stayed all night in "haunted" spots, but never glimpsed a shade in his 74 years, dying in 1929. Nevertheless, he was a fascinated believer in the supernatural and wrote and told endless brilliant ghost stories. Like one of his characters in *The Monk of St. Rules Tower*, he could...

spin yarns for hours about phantom coaches, death knells, corpse candles, people going about in winding sheets, phantom hearses and Lord knows what else.

Fife publishers J. and G. Innes have put out many editions of Linskill's marvellous, jokey *St. Andrews Ghost Stories*, which contains the following poem by the author:

There are ghosts and phantoms round us,
On the mountains, on the sea;
Some are cold and some are clammy,
Some are hot as hot can be;
They can creep, and crawl, and hover,
They can howl and shriek and wail,
And those that want to hear of them
Must read this little tale.

This is how St. Andrews can get you. That is how it got to William T. Linskill, the eccentrics' eccentric, who warmed the ancient spirits of St. Andrews.

In 1889, Linskill wrote *Golf* in the All-England series of sporting books published by George Bell of Covent Garden, London. His qualifications as author included starting the Cambridge University Golf Club in 1875. In the book he wrote:

As a lover of golf, I am constrained to say I think no man is more to be pitied than he who has not yet learned to play the game.

His renowned conviviality cannot be better revealed than in a sentence or two from a letter he wrote to a friend from St. Andrews in his sprawling, spidery hand. He apologised for being "Awful, terrible busy" and continued:

On. Wed. had a farewell supper at one of the clubs here, to the American professional golfers. Whisky in pails!, and only I did not suffer and sang comic songs till daylight in top-hole form.

Mr. Sutherland

Alexander Sutherland was a native of St. Andrews and member of the Royal & Ancient Golf Club no caricaturist could miss. Thomas Hodge recorded his inimitable presence many times for several publications.

In any other environment, he might have appeared simply a ramrod-straight, notably fit and trim elderly man about town. But given his intense Scottishness in dress and speech, and his fanaticism for golf, Mr. Sutherland became something remarkable to encounter.

Five pages of *Golf: A Royal and Ancient Game*, edited by Robert Clark, are devoted to this quaint Scottish golfer, under the title "Sutherlandia". John Blackwood, the publisher, said that for about 20 years he was the most famous figure on the links:

He was about 5ft 9in, very upright and his grey head was surmounted by a peculiar Scottish bonnet.

Sutherland lived golf throughout his waking hours and in his dreams. He and his kind held a simple, ancient faith that things could go on as they were, unchanged and perfect. They were wrong.

It was Sutherland, distraught, who made the following phrase immortal on the streets of St. Andrews the day of Allan Robertson's funeral, calling out repeatedly:

They may toll the bells and shut up their shops in St. Andrews, for their greatest is gone.

The saddest item of Sutherlandia concerns the new crowds who began to flood from the railway station across his sacred links turf. With arms spread wide, he would try to shepherd them off the grass. He once said:

It is disgraceful of the railway people bringing a parcel of uneducated brutes down here when they knew a real match was going on.

But then, to him, all non-golfers were untouchables.

He was really the direct successor of the remarkable Alexander M'Kellar, the "Cock of the Green", who used to hop about the Bruntsfield links all day and half the night in all conditions playing his own kind of golf. Sutherland studied the game all Sunday – when, of course, church duties prevented actual play. No weather conditions on earth could prevent his appearance on the links on Monday to try out his new ideas. "God bless me! Are you going to waste a Monday?" was his comment to golfers who said they had to work.

Once the ball maker Douglas Gourlay thought he would trick the old man, who was holding the plate outside the Episcopalian chapel where he was a lay official, and popped a feathery ball among the coins. But Sutherland was thrilled and couldn't stop talking about his luck.

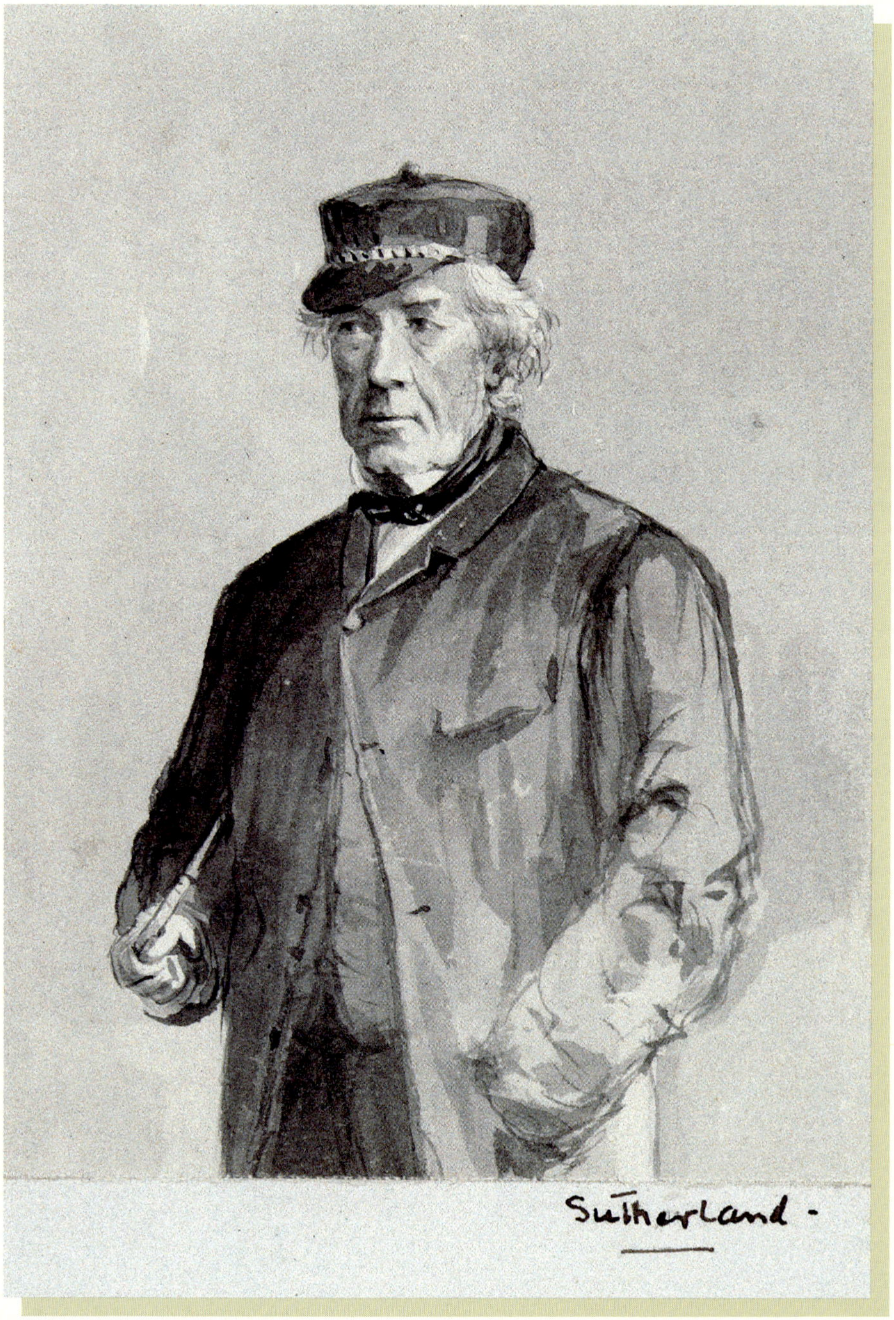

Above right: Mr. Sutherland, defender of another era.

Far right: Mr. Sutherland on patrol at St. Andrews.

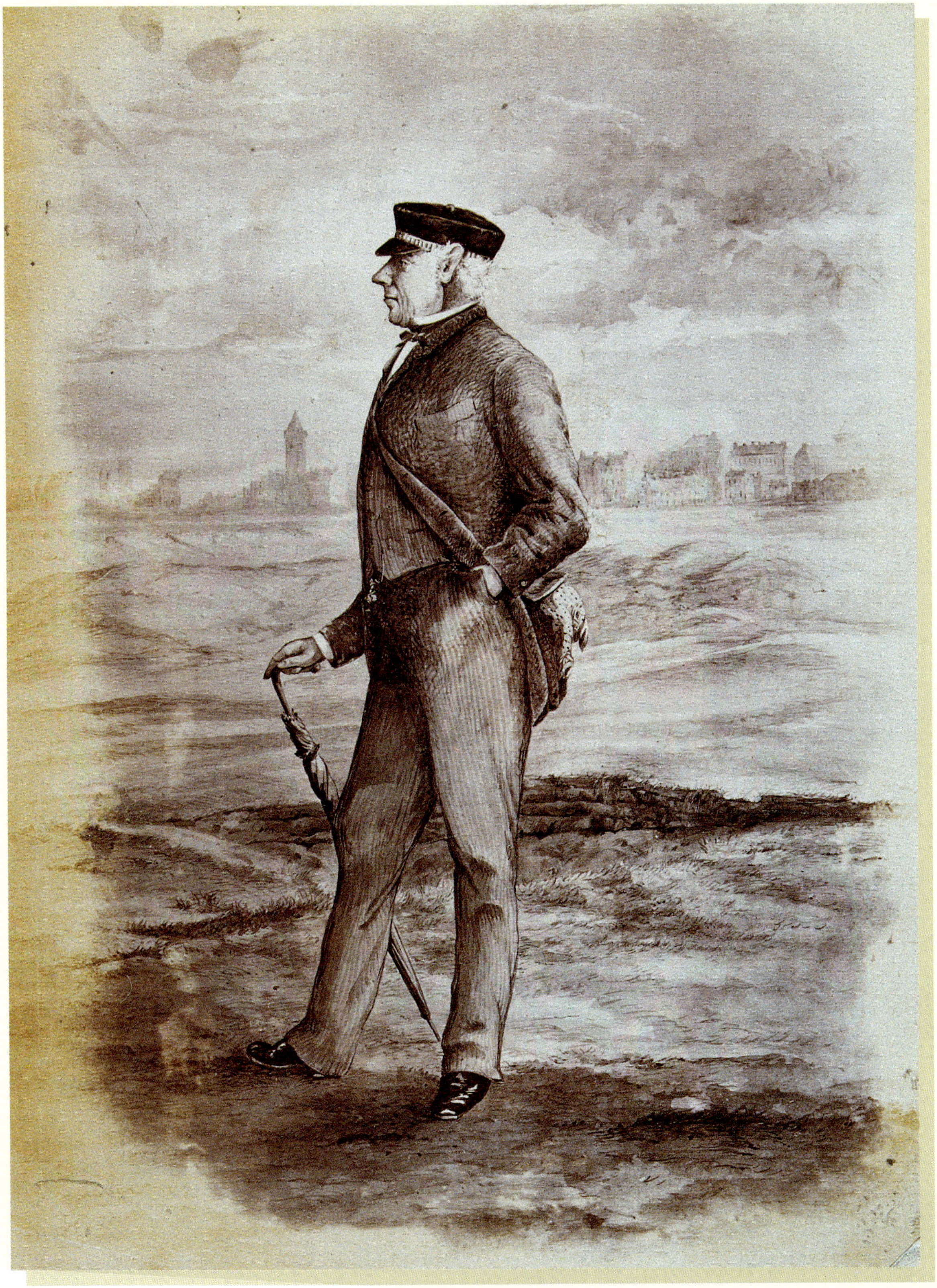

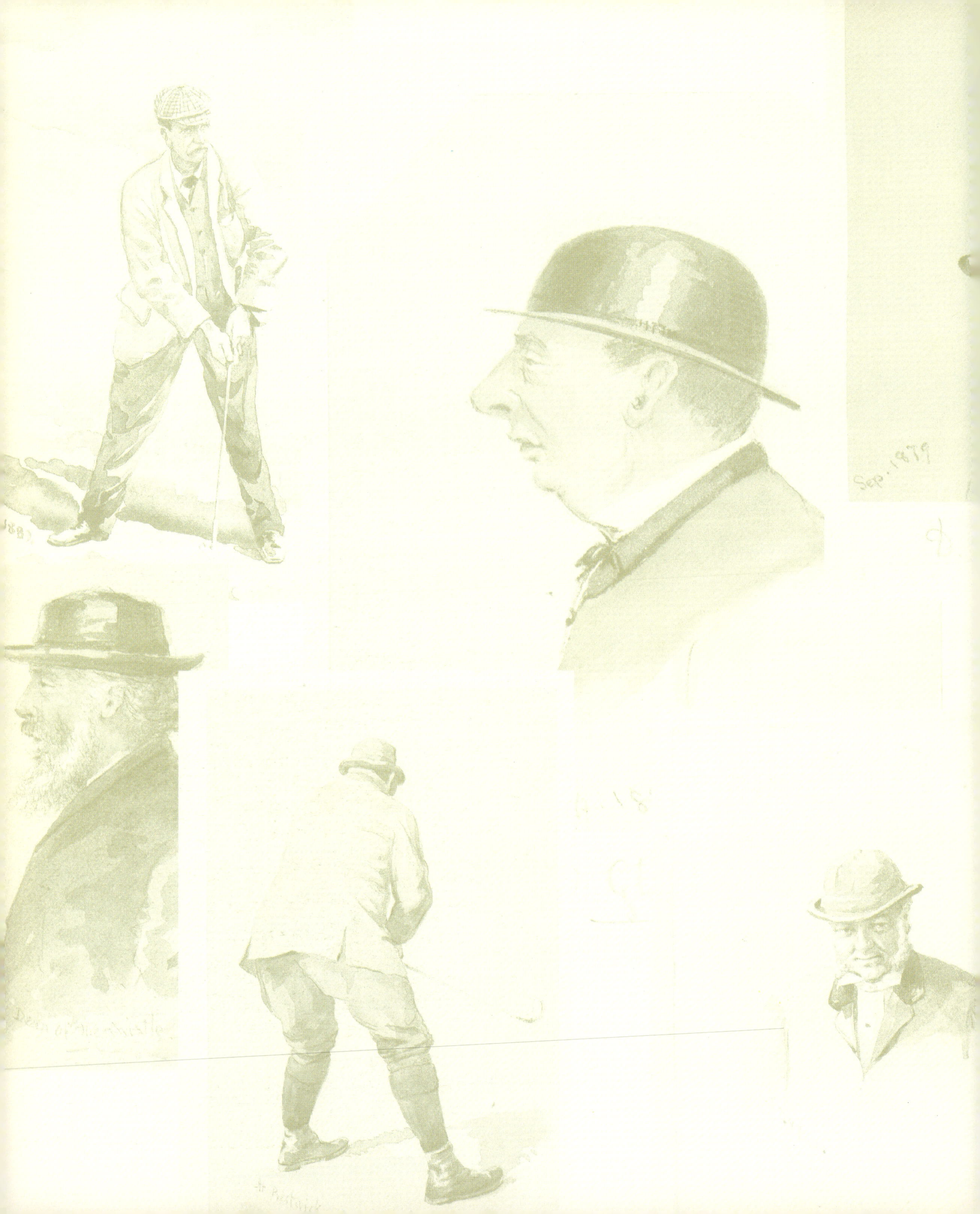
Sep. 1879

Gentlemen and Giants

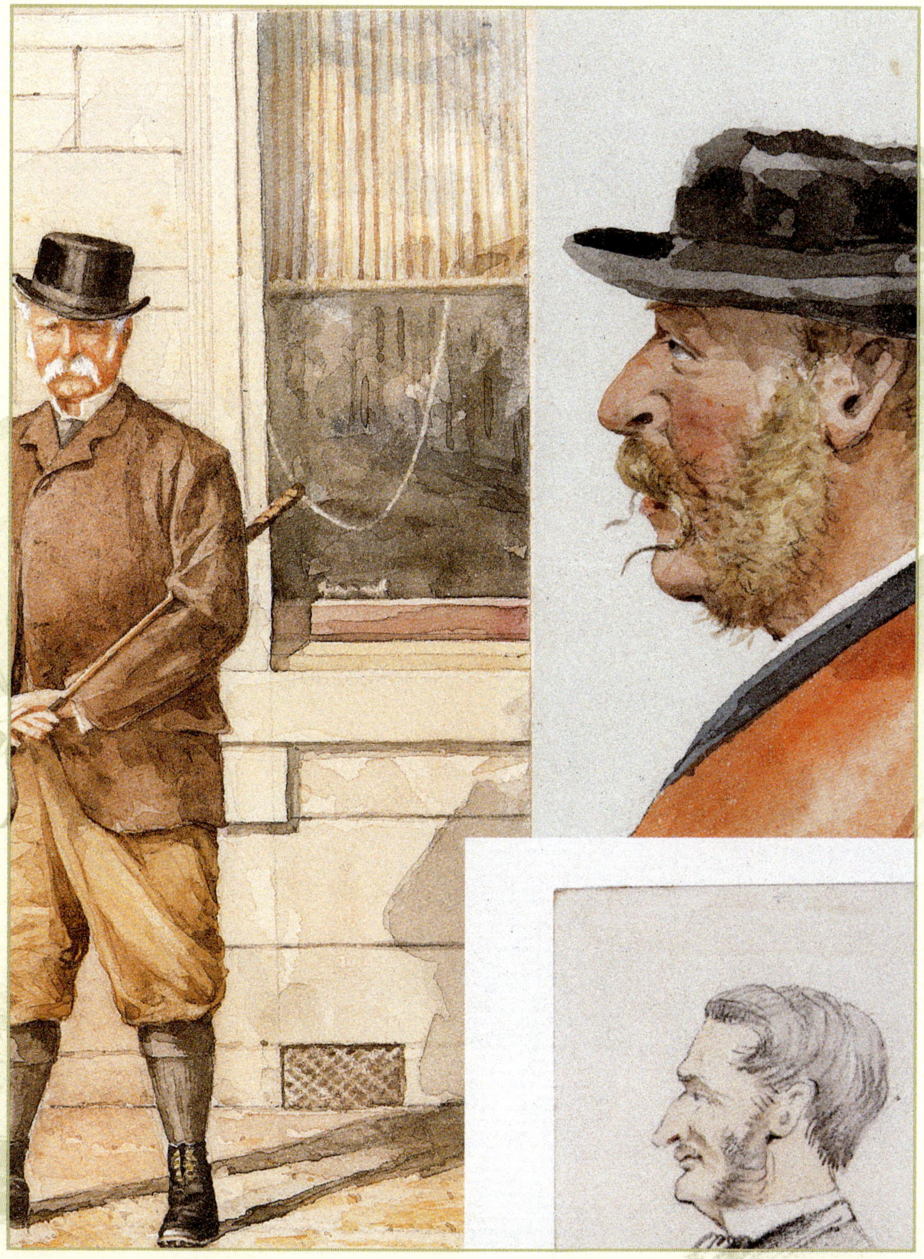

Gentlemen and Giants

Revisionist historians of the modern era would find the 19th-century members of the Royal & Ancient Golf Club, including Thomas Hodge, very easy targets. No doubt. Not many of their achievements, their battles, their attitudes would stand the challenges of present political correctness, or any other kind of correctness, racial, gender, pick whichever you like.

But of their time, they were reckoned men of honour. Many were pillars of the British Empire, that gigantic edifice not always dedicated to self-interest and exploitation, and today almost impossible to grasp in its complexity and strength. There is something about many of the old buffers, with all their faults, which remains resolutely Corinthian.

N.B. Most of the portraits illustrated are roughly 9cm x 8cm in the originals.

Below: several of Hodge's best portraits are of golfers not yet identified and some not even completed, as in this example.

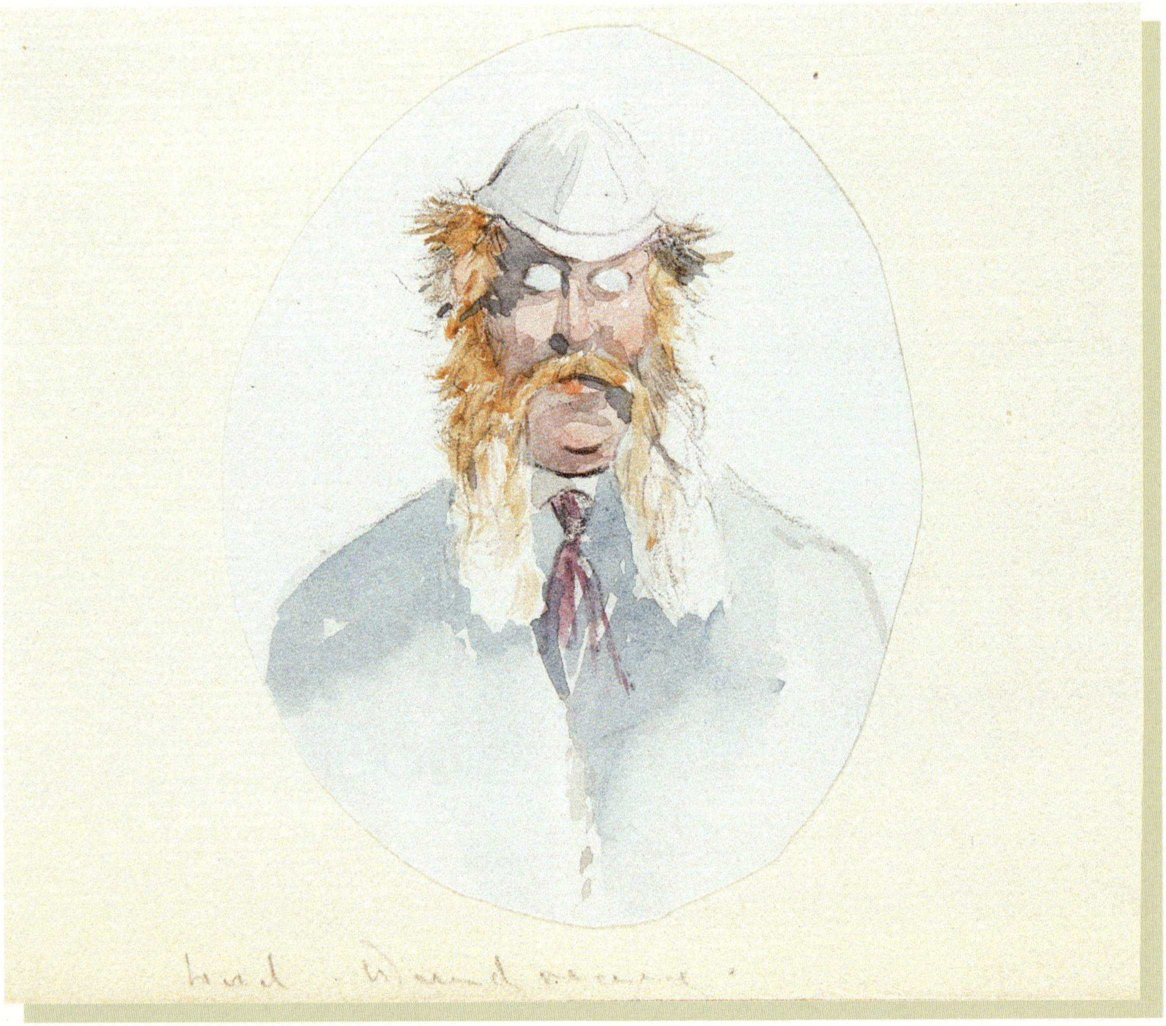

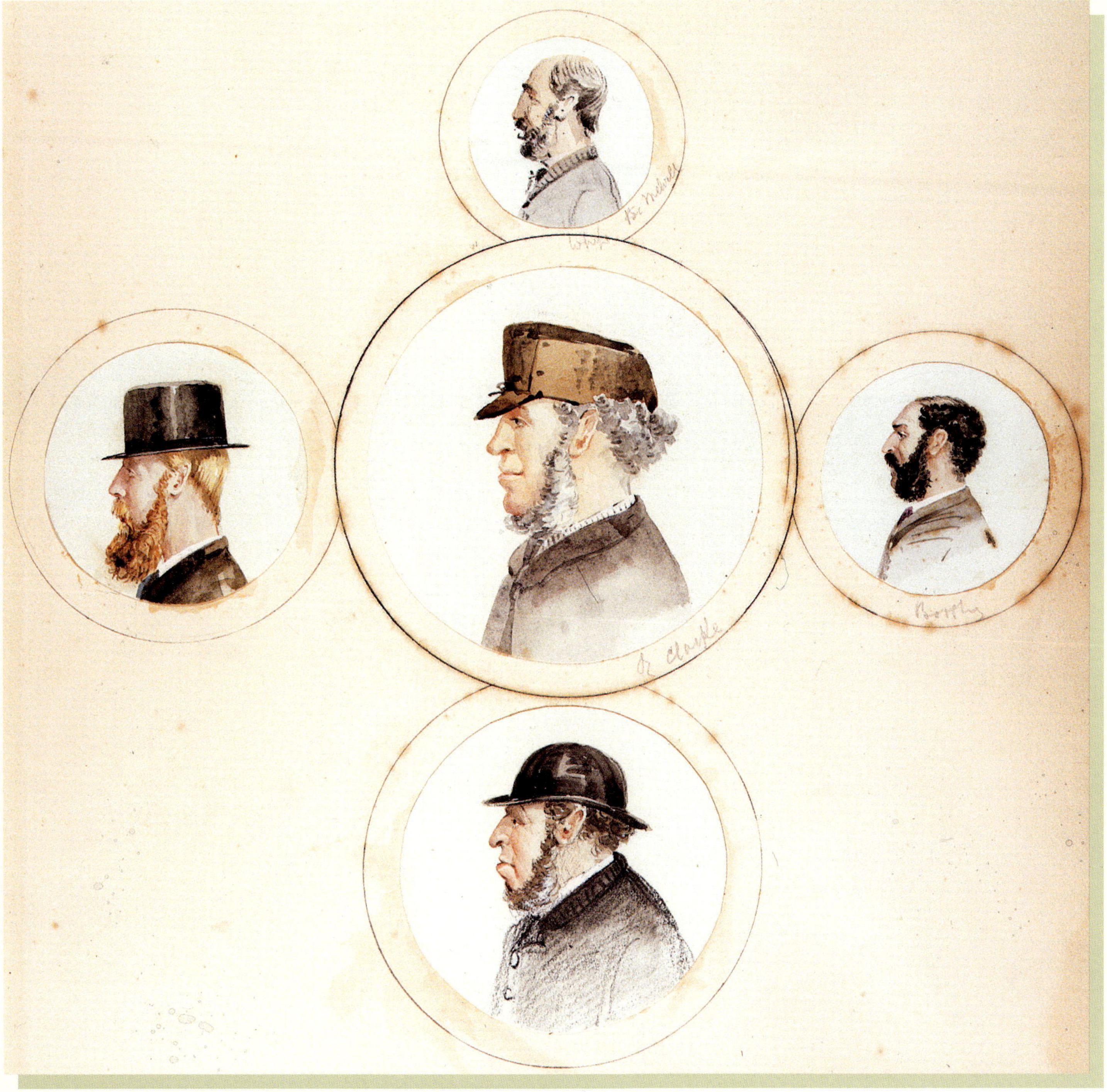

Above: thumbnail sketches often meant just that to Hodge as he dashed off tiny portraits of his golfing friends, often hardly an inch across and many still unidentified.

ROBERT CLARK

Described in one portrait as "The Slogger", Clark edited and published in Edinburgh 1875 *Golf: A Royal and Ancient Game*. Dismissively, he called it "scraps and patches", but his classic book contains much of the important writing on golf before 1875. Thomas Hodge, apparently, drew the fine map of the St. Andrews links (page 181) and also illustrated the poem "The Nine Holes of St. Andrews", with what must have been delightful watercolour vignettes before the engraver had his way. Clark as a golfer was described with unusual respect by that sharp-penned cleric critic, the Rev. J. Gordon McPherson of Ruthven. He wrote:

Robert Clark's club was short, stiff, heavy and strong; his swing was short, only half the average; and he put in the force by intense pressure with the wrist. No distinguished player used fewer clubs. His 'driver' had to do service for 'spoons' of all kinds; no 'brassie', no 'niblick' was required by him, so powerful was his wrist.

Below left: Robert Clark wearing a leather golf cap.

Below right: Robert Clark, as Hodge drew him for Badminton Golf.

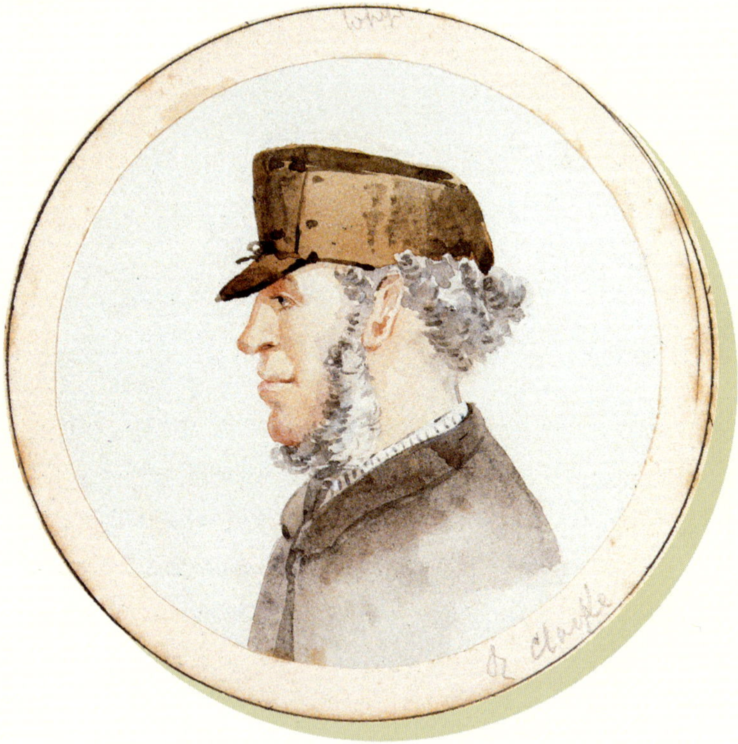

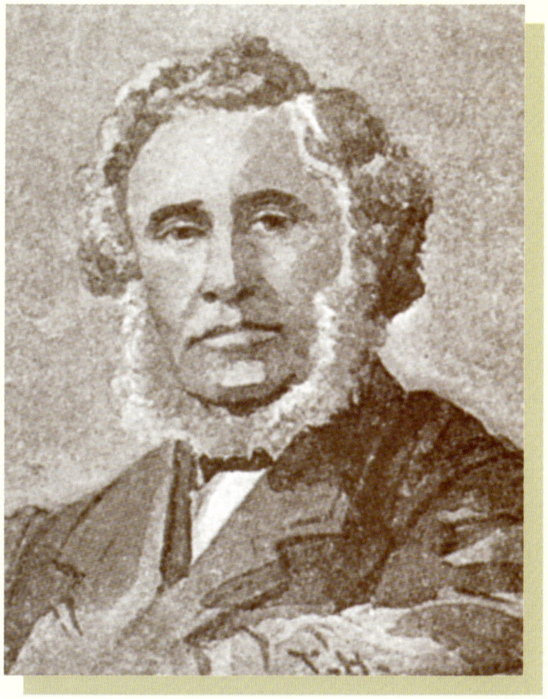

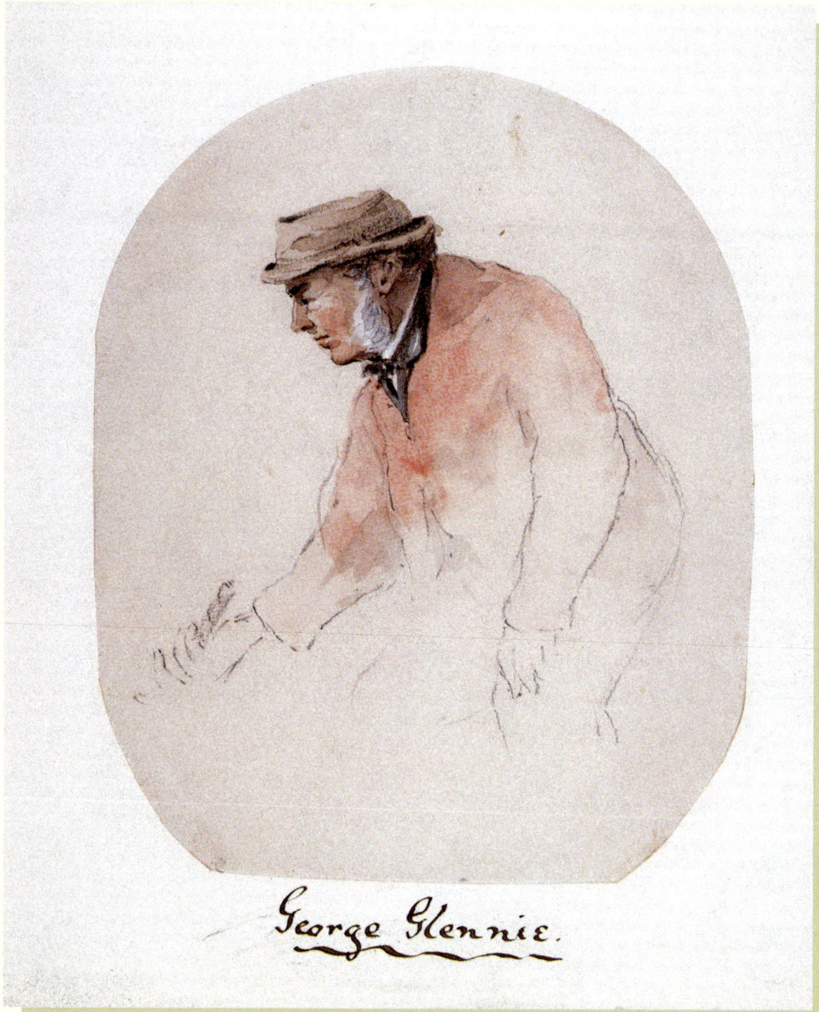

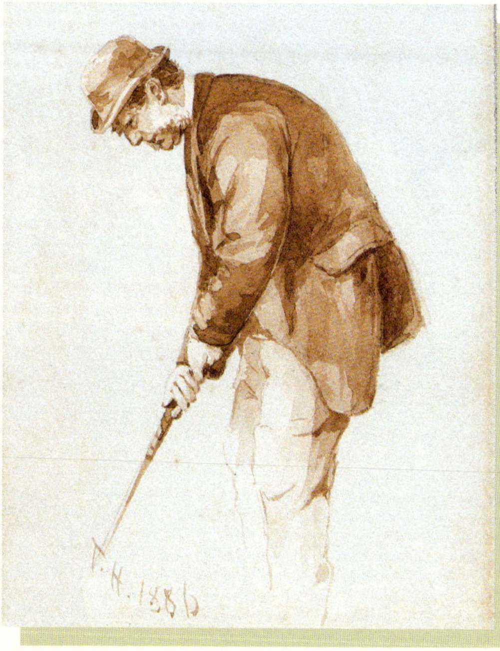

GEORGE GLENNIE

Two portraits; the first of which is perhaps Hodge's best period, the 1870s, showing Glennie leaning forward, club in hand, wearing a faded red jacket. The other portrait signed T. H. and dated 1886 was etched on to club medals. In a pencilled list of some of his sketches, Hodge wrote:

Mr. George Glennie. A most charming personality and a very prominent golfer at St. Andrews and Blackheath.

Glennie was also the driving force behind the creation of the Westward Ho! course. Harry Everard said of him:

Wherever he played he commanded admiration. A charming partner or opponent, Glennie's whole heart and soul were in the game of golf until the end of his days.

Above left: George Glennie by Hodge.

Above right: a monotone watercolour sketch of Glennie etched on to club medals.

His score of 88 at St. Andrews in 1855 was unbeaten by a club member until 1884.

An anecdote which illustrates Glennie's craggy humour involves Hodge, who was partnering him at St. Andrews. Glennie drove into Swilcan Burn, and the ball floated rapidly towards the sea. The athletic Hodge leaped into the water up to his knees and flicked the ball off the surface with his club for it to finish dead at the hole. The hole won, on the way back to the clubhouse Hodge forced himself to say eventually to the silent Glennie:

Well, what about that stroke?

Glennie replied:

No gowf at a'. Just monkeys tricks!

This incident recalls the dilemma of the Frenchman Jean van de Velde whose bravery cost him the 1999 Open when his ball landed in the water at Carnoustie. Van de Velde's general attitude would have warmed the old Cornishman's bones.

Glennie was a life member of Blackheath on the strength of winning, with John Campbell Stewart, a "Grand Tournament'" at St. Andrews in 1857 for the English club, upon which they described themselves as champions of the world. He was captain of Blackheath in 1862 and 1863, then secretary and treasurer from 1868 until his death in 1886. A civil engineer from Glasgow, he is the central figure in an oil painting by Heywood Hardy R. A. in the Blackheath clubhouse, where there is also a portrait by John Ballentyne R.S.A.

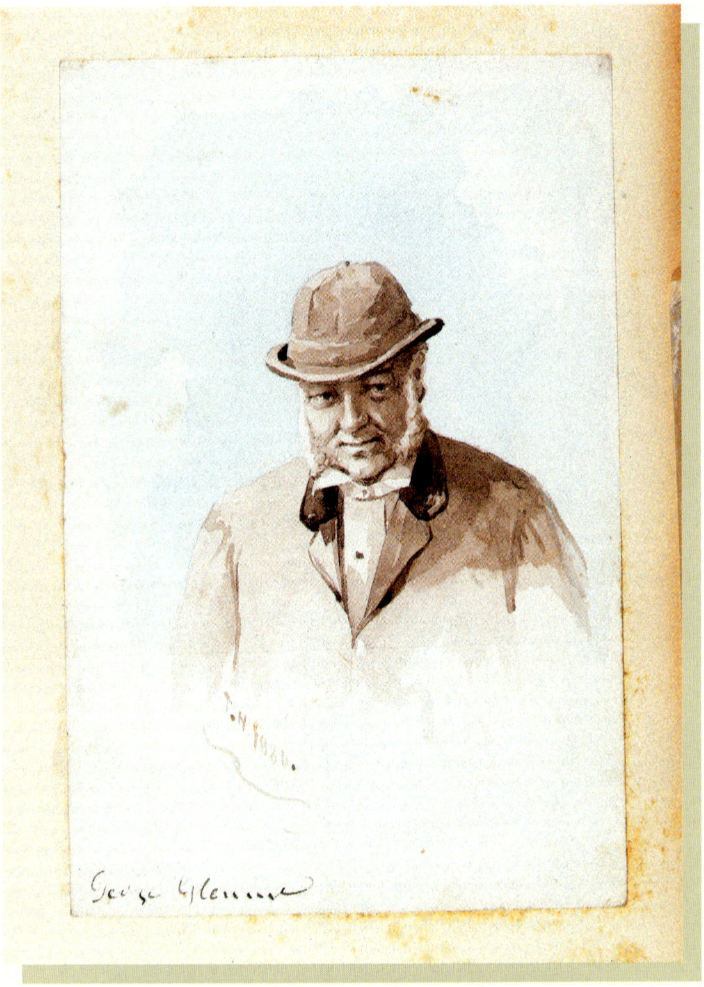

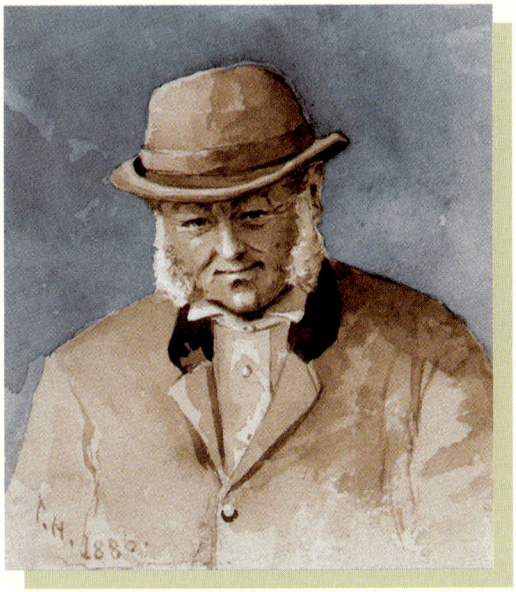

Right: another example of the way Hodge satisfied demand for his work. Two portraits, virtually identical, get a different background.

JOHN WHYTE MELVILLE

A book illustration used by Hodge in several publications, including *Badminton*. A portrait of Melville at the height of his golfing powers was painted for the R & A clubhouse by Sir Francis Grant. Melville played at St. Andrews for 67 years, was R & A captain in 1823 and nominated again in 1883, the year of his death at 86. The office was left open in his honour. He was reputed to have laid the foundation stone of the clubhouse in 1853. H. S. C. Everard said of him:

Never attaining a high degree of skill, his enthusiasm knew no bounds. From a hygenic point of view, he held golf to be absolutely unrivalled, and was frequently heard to declare his conviction that for keeping the doctor from the door the game was a specific. His matches, once they were made, had to be gone through with the most rigid inflexibility. On one occasion a foursome had been made up, but on the day there was such a gale of wind and snow that the rest of the party imagined, not unreasonably, that it was altogether unfitted for play. One of them, seeing a bank of snow drifting under his front door, betook himself to his smoking room; the second made preparations for wiping off arrears of business; the third stayed in bed. But they reckoned without their host, for in due course in came the dogcart from Mount Melville, carrying the owner with his accustomed cigar. Not finding a living soul in the club, he drove round to the residences of each of the absentees, and hauled them one and all ignominiously to the tee, though even he found it impossible after they did start to get further than the first hole.

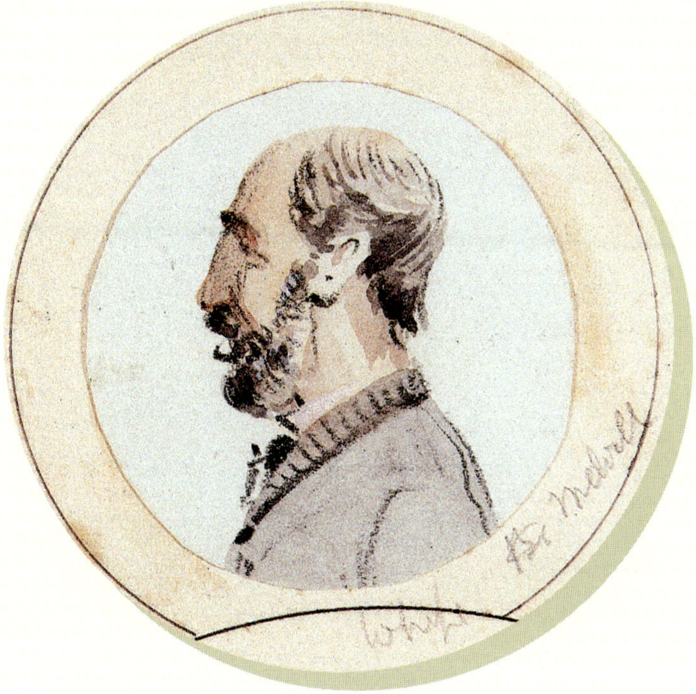

Above: John Whyte Melville.

His later years were shattered by the death of his son George, the famous field sports writer and novelist, killed in a hunting accident. There is what's left of an ornate memorial fountain dedicated to George in the centre of St. Andrews. George's most famous verse, now desperately out of kilter with modern attitudes, first appeared in *Baily's* magazine in 1871:

I have lived my life; I am nearly done;
I have played the game all round;
But I freely admit that the best of my fun,
I owe it to horse and hound.

George Whyte Melville also served a term as R & A captain in 1851. He was reputed to have predicted that "golf will become a monster engulfing St. Andrews", or words to that effect!

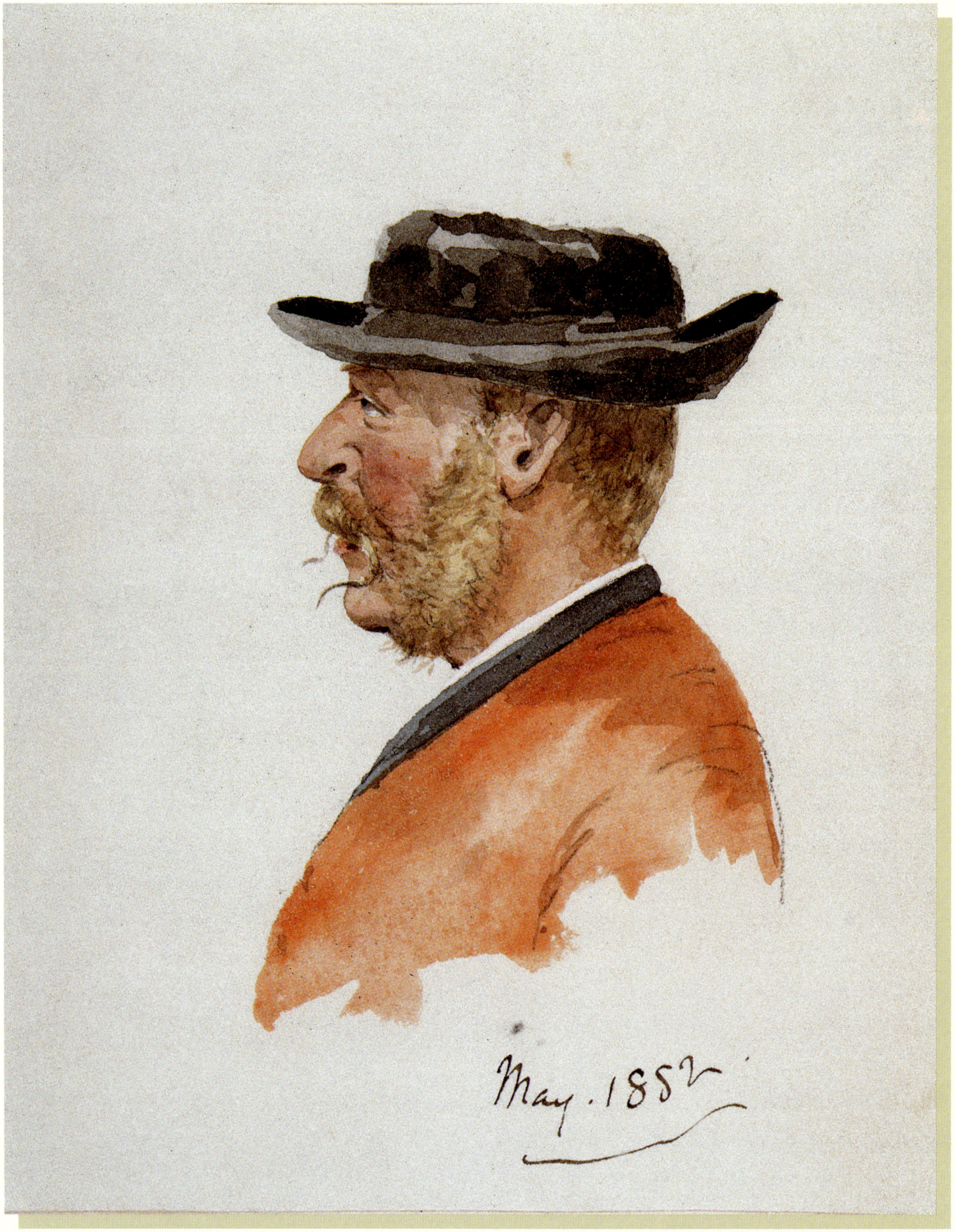
May. 1852

RANDLE JACKSON

Yet another of Hodge's best efforts, dated May 1882. Jackson, who sports luxurious ginger whiskers and wears red coat and black hat, was captain of the Royal & Ancient in 1881. He features in the artist's amusing series on "Conservation of the Links". Hodge had also served from time to time on the links committee.

SIR JAMES HOPE GRANT (1808–75)

A tiny watercolour portrait of one of the "first generation" of 19th-century stalwarts "in the forefront of every golfing battle" at St. Andrews and elsewhere. How Hope Grant ever found time and energy to play golf is something of a mystery. A senior officer with British forces in India and China and eventually a general, he was involved in countless desperate battles. The Indian "mutineers" in the 1850s regarded him as a humane opponent, unlike some of the British officers who supervised horrendous revenges for incidents like "the black hole of Calcutta". In 1860 he led the British contingent in the defeat of the Chinese and the capture of Peking. He had his men flogged for looting and was once imprisoned for six weeks after rightly accusing a superior officer of being drunk in charge of a battle. He introduced the war game and manoeuvres to the army.

His experiences in India made him intensely religious. In younger days he would join in the fierce betting at St. Andrews, when £5 a hole and £100 a round were commonplace gambles. Returning from India, he told fellow members at the start of play:

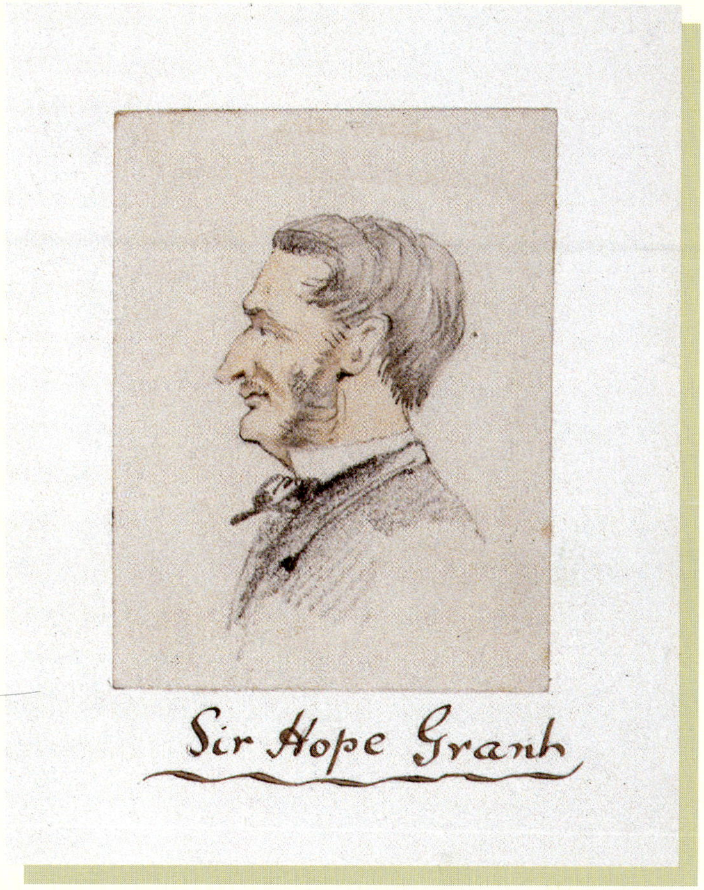

Above: Sir James Hope Grant.

In future I shall play for the golf's sake and nothing other.

His example is always in my mind, whenever I am tempted to do anything unworthy...

said a fellow officer. Brother of the the artist Sir Francis Grant, he was an accomplished musician but could hardly draw a straight line. Francis, on the other hand, couldn't play a note.

Far left: Randle Jackson.

HENRY A LAMB

A full-length watercolour study signed and dated T. H. 1886 and inscribed "second honours 86". Henry Lamb and his brother David are the Lambs also mentioned in the golf poem "Letter from the Rhine". They were rated among the first rank at the Royal & Ancient and elsewhere. Hodge was a frequent opponent (see: A. K. H. B. anecdote). Henry became the secretary of Royal Wimbledon and was also a founder of the St. George's Club, Sandwich.

A notorious aspect of his golf career was his claim to be the inventor of the new "bulger" club in the 1880s, which helped the eventual death of the long, sleek shape of club heads which the traditional craftsmen like Philp and Forgan had cherished. H. S. C. Everard wrote of Henry Lamb:

> *As inventor of the 'bulger' club, his name stinks in the nostrils of all who see a thing of beauty in the delicate curves of a real thoroughbred head.*

In the first issue of the magazine *Golf* in 1890, a poem appeared, written, as it turned out later, by Professor Tait, sniping lightheartedly at the "bulger". Henry Lamb wrote a verse in response, announcing himself as "the inventor" of the vilified new club.

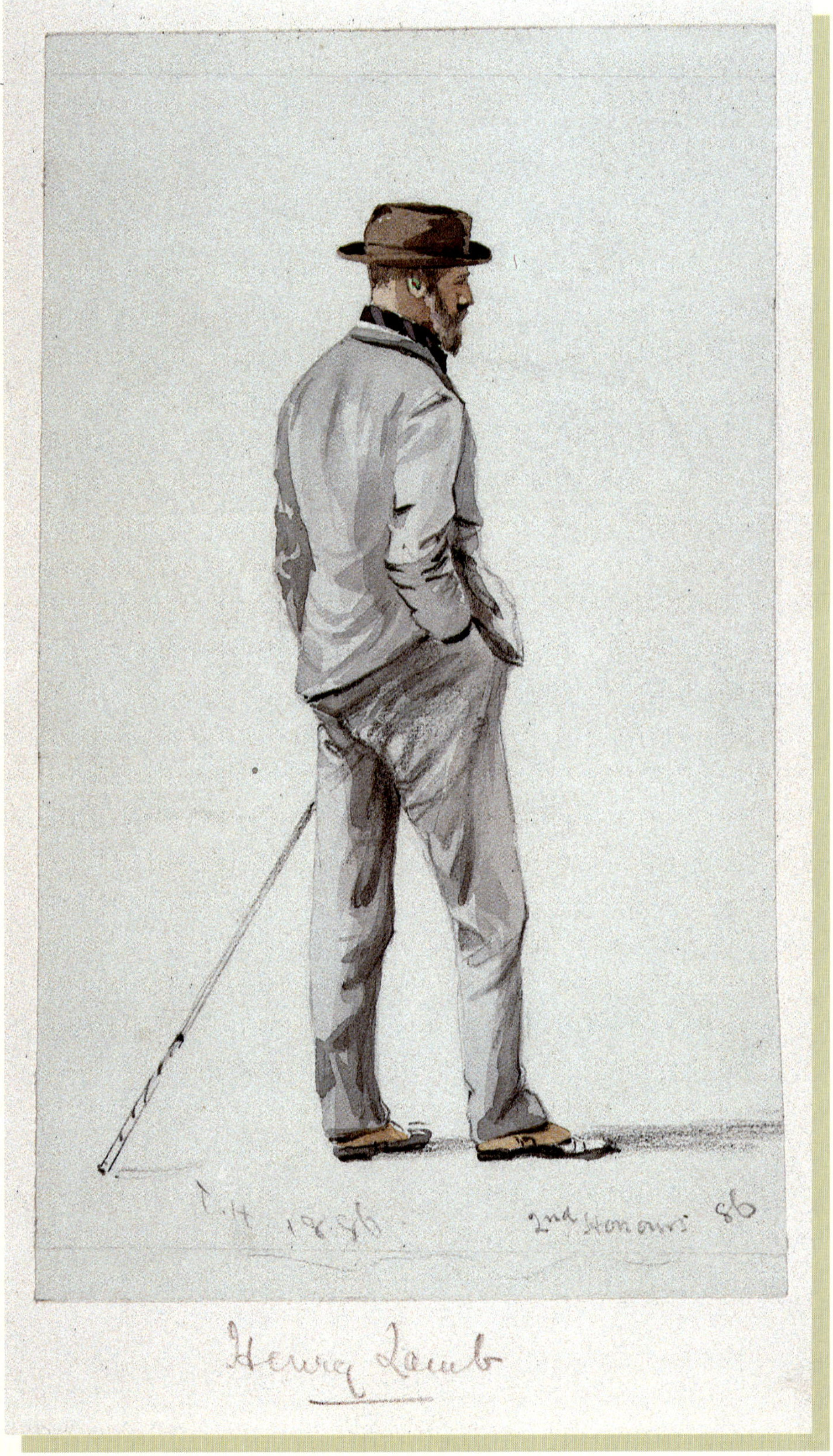

Then the storm broke. William Park Jr., describing himself as "ex-champion golfer", The Links, Musselburgh, intervened with a scathing letter, saying:

I see Mr. Lamb would like to make the outside public think that he was the inventor of the bulger. Now the fact is – and most golf club members know it – that I brought it out; and the only regret I have is that I did not take out a patent, which would have made a great deal of difference to me, financially at any rate.

Park, a member of the legendary Park family of professional golf champions, won the Open in 1887 and 1889. He was well known for making many unusual clubs based on his own theories. Unlike a high proportion of his less-fortunate professional colleagues, he was more than able to raise a pen in his hand instead of a golf club or a nip of whisky. He was also temperamental and argumentative and prone to threaten litigation when thwarted.

Not for the last time, what started as a fairly genteel argument suddenly turned rather nasty in the columns of *Golf*. Lamb replied angrily, defending his claims; Park returned to the fray with facts and dates when he had played with his version of the "bulger". He was furious at what he saw as a raw injustice. Golf caddies and professionals then had to know their place, but this was too much. Park's detailed statements ring true, but who actually first invented the despised and detested "bulger" may never be decided for certain.

Left: Henry A. Lamb.

Above right: Johnny Ball.

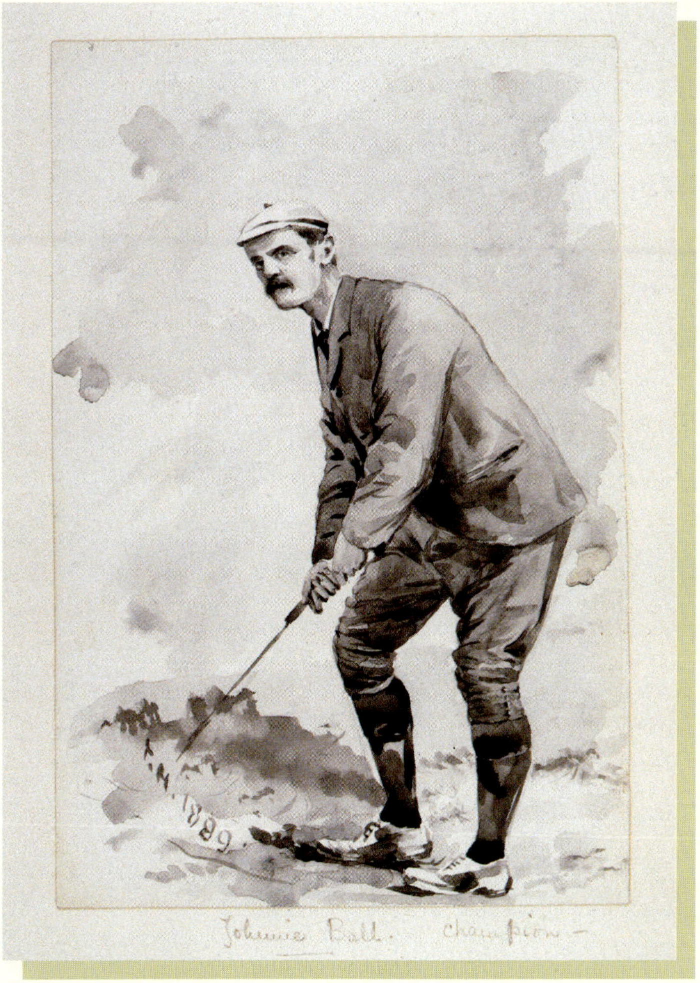

JOHNNIE BALL

Inscribed "champion", signed T. H. and dated 1889. A full-length grey wash drawing 17.5cm x 12cm which is very close to the Hodge portrait of Ball used on page 403 of the first edition of *Badminton Golf*.

John Ball Jr.. of Royal Liverpool was the first amateur to win the Open Championship, with a total of 164 (two rounds of 82) at Prestwick in 1890. The same year he won the Amateur Championship for the second time. Ball went on to win the Amateur title in 1892, 1894, 1899 (an epic against Freddie Tait), 1907, 1910 and 1912. Horace Hutchinson wrote of Ball, who became a subject of one of the series of famous *Vanity Fair* cartoons:

> *Mr. Ball's driving was the prettiest sight that golf had to give a man. I have never seen a player whose hitting was such a pleasure to watch, such a beautiful exhibition of grace and power, showing such ability to concentrate in a moment, and on the spot, all the muscular power that a human frame was master of.*

JOHN PENN

A full-length Hodge back-view, with Penn holding a long-nosed club, St. Andrews in the distance. Signed T. H. 1886. This illustration was used monotone on page 105 of *The Golf Book of East Lothian*. John Penn, born 1848, was M. P. for Lewisham from 1891 until his death in 1903. He lived at Archerfield in the winter and, as well as playing at St. Andrews, he was a prolific medal winner at the North Berwick links, taking the gold medal there in 1895. He was also a member of Royal Blackheath. A marine engineer with the family company of John Penn, Deptford, where he became chairman, he was also a serious collector of Thomas Hodge paintings and drawings, though the fate of his collection is yet another mystery.

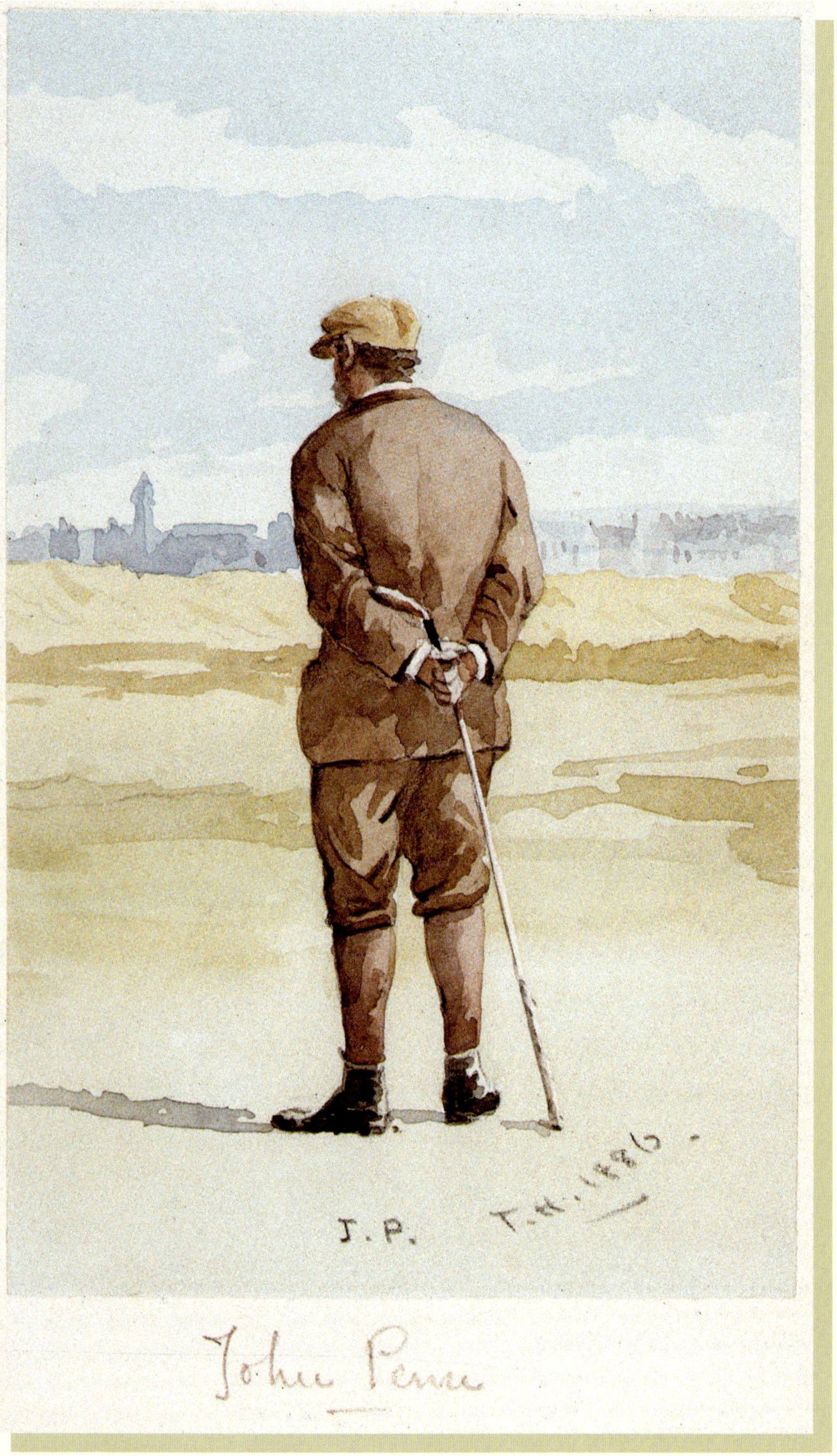

Above: John Penn.

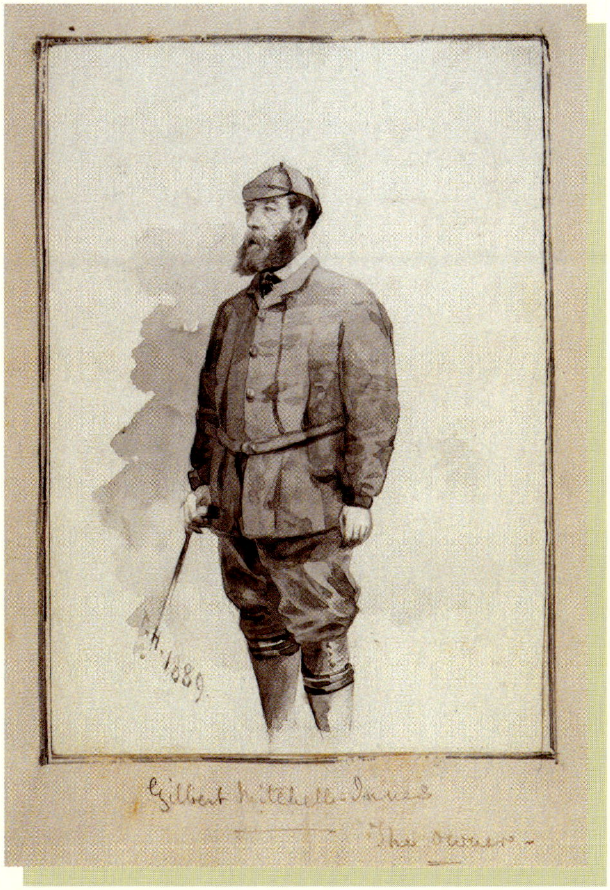

GILBERT MITCHELL-INNES

A three-quarter length portrait, signed T. H. 1889, with an inscription that appears to be in Hodge's writing: "Gilbert Mitchell-Innes. The owner." This was taken from the first album of Hodge paintings and drawings discovered in Camden in 1983 and probably means that particular collection once belonged to him. Mitchell-Innes did not play serious golf until he was over 30 years old. He was a frequent medal winner on the four leading Scottish links, coming first or second 22 times. His eternal problem with golf was that he refused to take it seriously enough for the game's faithful. Instead, he delighted in deer stalking in the Scottish highlands. Young Tom Morris once said:

> *I can NOT understand Mr. Innes, when he's playing as fine a game ony mortal man ever played, leaving gowf to rin efter a wheen stinking beasts and then coming back no able to hit a ba'.*

DR ARGYLE ROBERTSON

A full-length portrait signed T. H. 1891. This pale grey wash drawing is a very effective golfing image of the famous oculist, who was often in the honours list on medal days at St. Andrews.

Left: Gilbert Mitchell-Innes.

Below: Dr. Argyle Robertson.

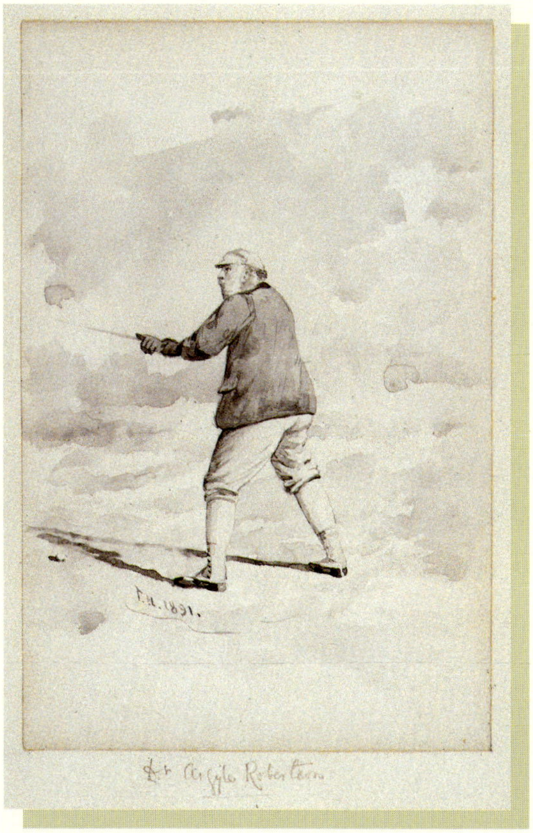

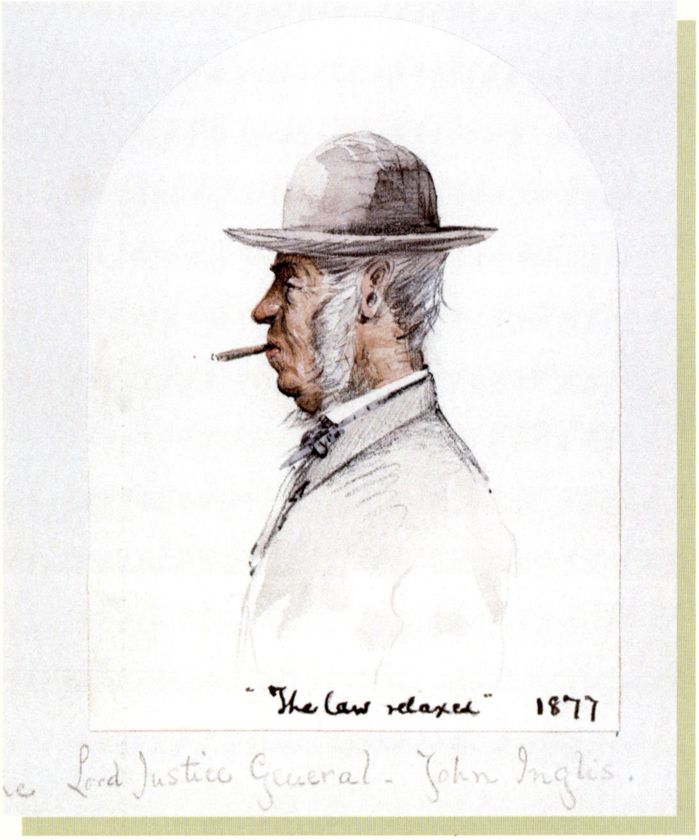

Above: the Lord Justice General – John Inglis.

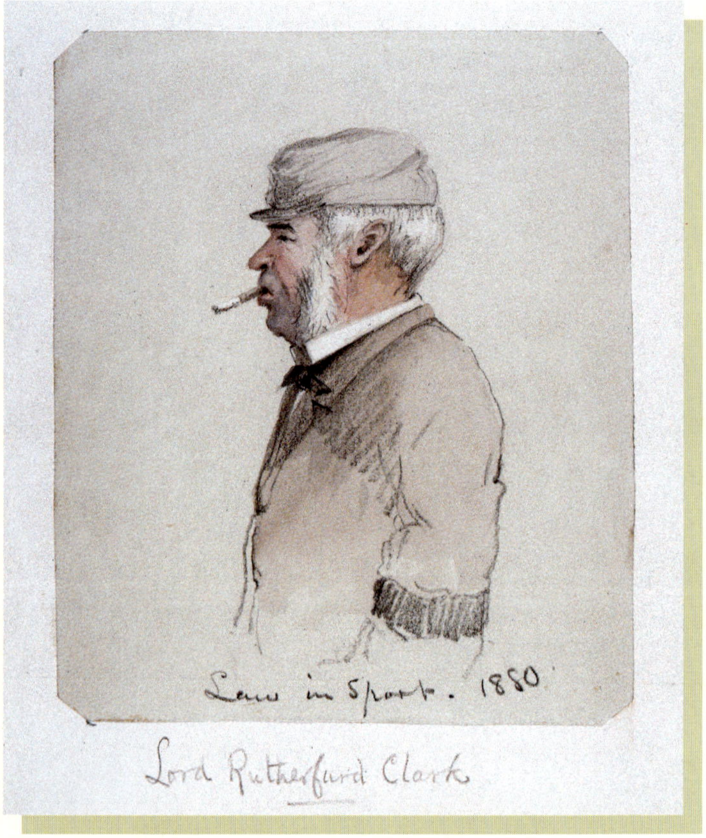

Above: Lord Rutherford Clark.

LORD RUTHERFORD CLARK

Two portraits, one inscribed "The Law Relaxed 1887", and "The Lord Justice General – John Inglis". The other is inscribed "The Law in Sport 1880". Here Lord Rutherford Clark wears a cap and pink golfing jacket. Writing of golfing style, Horace Hutchinson said:

> *A certain learned judge transfixes his ball, as he addresses it, with such a menacing coup d'oeil as threatens five years' bunker service at least. He brandishes his club with equal vigour for a putt of nine inches or for a drive of some hundreds of yards.*

Rutherford Clark rocketed to international fame when he defended Madeleine Smith successfully in one of criminal history's most notorious murder trials in 1857. Smith was accused of poisoning her lover with arsenic, but the verdict was a Scottish "not proven". The immense interest in the case was largely because of Smith's hypnotic personality and her bold attitude to sexuality far from Victorian morality of the 1850s. It was strongly hinted that the steely Rutherford Clark also fell under the spell of her "lustrous yet piercing eyes". His closing speech, said to have reduced listeners to tears, was hailed as one of the most rivetting in Scottish legal memory, though it reads much less dramatically today. In 1861 Smith married the artist George Wardle who was a close associate of William Morris. She bore Wardle three children and played the role of discreet London hostess for many years, her history unknown except to the world of Morris and his nearest artistic circle.

Smith died in America in 1928 aged 92, and was buried in the Mount Hope Cemetery, New York, as Lena Wardle Sheehy.

Below: a drawing, not by Thomas Hodge, of Madeleine Smith published during her trial.

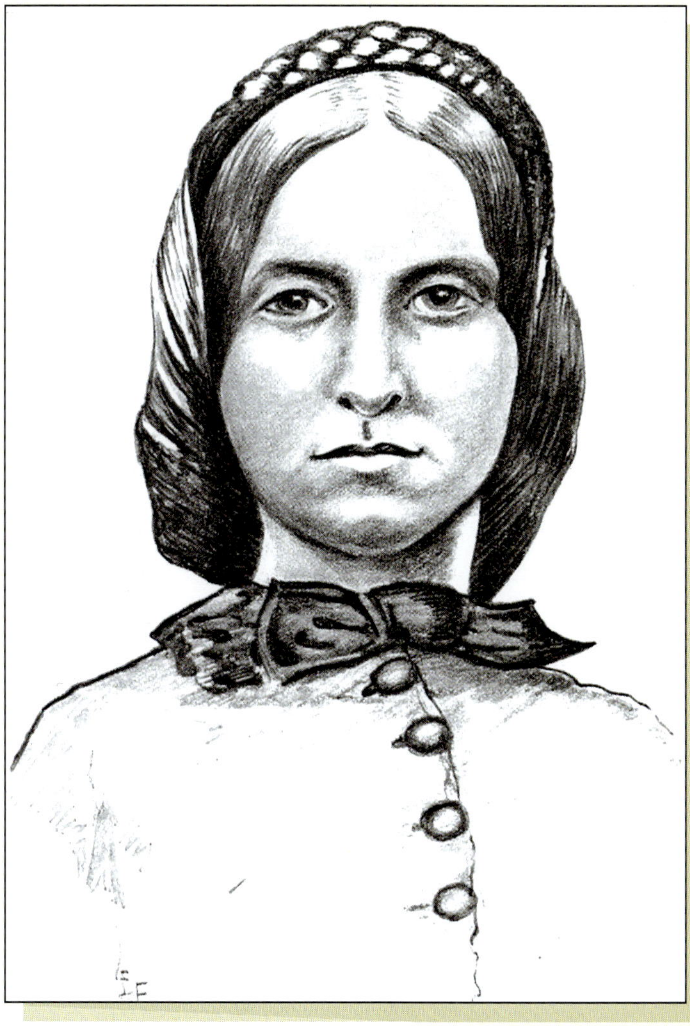

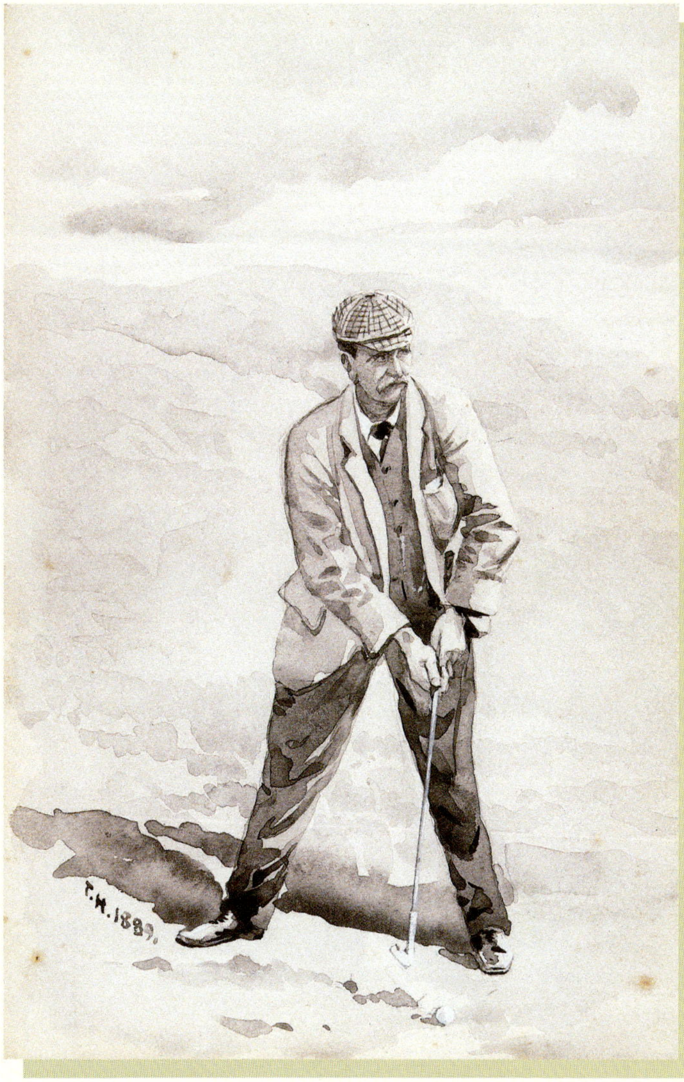

Above: the curious putting stance of Johnnie Laidlay.

JOHNNIE LAIDLAY

Two studies, one being another of Hodge's remarkably successful back view of golfers in action, used to capture character as well as playing styles. Laidlay is making a short putt "off the left leg", which was his method. Laidlay was one of the most successful golfers of the 19th century by doing everything the wrong way according to the style-book. Such was his success that he became a cult figure. "His miserable imitators swarm on every green in the Lothians", said one critic. Extraordinarily strong, he set records on many courses, and won the Amateur Championship in 1889 and 1891, losing the 1888 and 1890 finals to John Ball Jr., and the 1893 final by two holes to P. C. Anderson. He defeated Leslie Balfour Melville and Harold Hilton in his winning finals. The back view illustration was published on page 348 of *The Golf Book of East Lothian*.

Below: back view of Laidlay putting, his best (left) foot forward.

Right: a rare drawing of match action by Hodge.

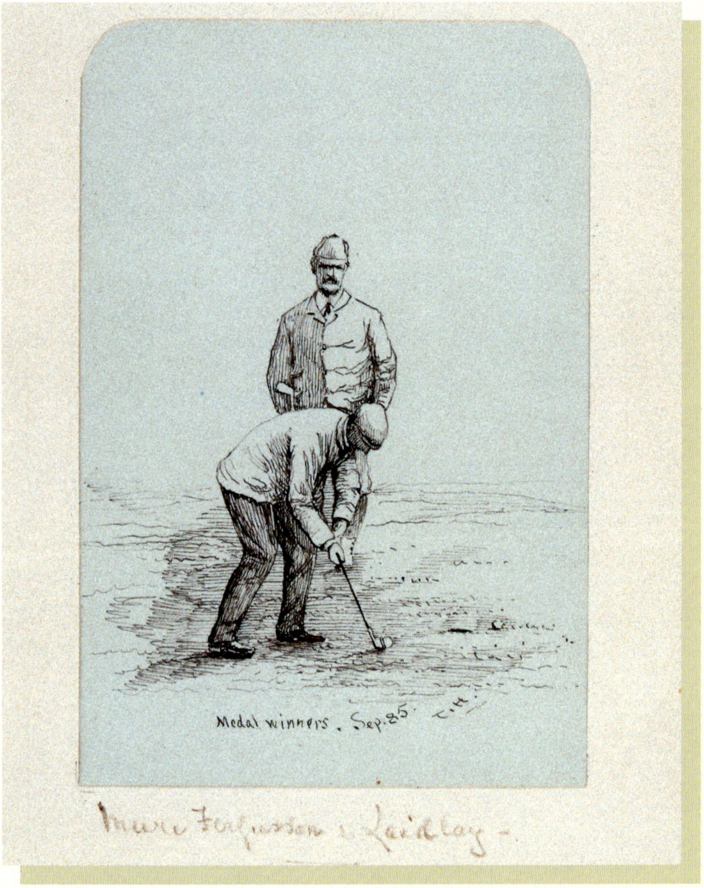

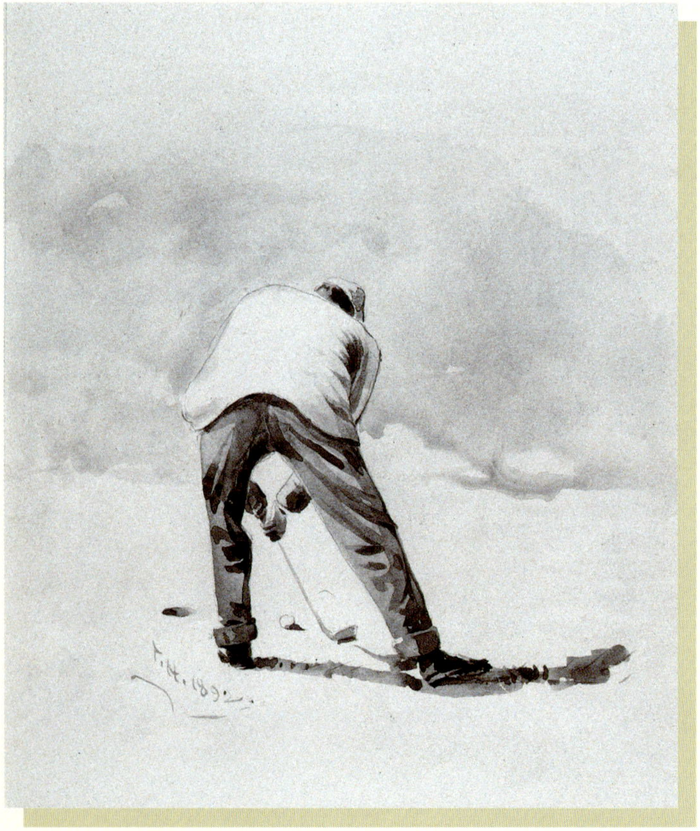

MURE FERGUSON and LAIDLAY

A pen drawing on blue card, inscribed by Hodge "Medal winners. Sept 85. T. H." Laidlay is shown putting with Ferguson's ball tight against the hole. In 1887, Laidlay won 11 competition medals, three with record scores. In the Open Championship, he was frequently close to the winner, never closer than in 1893 at Prestwick, when he was runner-up with a total of 324 for four rounds, against the victorious Willie Auchterlonie's 322. In this Open, Old Tom Morris, playing in his 33rd championship, said the rainy conditions were the worst he had seen since the start of the tournament in 1860.

SAMUEL MURE FERGUSON

A three-quarter-length watercolour portrait of the golfer who was the first holder of the Glennie Cup at the Royal & Ancient. He also won the King William IV gold medal in 1874, 1881, 1886, 1897 and (?) 1913. A prodigious driver and accurate putter, in his day he was among the best amateur players in Britain, playing frequently and with distinction in the British Open and Amateur championships. He lost the Amateur final by only one hole to John Ball Jr.. at Hoylake in 1894. R & A captain in 1910.

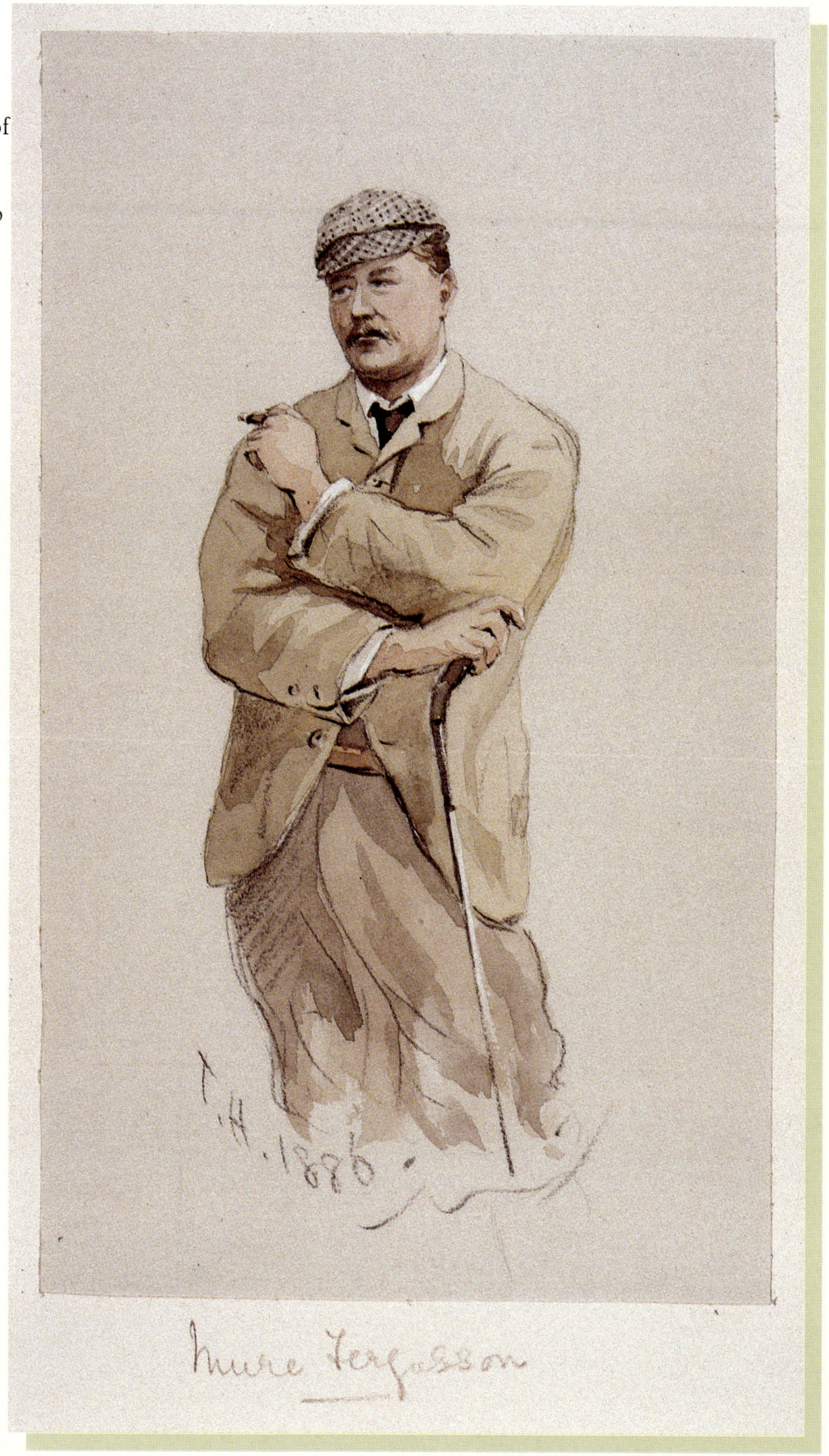

Right: Victorian golfing man personified; Mure Ferguson in 1886.

SIR ROBERT HAY

There are several fine watercolour portraits by Hodge of Sir Robert, including two ovals, one inscribed "Our Captain. 1876". A pencil sketch bears the inscription "Just my luck". (There is also a further portrait by Hodge on page 386 of *Badminton Golf.*) The lengthy poem called "Letter from the Rhine, a description of medal day at St. Andrews", has the lines:

And next come the fliers to show them the way;
There's Innes and Boothby, and lithe Robbie Hay.

Hodge also rates a mention in the epic poem.

Hay won medals in profusion at St. Andrews, other Scottish courses and Westward Ho! (He was Royal Devon president in 1874.) Tom Dunn, a judge of good players in the 19th century, said of Hay:

It is admitted on all hands by old golfers that Sir Robert's style was ideal. He would never take an iron club in his hand if he could help it. Give him his baffy, and to see him as I've watched him many a time approaching a hole, banging the shot up to the left and the ball dozing away round until it frequently lay dead, was 'a sicht for sair een.

Hay also rated highly with H. S. C. Everard:

By general consent one of the very prettiest players who ever handled hickory.

Hay was secretary of North Berwick from 1851 to 1864.

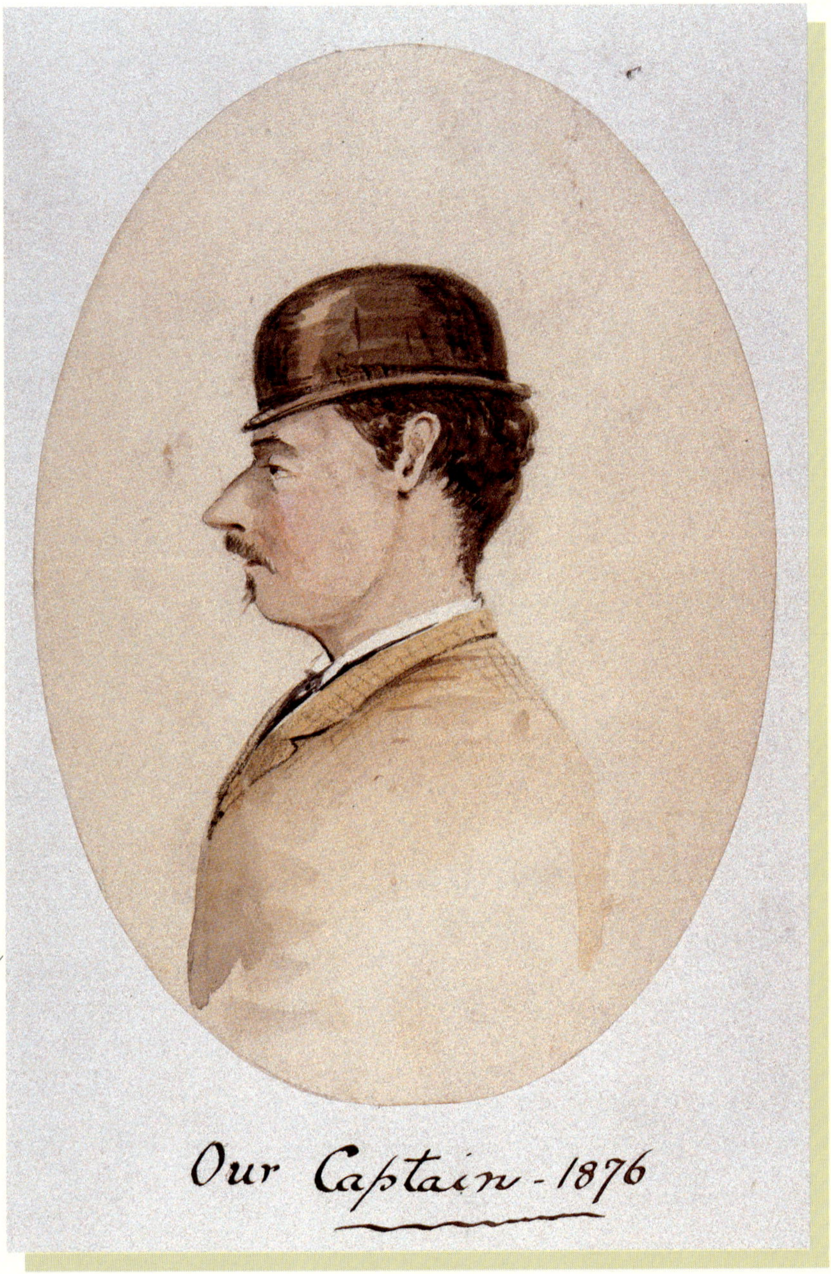

Above: Sir Robert Hay.

WALDEGRAVE LESLIE

It isn't always wise to dismiss Hodge's scraps lightly. Sometimes they record small gems of golfing history. Such a tit-bit is the sketch entitled "Valuable Fragment" done at St. Andrews in 1878 and captioned "Waldegrave Leslie". The Hon. George Waldegrave Leslie of the English Bar was a diplomat who worked in America and India and was twice Liberal M. P. for Hastings. In 1861 he married the Countess of Rothes. Elected captain of the Royal & Ancient in 1878, he was expected to take office by teeing off at the September meeting that year, thus collecting the Royal Adelaide medal and the Silver Club. Unfortunately, on the eve of the ceremony he was injured in an accident in Edinburgh, breaking small bones in his right hand and dislocating his right thumb. He arrived at the first tee with his playing arm in a sling and struck off with his left. "Under the circumstances the hit was a good one, the ball being raised and sent rolling on", wrote the *St. Andrews Citizen*. Hodge, partnered by Major Boothby, returned a score of 100.

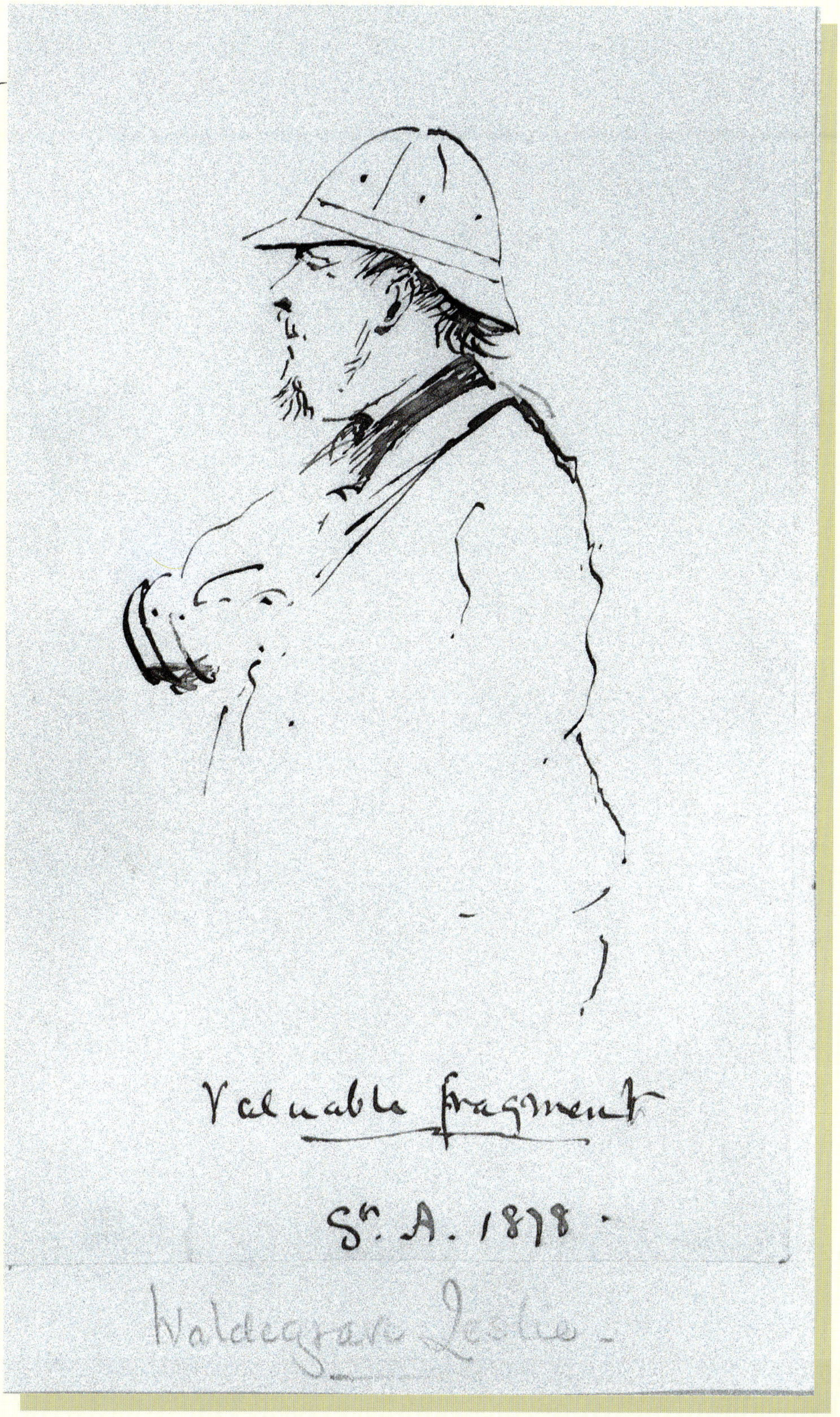

Right: Waldegrave Leslie.

BOB CATHCART

Portrait with Hodge's inscription: "Left hand down, Sept 1880". Robert Cathcart of Pitcairlie was a tall, angular figure who can be seen on some of the early group photographs of Royal & Ancient members, caddies and professionals, posed on St. Andrews links. The left-hand down phrase refers to Cathcart's strange method of holding his clubs left hand below the right while making shots as a right-hander.

Right: Robert Cathcart.

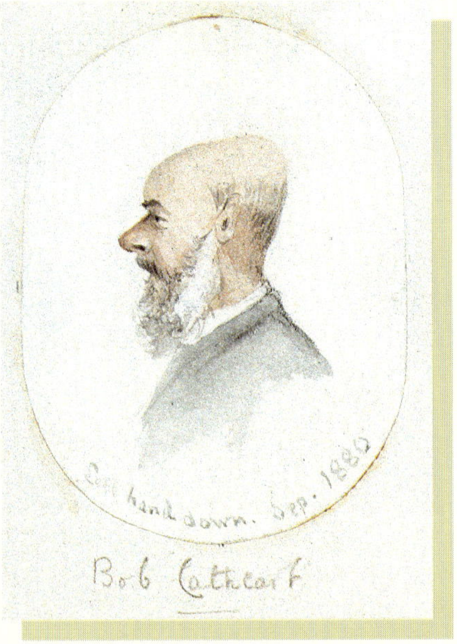

Below: Andy Stuart, record breaker.

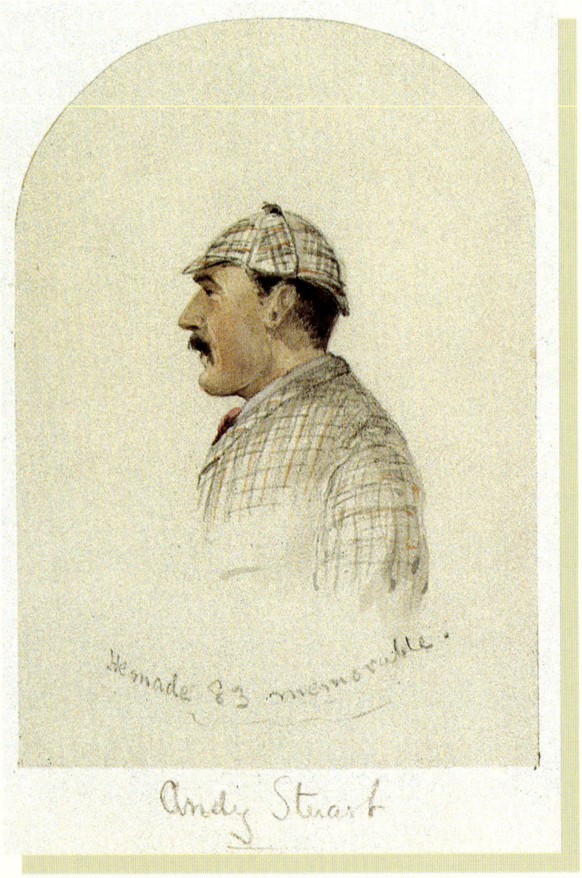

Not a brilliant player, he was nevertheless an important member of the R & A., convenor of the St. Andrews green committee and a tireless official "at the ropes" when championships and big matches were staged. Captain of the R & A in 1857, he was elected again in 1906 though ill-health prevented him accepting. He was a J.P. and Convenor of the County of Fifeshire after being an officer with the 74th Highlanders who fought in the "Kaffir War" of 1852–53. He cultivated the famous flower gardens at Pitcairlie. He died on the same day as Hodge, aged 76.

ANDY STUART

A head and shoulders watercolour portrait, with Hodge's inscription: "He made 83 memorable". This is a double reference by the artist to Stuart's record score for the St. Andrews medal of 83 in 1883. Reckoned a dangerous player on all Scottish courses, he was also a winner of the Glennie Cup and King William IV golf medal at St. Andrews.

MAJOR ROBERT BOOTHBY

Robert Boothby was a close friend and playing partner of Hodge for many years. Boothby, father of Harry Everard's wife Annie, was an active member of the greens committee responsible for the condition of the links. Boothby and Hodge made an annual pilgrimage to the national rifle shooting championships at Wimbledon for some years.

Right: Robert Boothby.

Below: James Balfour, who hated change.

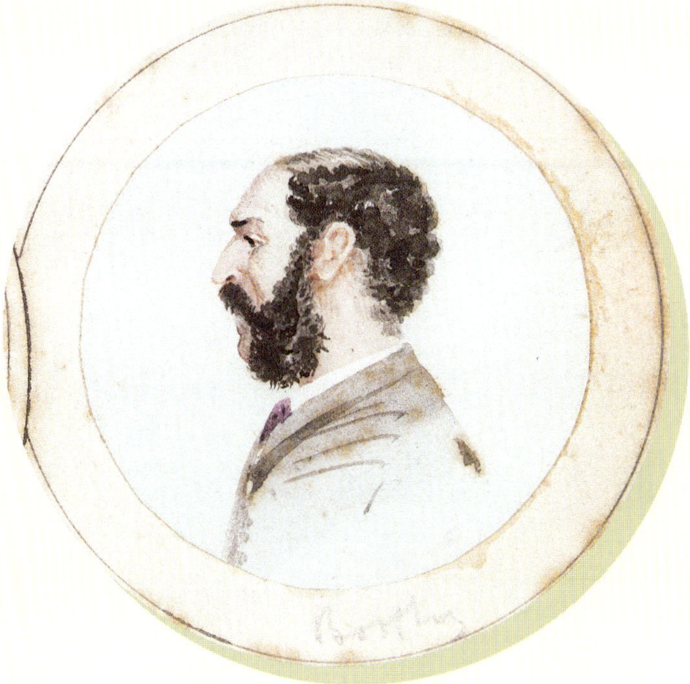

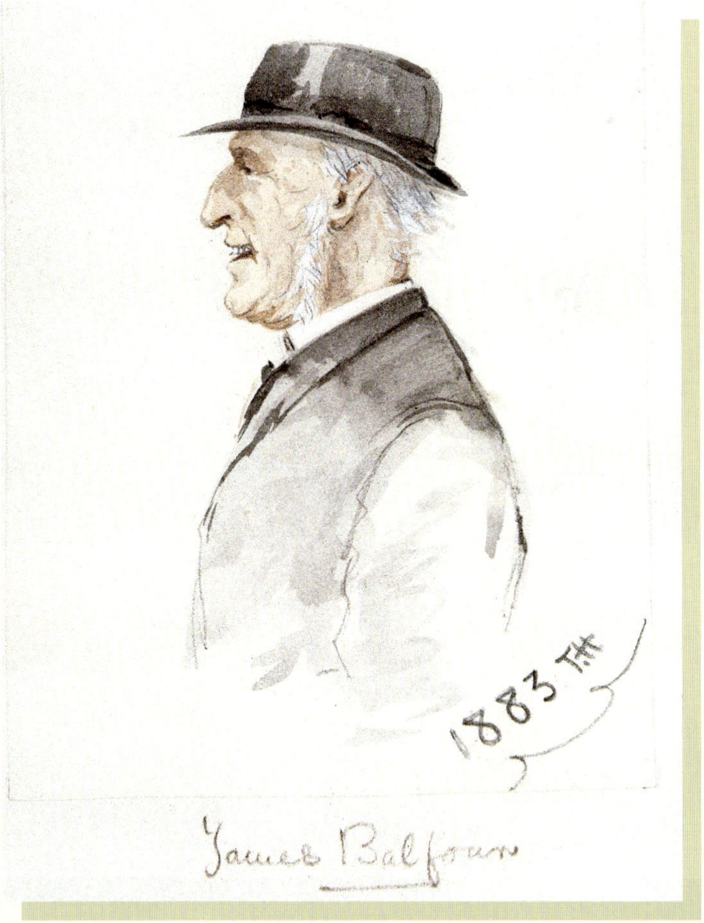

JAMES BALFOUR

Watercolour signed T. H. 1883. James Balfour was a medal winner three times in the Royal & Ancient lists. He was the father of Leslie Balfour-Melville, who won the Amateur Championship in 1895, defeating John Ball Jr. at St. Andrews in the final at the 37th hole. James Balfour was the author of *Reminiscences of Golf on St. Andrews Links* published in 1887, 68 pages, now a great rarity. Balfour recalled that when he began playing in the early 1840s, the golfers were "just a few resident gentlemen and occasional strangers from Musselburgh, Perth and Leith". They met in the Union Parlour, Golf Place, St. Andrews about midday and arranged matches. His sadness was that the gutta ball and the railway through Fife made St. Andrews "hitherto a retired place of learned and ecclesiastical leisure, much more accessible, and destroyed the exclusive and patrician tone of the game".

"DEAN OF THE THISTLE"

Another exceptional portrait dated 1882 and signed T. H. This is the Very Rev. Principal Tulloch, chaplain of the Royal & Ancient, who had been a member for 30 years at his death in 1886. Both he and the Rev. Boyd were greatly-admired props to a little community which suffered anguishing blows of misfortune. Principal Tulloch, Dean of the Thistle and vice-chancellor of the University of St. Andrews, wrote the inscription which appears on Young Tom Morris's memorial:

In memory of Tommy, son of Thomas Morris, who died 25th December 1875, aged twenty four years. Deeply regretted by numerous friends and all golfers. He thrice in succession won the Champion belt and held it without rivalry, and yet without envy, his many amiable qualities being no less acknowledged than his golfing achievements. This monument has been erected by contributions from sixty golfing societies.

The monument was erected in the cathedral churchyard, St. Andrews.

H. J. WHIGHAM

A full-length, typical "Hodge" back view, captioned by the artist "At Prestwick, T. H. 1886". The sturdy Whigham was a British journalist who won the American Amateur Championship in 1896 at Shinnecock and successfully defended it at Chicago the following year. He married the daughter of Charlie Macdonald, the first official amateur champion of the U.S.A. In 1898 he failed to qualify for the American Amateur as he had only recently returned from Cuba and the Spanish-American "war" which he had been reporting as a special correspondent. He came back suffering from malaria, and it was claimed that he had been at one point captured by the enemy, to be ransomed at the rate of a general "because he was a champion golfer".

Right: Principal Tulloch, community hero.

Below: Whigham from the rear.

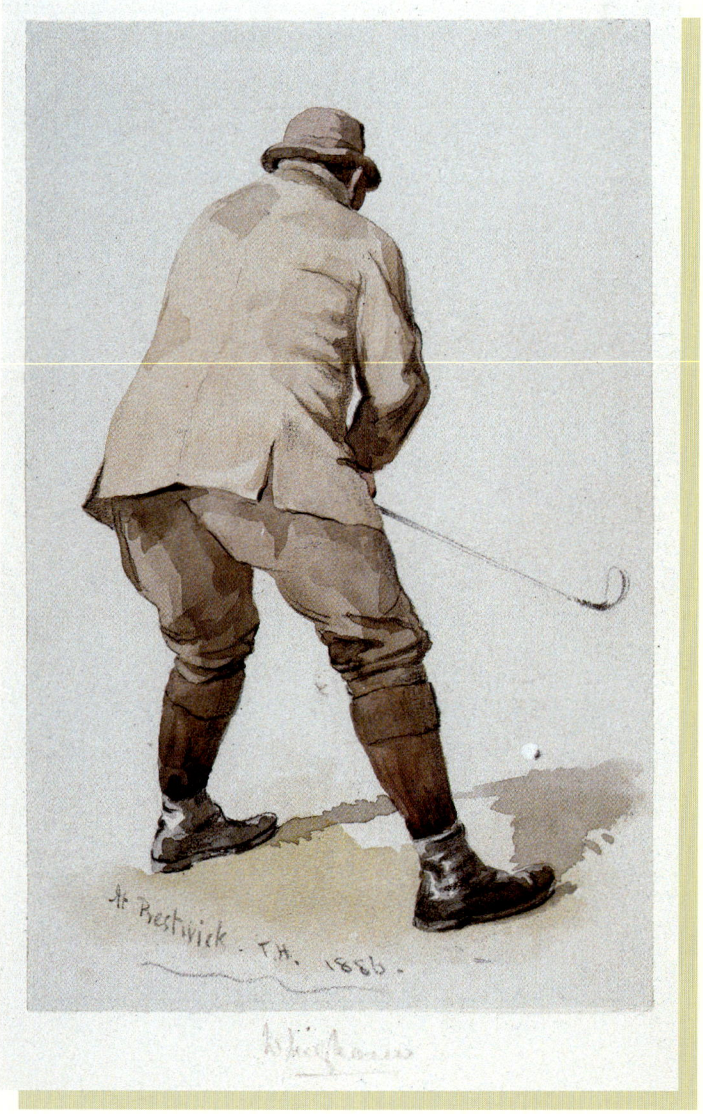

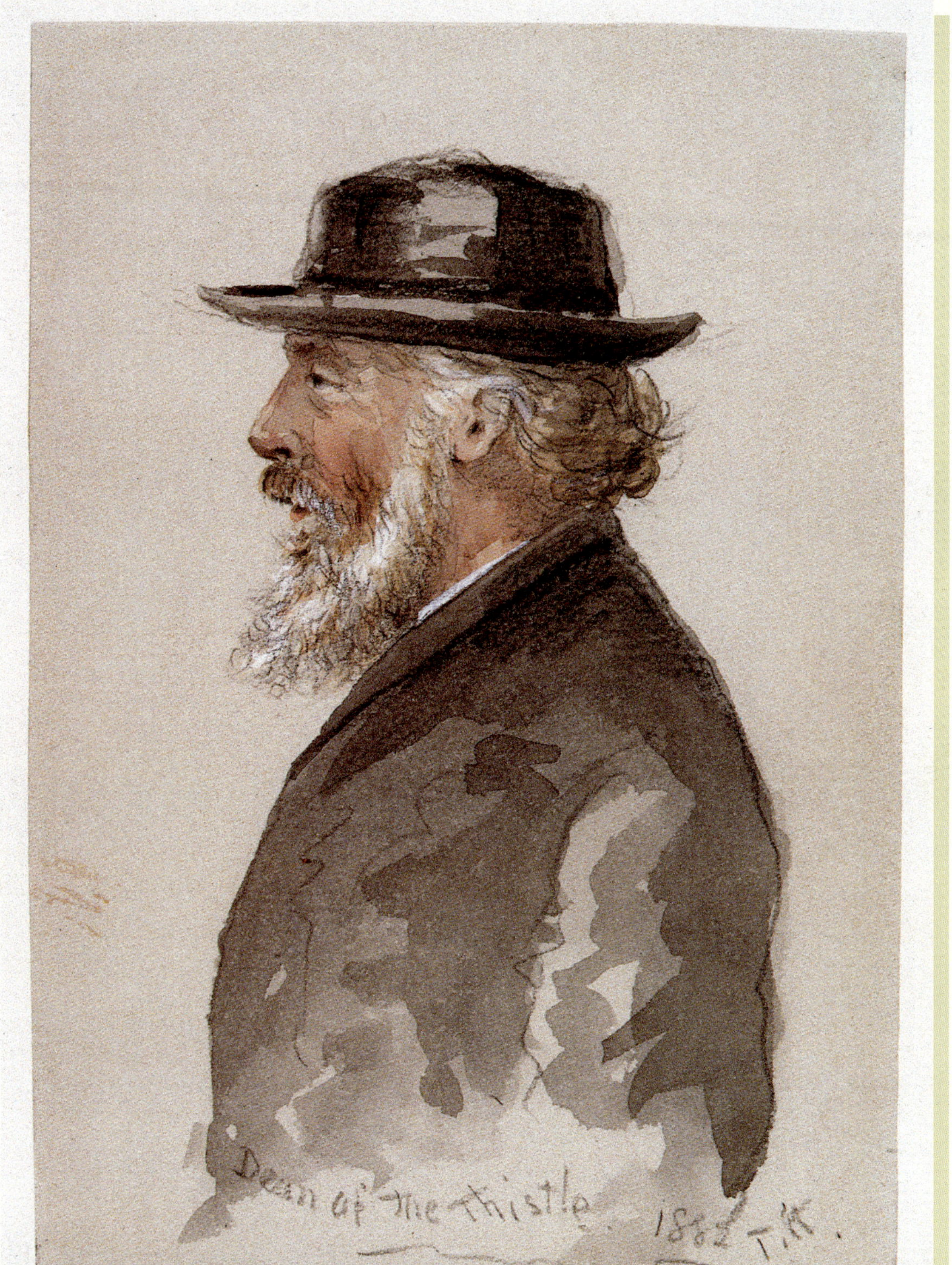
Dean of the thistle. 1862 T.H.

JOHN BLACKWOOD

Two watercolours, the first showing Blackwood in a red jacket and a cap, smoking a cigar and dated 1873. The second is on blue card and inscribed "The Editor – John Blackwood" in Hodge's handwriting. In this 1880s image he wears a black bowler and jacket.

Named as "No. 5" on Hodge's pencilled list found with the Camden Lock paintings in 1983, Hodge wrote:

Mr. John Blackwood (Blackwood's Magazine). Very short, but a celebrated putter and a good foursomes player.

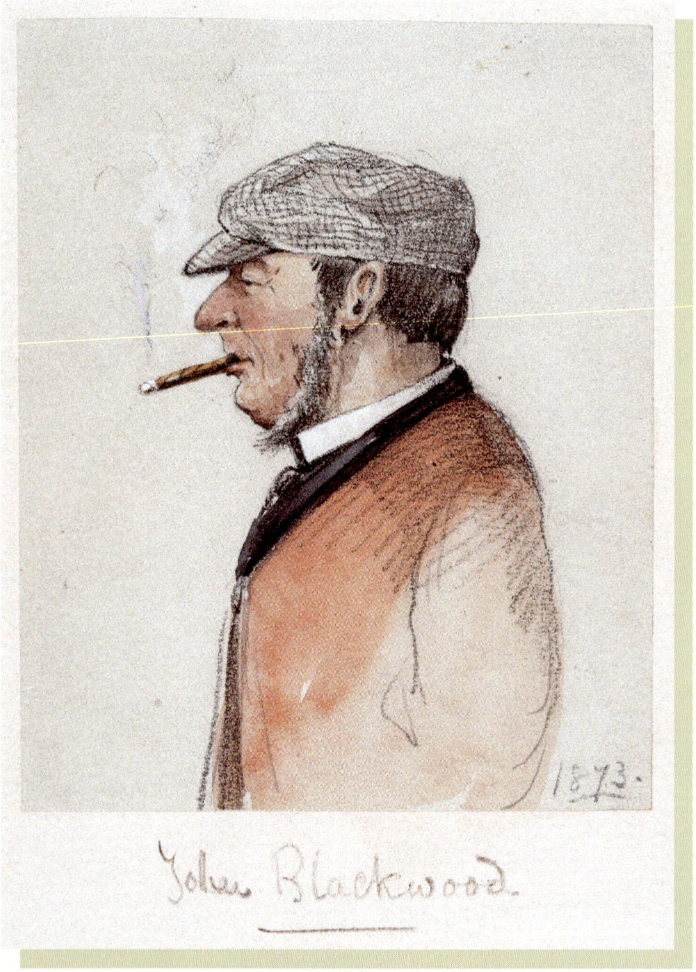

The Blackwoods lived at Strathtyrum Woods, St. Andrews, their best-known publishing venture being the magazine carrying their name ("prose in precis for the Empire"). John was captain of the Royal & Ancient in 1871. As a golfer, Horace Hutchinson recalled:

He putted in a style which was contorted almost to the point of anguish – facing the hole at which he was playing, with feet close together, the right heel raised from the ground and the right knee bent forward. The ball was to the right of the right foot and the putter was held away to the right side with vertical shaft, and only the extreme toe resting upon the ground.

In this attitude of unspeakable discomfort he used to putt with a deadliness which was of world-wide renown.

Blackwood once dryly pinpointed the nature of St. Andrews as a haven from the world's woes when he wrote to an English friend:

We are more occupied in debating whether to build a bridge in part of our links than in the question whether Russia will lick Turkey or Turkey Russia!

Left and right: John Blackwood.

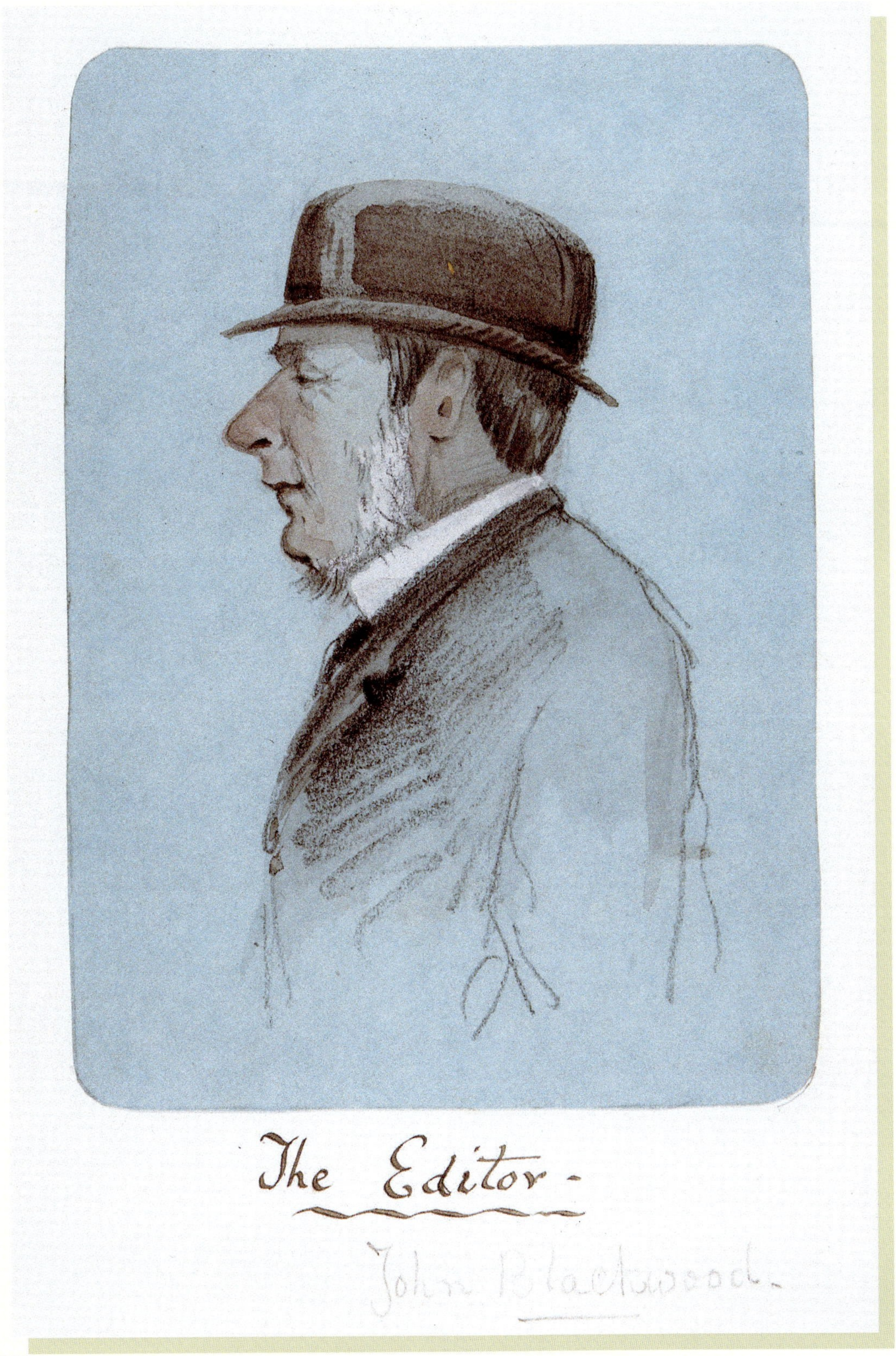
The Editor -
John Blackwood.

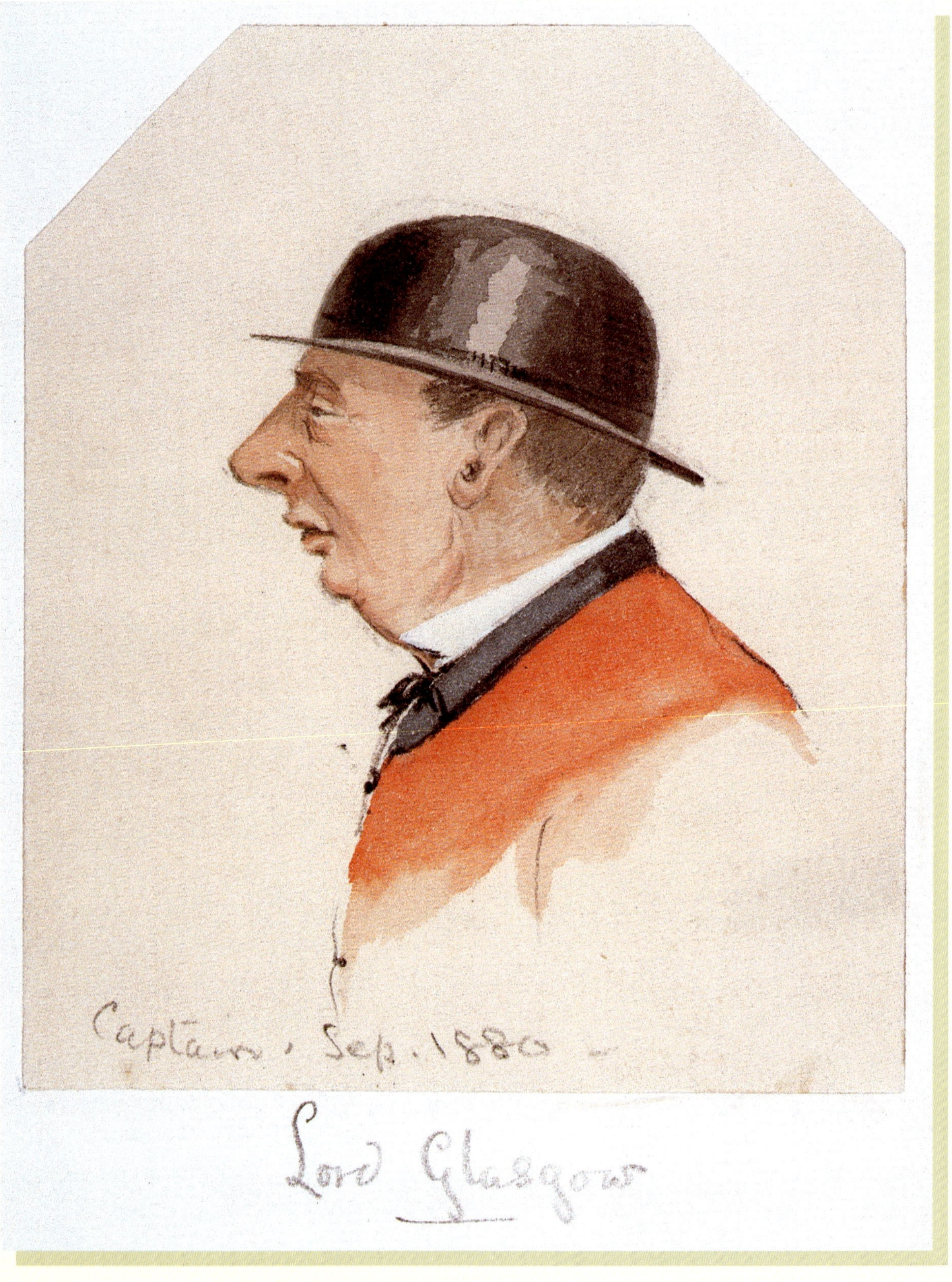
Captain. Sep. 1880
Lord Glasgow

LORD GLASGOW (The Right Hon. the Earl of Glasgow)

A distinctive profile inscribed "Captain Sept 1880". A black bowler complements his red Royal & Ancient golfing jacket with navy blue collar. In his book *A Royal and Ancient Game*, Robert Clark recalled an incident involving Lord Glasgow's predecessor and George Fullerton Carnegie, author of *Golfiana* in the 1830s. Carnegie was a wealthy wastrel of immense charm and ability. Very small and ferociously tough, he burned up the then colossal inheritance of £5,000 per annum among the Edinburgh wild set of gamblers, hunters and racehorse owners. Dining one day with Glasgow and others at the Royal Hotel, Princess Street, they took offence at one of the waiters and threw him out of a window. Told by the management that the poor man was grievously hurt, the party replied:

Put him on the bill.

Gentlemen could be hooligans, too.

Left: Glasgow's piercing profile.

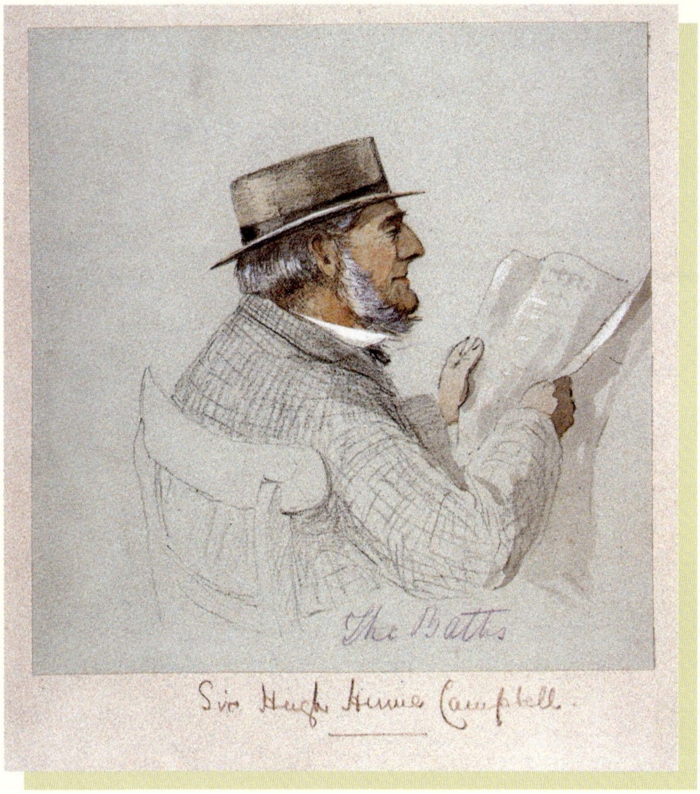

Above: Sir Hugh, paintings collector.

SIR HUGH HUME CAMPBELL of Marchmont

This is inscribed by the artist "The Baths", and was used on page 96 of *The Golf Book of East Lothian*, where, in addition to being a member of the R & A, he is described as "quite a type of the old golfing country gentleman". Sir Hugh was also a member of Blackheath, which he captained in 1850, and also joined the North Berwick club in 1839. An outstanding foursomes player, he was a collector of paintings and one of his acquisitions, *The Golf Players* by P. de Hooch is recorded as being sold in June 1894 for 600 guineas.

"BOB BETHUNE"

An eccentric portrait of a golfer in a turban and inscribed by Hodge "Curry-powder 1880". Alexander Bethune, captain in 1869, was a member of the Bethune family with long associations with the Royal & Ancient and Fife. In 1864, Admiral Bethune was more conscious than most members of the mass of old golfing clothes and equipment heaped in the corners of the clubhouse. He suggested they should be displayed in cabinets and preserved. They were, eventually. Any golfing outsider lucky enough to glimpse these treasures today cannot help but be a humble admirer. In 1858, "Mr. Bethune of Blebo" went round the links with Allan Robertson when the master golfer set his record score of 79.

Below: Bob Bethune of a famous golfing family.

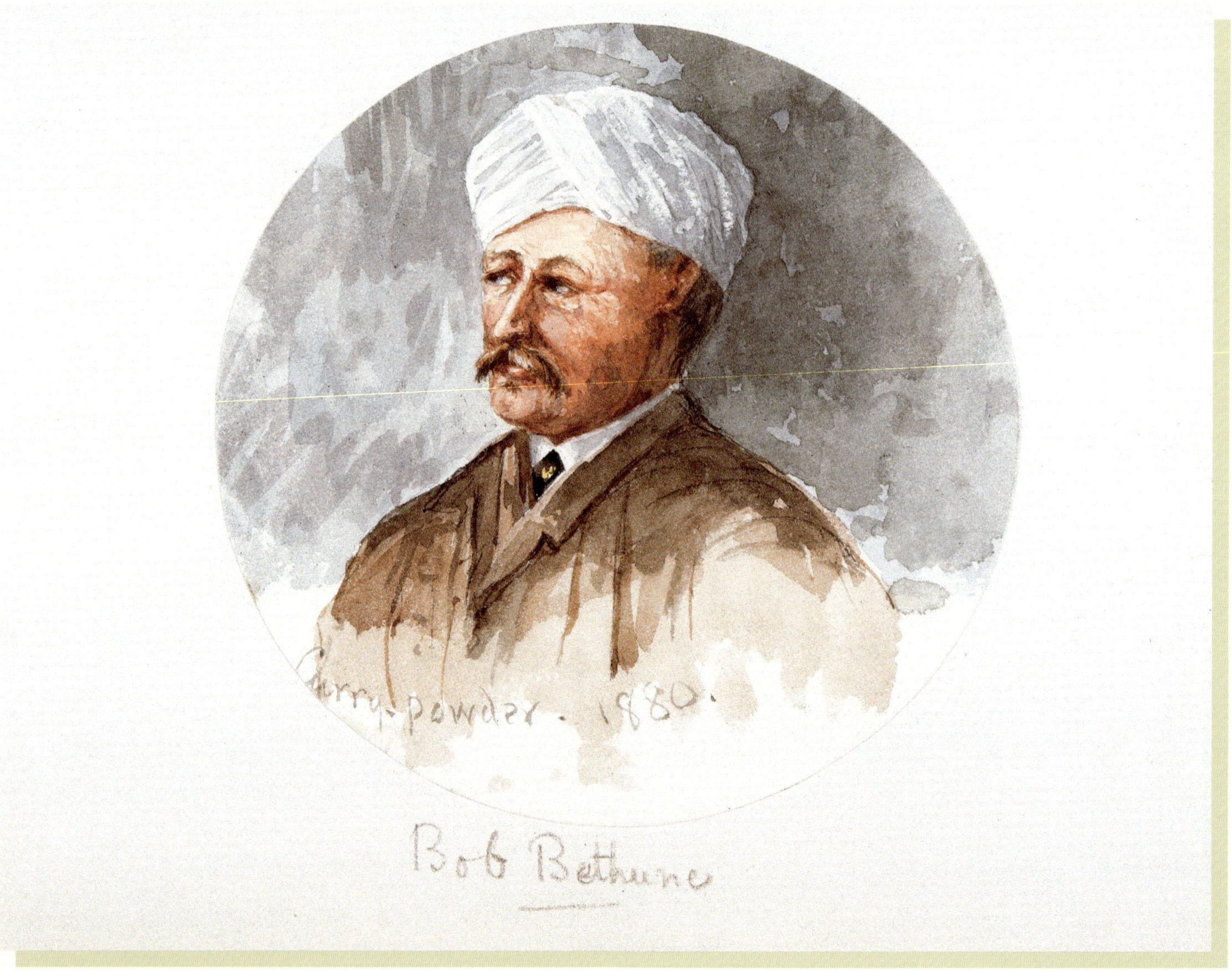

MR GRAY

Inscribed by Hodge "The Giant. 1877". A mid-length watercolour portrait of a man in a blue jacket with a straw hat swathed in white cloth. A note on him in Hodge's handwritten Camden Lock list says: "No. 6. Mr. Gray. 6ft 6 inches and most erratic". This dramatic height for the era enabled Hodge to produce one of his sly jests in his panorama of the 1862 October meeting at St. Andrews, when he measured Mr. Gray and the towering caddie "Lang Willie" standing side by side in the crowd at the last green.

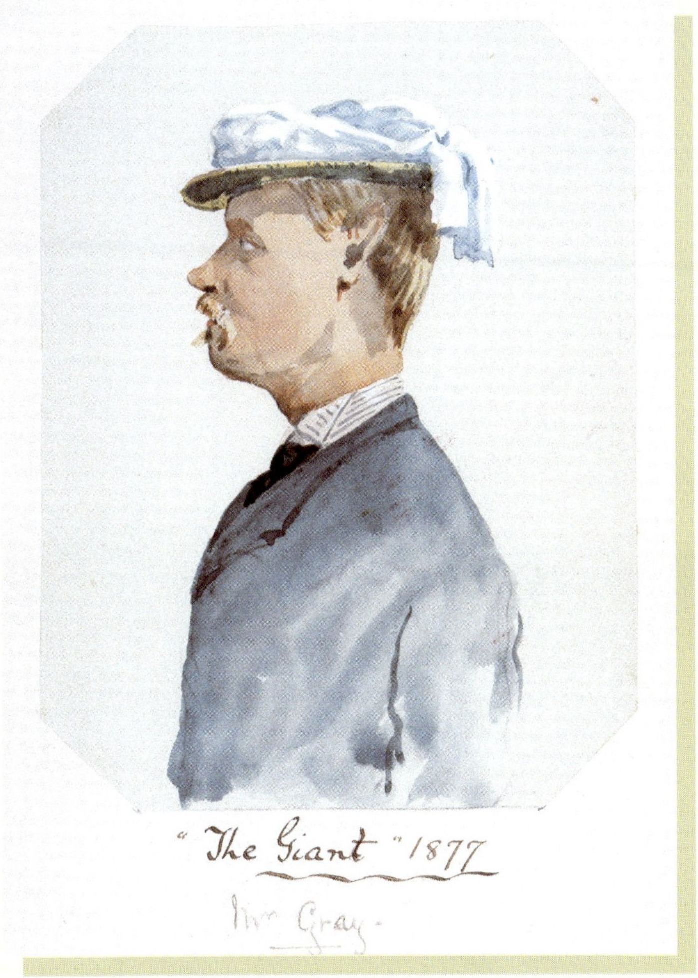

Above: Mr. Gray.

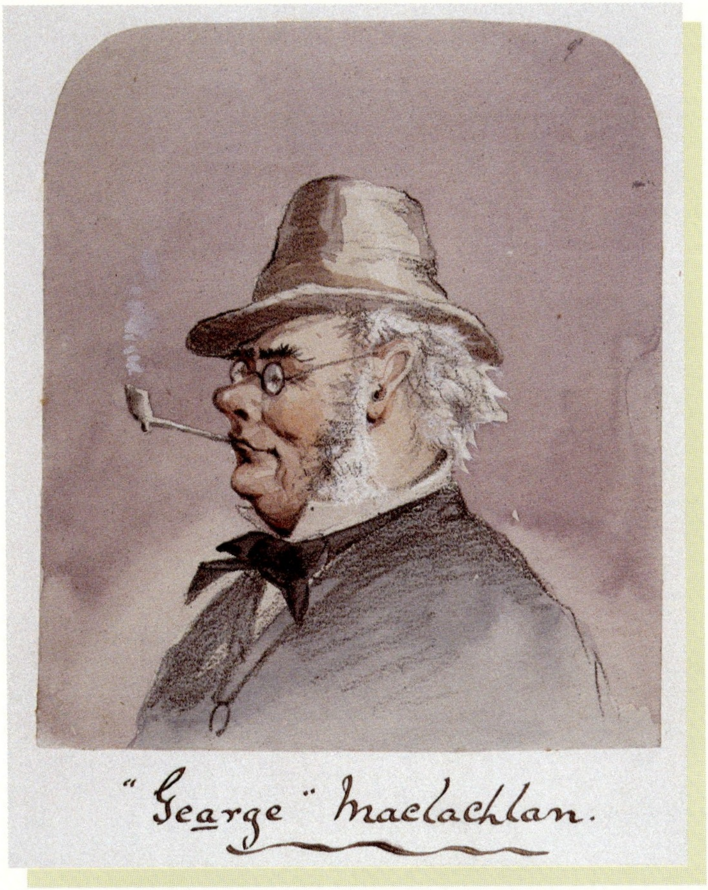

Above: Gearge Maclachlan.

GEARGE MACLACHLAN

(Hodge has underlined the A in Gearge.) This superb portrait is, judging by its quality, from the 1870s. The subject, in spectacles, smoking a clay pipe, wearing a blue jacket and a jaunty hat, also has a medal round his neck. Hodge's list says:

The MacLachlan of Castle Lachlan,
Strathlachlan. (To be said quick).

MR SIBBALD

John Sibbald of Edinburgh, his portrait inscribed by Hodge "Courtesy and Tobacco. T. H. 1882". An enigmatic legend for this character in his black hat, muttonchop whiskers and pince-nez, smoking a cheroot in a holder.

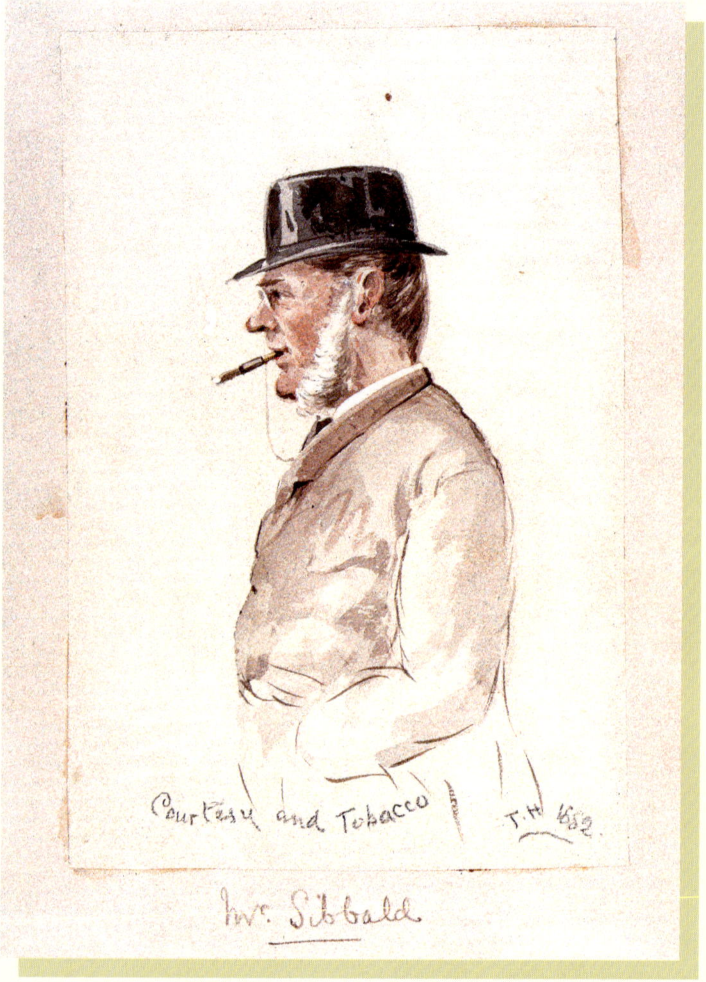

"SOCRATES HAD SIMILAR FACIAL LINES"

Dated September 21, 1880. A strong candidate for this deft portrait is Colonel Shortread, although this identification is not certain.

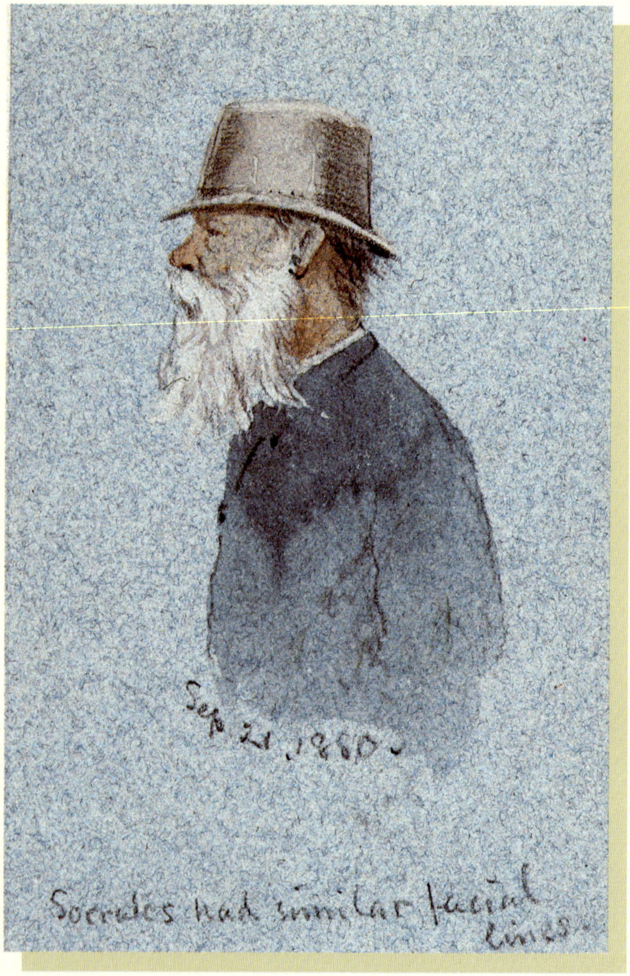

Above: John Sibbald.

Left: probably Colonel Shortread.

Right: D. B. Wauchope.

D. B. WAUCHOPE

Inscribed by Hodge "Juice of the grape, Sep 1879". Wauchope was captain of North Berwick in 1896.

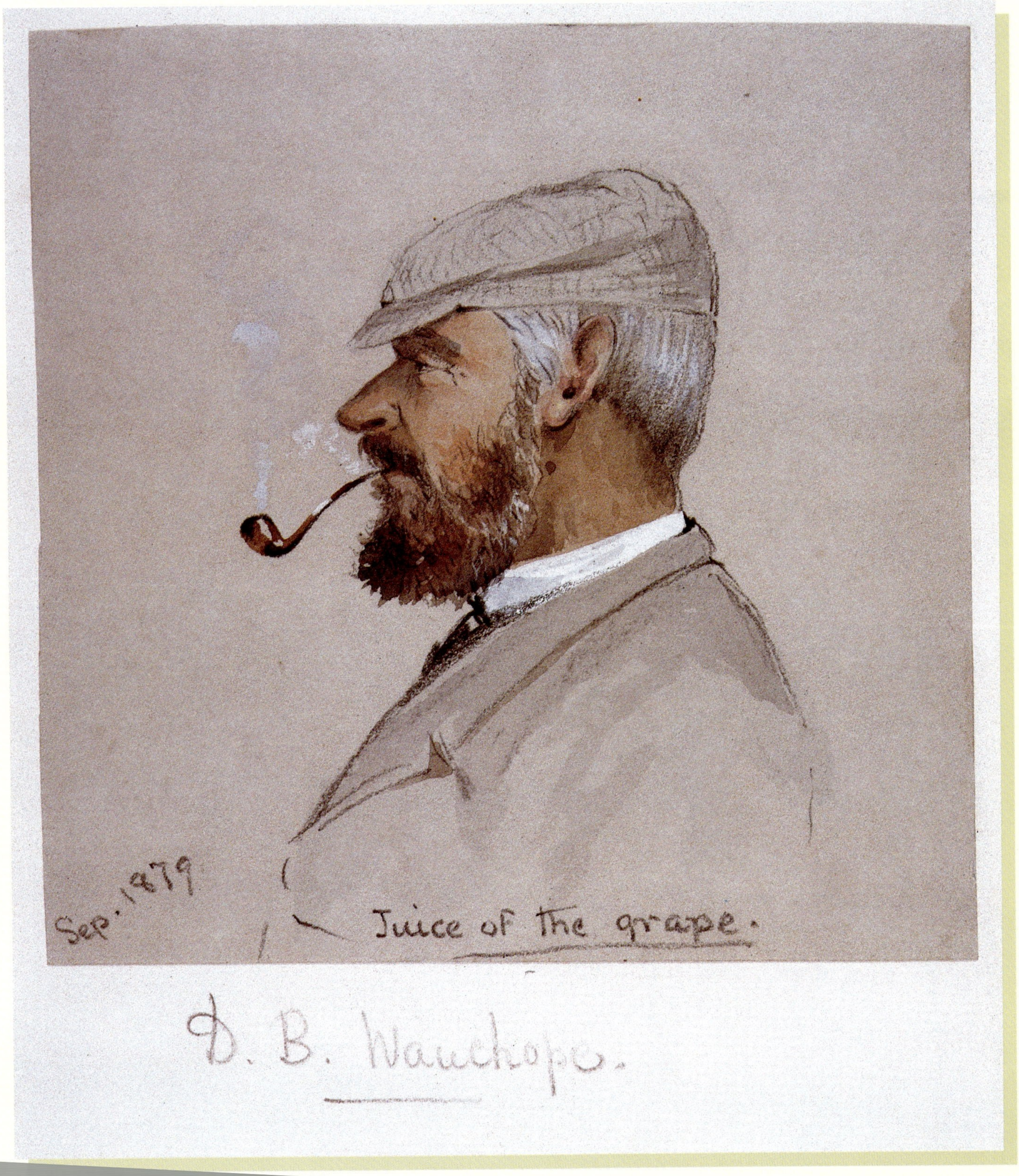
Sep. 1879
Juice of the grape.
D. B. Wauchope.

"MR. BENNETT"

Signed T.H. 1885. Probably Andrew Bennett, author of *The Book of St. Andrews Links* published in St. Andrews in 1898.

JOHN BUCHANAN HAY

Inscribed in Hodge's handwriting "That bright and particular star". Hay gained several mentions in the 19th-century records as a sportsman with a spectacular physique.

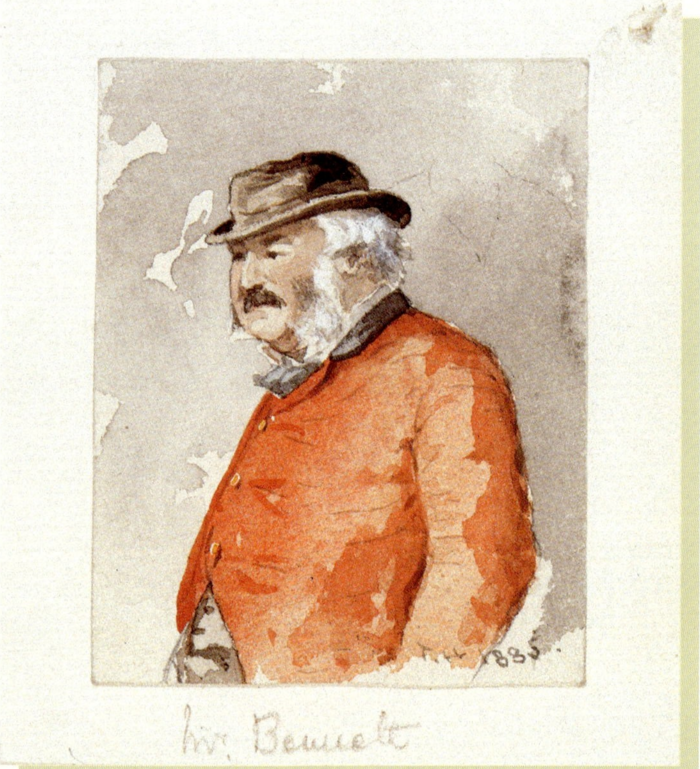

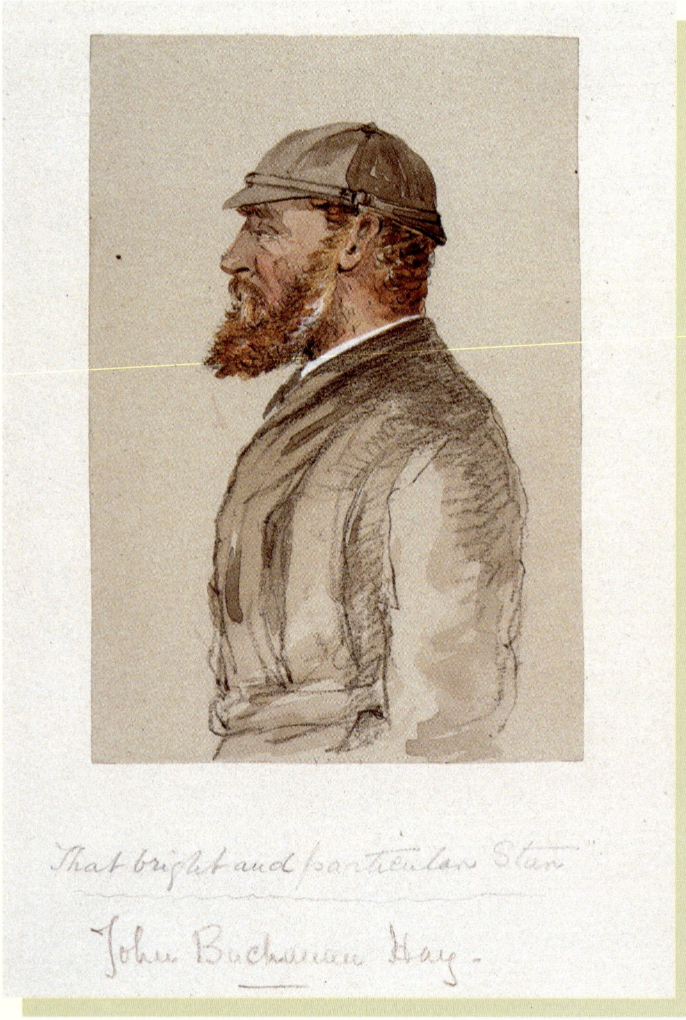

Above: Andrew Bennett.

Left: the massive John Buchanan Hay.

Right: Mr. Blackwell.

MR. EARNLEY BLACKWELL

An imposing full-length portrait of Earnley Blackwell standing in front of the Royal & Ancient clubhouse in 1885.

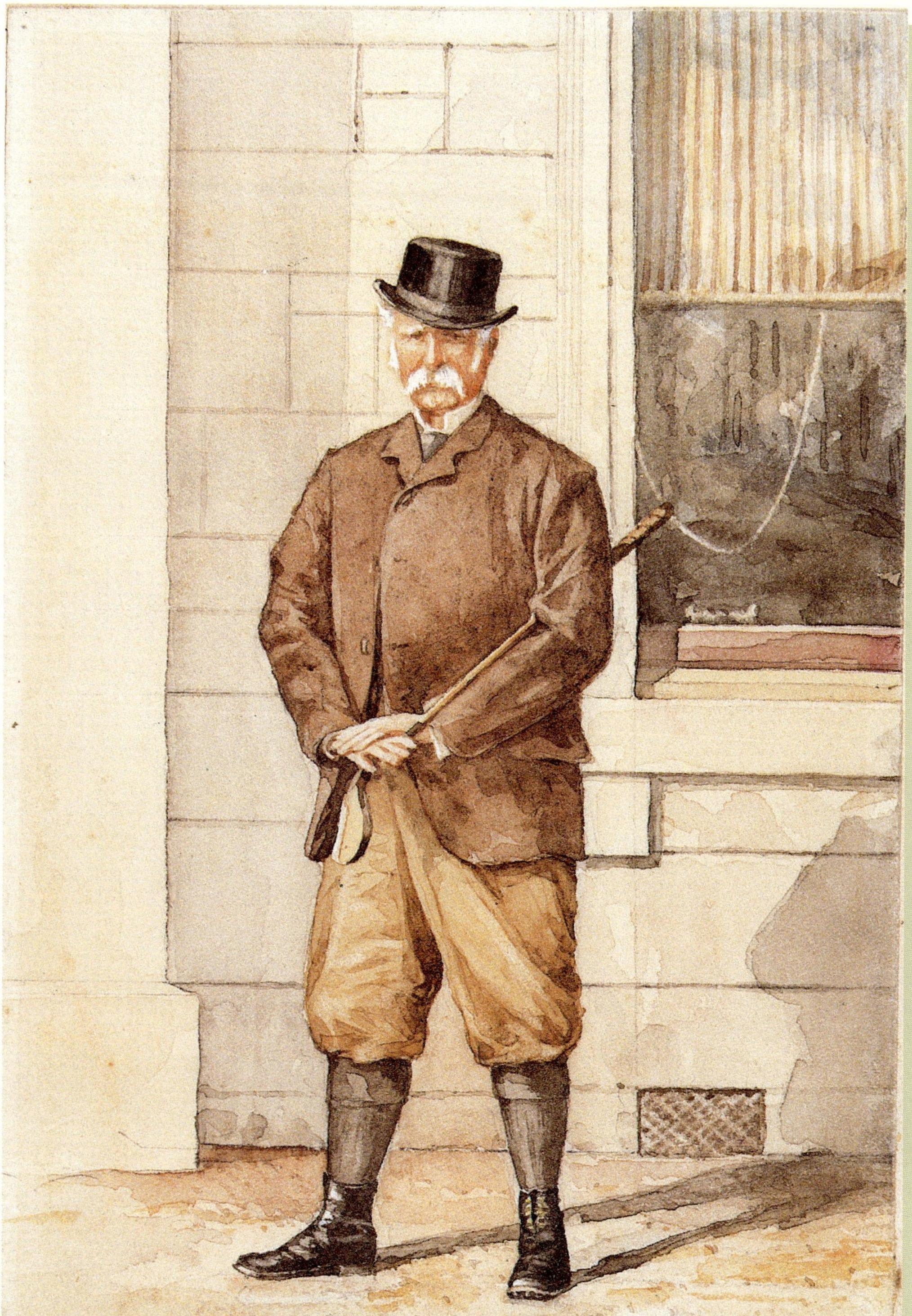
F.H. 1885

"WILLIE BURN"

This full-length portrait signed T. H. 1885 shows Captain W. H. Burn standing on the links with St. Andrews away in the distance.

TOM MACKAY

Hodge notes that the hefty Mackay was a medallist at St. Andrews in 1874.

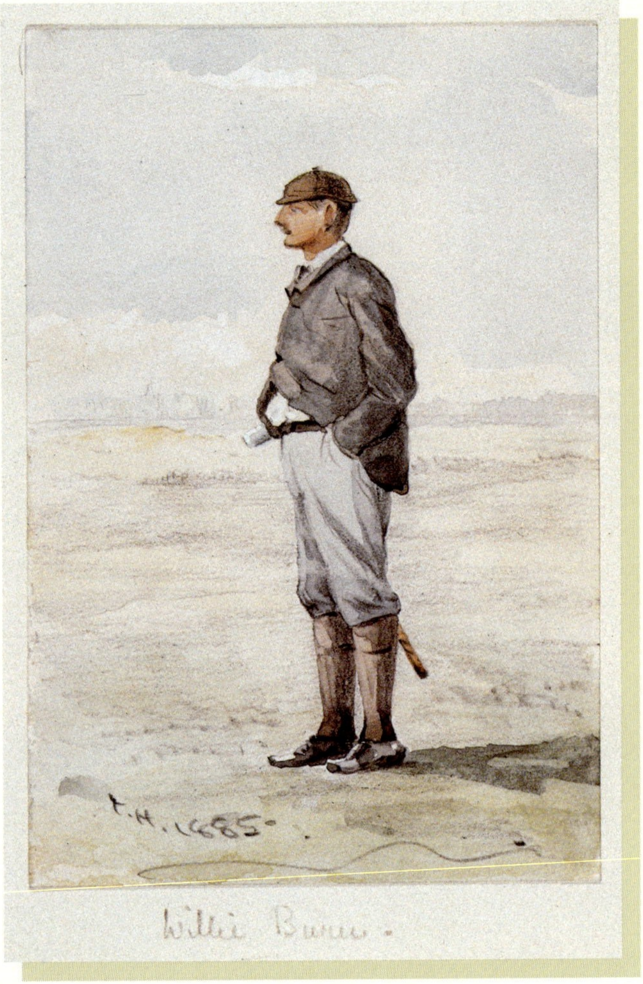

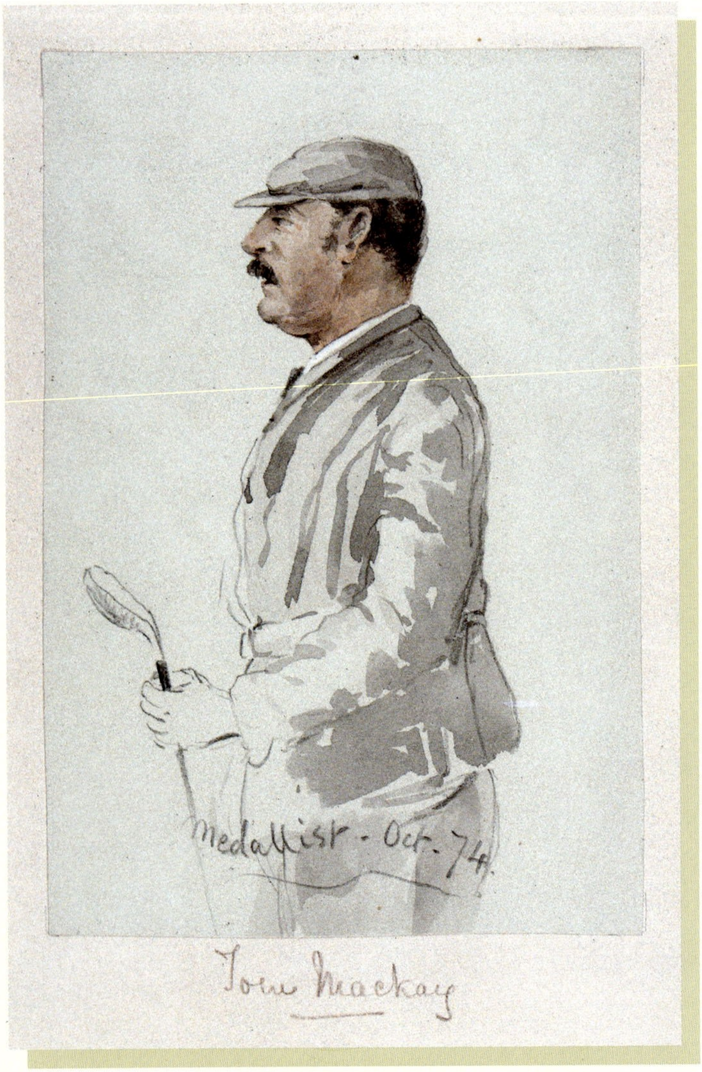

Above: Willie Burn.

Left: Tom Mackay.

Right: Alec Kinloch.

ALEC KINLOCH

Inscribed by Hodge "An old captain. T. H. May 1882". Alexander Kinloch of Gilmerton was R & A captain in 1872.

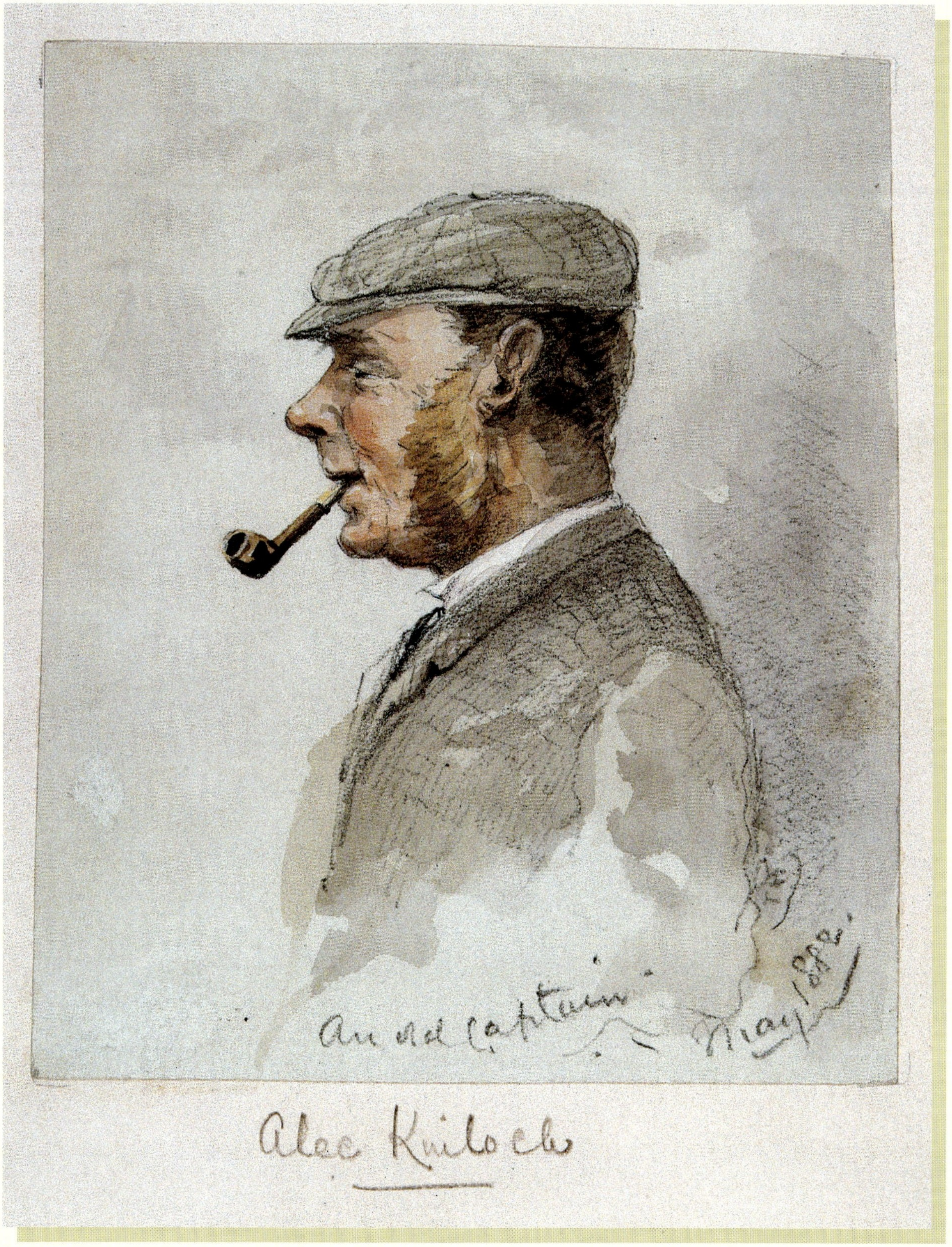
An old captain
May
Alec Kinloch

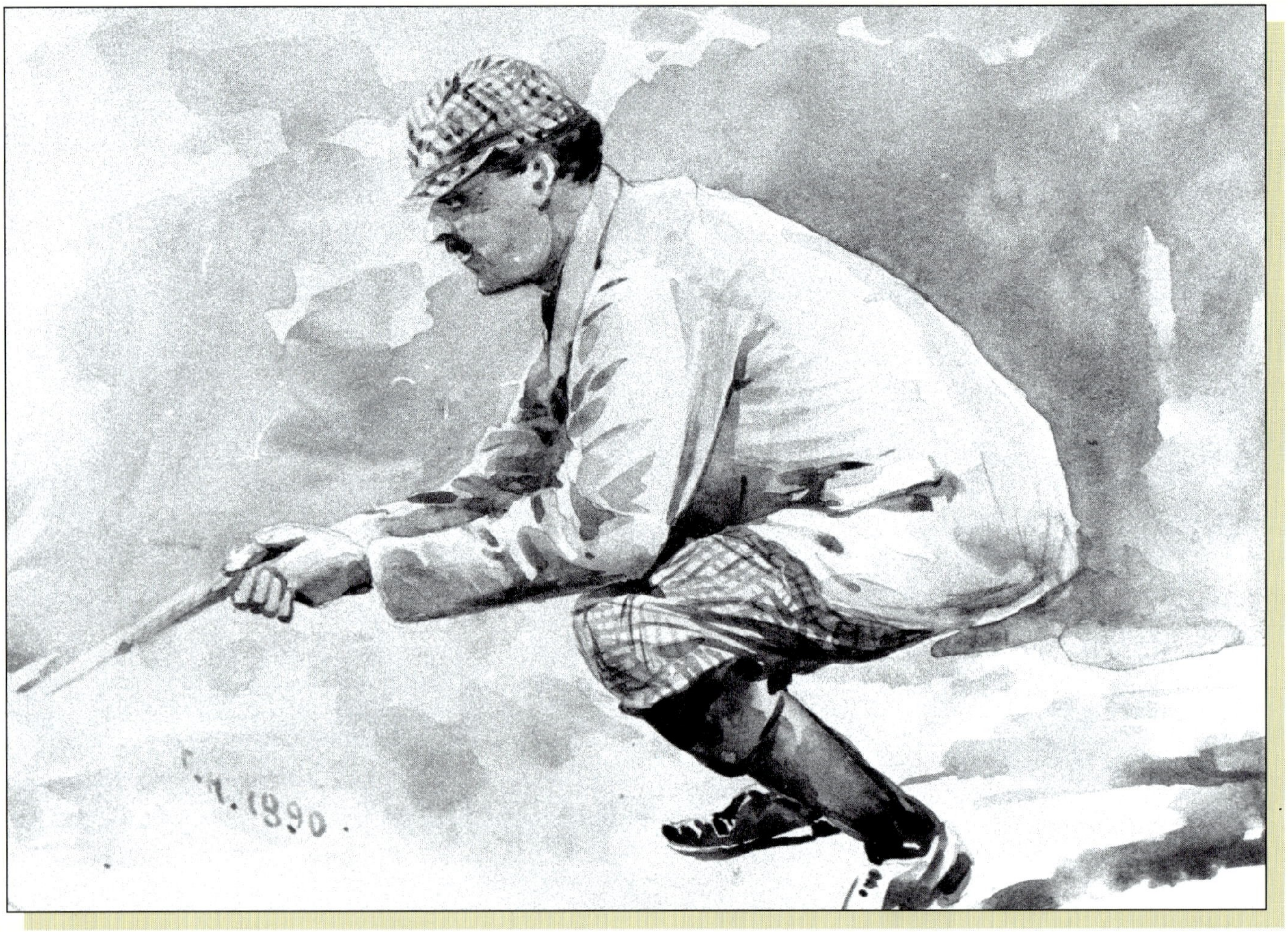

Above: Hutchinson studies the terrain.

HORACE G. HUTCHINSON

Described many times as one of golf's "great statesmen", Hutchinson was a fine golfer who won the Amateur Championship in 1887, having the temerity to overcome John Ball by one hole in the final at Hoylake. Though he had also won the Amateur in 1886, he is better-known over a century later as a prolific writer and editor of books and articles on the game. The most famous, the *Badminton Golf* edition of 1890, was illustrated by Hodge and Harry Furniss. The faint memory of Hodge when he was rediscovered in the 1980s sprang mostly from the works in Badminton. These were disparaged unfairly by some people as "merely copies of photographs".

Hutchinson was captain of the Royal & Ancient in 1908, the second Englishman to be so honoured. Born in 1859, he died in 1932, spending the last 18 years of his life as an invalid.

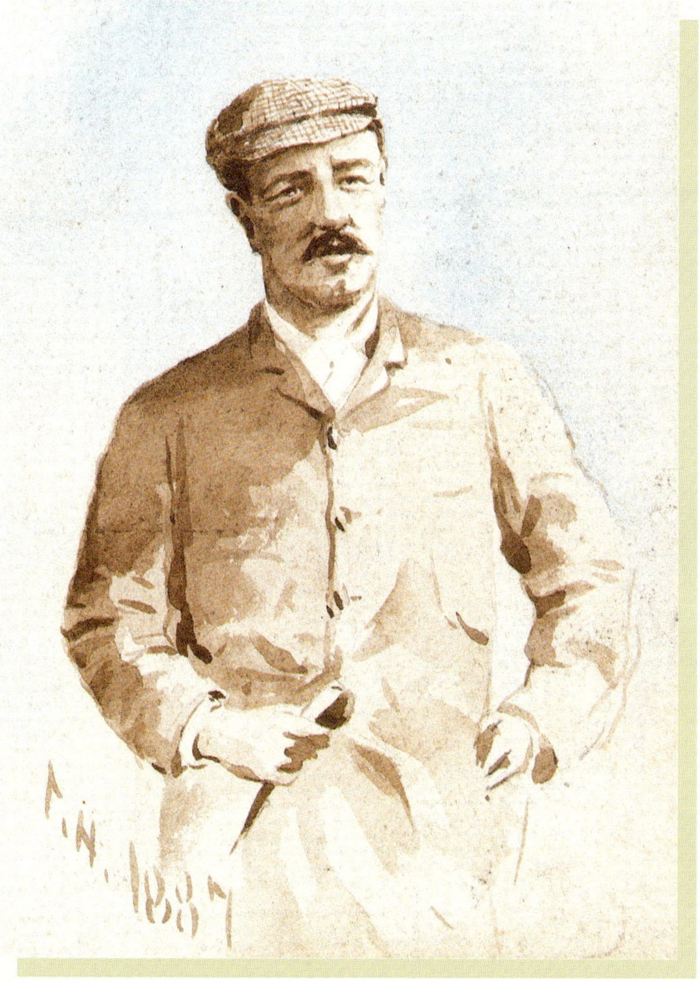

Above: *an untitled portrait, probably Hutchinson.*

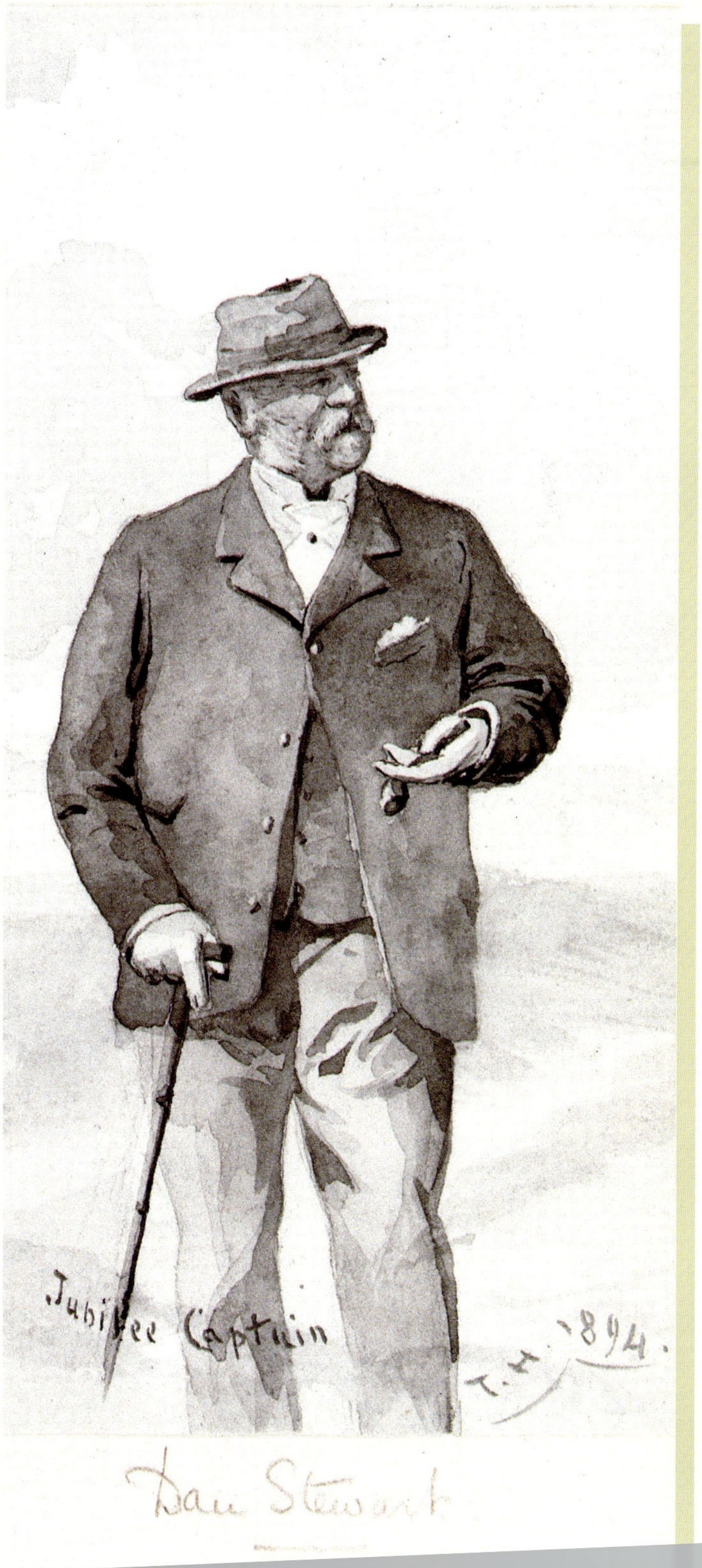

Right: an elegant figure on the course, Dan Stewart.

DAN STEWART

"Jubilee Captain" of the Royal & Ancient, pictured by Hodge in 1894, some time after he had ceased to live in St. Andrews.

Mr. Hodge will have his little joke...

Thomas Hodge had the reputation of a gentle jester among those of the St. Andrews fraternity friendly towards his artistic subjects. Here are three of his jokes. The unknown with his dog is Mr. Bethune (see photograph, page 53). Laidlay, the golfer, was notorious for his phlegmatic lack of reaction to any playing circumstance. The wild billiards player is a joke on Hodge by Hodge. Something of a wizard on the R & A green baize, he is probably reacting to the not infrequent tiffs over members' behaviour as they swapped clubs for cues.

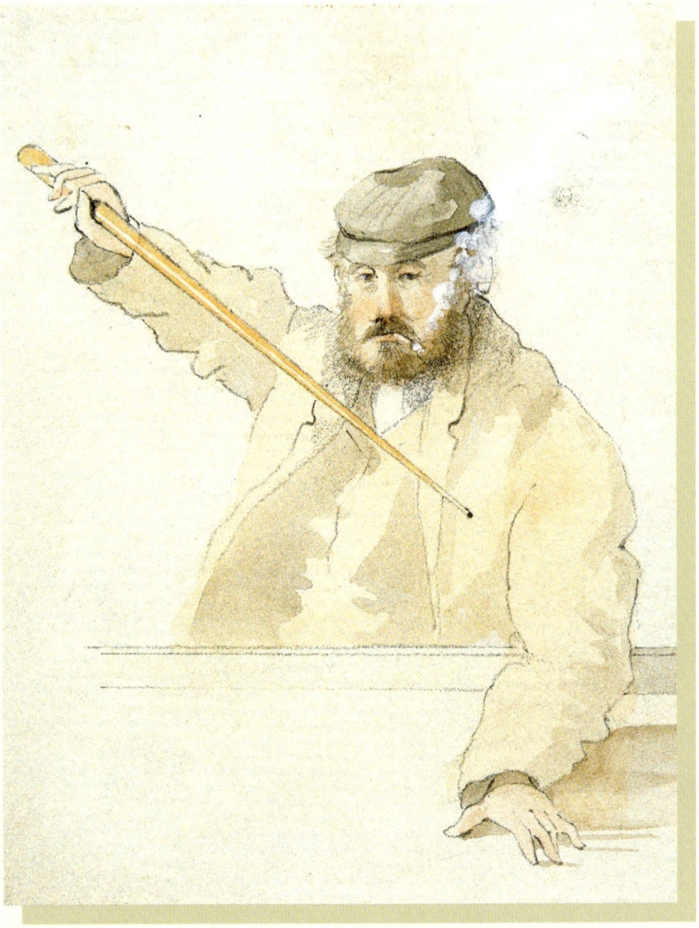

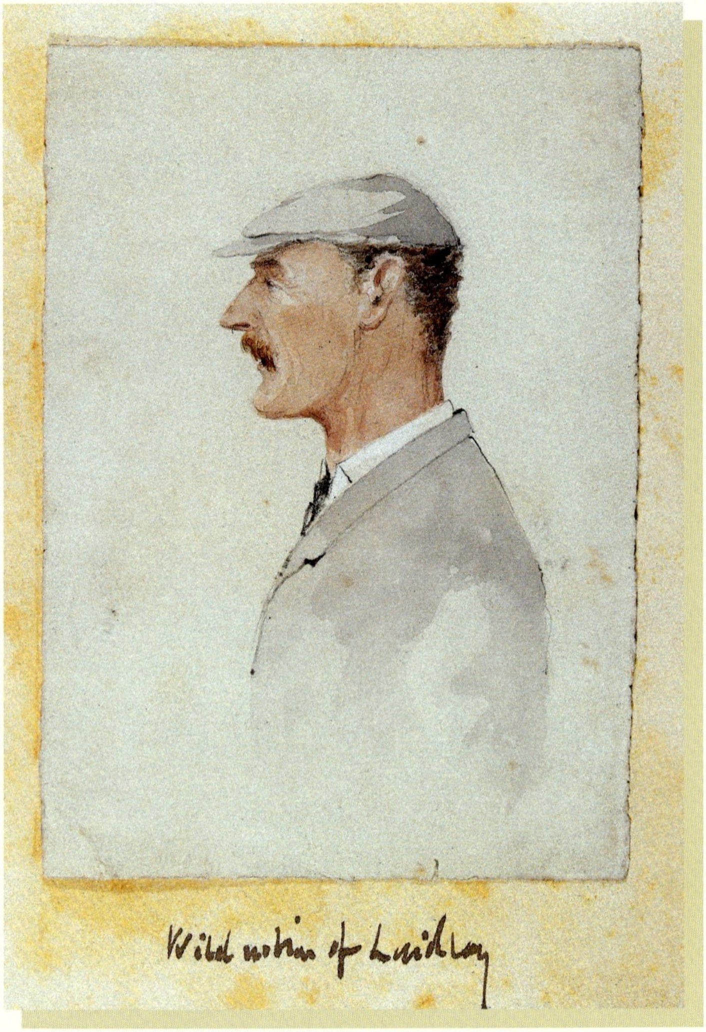

Above: "Wild notion of Laidlay" says T.H.

Left: the exuberant billiardeer – Hodge, by Hodge.

Right: an in-joke on Mr. Bethune.

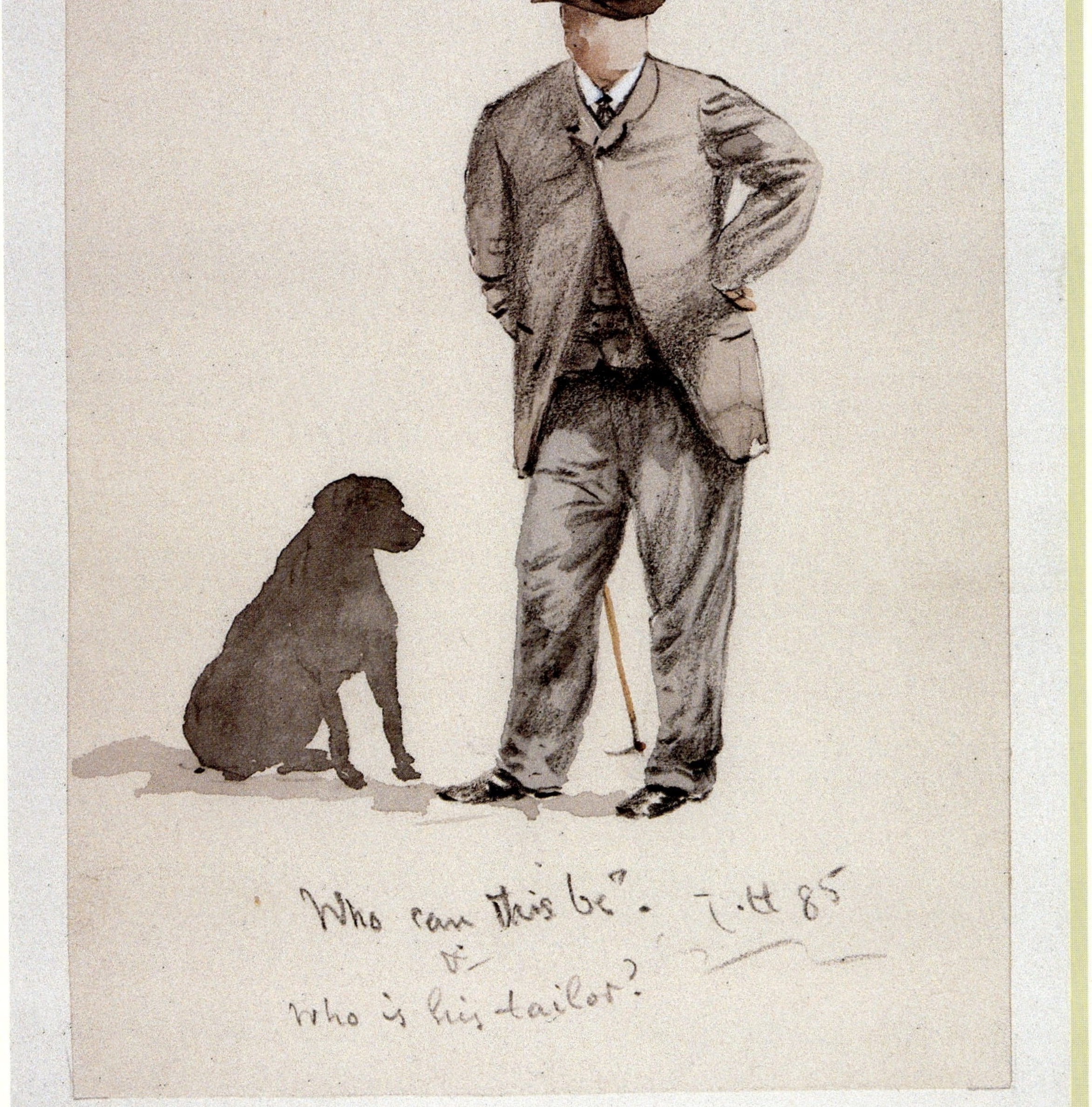
Who can this be?. T.H 85
&
who is his tailor?

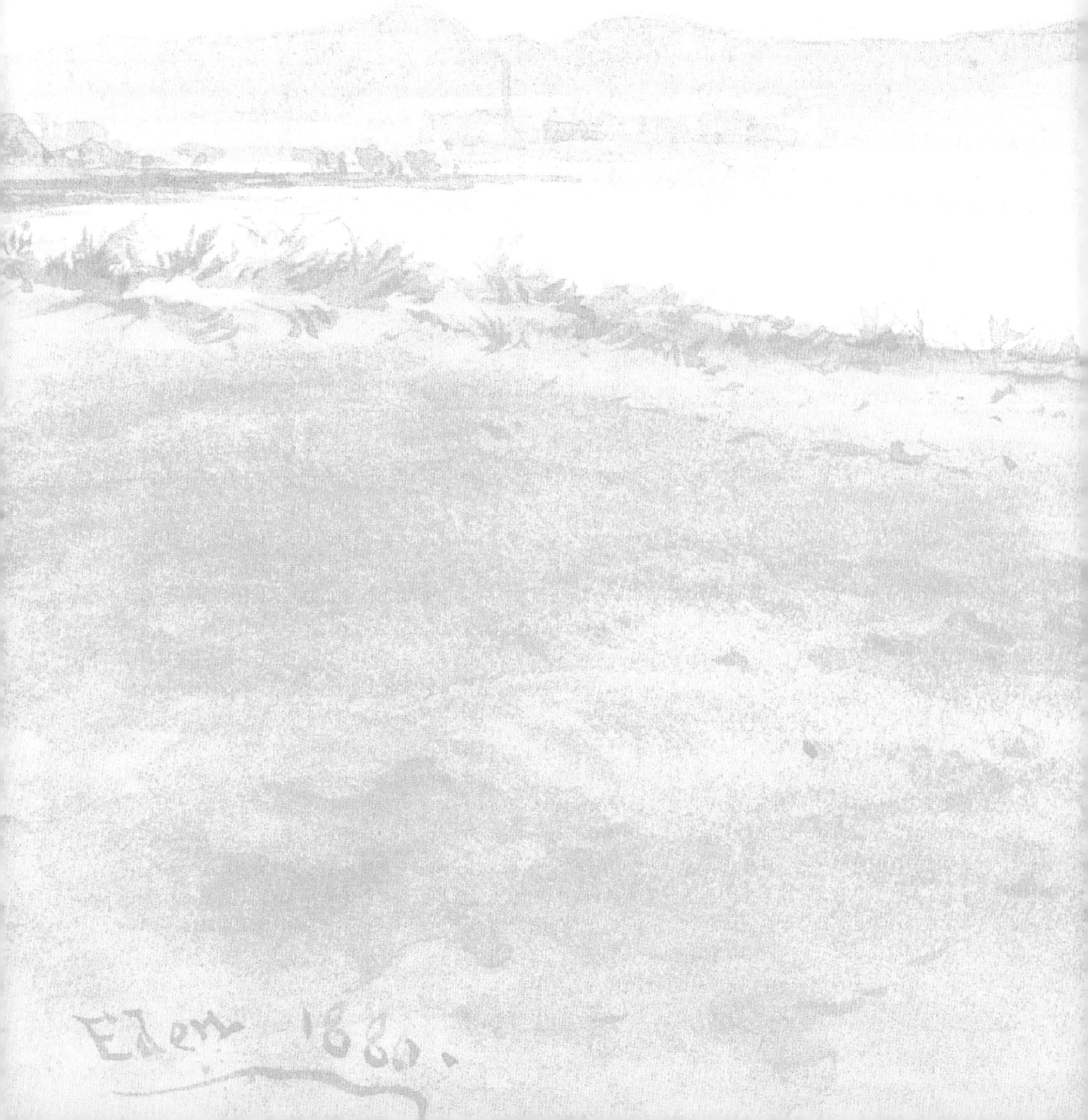
Eden 1860.

Pat Alexander and the Nine Holes of St. Andrews

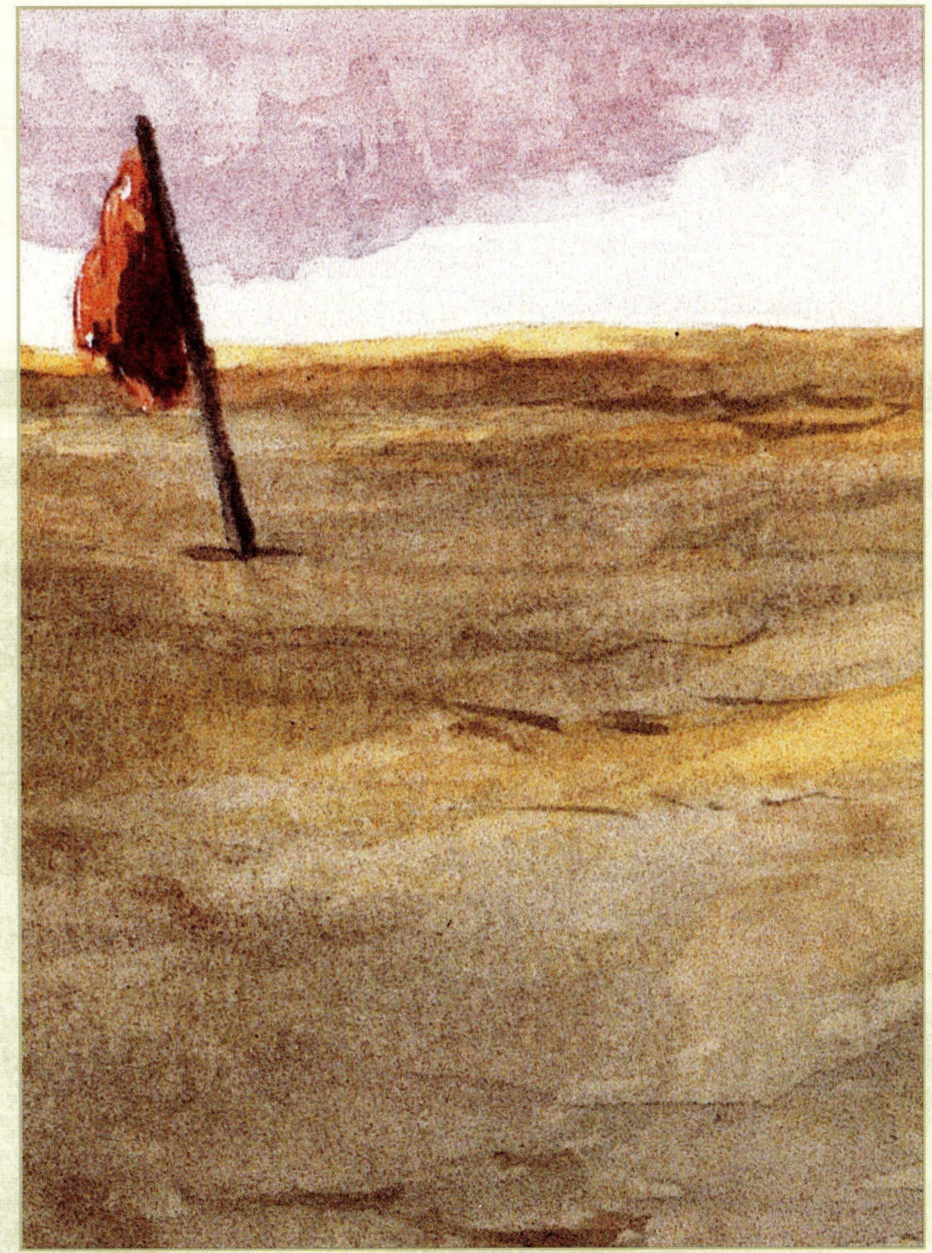

Pat Alexander and the Nine Holes of St. Andrews

Golf's Bohemian

No-one fitted more neatly into the sheltered academic coterie attached to golf and the Royal & Ancient of Thomas Hodge's era than Patrick Proctor Alexander. Hodge admired Alexander's "bohemian" lifestyle as a professor at St. Andrews University and his easy-going disdain of fame and fortune. W. W. Tulloch summed up his friend, painted here in a club armchair in 1883, along the lines of:

Poet, professor and the best of jolly good fellows.

Alexander was the joint author, with Robert Chambers and Chambers' son, also Robert, of the famous golf poem, "The Nine Holes of St. Andrews".

Nine verses, each describing a hole on the Old Course, were illustrated by Thomas Hodge. Unfortunately, the six illustrations, which must have been gemlike examples of Hodge's miniature landscapes done in watercolour, were engraved in depressing fashion by a man signing himself T. Robertson. Hodge's discreet signature is hardly to be seen. Sadly, the whereabouts of the original watercolours is not known. The next few pages show the poem with four of Hodge's illustrations in Robert Clark's *Poems on Golf*, published in Edinburgh in 1867.

Right: Pat Alexander by Hodge.

Below: one of the images by Hodge used in Robert Clark's book.

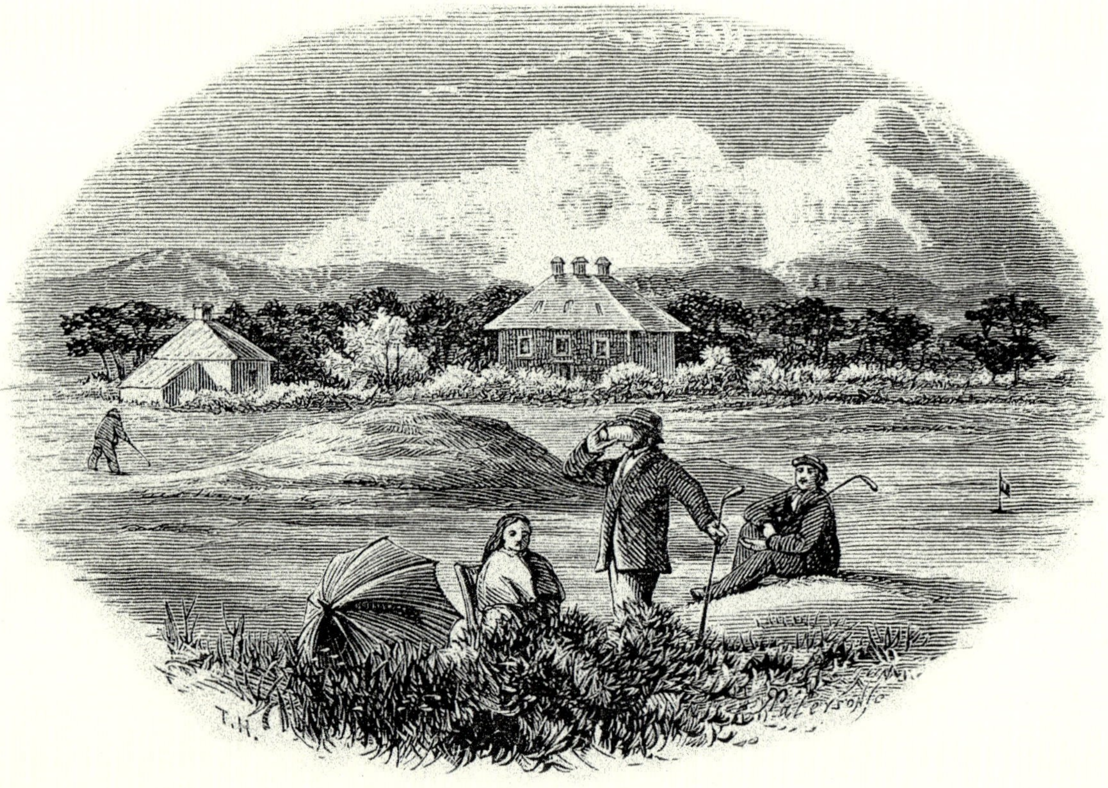

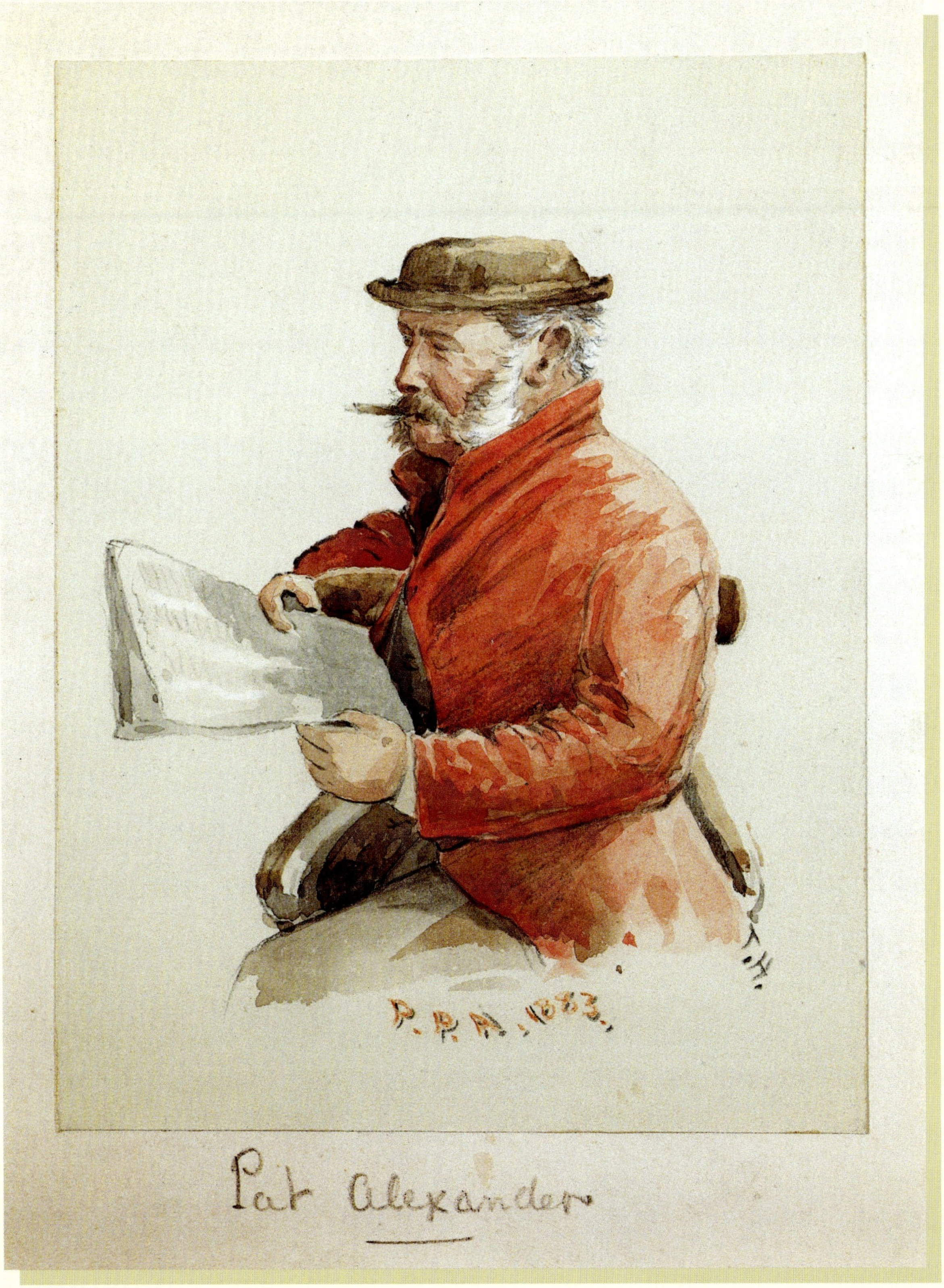
P.P.A. 1883.
Pat Alexander

The Nine Holes of the Links of St. Andrews

THE FIRST OR BRIDGE HOLE – R. C.

Sacred to hope and promise is the spot –
To Philp's and to the Union Parlour near,
To every Golfer, every caddie dear –
Where we strike off – oh, ne-er to be forgot,
Although in lands most distant we sojourn.
But not without its perils is the place,
Mark the opposing caddie's sly grimace,
Whispering: "He's on the road!" "He's in the burn!"
So is it often in the grander game
Of life, when, eager, hoping for the palm,
Breathing of honour, joy, and love and fame,
Conscious of nothing like a doubt or qualm,
We start, and cry: "Salute us, muse of fire!"
And the first footstep lands us in the mire.

THE SECOND OR CARTGATE HOLE – R. C.

Fearful to Tyro is thy primal stroke,
O Cartgate! For behold the bunker opes
Right to the teeing-place its yawning chops,
Hope to engulf ere it is well awoke.
That passed, a Scylla in the form of rushes
Nods to Charybdis which in ruts appears;
He will be safe who in the middle steers;
One step aside, the ball destruction brushes.
Golf symbols thus again our painful life,
Dangers in front, and pitfalls on each hand;
But see, one glorious cleek-stroke from the sand
Sends Tyro home,and saves all further strife!
He's in at six – old Sandy views the lad
With new respect, remarking: "That's no bad!"

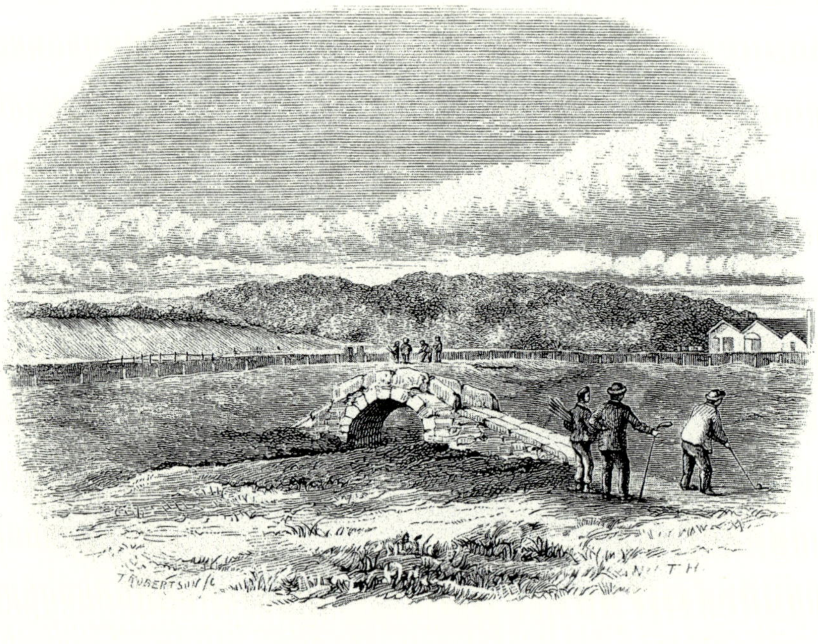

THE THIRD HOLE – R. C.

No rest in Golf – still perils in the path;
Here, playing a good ball, perhaps it goes
Gently into the Principalian Nose,
Or else Tam's Coo, which equally is death.
Perhaps the wind will catch it in mid-air,
And take it to the Whins – "Look out, look out!
Tom Morris, be, oh be, a faithful scout!"
But Tom, though links-eyed, finds not anywhere.
Such thy mishaps, O Merit: feeble balls
Meanwhile roll on, and lie upon the green;
"Tis well, my friends, if you, when this befalls,
Can spare yourselves the infamy of spleen.
It only shows the ancient proverb's force,
That you may further go and fare the worse.

THE FOURTH OR GINGER-BEER HOLE – P. P .A.

Though thou hast lost this last unlucky hole,
I prythee, friend, betake thee not to swearing,
Or other form of speech too wildly daring,
Though some allege it tendeth to console.
Rather do thou thy swelling griefs control,
Sagacious that at hand a joy awaits thee
(Since out of doubt a glass of beer elates thee),
Without that frightful peril to thy soul.
A pot of beer! Go dip thy angry beak in it,
And straight its rage shall melt to soft placidity,
That solace finding thou art wise to seek in it;
Ah! Do not thou on that poor plea reject it,
That in thine inwards it may breed acidity –
One glass of Stewart's brandy will correct it.

THE HELL HOLE – P. P. A.

What daring genius first did name thee Hell?
What high, poetic, awe-struck grand old Golfer?
Misdeem him not, ye pious ones, a scoffer –
Who-'er he was, the name befits thee well.
"All hope abandon, ye who enter here"
Is written awful o'er thy sandy jaws,
Whose greedy threat may give the boldest pause,
And frequent from within come tones of fear –
Dread sound of cleeks, which ever smite in vain,
And – for mortal patience is but scanty –
Shriekings thereafter, as of souls in pain,
Dire gnashings of the teeth, and horrid curses,
With which I need not decorate my verses,
Because, in fact, you'll find them all in Dante.

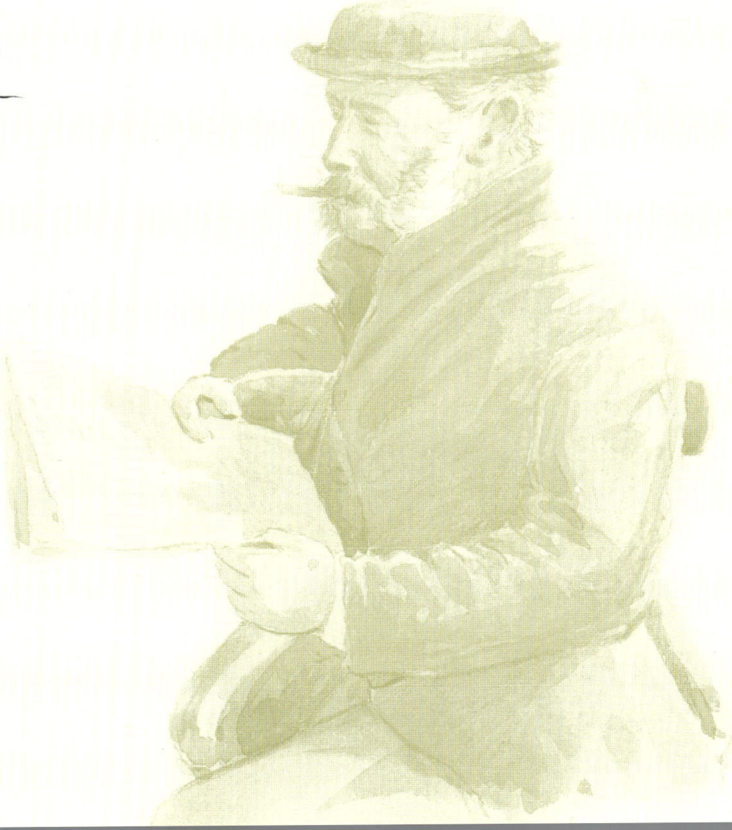

Pat Alexander and the Nine Holes of St. Andrews

THE HEATHER HOLE – P. P. A.

Ah me! Prodigious woes do still environ –
To quote verbatim from some grave old poet –
The man who needs must "meddle with his iron";
And here, if ever, thou art doomed to know it.
For now behold thee, doubtless for thy sins,
Tilling some bunker, as if on a lease of it,
And so, assiduous to make due increase of it;
Or wandering homeless through a world of whins!
And when, – these perils past, – thou seemest dead,
And hop'st a half – O woe! thy ball runs crooked,
Making thy foe just one more hole ahead,
Surely a consummation all too sad,
Without the sneering devilish "Niver lookit",
The closing comment of the opposing cad.

THE HIGH OR EDEN HOLE – J. C. Jr.

The shelly pit is cleared at one fell blow,
A stroke to be remembered in your dreams!
But here the Eden on your vision gleams,
Lovely, but treach'rous in its solemn flow.
The hole is perched aloft, too near the tide,
The green is small and broken is the ground
Which doth that little charmed space surround!
Go not too far, and go not to a side;
Take the short spoon to do your second stroke;
Sandy entreats you will the wind take heed on,
For, oh, it would a very saint provoke,
If you should let your ball plump in the Eden.
You do your best, but who can Fate control?
So here against you is another hole.

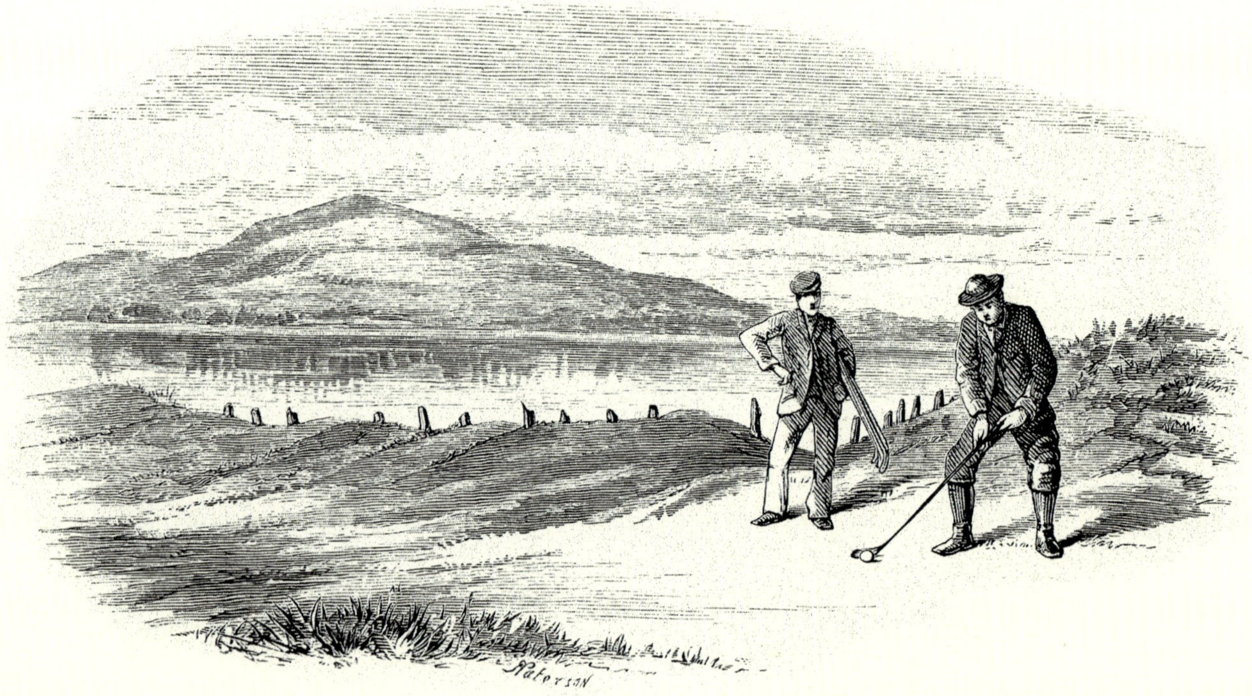

The Short Hole – J. C. Jr.

Brief but not easy is the next adventure;
Legend avers it has been done in one,
Though such long steals are now but rarely done –
In three 'twere well that you the hole should enter.
Strangely original is this bit of ground,
For, while at hand the smooth and smiling green,
One bunker wide and bushy yawns between,
Where Tyro's gutta is too often found.
Nervous your rival strikes and heels his ball –
From that whin-bush at six he'll scarce extract it;
Yours, by no blunder this time counteracted,
Is with the grass-club lofted over all.
There goes a hole in your side – how you hug it!
Much as th' Australian digger does a nugget.

The End Hole – R. C. Jr.

The end, but not the end – the distance post
That halves the game – a serious point to thee,
For if one more thou losest, 'twill be three;
Yet even in that case, think not all is lost.
Men four behind have been, on the return,
So favoured by Olympus, or by care,
That all their terrors vanished into air,
And caddies cried them dormy at the burn!
I could quote proverbs, did I speak at random.
Full many a broken ship comes into port,
Full many a cause is gained at last resort,
But Golf impresses most, Nil desperandum.
Turn, then, my son, with two against, nor dread
To gain the winning post with one ahead.

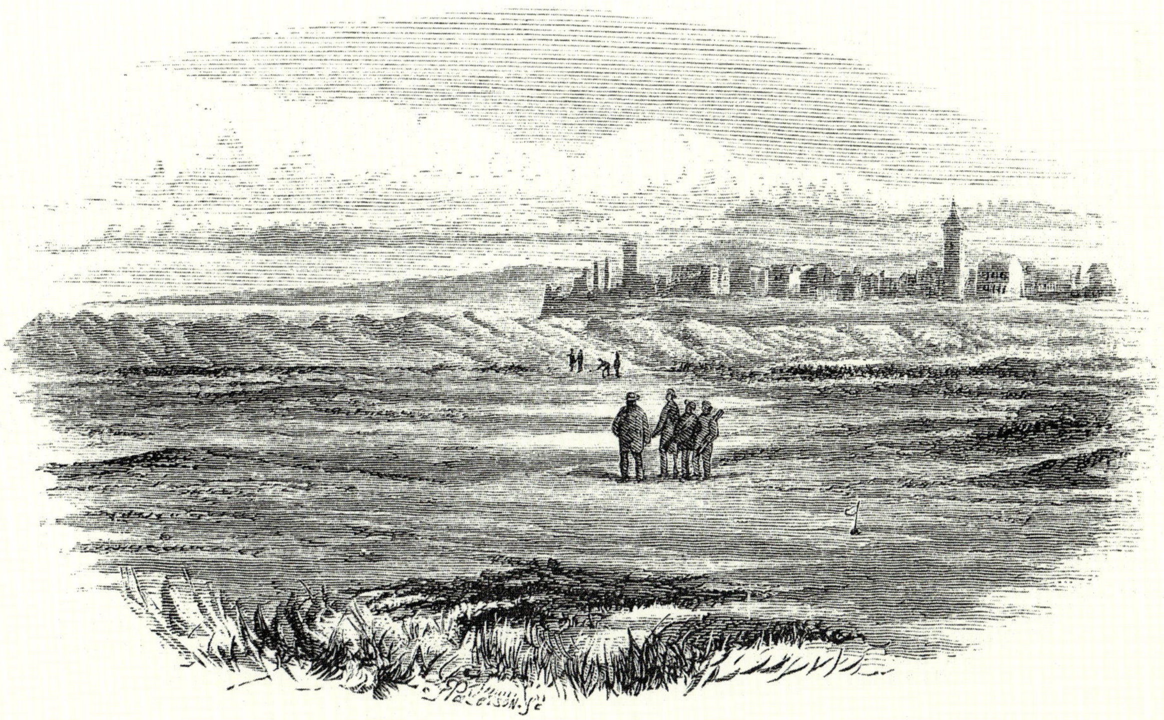

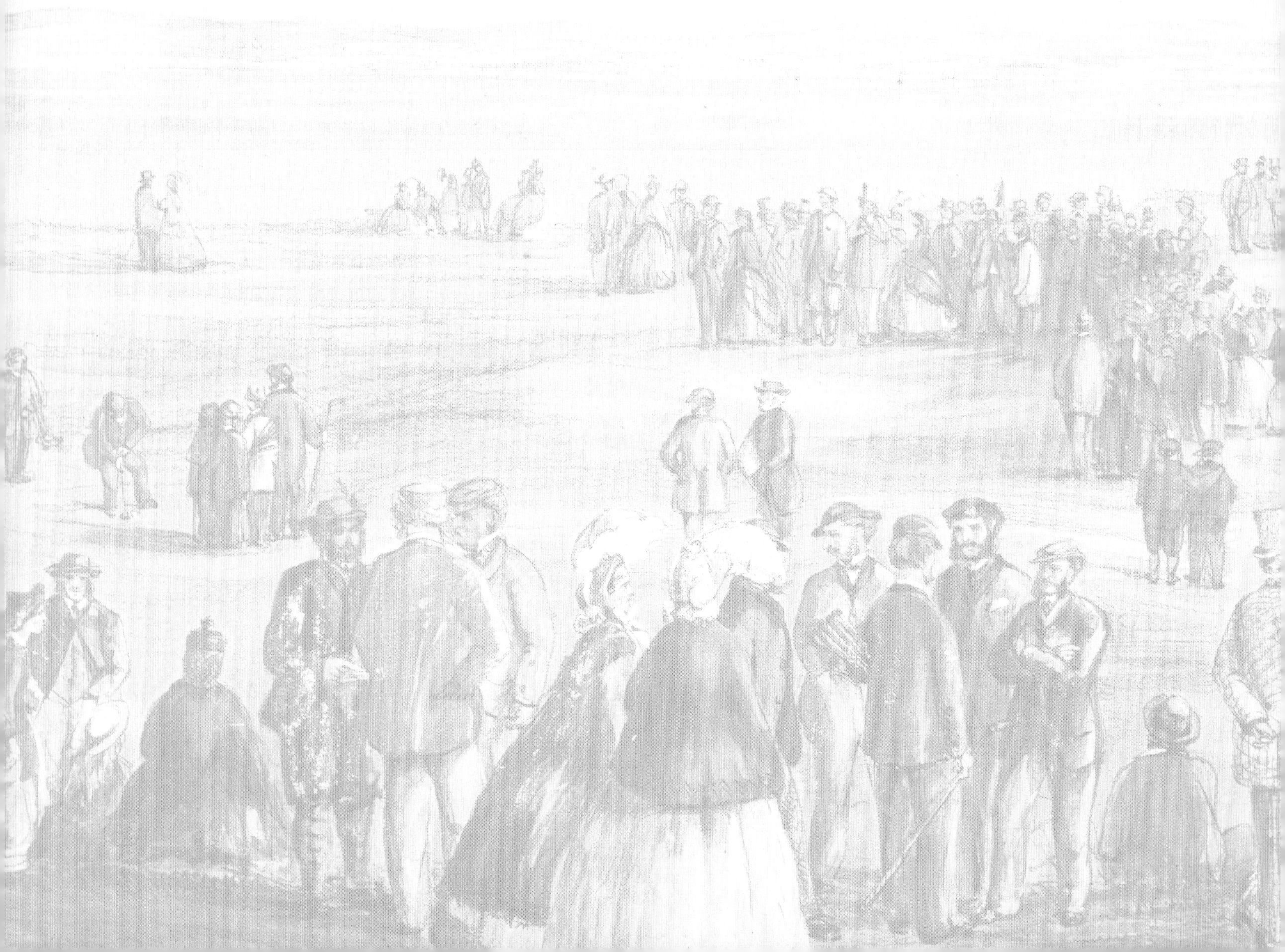

The Home of Golf

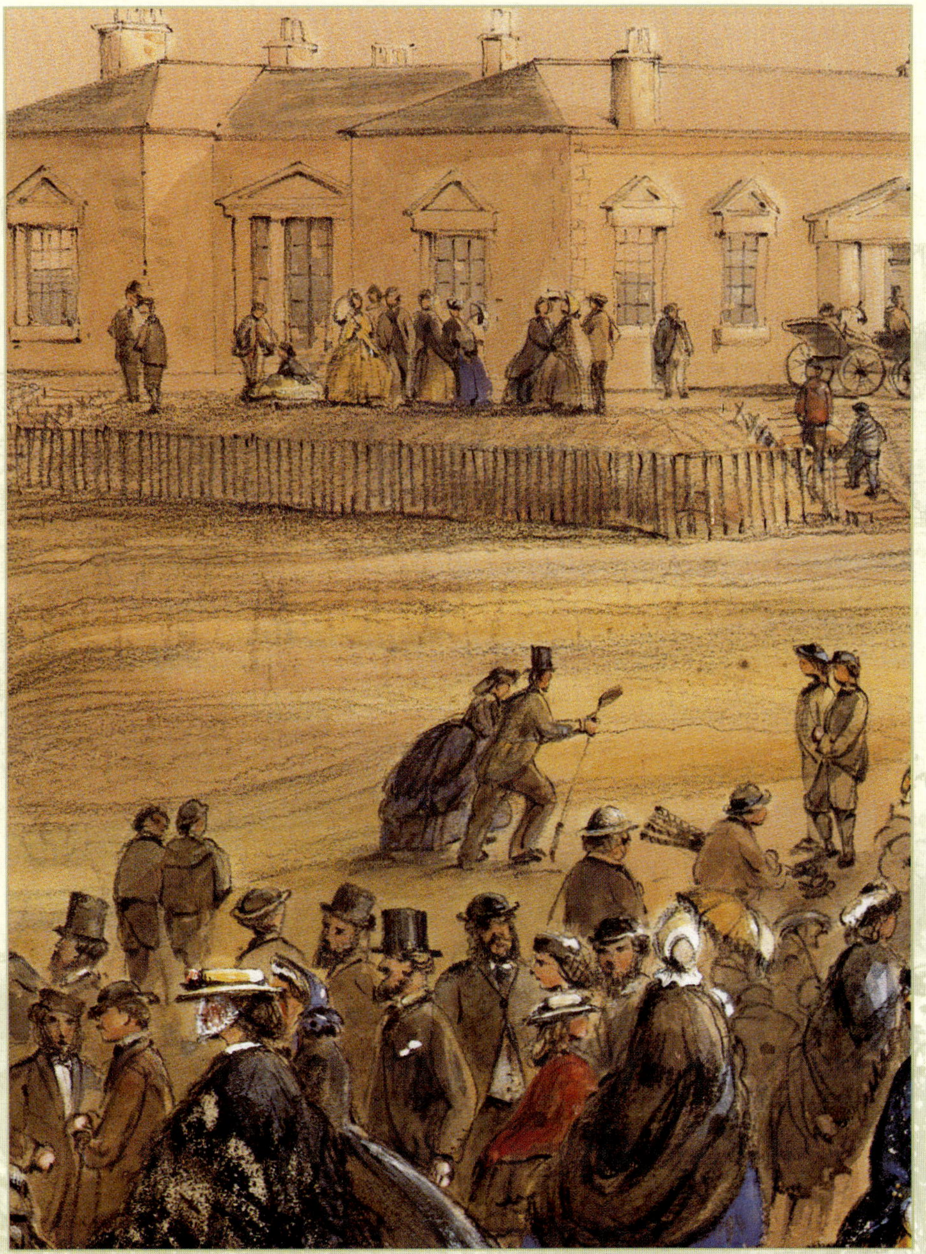

The Home of Golf

The noted turf of Saynctandrewys (an ancient spelling of St. Andrews) buries its roots into sandy soil and rubbish. It does miraculously well. This turf always has been coveted. Mature and educated men have snarled over it like dogs after the same bitch. Even so, pretty well all it was ever fitted for, yet supremely well fitted, was golf.

Whichever path of sporting history the scholarly care to wander (that old club and ball games were imported from Europe; or that golf evolved as the prudent Scot's alternative to violent brawls like shinty), none can deny that Scotland's seaside terrain moulded golf into its present character.

Thomas Hodge's known paintings of this territory, particularly of St. Andrews' oldest links, start here with his view of the Royal & Ancient's October meeting in 1862. For all its fragile, time-stained appearance, this watercolour, the biggest painting in the Norah Sheward collection given to the R & A in 1985 at roughly 50cm x 35cm, is one of the most important single golf paintings ever rescued.

A great deal of the colour had been burned out of the painting by its being hung in harsh daylight over the years, suggesting that at some time it might have been taken abroad. There was no blue left in the sky, no green in the grass. An ill-advised retoucher splodged white paint over the distant sea and horizon. Nevertheless, it was a bit like the salvage from an ancient merchantman – half the unique treasure saved from the wreck is infinitely better than nothing. The painting, cleverly restored by Fiona Butterfield to something like its original state, now hangs in the R & A secretary's office.

The main illustration on the following two pages shows the painting as it first resurfaced, the beaten-up charm of Hodge's scene holding a massive bonus because of the information it contains. The Royal & Ancient clubhouse had been built only eight years earlier, and is revealed as the plain though dignified stone box which was trimmed up during subsequent decades until it achieved its present outline.

A fence at the far boundary of the clubhouse appears to rest almost at the edge of the beach, which was exactly so at this time. The sandy expanse just beyond the farthest group of spectators is also the beach. Worthy reclamation works in the ensuing century, largely based on old fishing boats filled with rocks and rubbish, built up this area into land fit for car parks. It also gave the clubhouse, and eventually the new museum of golf, room to breathe.

Hodge's lively horses draw carriages to the entrance of the club. About 50 of the 200 or so spectators are women and children. In the foreground are characters of the era. Fifth from the left is Hodge himself. He wears a blue mountain-walker's suit, a Tyrolean hat complete with feather, and broad military puttees round his dramatic calves. Now 35, he sports a full beard; perhaps he is just returned from his annual European holiday. In his hands, we are entitled to speculate, can just be spotted a small sketch pad.

Hodge's speckled appearance and that of one or two others may be caused by an old coating of gum arabic (varnish) cracking and falling off the picture surface. Hodge is seen talking animatedly with two fellow members, one of whom may be Henry Lamb (red coat).

The caddie with a bundle of clubs under his arm is "Old Daw" Anderson, well known later for his ginger beer refreshment cart on the course. He is talking to Major Boothby and John Whyte Melville (arms crossed), the captain of the club in 1823 who laid the foundation stone of the clubhouse. On their left (red coat) is Sir Robert Hay, most elegant of gentlemen players.

In the centre of the foreground, puffing notorious smoke clouds from his cigar, is Scotland's famous lawyer of the age, John Inglis. One of the little Hodge jests that can be picked out is the placing of two giants of the golfing day, in stature that is, side by side at the final green. Mr. Gray ("Six foot, six in, and very erratic" wrote Hodge once) and the lugubrious Lang Willie, a top-hatted local caddie, are sized-up and Hodge's verdict on the question of height goes marginally to Mr. Gray.

Below: the restored Hodge painting.

Overleaf: Hodge's masterpiece in its original form before conservation work. The Dundee Courier and Argus reported on Thursday October 2, 1862 that the weather was fine, though a good, stiff breeze was blowing, and "A large assemblage of ladies and gentlemen congregated on the Green to witness the commencement of the competition. About a quarter before 12 o'clock the noble Earl made his appearance on the links and the cannon was fired, being the signal to start the competition. Lord Dalhousie then, as Captain of the Club, went through the form of playing off the first ball, by which he had the honour of winning the Silver Club and the Royal Adelaide medal. Altogether this has been the most successful meeting of the St. Andrews Royal & Ancient Golf Club we have seen for several years past."

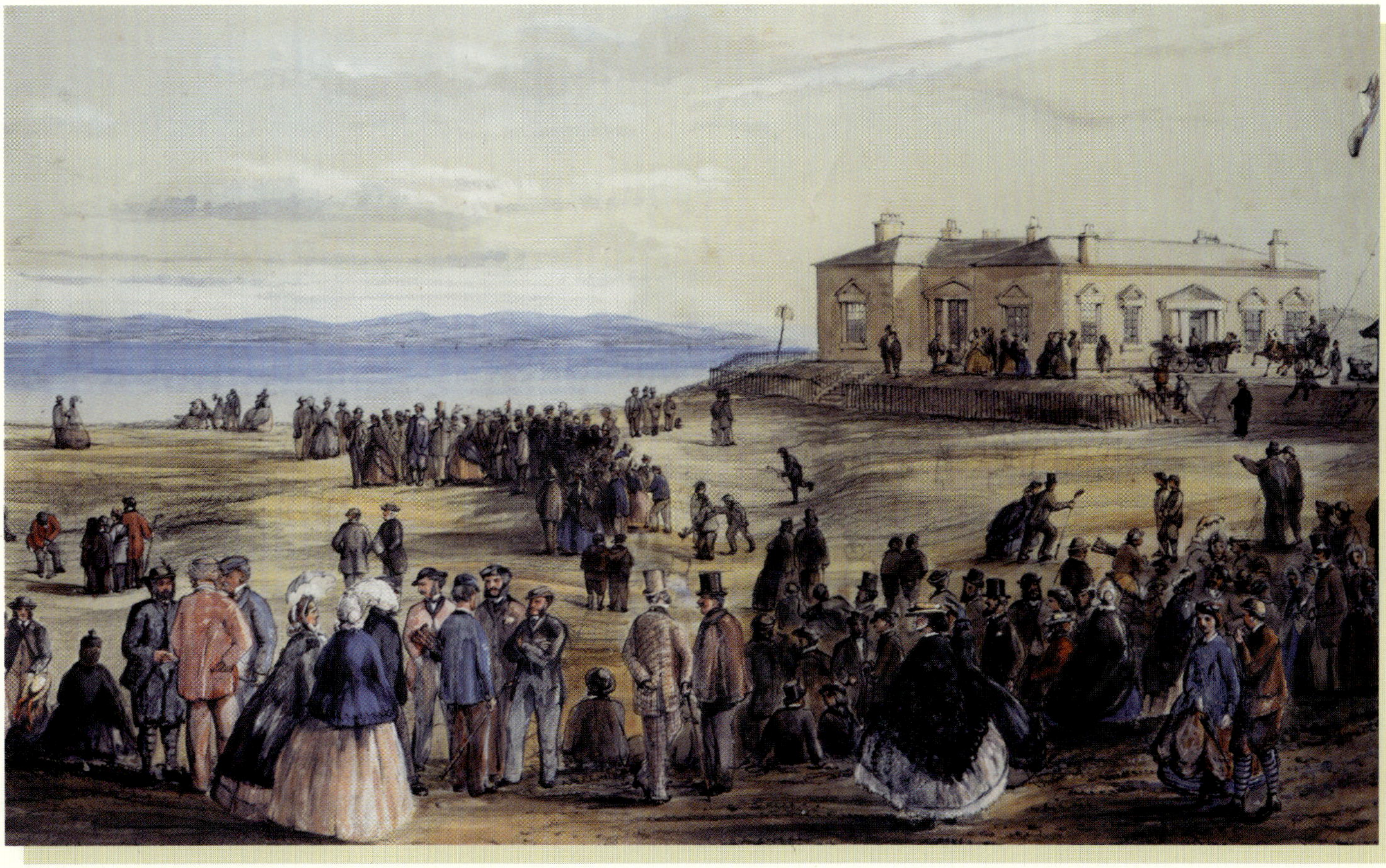

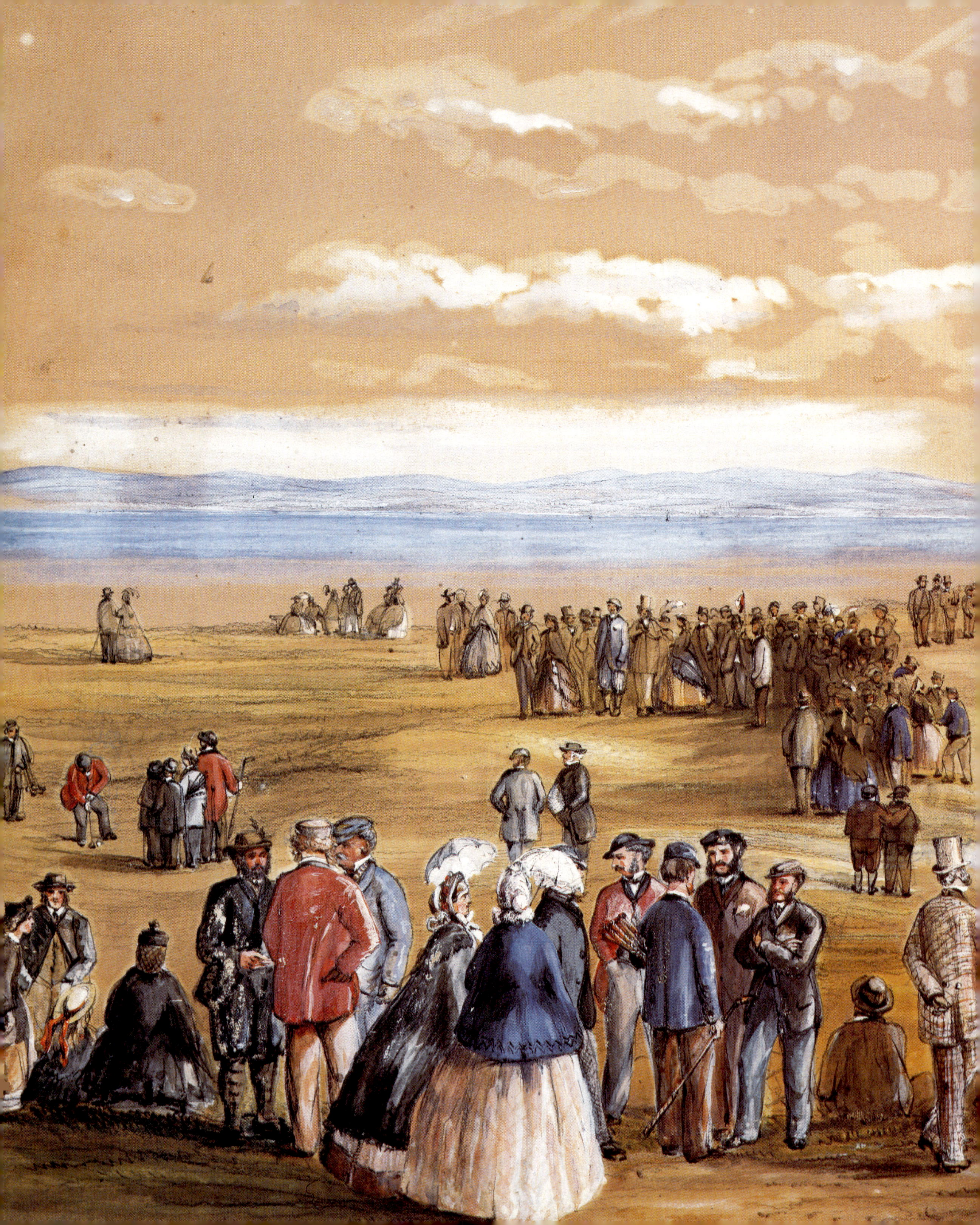

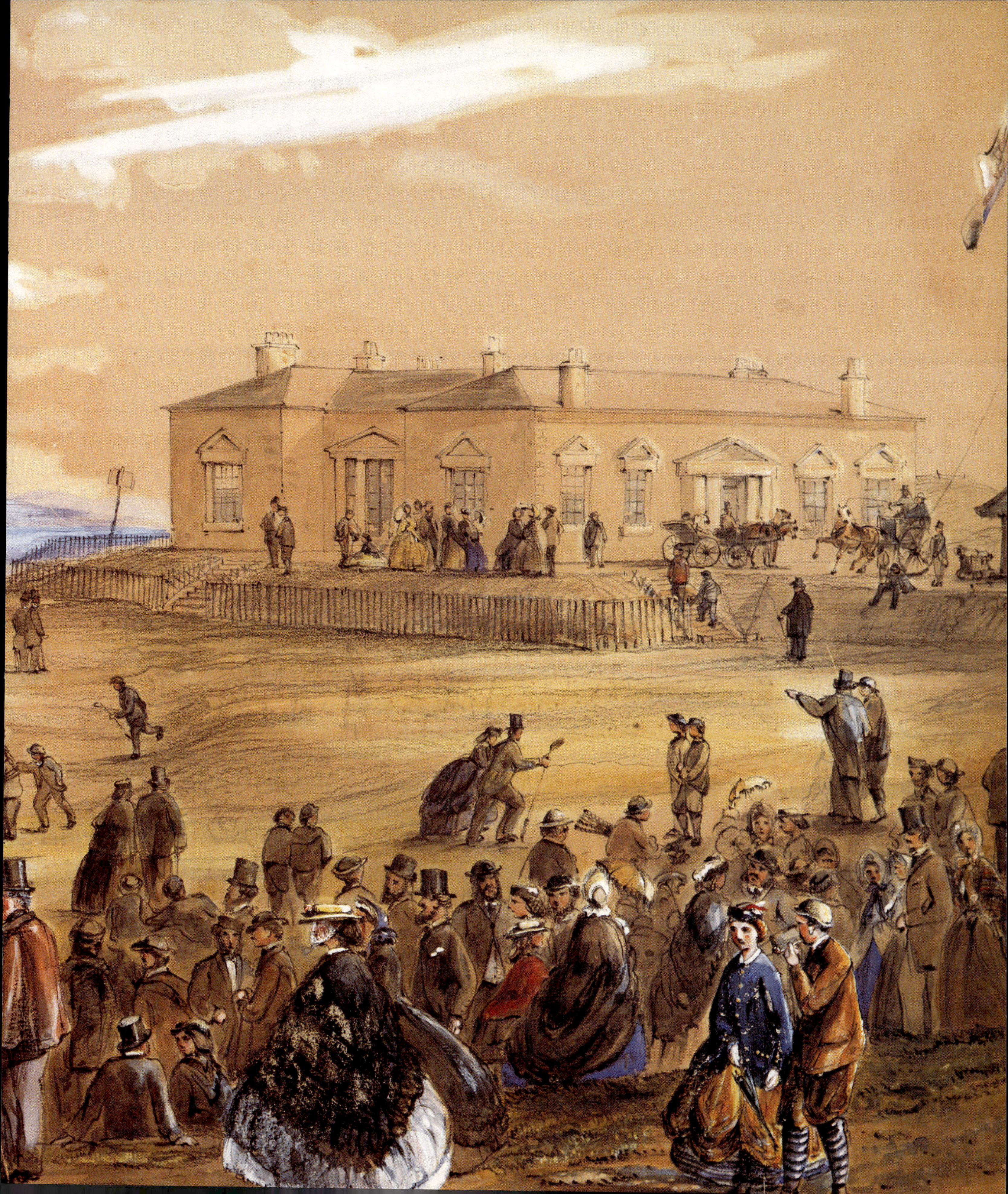

The Scenic Series

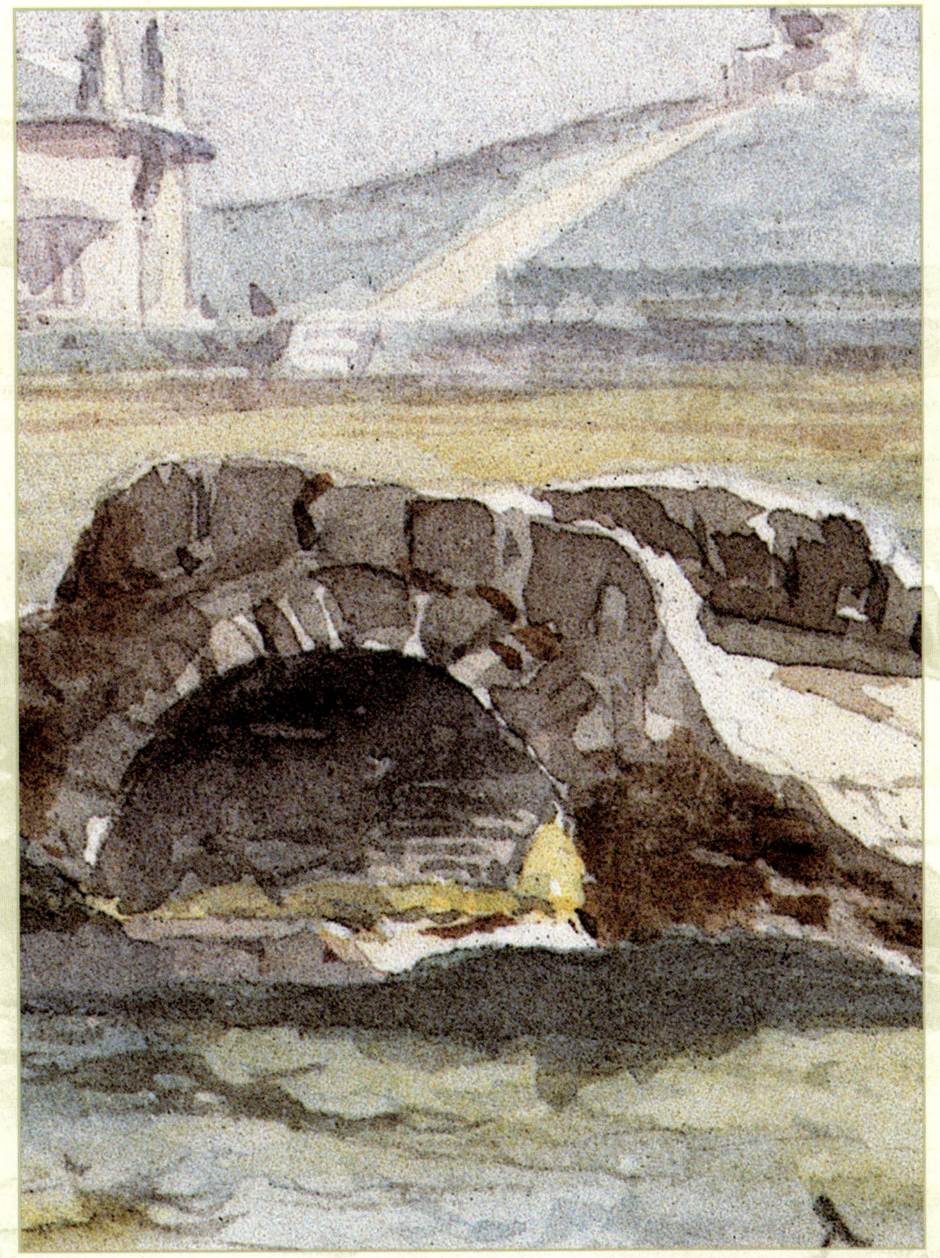

The Scenic Series

If you are dreaming of the perfect course, golfer, let your eye dwell on the following miniature paintings by our artist hero of St. Andrews.

SCENIC SERIES No. 1

In 1879, Thomas Hodge started to paint what he entitled his "Scenic Series". First of all, he pictured the Royal & Ancient clubhouse from the other side of Swilcan Bridge. Some conservationists might wish a structure as ancient and historic as this worn stone bridge to be protected now under bulletproof glass or plastic. It isn't. Once the only link between St. Andrews and its former harbour at the Eden rivermouth, it is still in daily use as part of the golf course though 800 years old.

Hodge's handwritten caption to this most delicate landscape reads like a quotation from an unknown club dignitary:

Well, architecturally it certainly is an ugly mixture, but familiarity has softened that, and I doubt if any more patching will improve it.
(Before the alterations).

As in Hodge's 1862 painting of the clubhouse 17 years earlier, the steep fall into the sea at the building's right remains alarming. Sir Hugh Playfair, a captain of the Royal & Ancient and legendary mayor and patron of St. Andrews, and a genius called George Bruce were visionaries who pushed the sea backwards with homespun reclamation schemes which included filling old fishing boats with stones and blocks of cement and burying them at the edge of the shallow cliffs.

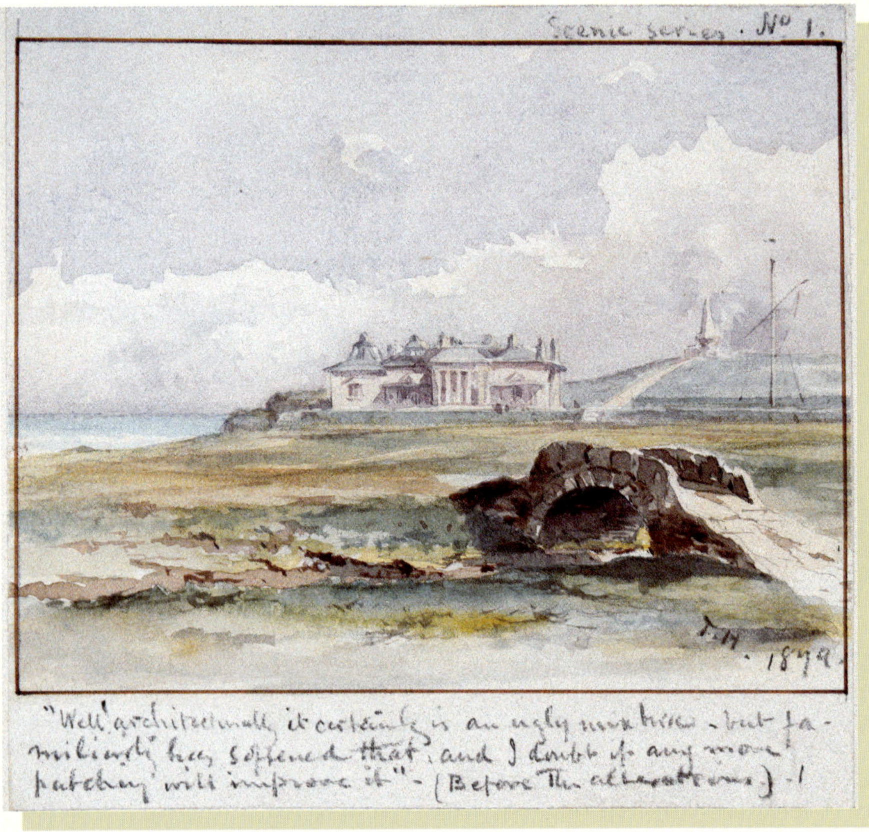

Left: the Royal & Ancient as seen by Hodge from Swilcan Bridge.

SCENIC SERIES No. 2

Curious composition though it is, this also contains a mine of information. Hodge's inscription reads:

Taking the opposite view of the matter.

Underneath that, he has written:

From the club-house window.

All this series of watercolours is on a miniature scale, often less than postcard size, which underlines the opinion that Hodge was hoping to publish a book well over a century ago. Small, yes, but with detail that is educational.

For instance, it is often remarked how the old Swilcan Burn, whose now trimly tailored banks still dissect the Old Course, once had its mouth not 50 yards from Swilcan Bridge. This might have seemed unlikely on viewing the wide expanse of land between the bridge and the sea in the last days of the 20th century. Yet here is the evidence; the old mouth of the burn clearly is close to the bridge, with its steep banks of golden sand waiting both to trap the careless shot and to provide tees for the players' drives.

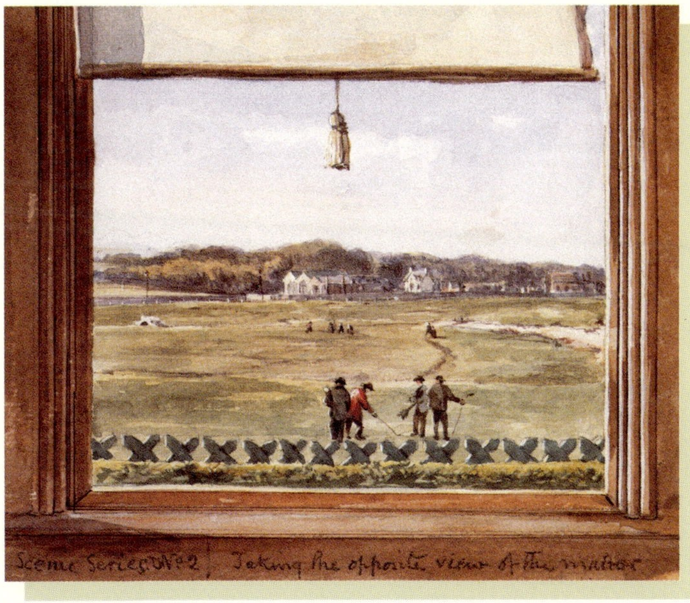

Above: through the clubhouse window in the 1880s.

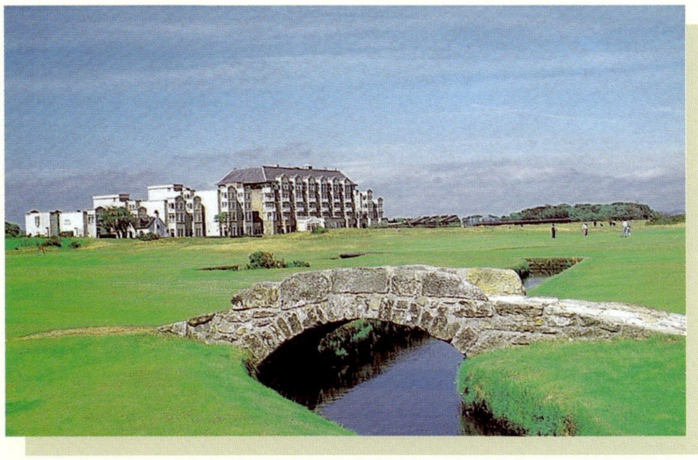

Above: through the clubhouse window in the 1980s, the giant hotel.

Hodge's quaint vision of the links through the front window of the R & A holy-of-holies has a deeply ironic twist. He is saying that this is a prospect sacred to golf and golfers. Untouchable. Timeless. Well it was – for a century, until the 1980s – when suddenly the Old Course Hotel was planted right at the edge of Hodge's heaven. It's a remarkable hotel in a remarkable place. Any golfer would thrill to a weekend there. Don't ask how it happened, just start saving up for a visit if you are the complete golfing hedonist. They'll be happy to send you a price list.

No-one can know how the old diehard R & A members would have reacted (perhaps suicide?) to the information that in some years this American-designed palace that has been plonked into the dead-centre of their horizon receives up to 27,000 international visitors. And the first and greatest moment these tourists enjoy is the spellbinding panorama of St. Andrews and the Royal & Ancient clubhouse, from THEIR windows.

Four years after recording the view from the clubhouse window, Thomas Hodge produced this painting of a match in progress on the outer limits of the course, signed T. H. 1884. St. Andrews is a hazy silhouette on the horizon and the rest of the world is a million miles from the peaceful encounter. Unfortunately the artist's caption is lost, so that the identity of the players can only be a strong guess. The man putting could be one of the Balfours, with Gilbert Mitchell-Innes watching. The most interesting thing about the scene, which Hodge has invested with a nice sense of space and distance, is the caddies' equipment. They are each carrying their players' clubs in rough bags, one of the earliest notes of such as innovation. Previously, as can be seen from the 1880 painting from the clubhouse window, caddies wrestled with their patrons' clubs under one armpit, held club-heads foremost, of course. Sometimes a narrow strap helped keep the clubs together. The exact year golf bags were introduced around the 1880s seems unknown. One caddie in the "window" painting appears to have a carrying bag, the other does not.

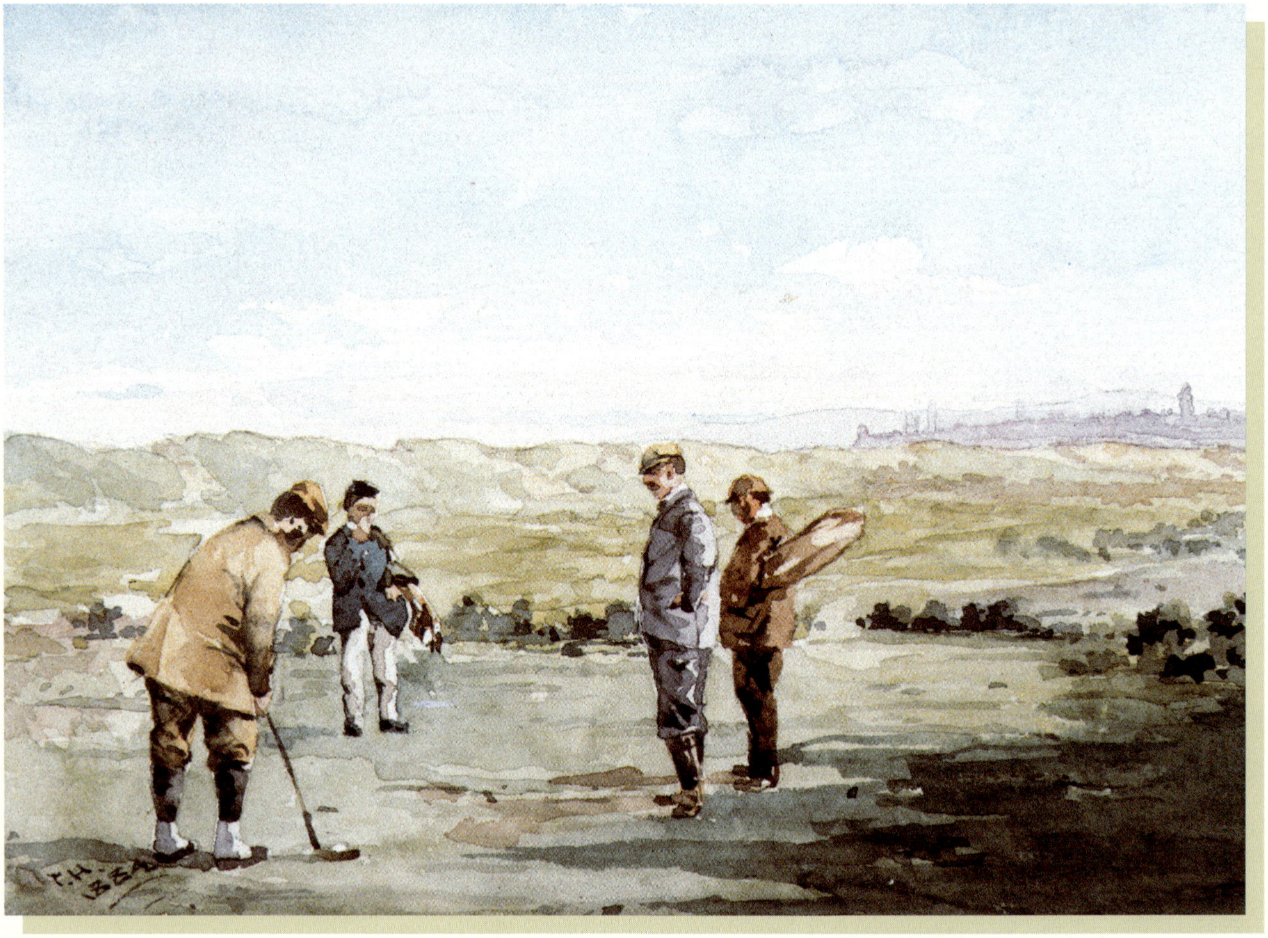

Above: a quiet match in perfect surroundings, 1884.

SCENIC SERIES No. 3

When Thomas Hodge made this enigmatic sepia wash drawing in 1880, he inscribed it:

Famous road(?) at St. A. A near cut to the House of Lords through the Courts of Session.

This is jokey allusion to the most uproarious rumpus over the St. Andrews links he and thousands of others witnessed there in February 1880. The conflict roused such passions that it was said by a Mr. Oliphant in the Town Council chamber to have caused "More bad blood and bitterness than anything in the town in the memory of living man".

St. Andrews and Scotland were particularly short on laughter that winter. On December 28, 1879, only a month earlier, on the last Sunday night of the old year, in a peculiar hurricane which would rage one moment then almost be still the next, the last train left the village of Leuchars, six miles outside St. Andrews with about 100 passengers on board. All died a few minutes later when the

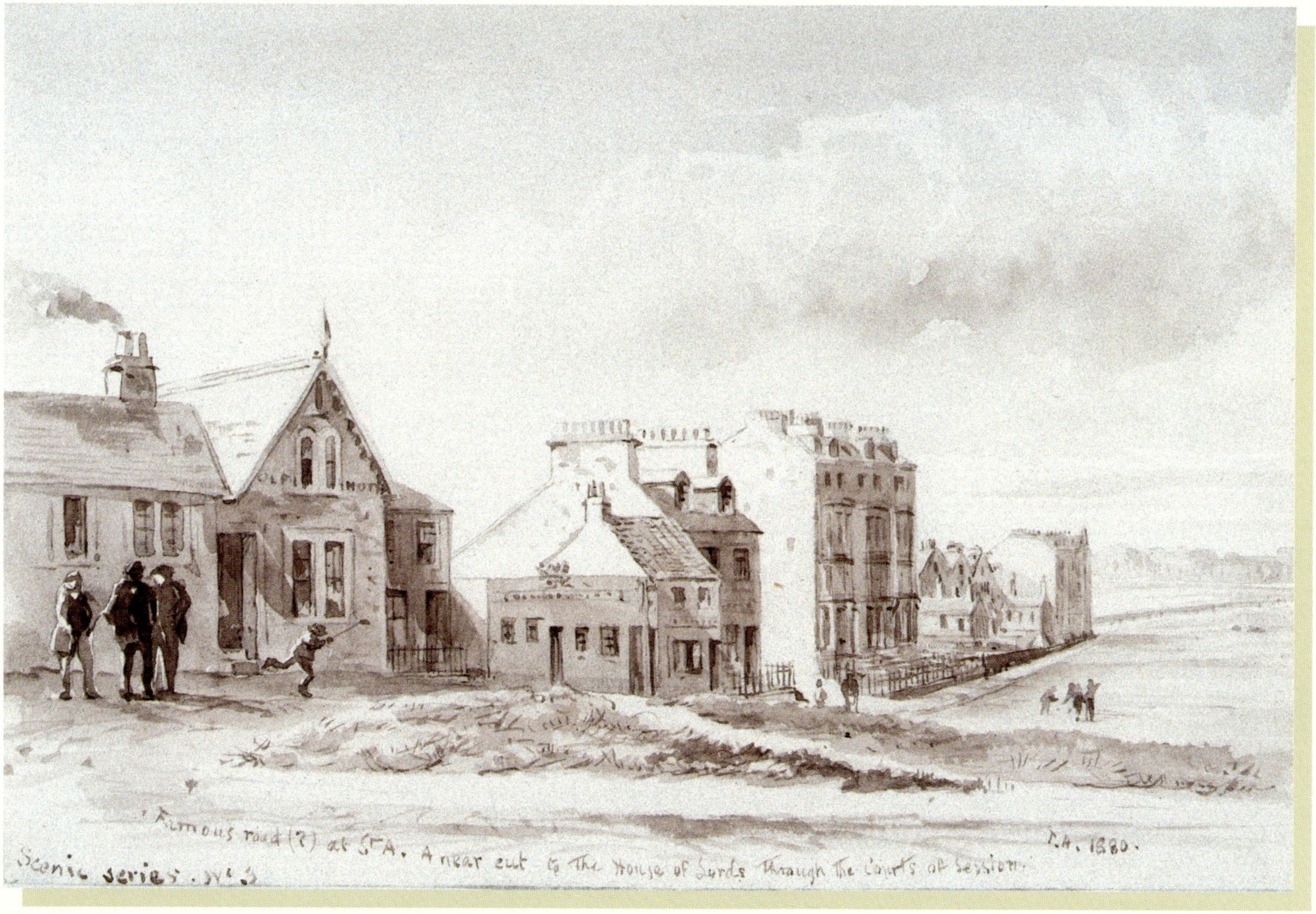

Above: a conflict which caused "More bad blood and bitterness than anything in the town in the memory of living man"...

train fell in a brief spray of sparks through the pitch darkness down into the river ... the Tay Railway Bridge disaster.

Bodies were still being recovered amid general mourning, when St. Andrews Town Council obtained the legal go-ahead to "make up" a hotly disputed pathway at the edge of the golf links. This was to become Links Road. Opponents of a permanent road surface, resident members of the Royal & Ancient and others who felt this was taking a slice from the golf links illegally were caught napping.

The weekend after receiving permission, a gang of labourers and councillors quickly levelled and metalled the better part of the road. Sunday was a rest day, except for plotters, and on the Monday, battle began. The local newspaper, the *St. Andrews Citizen*, reported:

On Monday morning, these operations were resumed; but to the amusement of many, and anxiety of others, an opposition squad of men, horses and carts put in an appearance and removed the metal, depositing it on the road across the links quicker than the other side could put it down.

Finding themselves outnumbered and outmanoeuvred, those in favour of the road suspended operations. The police were appealed to, but as the case was a civil one they were powerless.

About two in the afternoon another attempt was made to have the road macadamised; but the opposition and carts again appeared, and though Councillors Oliphant and Aikman tried to prevent them interfering, they were unsuccessful and something like a melee ensued for a short time, and the road was again cleared.

The road party were more successful in a third attempt. At six o'clock a large portion of the road was again installed. A large number of carts were then expected from a distance, to remove the metal, and until they arrived it was being lifted and removed in barrows.

The utmost excitement prevailed in the city, work being almost entirely suspended, and the Links in the neighbourhood crowded with spectators to witness the unusual proceedings. Several attempts were made to remove the metal, and several skirmishes occurred between the opposing parties; but happily no injuries of a serious nature were inflicted.

A strong body of police constables was on the ground, and their presence was sufficient to prevent any incipient attempt at rioting. Liquor being freely supplied to the labourers, a large number were much intoxicated as the evening advanced, and their eccentric movements added to the ludicrousness of the scene.

Another account in the same newspaper said:

The scene on Monday evening was most discreditable to St. Andrews. The shouting, profane swearing, and general conduct indulged in, were such that it is hoped will never be again witnessed or heard in St. Andrews.

The turning point in favour of the road makers had been the simple resort to bribery. Carters were offered more money to change sides. A new wave of carts sent in by the anti-road side were lifted off their wheels or had their harness cut and destroyed. An eye-witness counted over 50 men lying drunk on the links at the end of the day. Police reinforcements were called in from all round Fifeshire to prevent further incidents during the following week. A local man, W. A. Dick, painted a cartoon lampooning the incident, photographs of which sold quicker than they could be printed. This primitive painting by Mr. Dick recording the ludicrous events is held by the St. Andrews Preservation Trust Museum in North Street. It seems to be dated 1878, which must be a mistaken afterthought caused by the prolonged nature of the dispute which had been going on throughout the late 1870s.

Dick's weird stab at satire, showing a donkey leading an elephant, must be his opinion of the two opposing factions. If Hodge sketched the battle, nothing has been found yet.

Below: the painting by St. Andrews shopkeeper W. A. Dick lampooning the great Links Road battle. The painting, now exhibited in the St. Andrews Preservation Trust Museum in North Street, was sold widely as a print, presumably photographic.

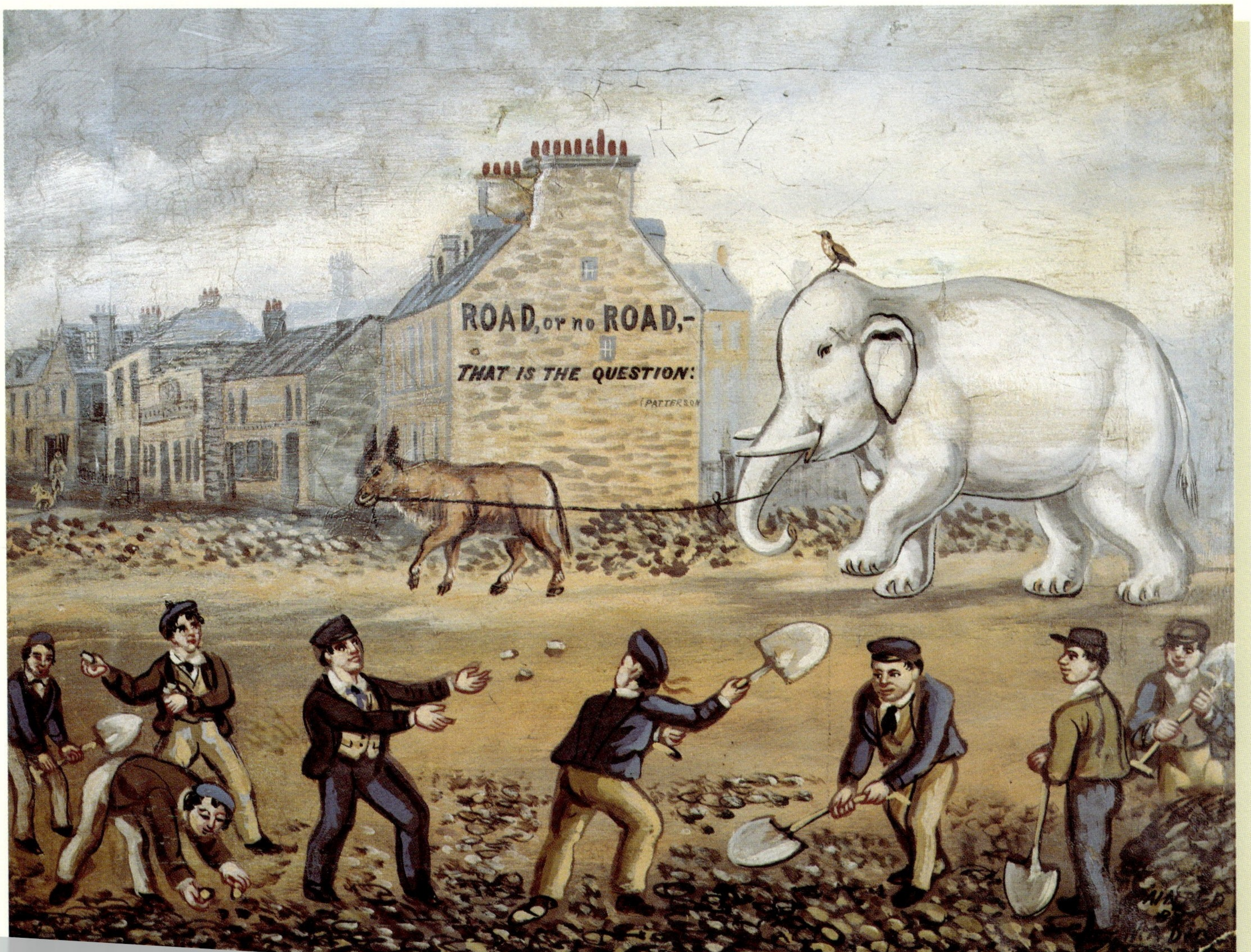

Hodge's desire to record the nature of St. Andrews links in the early 1880s may have sprung from the battle of the road. Certainly the "resident" members of the Royal & Ancient club were particularly anxious about the treasured acres. The links had been sold by St. Andrews Town Council to avoid bankruptcy in what were days of dire poverty for many areas of Scotland at the close of the 18th century. The absolute right of all inhabitants, and any others, to go to the links and play golf was reserved.

Inevitably, there were many skirmishes over the use of the land as the local golfers clashed with proprietors and tenants who, among other things, converted a large area into a rabbit warren.

The black and white rabbits may have been profitable delicacies to the owner, a Mr. Dempster, but to the golfers they were a destructive horde of pests. Fisticuffs between servants of Mr. Dempster and irate citizens are recorded, plus allegations of the poisoning of dogs used to hunt the burrowing bunnies.

The Royal & Ancient (until 1834 known as The Society of St. Andrews Golfers) led a victorious legal attack against the rabbits in 1813. The traditional rights of golfers on St. Andrews links were confirmed. The role of watchdog over the links well became the R & A during the next decades. The links extended beyond the boundaries of what is seen today as the Old Golf Course, and there was a conflict of interest between a town council which wanted to permit building to obtain revenues and the club which defended the golfing acres. In one major trade-off, the club obtained the land for its clubhouse in return for not fighting one of the council's house-building projects.

If memory runs deep anywhere, it is in St. Andrews, and the battle of the road in 1880 aroused old suspicions and enmities. Whether Thomas Hodge was one of the small group who wanted the R & A to buy the links when they came up for sale rather secretively in the late 1880s is another matter. Certainly he, Harry Everard, Major Boothby and other traditionalists were "resident members", that's to say among the 100 or fewer who lived in or near St. Andrews out of a total of between 700 and 800 members. Many of these residents regarded the soaring popularity of the game with dread rather than joy.

In 1891, the then owner, Mr. George Cheape (Laird of Strathtyrum, a property adjoining the links now a luxury hotel. It houses the biggest, in all senses, painting in golf's history, *The Golfers* by Charles Lees, "Not for sale even for a million pounds"), offered the links to the Royal & Ancient. The deal fell through. Two years later, just at the point Thomas Hodge and Andrew Lang were being roasted alive by the local historian David Hay Fleming over their careless book about St. Andrews, Cheape again offered the links to the club for £5,000.

Subsequently, the truth of events became rather blurred. The club and the town council met, after which each accused the other of "intervening" in negotiations with Mr. Cheape. An angry public meeting found David Hay Fleming slaying dragons once more. He was cheered when he said:

The action of the club in trying to forestall the town council in the links is desperately shabby. Although they keep up the links, they have not always done so. It is owing to the citizens that the links are still in existence ... the town has much the deeper interest in preserving the links for all golfers whether members of the club or not.

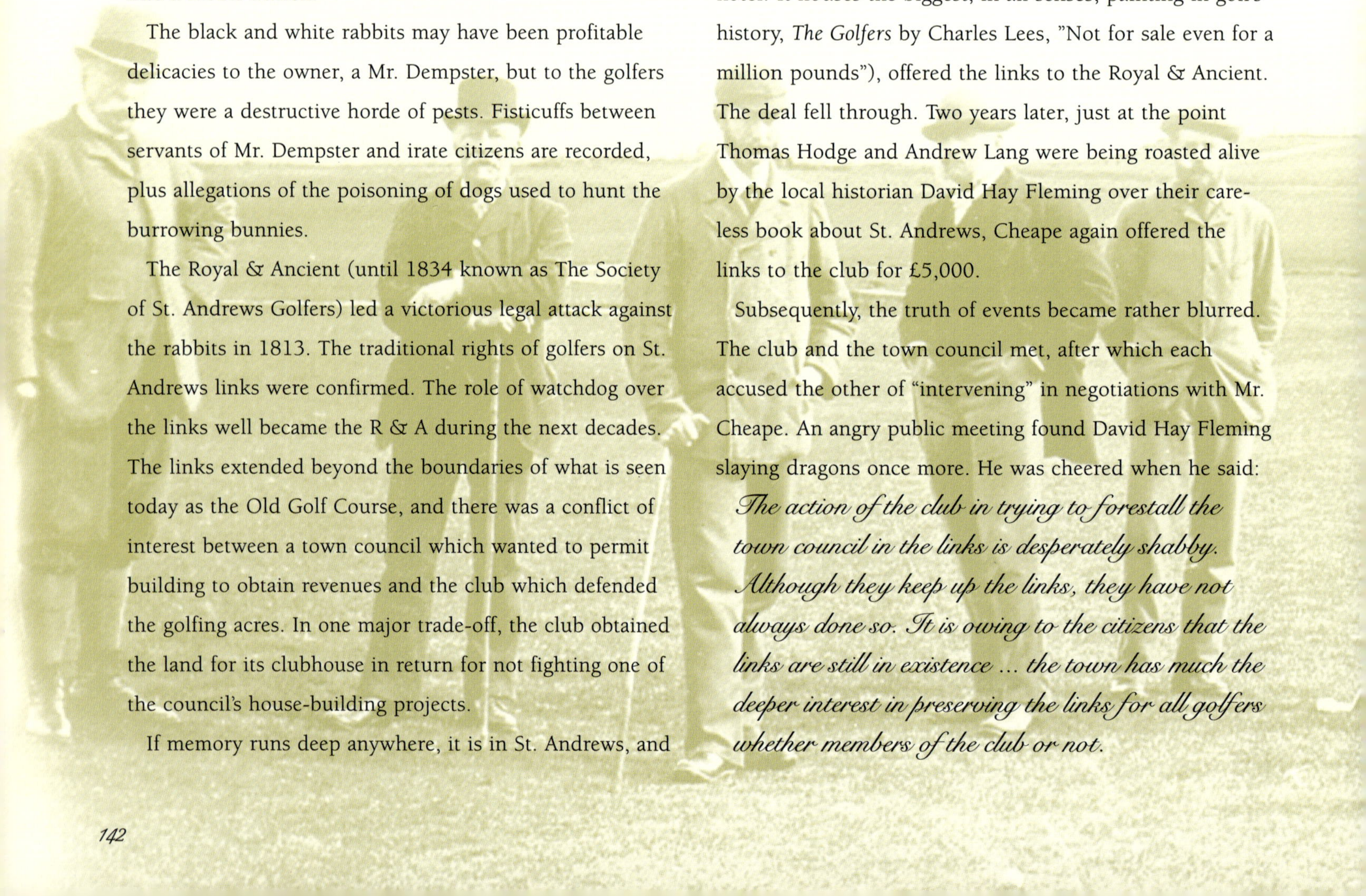

It is often said that the Royal & Ancient has never owned the great golf course, but this isn't strictly true because they went ahead with the purchase. Their proviso was that they would re-sell it to the town if the council could obtain the necessary Act of Parliament and subject to the club keeping its playing rights and voluntary duty to maintain the course.

The conflict roused many a quivering nib from the ink-pots of Fife, so that letters stung the participants from the pages of local newspapers like slaps in the face. Take that, sir! And take that! Householders complained of the cost to St. Andrews. "Why not clean up our disgraceful drains instead", wrote one anxious mamma.

Worried about the increasingly bitter tone the dispute was taking, the *St. Andrews Citizen* ended an editorial on the matter with the comment:

It would be suicidal and fatal for the Town and the Club to quarrel.

Nevertheless, the dispute could not be settled amicably before both parties had attended a committee meeting of the House of Commons on April 25, 1894 when the town council's petition for permission to buy the links, opposed by the R & A, was heard. After listening to both sides, the committee wearily said they thought the two parties should be able to reach agreement by themselves. Which they then did! Thus the links are held today by a Trust. This has survived changes in local government administration throughout the 20th century and other hurdles simply because, in the end, both golf club and St. Andrews know they are fated to share the same sweetheart always.

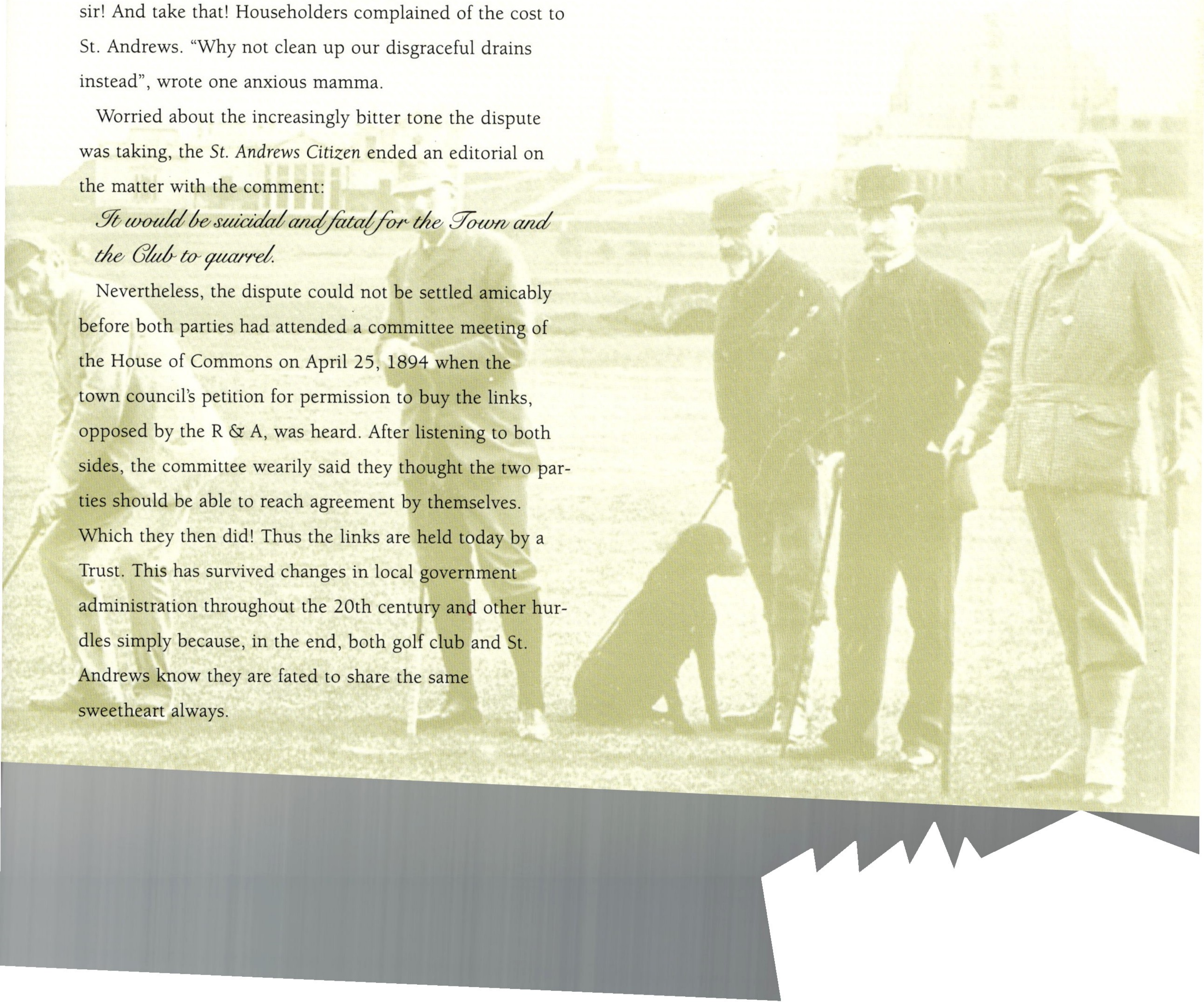

SCENIC SERIES No. 4

A watercolour landscape of part of the Old Course (size 22cm x 17cm). The caption in Hodge's hand reads:

Twenty years ago the lower course under the Elysian fields approaching the hole o'cross wore this aspect. At that time there was also more sky, and a large breed of sheep. Octr. 1880.

The latter sentence is doubtless one of Hodge's mildly sarcastic digs, possibly at the way the course was being smoothed out and tailored, and the increase in peripheral building. How he would have reacted over a century later with half of Fife laid out as golf courses with their attendant facilities is not difficult to imagine.

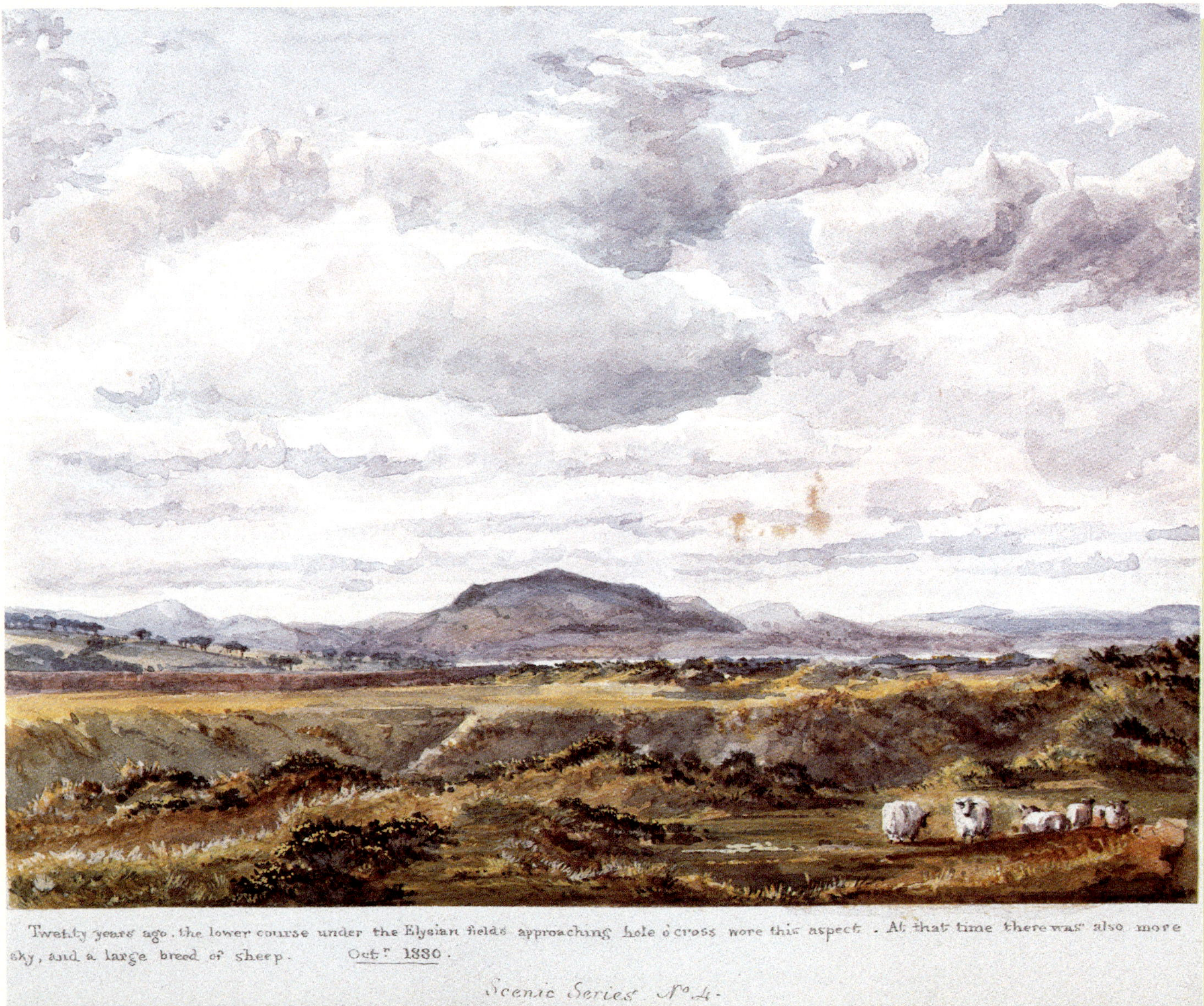

SCENIC SERIES No. 5

Inscribed by Hodge *"Eden 1880"*. This is an odd-looking landscape for the non-golfer to appreciate.(size 23.6cm x 9.9cm). It is the point of the Old Course at St. Andrews overlooking the mouth of the River Eden where the 7th and 11th holes were close together. The painting emphasises the rugged, tricky nature of the putting greens in the late 19th century. The flagpole was equally homely.

Left: the Old Course pictured here by Hodge in 1880.

Below: part of the Old Course at St. Andrews overlooking the River Eden.

SCENIC SERIES No. 6

Watercolour landscape (21.3cm x 13.4cm) of a beached wreck with St. Andrews in the background (see next page). Signed T. Hodge and dated 1881, "Relic of Mch 5". The caption in Hodge's script reads:

The Harmony of Mandal in Norway was beached as above. Crew saved.

The sea was ever part of St. Andrews' history, the British Navy frequently resting at anchor in the bay adjoining the golf links. Hodge's painting recalls the story of another R & A golfing hero, Admiral Maitland Dougall, who took the stroke oar in the St. Andrews lifeboat on the morning of the October meeting in 1860. After helping to rescue the crews of several fishing boats in the bay in a ferocious gale, the intrepid admiral went back to the golf tournament and won the gold medal that same afternoon. Gourlay, the ball maker said:

What nerve he must have for the game.

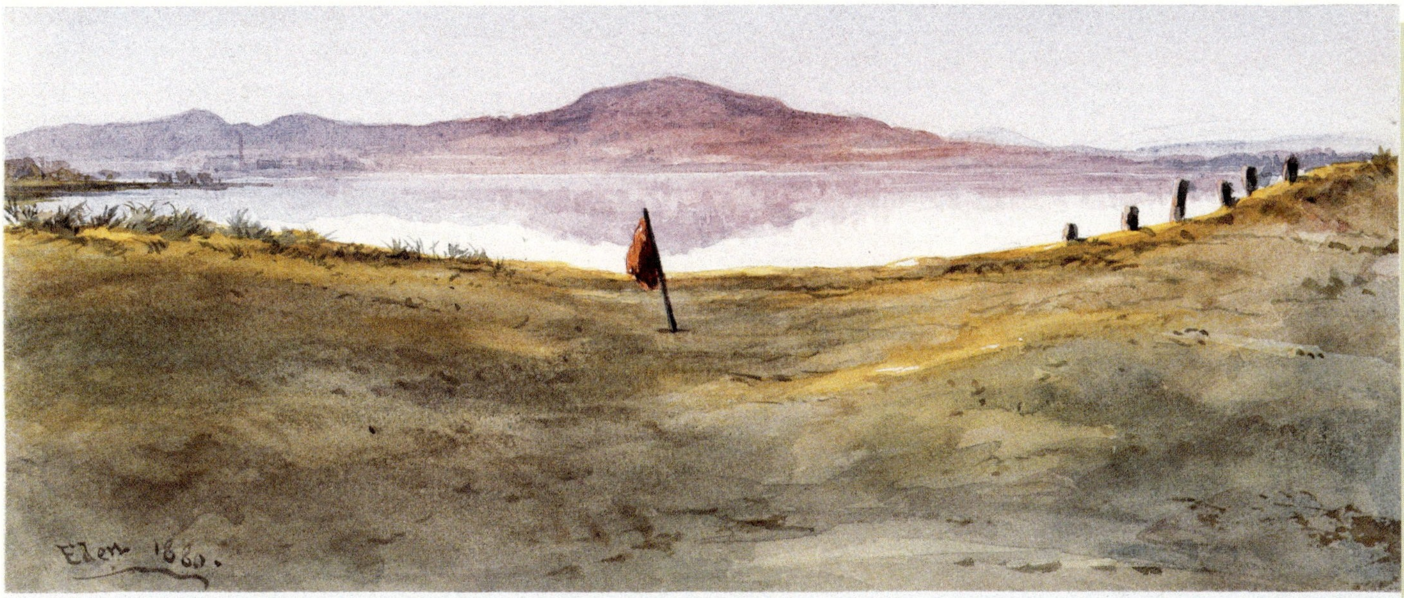

Scenic Series No. 5...

Thousands of people gathered on the West Sands to watch the drama of the *Harmony*, driven to the shore in a snowstorm with hurricane-force winds. In immense seas, the lifeboat *Ladies Own* rescued the crew of four men and a boy, returning to the beach to the crowd's cheers. Later that day a large boat was seen drifting on to the rocks to the north of St. Andrews, the crew clinging to the rigging. The Life Brigade discharged a rocket which would have meant all being saved. But suddenly the vessel, the *Merlin* of Sunderland, lurched massively in the giant waves, and the five remaining crew

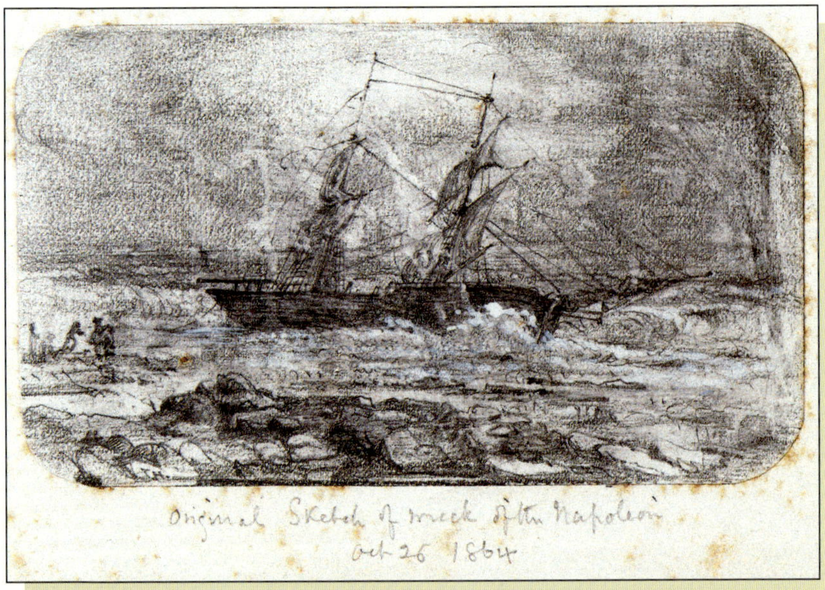

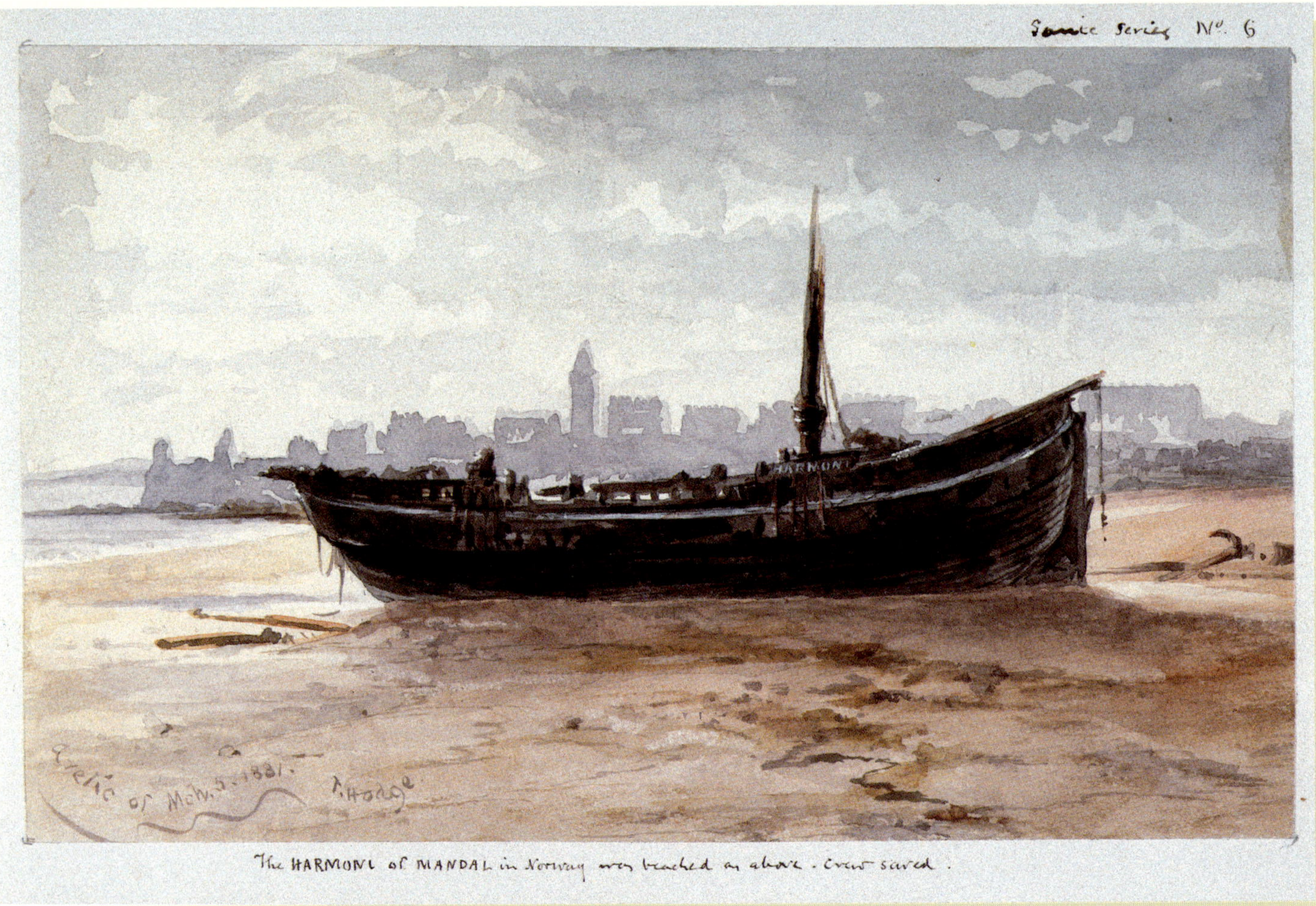

were drowned as the crowd on shore wept at their screams. The *Merlin* was "smashed to matchwood" on the rocks.

Never was a wreck more complete

wrote the *St. Andrews Citizen*.

SCENIC SERIES No. 7

Watercolour view (13cm x 20.1cm)of the approach to the 17th hole at St. Andrews, signed T. H. and dated '81. The wall to the station-master's house is on the right. That wall and the garden beyond created dreaded penalties for the players. Hodge's caption reads:

When all square and 2 to play, give this place a wide berth.

When Hodge painted the same house three years later, its fence had been raised (against golf balls and golfers?) among other changes. The ruts in the path caused by carts and carriages bred the heavy rut irons now prized so highly by collectors of old clubs.

Above left: the wreck of a ship, the 'Napoleon' captured by Hodge in a pencil sketch.

Left: the 'Harmony', wreck painted by Hodge in 1881.

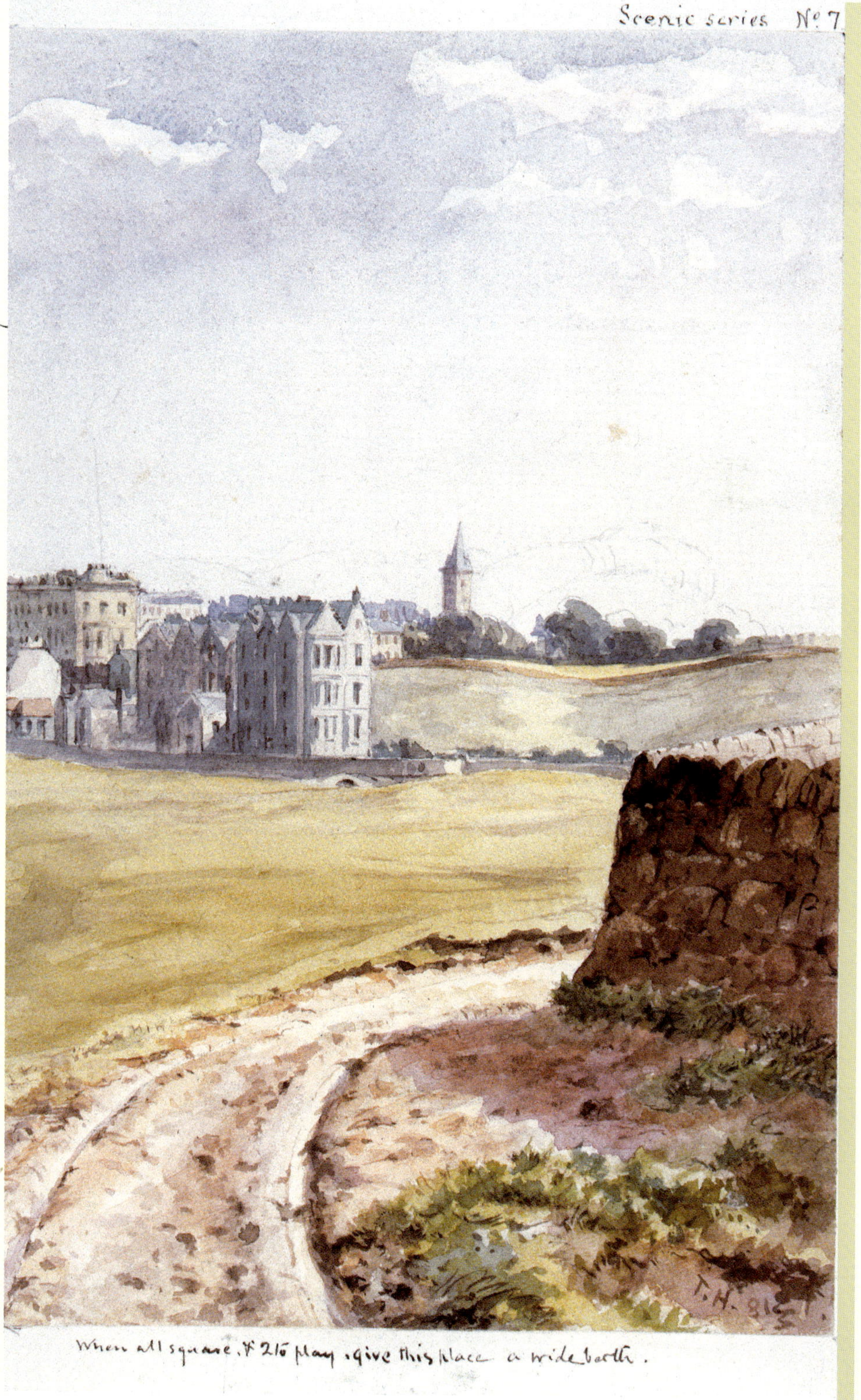

Right: the birthplace of rut irons.

ST. ANDREWS

A wintry, sepia-wash landscape of St. Andrews viewed from the old edge of the links. Signed T. H. 1884. St. Andrews, ancient ecclesiastical capital of Scotland whose university was established in 1410, includes in its history the legend of a Greek monk called Regulus. In 370 AD he was said to have brought with him relics of St. Andrew (arm bone, three fingers, three toes) by boat from Greece. After a two-year journey, he and his crew were shipwrecked in St. Andrews Bay. The city he and succeeding ancients built up became known as "the capital of the kingdom of darkness". No disgusting horror of torture and execution by ghastly means was left untried by its religious fiends. Up to the 18th century witch-hunting and superstition was rife. And then there was golf!

Below: the fringe of the Links in 1884.

Right: St. Andrews under snow.

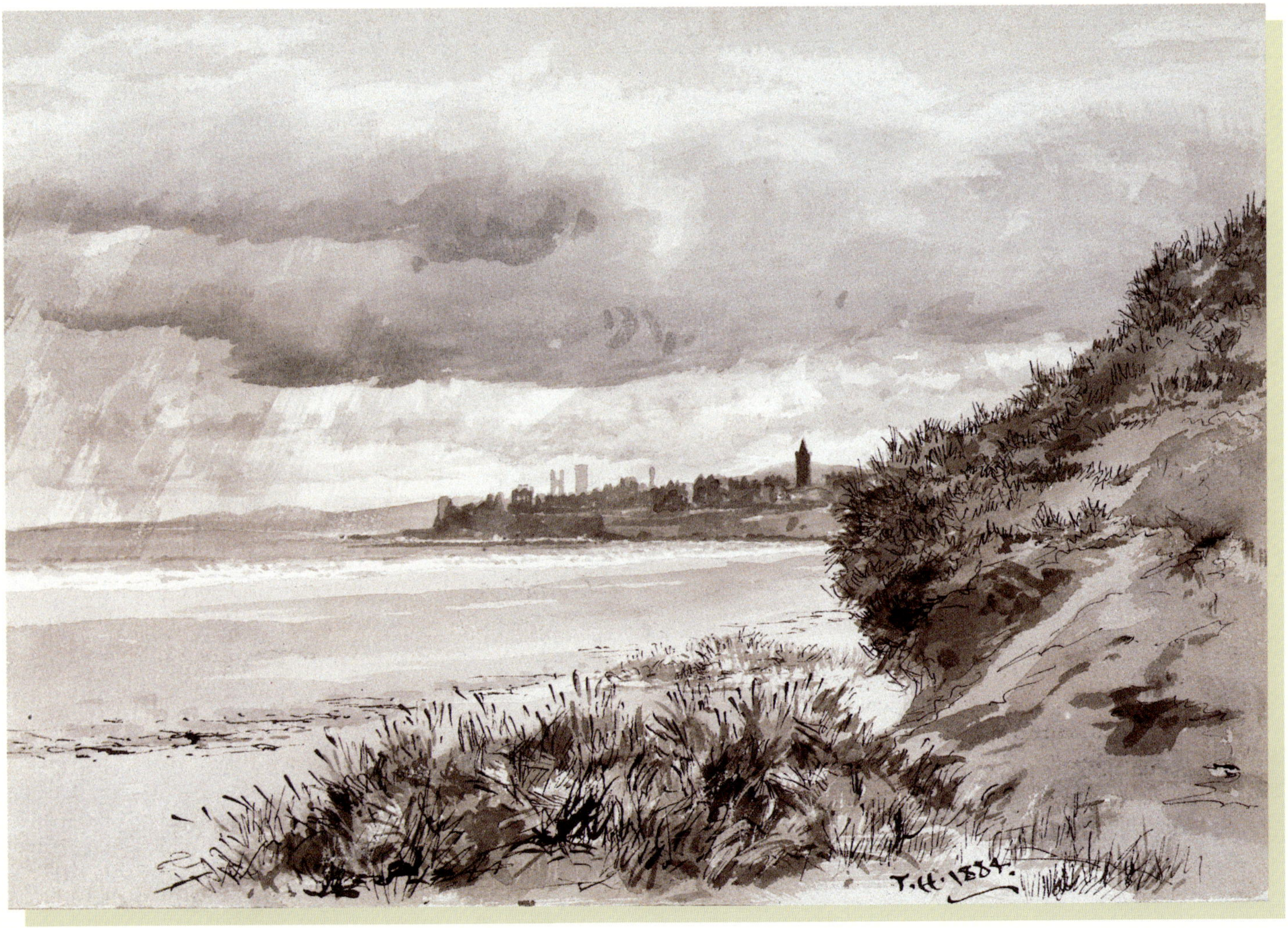

ST. ANDREWS UNDER SNOW

Watercolour (14.1cm x 10.1cm), signed T. H. 1884, with an inscription in the artist's hand:

Auld Tom + G.M.-I., Frozen out Golfers.

Old Tom stands on the left, wearing a heavy overcoat and his cap, hand on flag and faced by the famous amateur sportsman Gilbert Mitchell-Innes. Apart from the wintry bleakness, the painting shows additions made to the club-house since Hodge painted it in 1879.

It took Arctic weather to keep the more fanatical members of the Royal & Ancient from their rounds of golf. Some of the winters in the 1880s were particularly cruel. Parish minister A. K. H. Boyd wrote of "an unutterable chill the like of which no man remembered" and snowfalls six feet deep. He recalled an impoverished lecturer desperately trying to get a paying audience to one of the St. Andrews' halls in Siberian conditions because he had to get money to support his starving family. The locals nobly packed the hall, but the lecturer died shortly afterwards from a fever made fatal from walking the bitter streets selling tickets. On another occasion, St. Andrews was cut off for three days, and one of Boyd's sons walked home the six miles from Leuchars "with the snow sometimes over his head" after being stranded at the railway station overnight by a March hurricane.

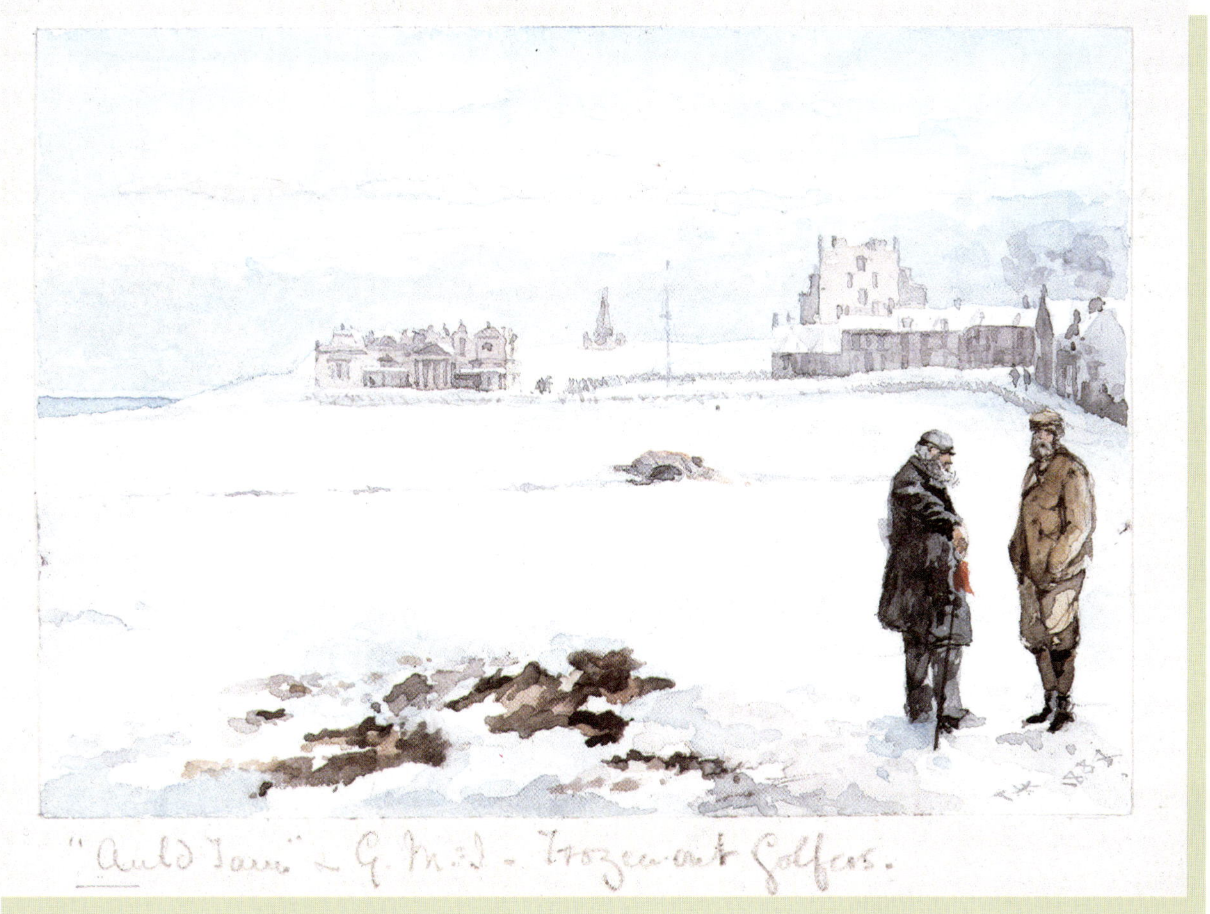

THE LADIES' LINKS

Watercolour (13.7cm x 9.8cm), signed T. H. '85. Two women golfers at play on a small, rough patch of grass which served as the green in 1885. A flag bearing the number 18 is alongside. The matronly figure putting is more than likely Mrs. Hodge. The St. Andrews Ladies Golf Club, formed in 1867, was the first of its kind in the world.

As it was over a century ago, the Royal & Ancient clubhouse remained in the late 1990s a preserve where few females trod unless paid to do secretarial work or perform menial tasks. Advised in 1986 that she might not be able to see her grandfather's pictures actually hanging in the clubhouse, Thomas Hodge's granddaughter, who had just gifted them the treasures, replied:

Quite right! The men need a rest from women sometimes.

When T. H. painted this charming scene, the dozen or so "Ladies' Links" then in Britain were essentially putting greens fringing the main courses and aimed at keeping the dear little things contented but at a distance. Jolly packs of "New Women" in tweeds, smoking cigars, or busty golfing belles in bloomers were the stuff of cartoons drawn for London society magazines. The boring reality for many British women was their newly coined status as "golf widows".

In 1890, one wife found the courage to write to the new magazine *Golf* that:

A little of Hoylake goes a long way. A week of Felixtowe is, we think, as much as human nature can be expected to endure ...

The main reply from a golfer (do we detect the unruly pen of Professor Tait here?) was intended to amuse:

One observes a disagreeable, rebellious sentiment in woman. She seems to think that she has a right to be heard on this subject, namely Golf, a topic which should be tabooed to her. She is so constituted as to like living in town, which is hateful to every well-civilised man. There she has the shops, the dinners, gossip about trivialities, the smoke, the noise, the general artificiality. She might put her private tastes aside in the holidays. But she does not.

In regard to all manly diversions, woman is singularly a mistake. Say it is fishing, she hates getting her feet wet; she hates a boat, in which she is not very well; she hates cruelty; she is glad when a trout or salmon gets away. We are speaking of married women of course. Girls are much better behaved and know their place.

On the links, she chatters, she speaks to a man on his stroke....she keeps everyone back by her inefficiency. She should be content with the Ladies Links, where, very likely, some quiet young man may practise putting with her. The female intellect, keen enough in trifles, is incapable of a mature and reasoned interest in golf. Can we not have a colony for wives in the holidays?

Clearly he did not know or care that Mary, Queen of Scots, was a keen golfer and played at St. Andrews in the 16th century.

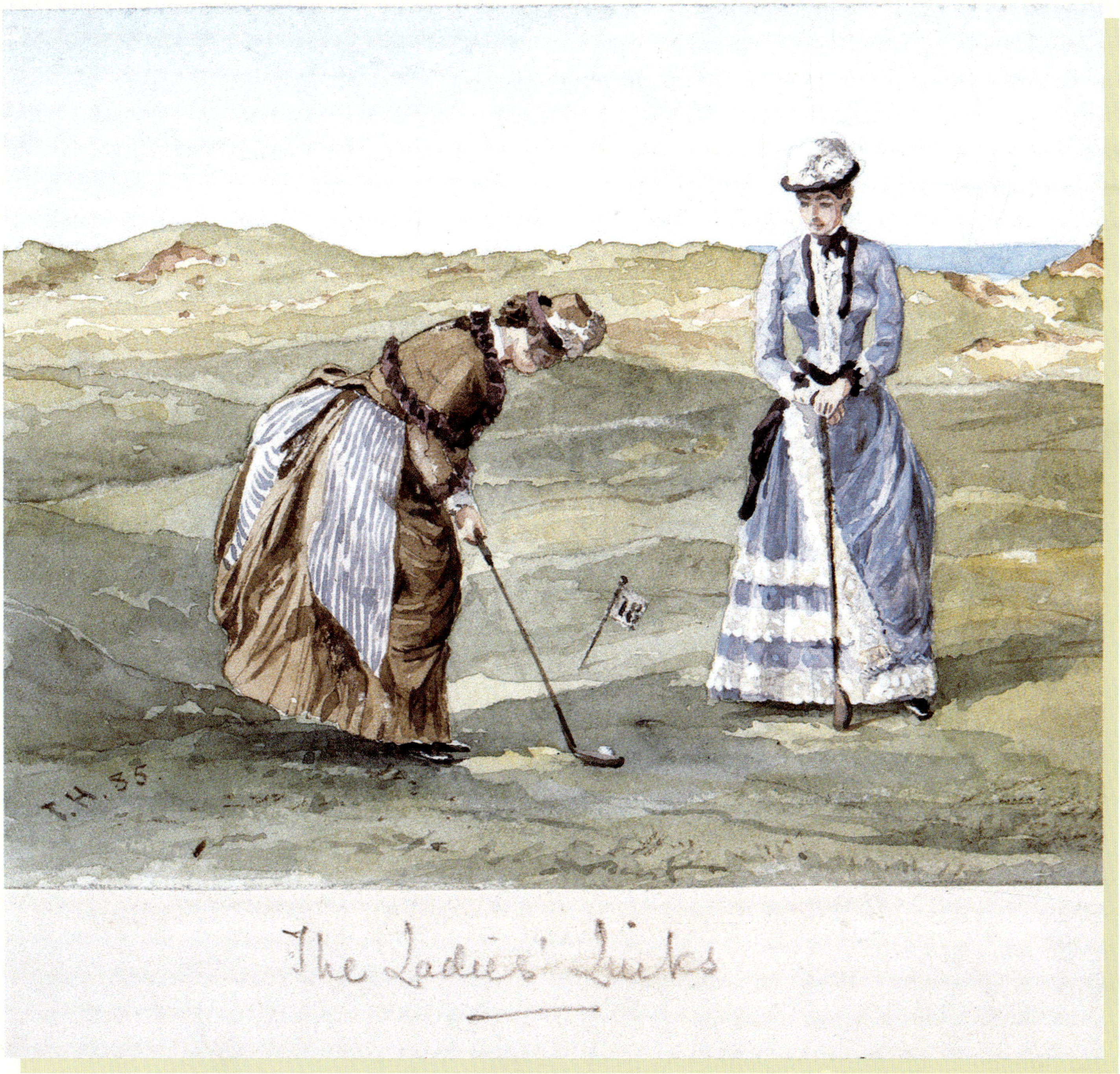

Above: ladies playing at St. Andrews in 1885.

Another golfer wrote:

... his devotion to the game keeps the golfer within reach of his better-half, and gives her the comforting assurance that he is not playing the part of the gay bachelor in Paris ...

The wife replied:

Rip van Winkle does not seem to have heard of educated women, or literary women, of artistic women; he does not know that a woman beat the men at Harvard and at Cambridge ... that women are beating the men all round whenever they are able to get a chance of the same advantages of training which men enjoy and try so hard to keep to themselves.

But woman's day is coming when she will have her revenge for centuries of oppression. Men know it, all except the best of them, who have no need to fear. Hence their bitterness.

Golfing man was given the last word by an editor possibly embarrassed that, yet again, what had started as a fairly innocent argument in the pages of *Golf* was turning extremely nasty. He wrote:

I have heard of literary women, and very little good of them; they are the bane of my existence. The sex has produced putters – ladies who putt well – I admit, but it is also rich in such poets, and painters, and amateur novelists, as the world could well dispense with.

Yes, I have heard that a lady 'beat the men at Cambridge'. Ladies occasionally mention the circumstance. But mark, it was at Cambridge!

The poet observes:

This was not Oxford's case, These were but Cambridge men. What has all this disquisition got to do with golf? Women's day is coming indeed; it has come when woman drags golfing man in his few hours of leisure from the links.

Right: after exercise, refreshment! And where better for Thomas Hodge (at the rear) and his oldest son Donald to halt than at "Old Daw's" ginger beer cart on the St. Andrews links. This sketch was done by Hodge in 1891. Donald appears to have a large box camera in his left hand as he sups Daw's nectar.

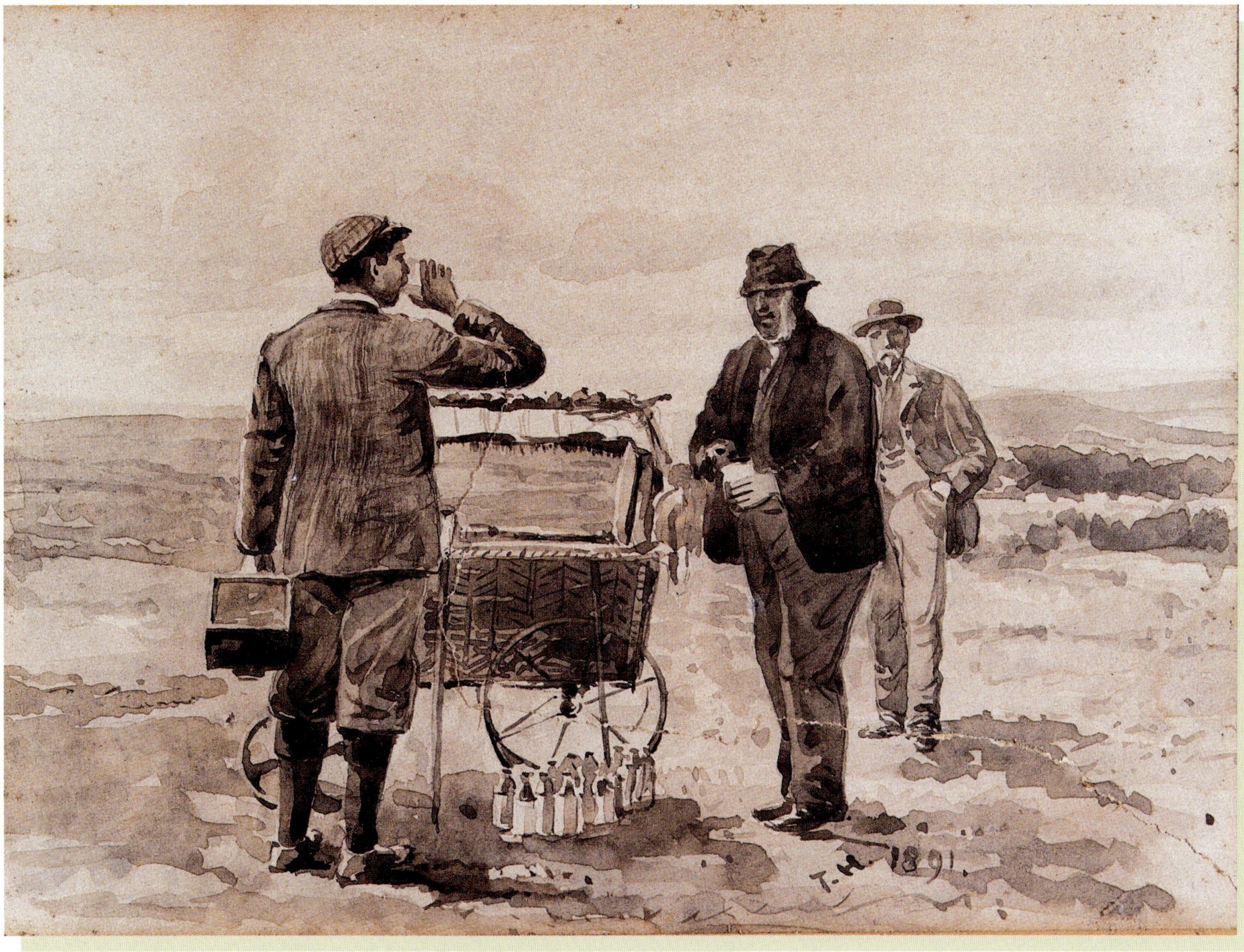
T. H. 1891.

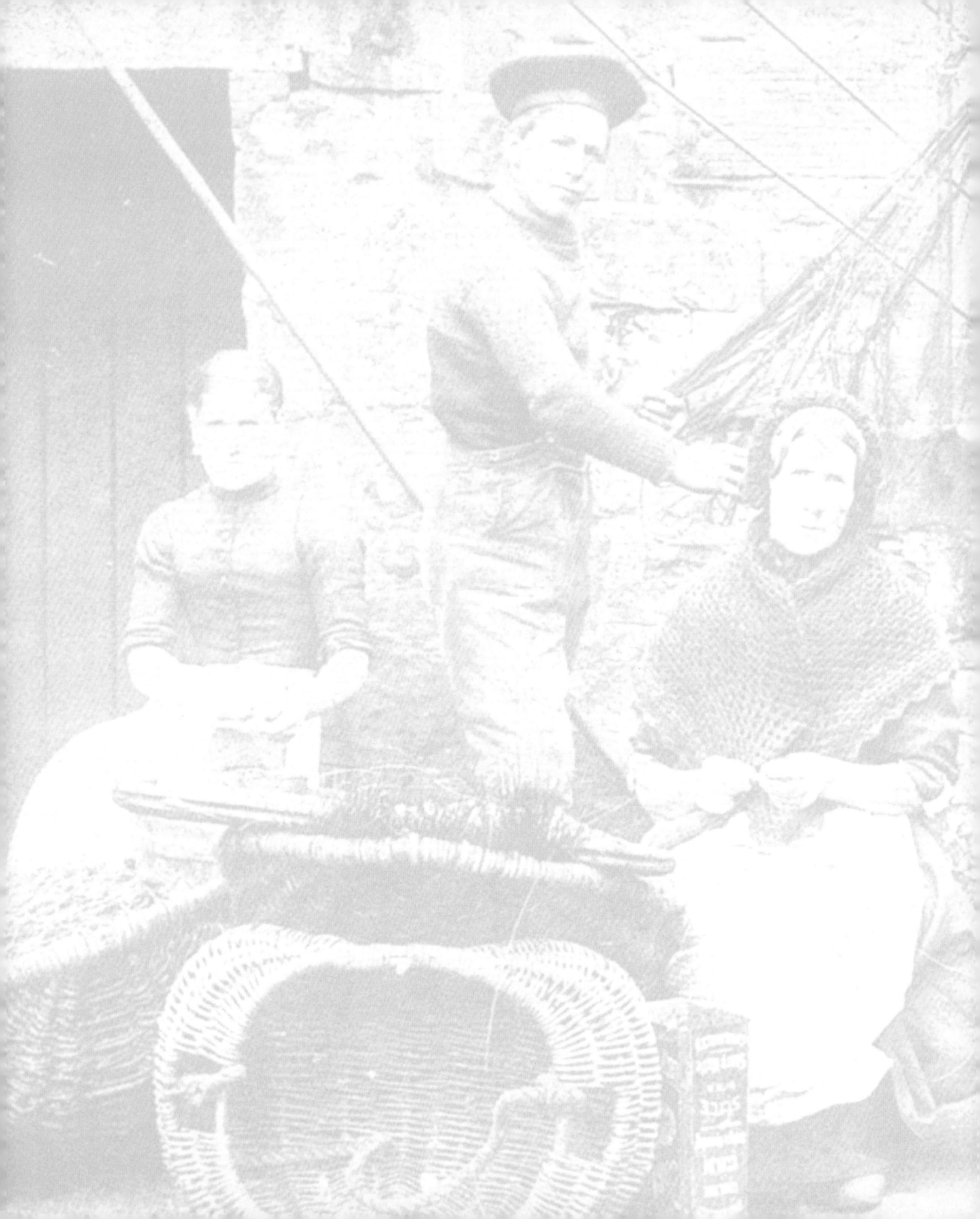

Caddies Comedians and Champions

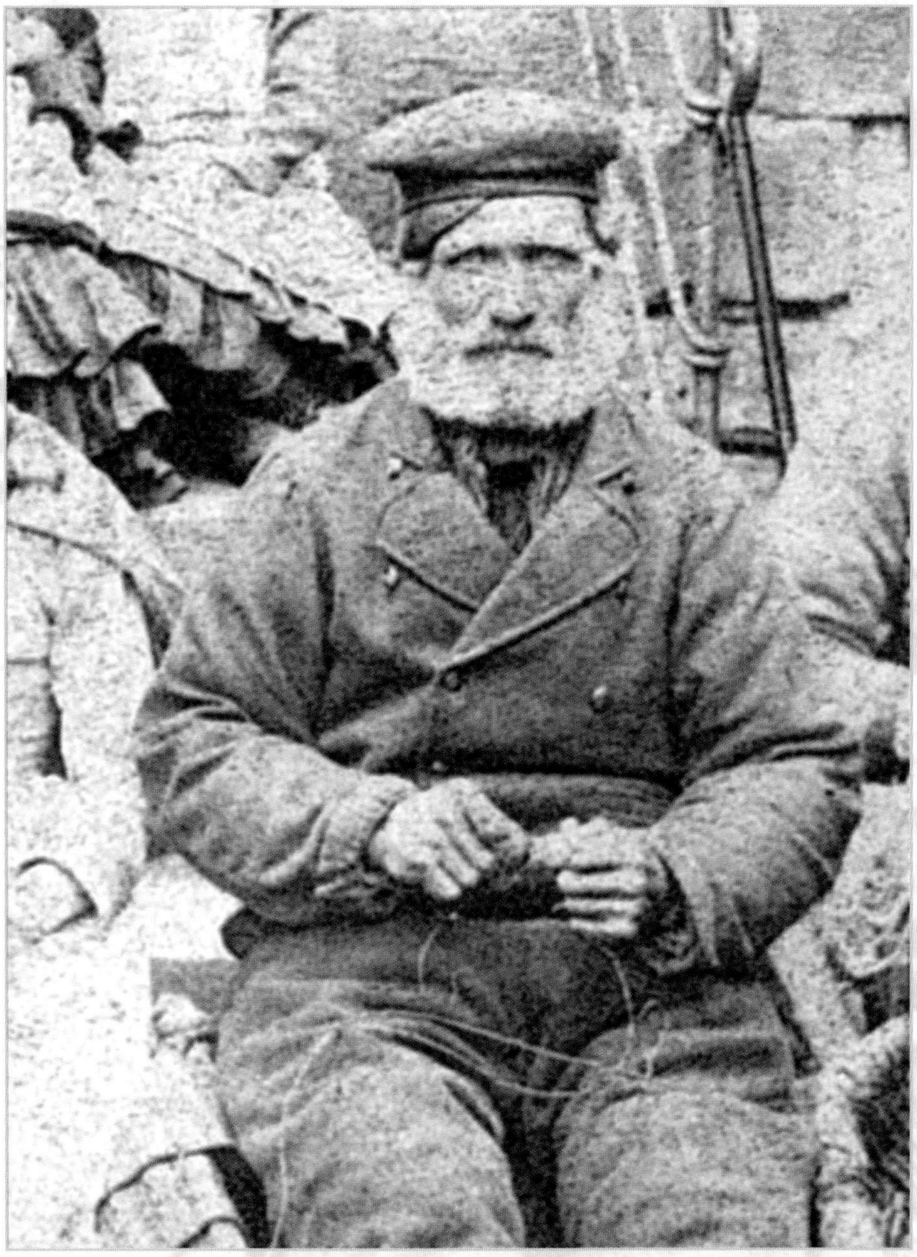

Caddies, Comedians and Champions

“THE SKIPPER”, DAVID FENTON

With his peaked cap contorted into an impossible shape, David Fenton, nicknamed The Skipper, features in dozens of ancient photographs of golfing groups in the 19th century. Hodge drew and painted him many times, a caddie of fearsome knowledge and dry wit whose services were always in demand. He belonged to that family of St. Andrews golf which, on the links at least, readily encompassed both rich and threadbare.

Certainly the most charming Hodge watercolour discovered in 1983 is “Stymie”, a study of three boy golfers posed in front of Old Tom Morris's shop at St. Andrews in 1882.

Whether the artist is commenting on the childish nature of the old golfing hazard (when one ball obstructed the path of another), which some members of the Royal & Ancient tried to remove from the rule book without success for generations, is anyone's guess.

What Hodge has left for certain is an early portrait of Sandy Herd, the boy kneeling, who became Open Champion at Hoylake 20 years later in 1902. He was 13 when Hodge painted this picture.

The boys are dressed in warm hand-me-downs with good, solid black boots, successful paid golfers to be, luckier members of the squad of caddies that haunted the links scratching a slight living and thankful to be wry court jesters to the gentlemen.

In the story of his golfing life published in 1923, Herd said:

The first golfer I caddied for was Mr. Thomas Hodge, who kept a boarding school at St. Andrews. He carried so many clubs – there were no golf bags at that time – that my arms were not long enough or strong enough to hold them and Mr. Hodge had often to turn back for clubs I had dropped on the links. ‘Dropping strokes is bad enough, laddie, but dropping clubs is worse’, Mr. Hodge used to say. Great was my mother's joy when I put the first five shillings earned as a caddie in her hands.

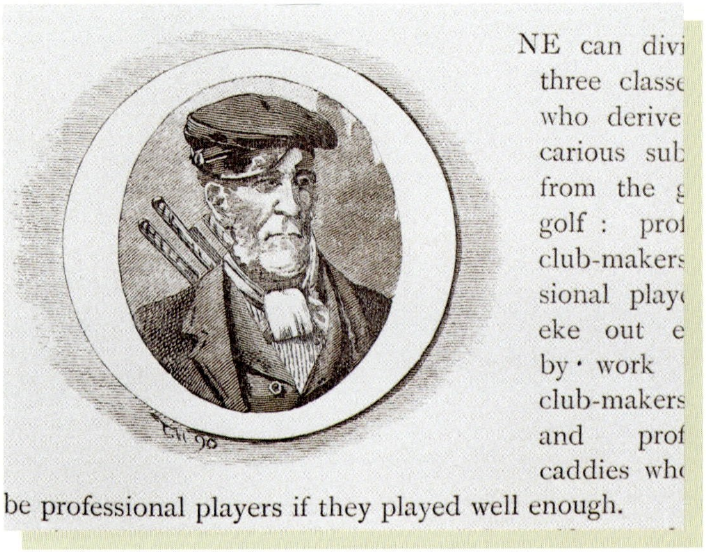
NE can divi
three classe
who derive
carious sub
from the g
golf : prof
club-makers
sional playe
eke out e
by · work
club-makers
and prof
caddies whe
be professional players if they played well enough.

Above: an illuminated letter used in the text of Badminton Golf 1890 bears the portrait of “Skipper” David Fenton.

Right: future champions, 1882.

Herd and his friends scavenged champagne corks from the rubbish tip behind the Royal & Ancient clubhouse and shaped them into golf balls. The corks were loaded with bits of metal and when painted became fair imitations of the real thing. Although there was an impassable social gulf between these lads and the club members, it did not prevent them from playing practical jokes. A favourite trick was to substitute plaster balls made in the old gutta moulds, when teeing-up for R & A members.

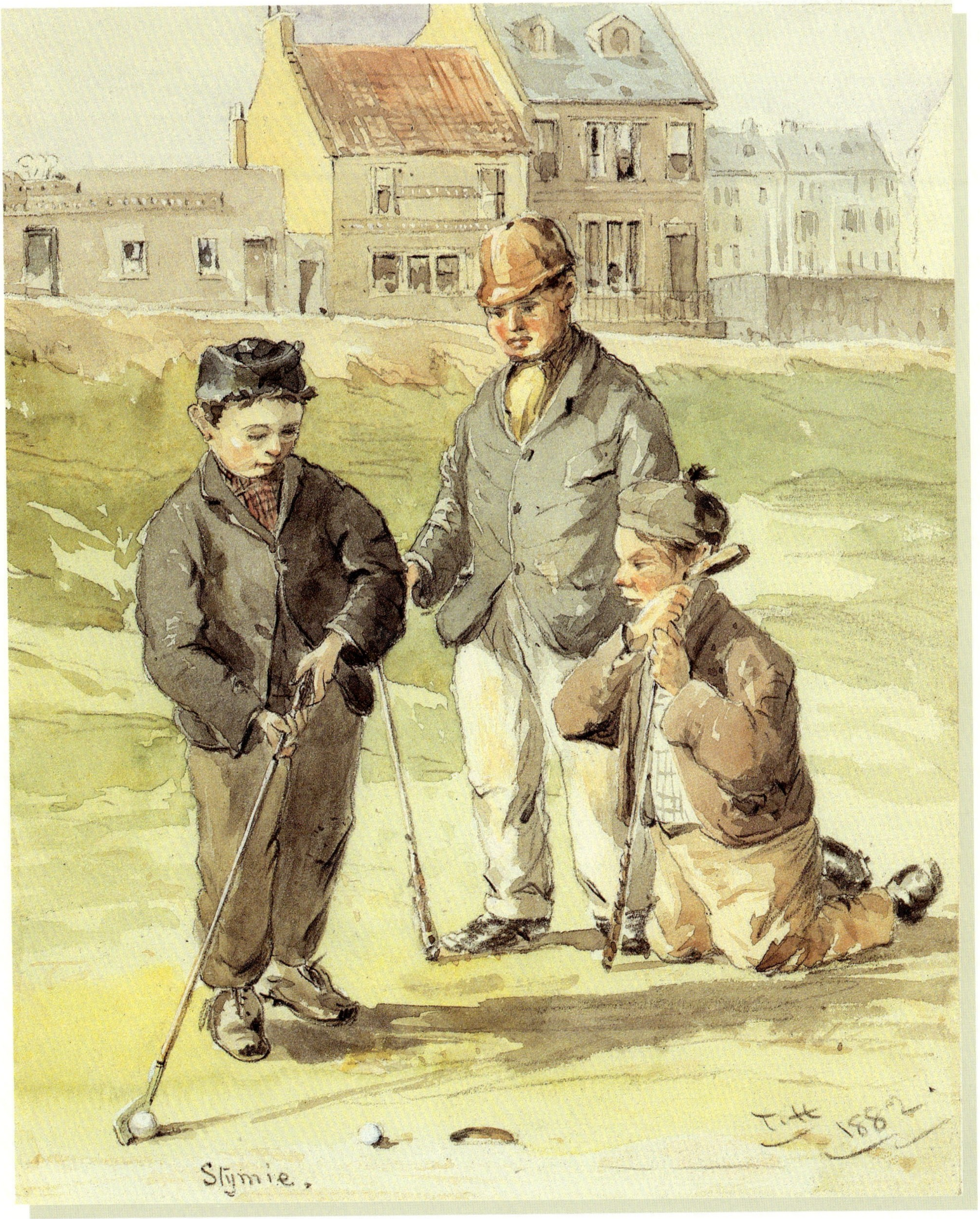
Stymie.
Tait 1882.

These exploded into a cloud of powder on the impact of the club and often began a chase across the course to avoid the wrath of the victim.

Humour could be a cruel and stupid brute in Victorian times as well. Herd and friends thought it a great laugh to throw pathetic creatures like the kilted and sporranned hanger-on Donald Blue, fully dressed and howling with rage into the waters of Swilcan Burn.

Blue clearly invited the ducking at times in return for a few coins and drams.

The other boys in Hodge's picture are not so easily identified. It has been suggested that the large youth in the centre, watching his friend try to trickle the ball round that of his partner, is one of the Kirkaldy clan. If so it must be Hugh Kirkaldy. Hugh and Andrew ("Andra") Kirkaldy – there was another golfing brother called John – were brilliant St. Andrews players. Hugh won the Open Championship in 1891 – the year Thomas Hodge produced a sepia wash portrait entitled "Kirkaldy – professional". Andra, the likely subject of this portrait, was twice runner-up, once to his brother in 1891. There was the little matter of fighting as one of Her Majesty Queen Victoria's soldiers in Africa which reduced Andra's opportunities.

Kirkaldy's chief claim to fame was as a long-reigning Goliath of the old links, second only to Old Tom Morris as a formidable presence, though a patriarch of an entirely different temperament.

Andra swore constantly like the rough trooper he once was. All his life he damned and blasted – and worse – at the high and mighty and got away with it because of the wicked imp of mischief in his eyes and his fiendish sense of timing. "For pity's sake dinna make me laugh, Andra", opponents would plead as they went round the course with the cunning old demon.

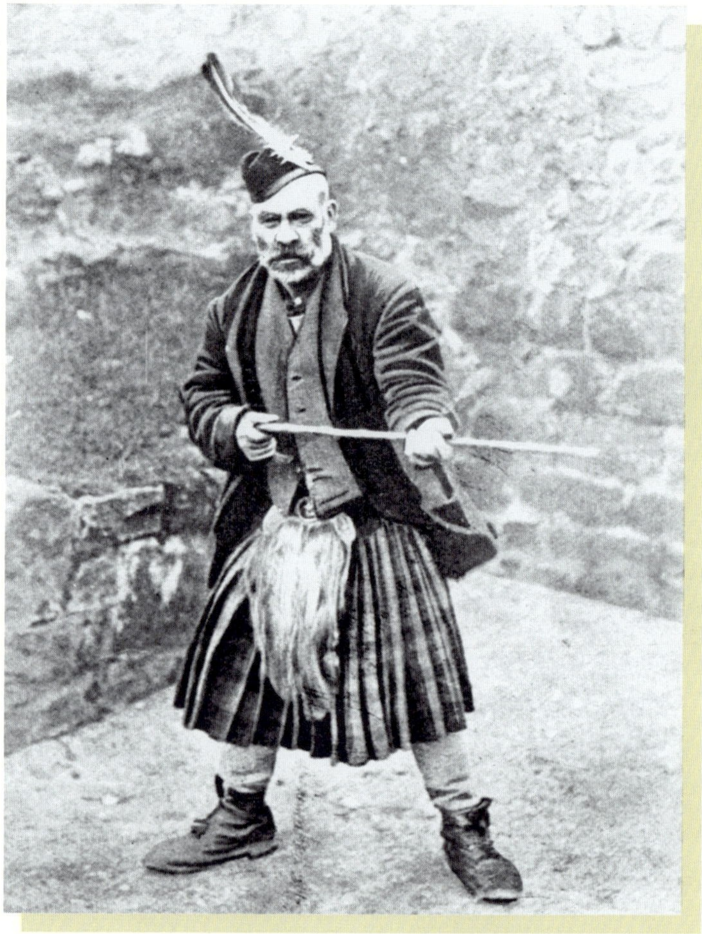

Above: Donald Blue, a slim-witted St. Andrews character whose fate was to be chased round the links and thrown into Swilcan Burn on high days and holidays. But there is plenty to suggest he encouraged the pantomime for the sake of a few coins and drams.

Andra's devil-may-care attitude served him well in the Highland Light Infantry, which he ran away to join as a boy in the late 1870s. He was twice shot in the leg and once in the arm at Tel-el-Kebir in the Egyptian campaign, where he narrowly escaped with his life at the hands of an Arab spearsman.

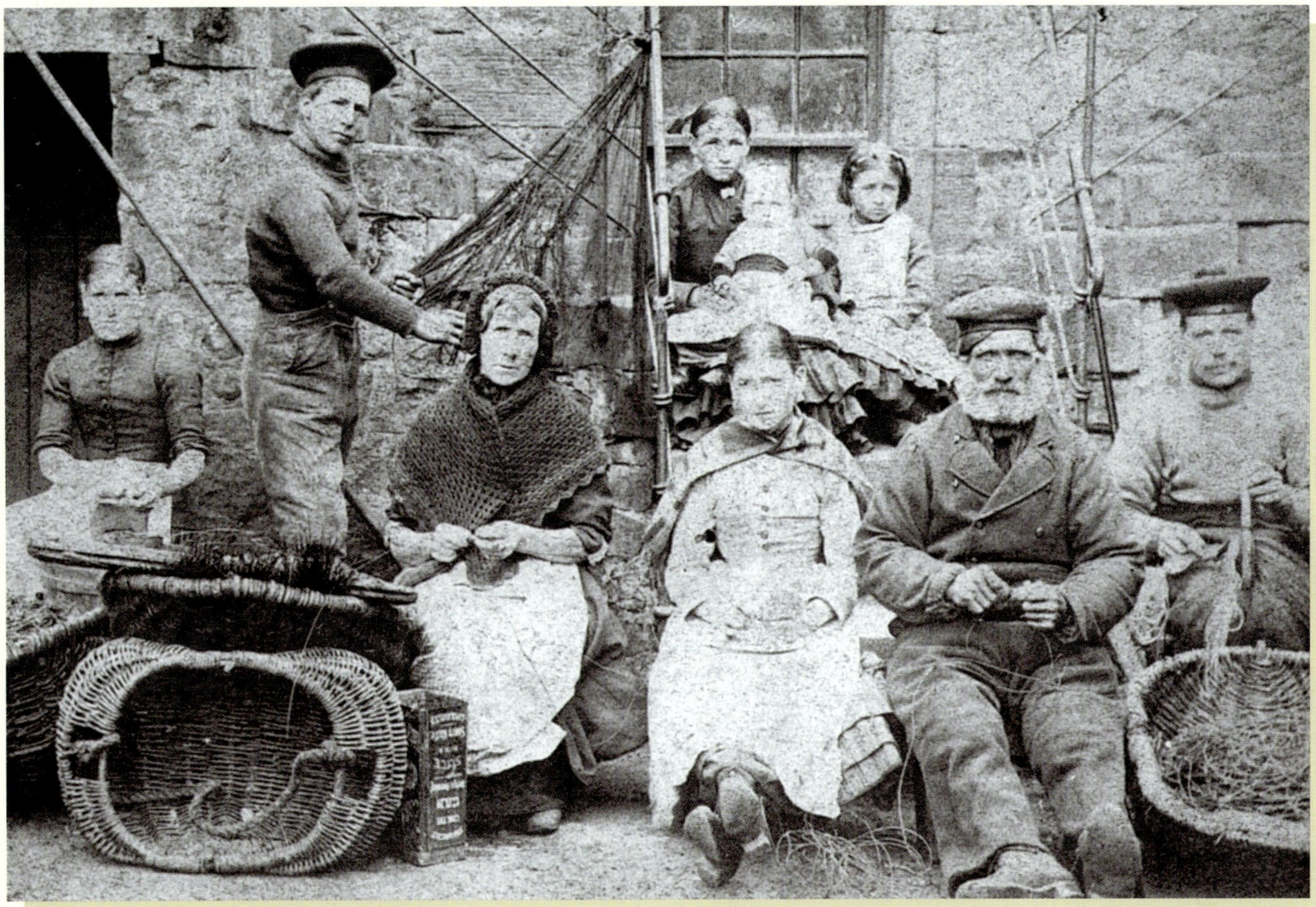

Above: caddies and champion golfers sprang from the poor fishing families of Fife. These are the Gourlays in 1890, dourly respectable.

An image Thomas Hodge always carried in his memory of St. Andrews links was that of a boy caddie eternally racing in the direction of his master, brandishing a fresh playing club. This nostalgic vignette, used several times, is reminiscent of the fluent oil sketches by Charles Lees that hang in the Royal & Ancient clubhouse, arguably the most lucid of all works of art on the game. Hodge must have admired Lees' gems throughout his long membership of the club.

In sport there are many relationships that can seem curious, if not verging on the ludicrous, to an outsider. And on the face of it, there is none odder than that of the golfer and his caddie. The caddie, or club carrier, is the golfer's course servant and guide, though often the caddie is a far better golfer than the man who is paying him. This was overwhelmingly true in the years of the first great golf boom in the 1880s and 1890s, spawning a thousand jokey cartoons for the likes of the London magazines *Punch* and *The Graphic*.

Yet given the curse of class division in Victorian British sports, especially in cricket, soccer and rugby, the gentlemen golfers in the St. Andrews of Hodge's day were comparatively decent in their treatment of those in their pay who were most crushingly unequal. When feckless and penniless Jock might be seen wearing his lordship's cast-off breeches and boots, it was accepted by many as being as close to an act of friendship as one of charity.

The caddies also maintained some self-respect by inventing an encyclopedia of bitter-sweet comment about their masters which helps fill scores of those little booklets on golf humour still sold in St. Andrews and elsewhere. Those who were of sterner stuff left Britain permanently to export golf to all points of the globe before the temptation to drown their sorrows in malt whisky could wreck their health and hopes.

JAMIE ANDERSON

A stern watercolour profile inscribed by Hodge *"Semper rid. May 80"*, which, it can be guessed, translates as "always laughing". The number 87 in a circle is probably a scoring total. The dour Anderson was Open Golf Champion in 1877, 1878 and 1879. This portrait was painted when he was 38 years old in 1880. Curiously enough, that year, Anderson refused to defend his title at Musselburgh

due to the shortness of notice given of the venue.

In fact, the hazards at Musselburgh for visiting professional golfers had nothing to do with the links, but everything to do with gangs of violent spectators.

Jamie's portrait reflects his nature. His machine-like play seldom faltered; plain driving, perfect approach shots, sure putting. He was born into the caddying world of St. Andrews in 1842, the son of "Old Daw" Anderson, a famous character-landmark of the links who sold ginger beer to the players from a wheeled wickerwork cart he pulled round the course. Jamie was an excellent club maker, working in St. Andrews, Ardeer and Perth, then back in St. Andrews. For all his steadiness, he died in Dysart Combination Poor House at Perth aged 63 in 1905.

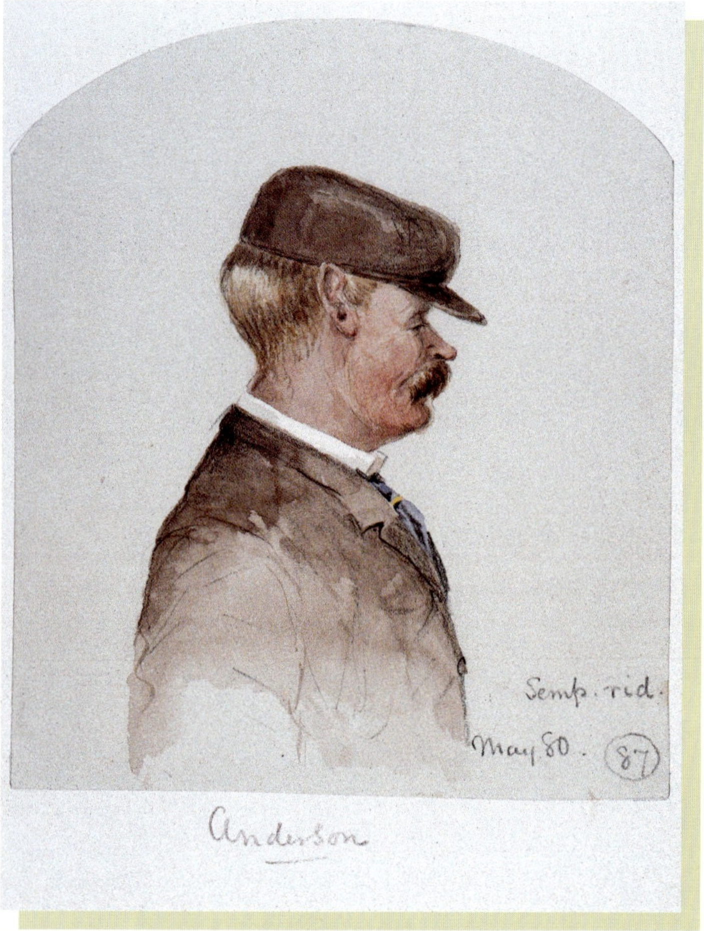

Above: Jamie Anderson by Hodge.

Right: "Daw" Anderson by Hodge.

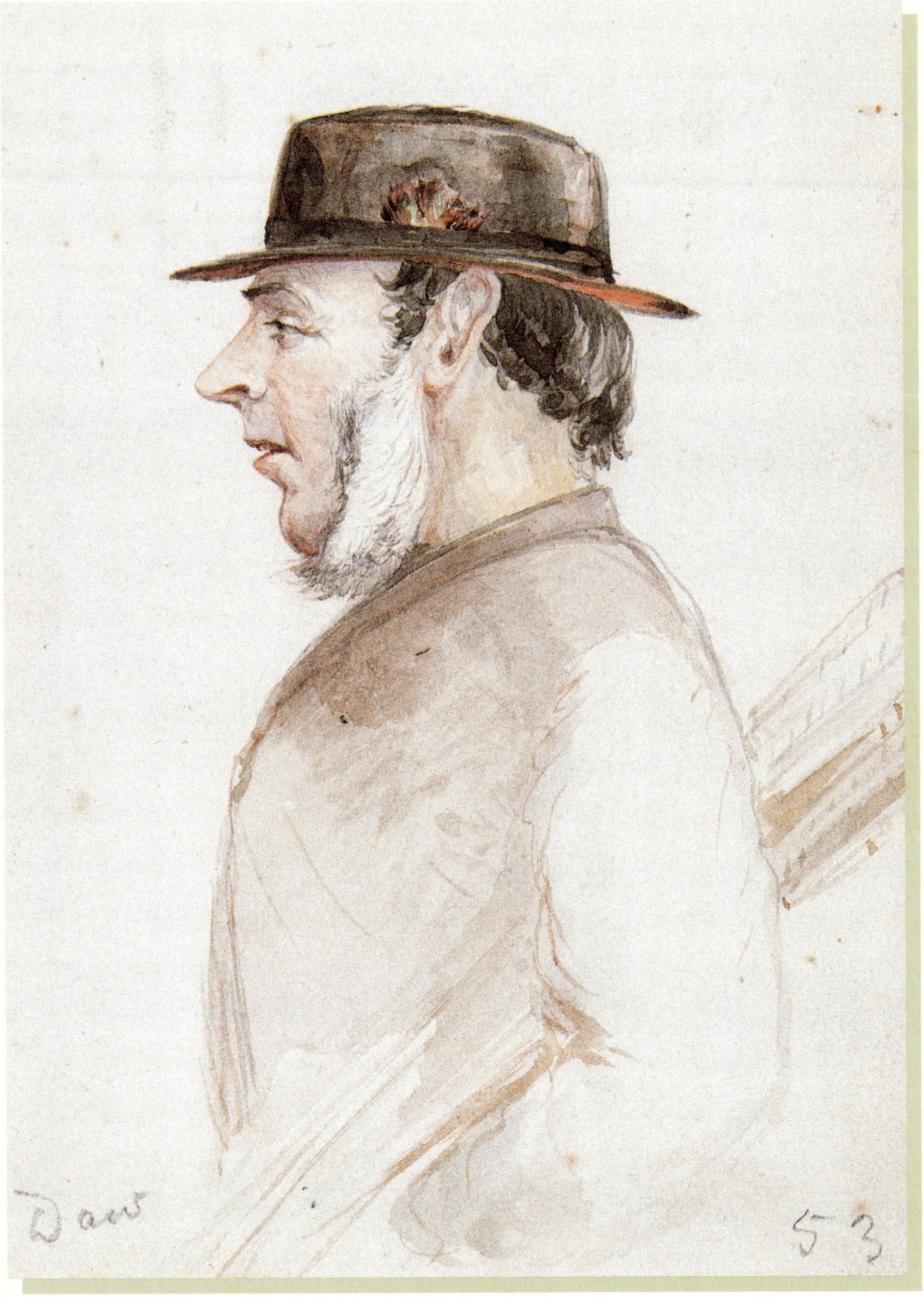
Daw
53

Anderson's brother David was the founder of D. Anderson and Sons, club and ball makers, who exported golf equipment world wide. Old Daw, a skilled feathery ball maker in his day, died in 1901 aged 80.

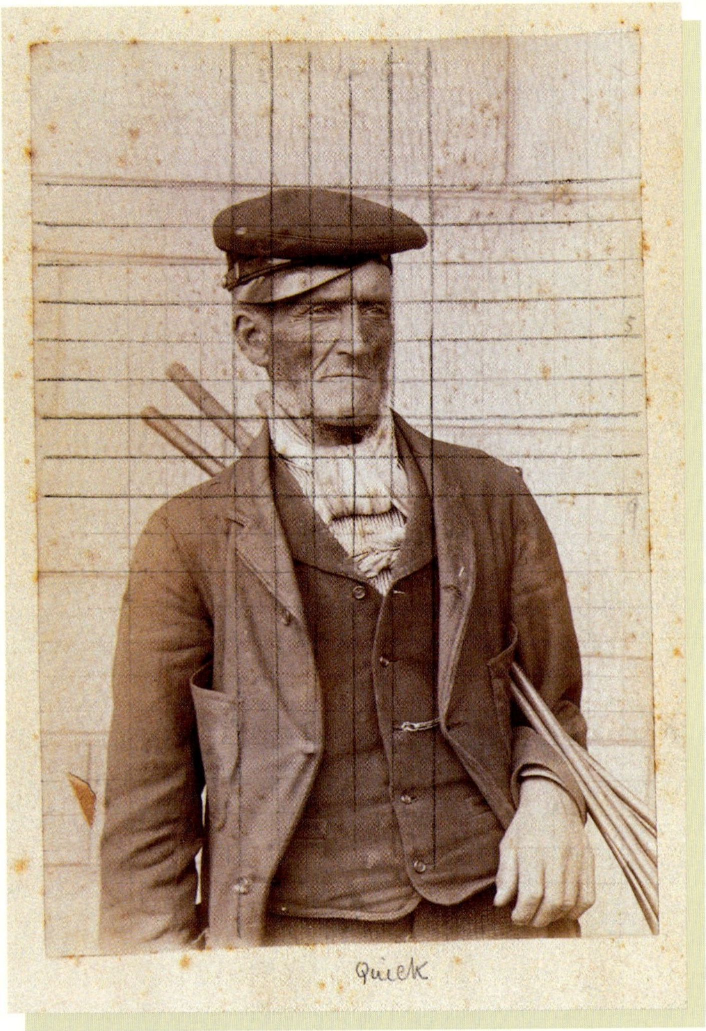

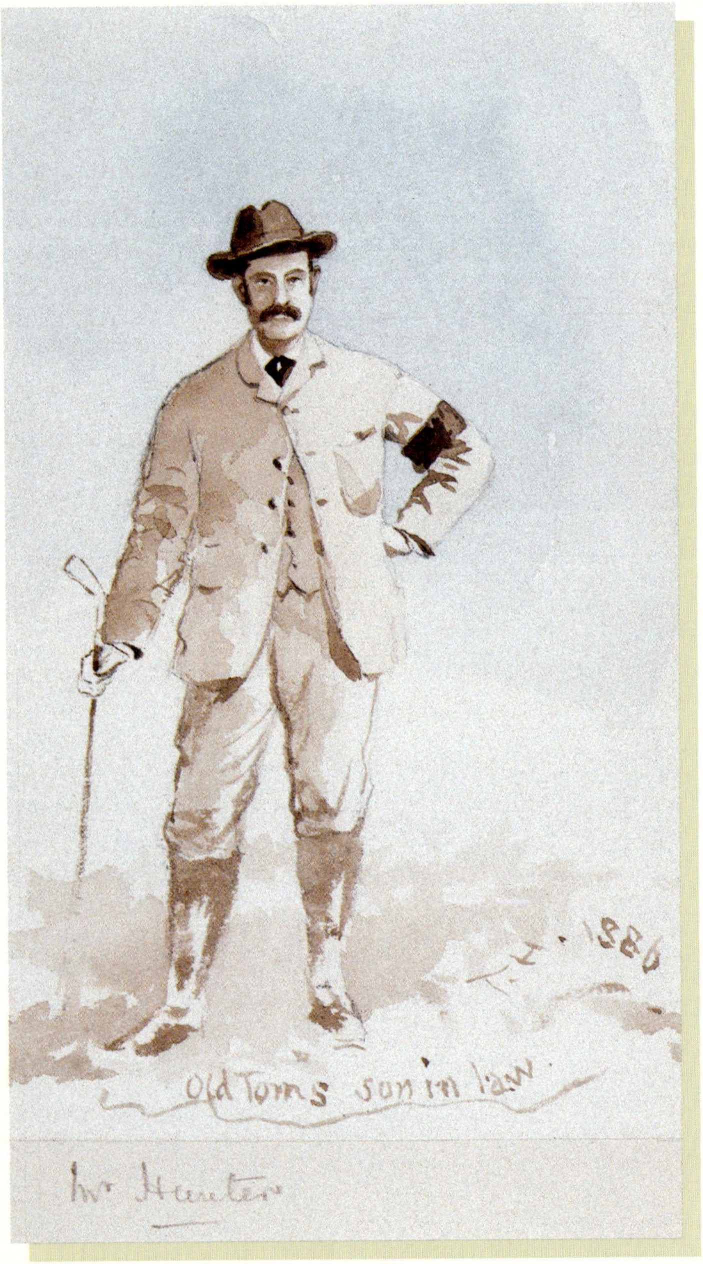

Above: this photograph from a Hodge album shows how he squared up his reference ready for a quick drawing or painting if requested by a publisher. This image of David Fenton, "The Skipper", was always in demand.

Left: Mr. Hunter, Old Tom Morris's son-in-law, and a "good golfer".

ROBERT FORGAN

Thomas Hodge's portraits were occasionally close to works of genius. Unfortunately, in the 90 years of their total neglect and casual dispersal Lord knows where, many were also divorced from Hodge's captions. This St. Andrews stalwart with the monumental white whiskers has lost his neat Hodge title. However, he bears a striking resemblance to the club maker Robert Forgan (1824–1900) who continued the peerless work of his uncle Hugh Philp on Philp's death in 1856.

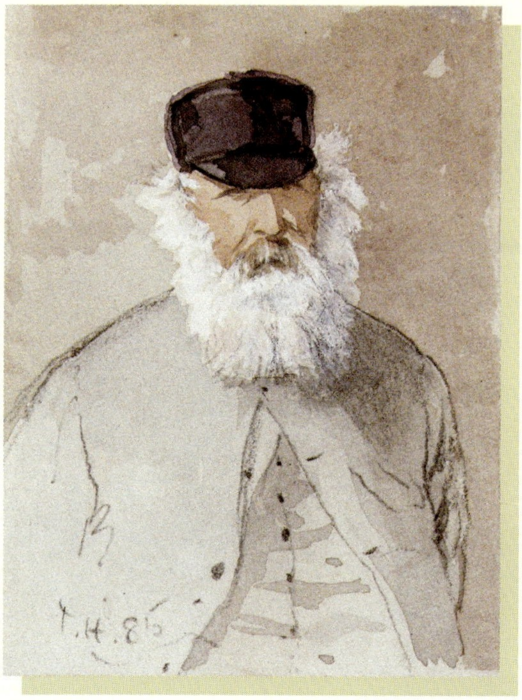

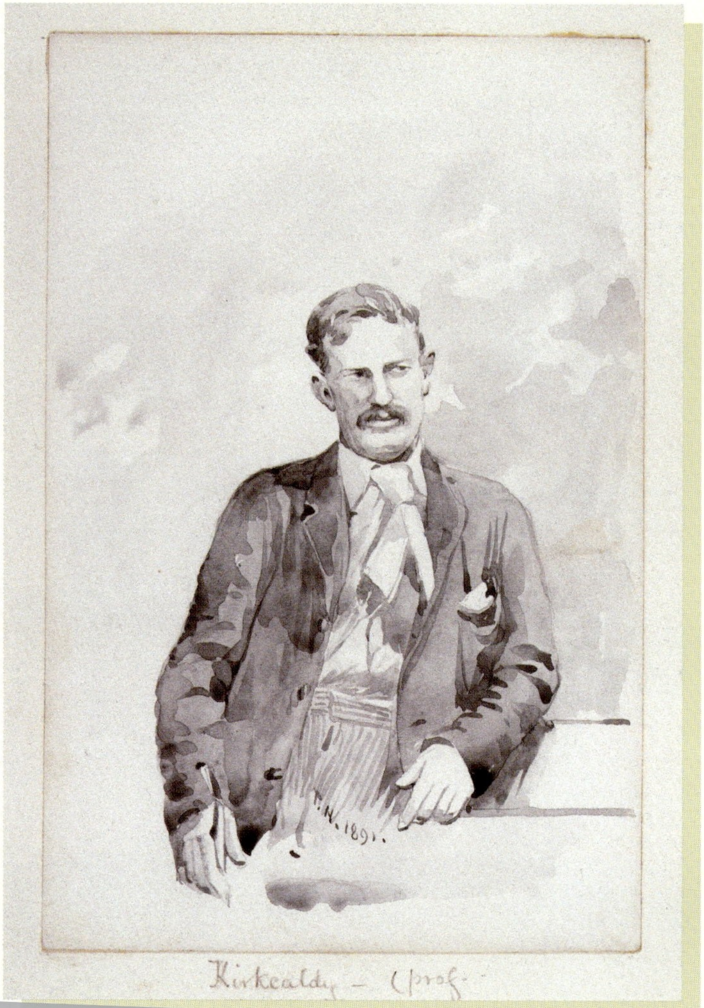

KIRKALDY

Hugh Kirkaldy, winner of the Open Championship held at St. Andrews in 1891, or his brother Andrew who finished second two strokes behind him in that year. Hodge has captioned the sketch simply *"Kirkaldy – 'prof'."* However, the quizzical cock of the head and the narrow glance suggest strongly that this is indeed the terrifying Andrew (or Andra!) as a young man. After finishing in the top echelons of the Open throughout the 1890s, Andra eventually became the custodian of St. Andrews' links for the Royal & Ancient. His worldwide fame earned a giant oil painting on the walls of the Royal & Ancient club house.

Above: possibly club maker Robert Forgan.

Left: the look of Andra Kirkaldy.

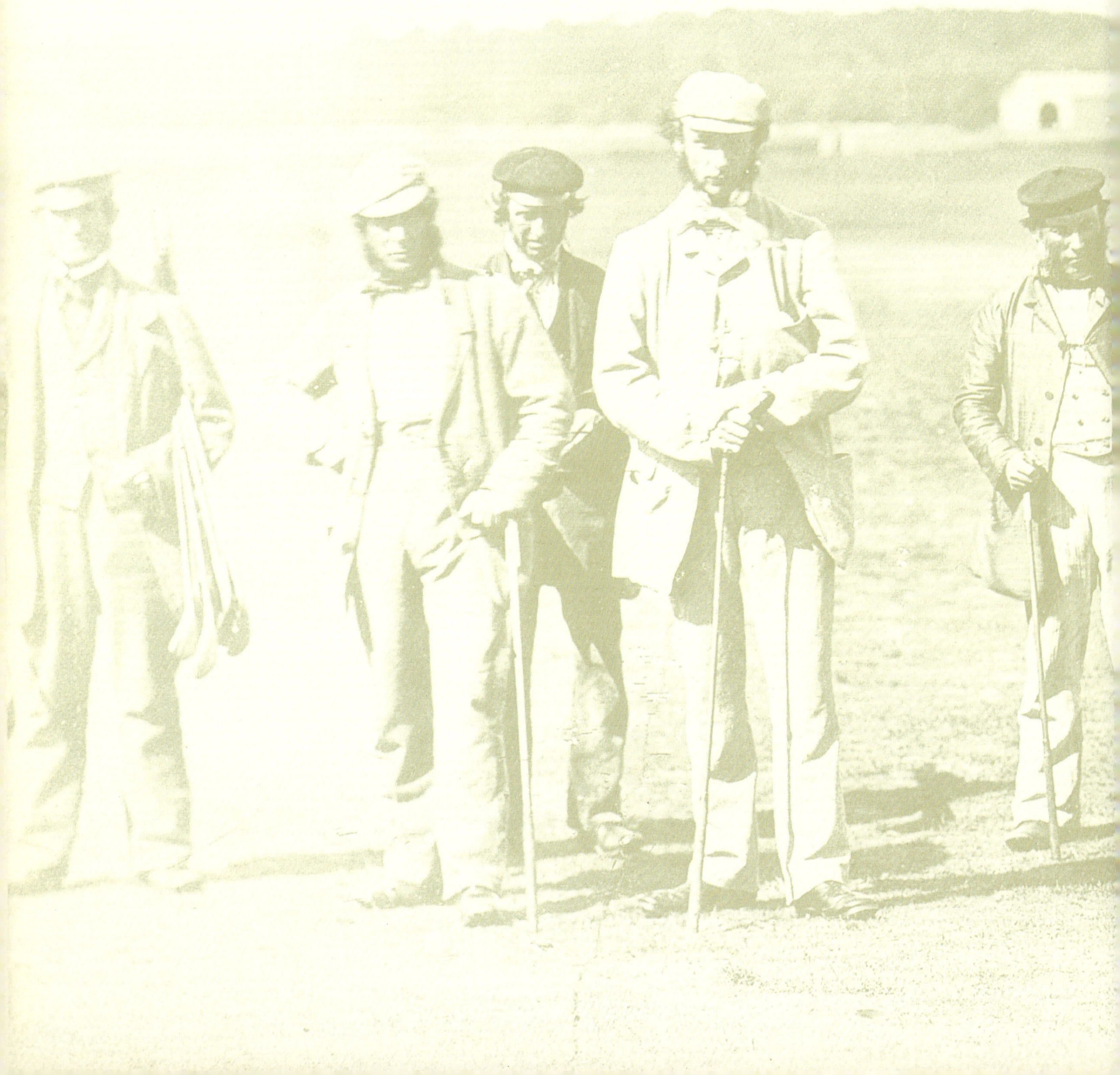

Ghostly Images of Golf

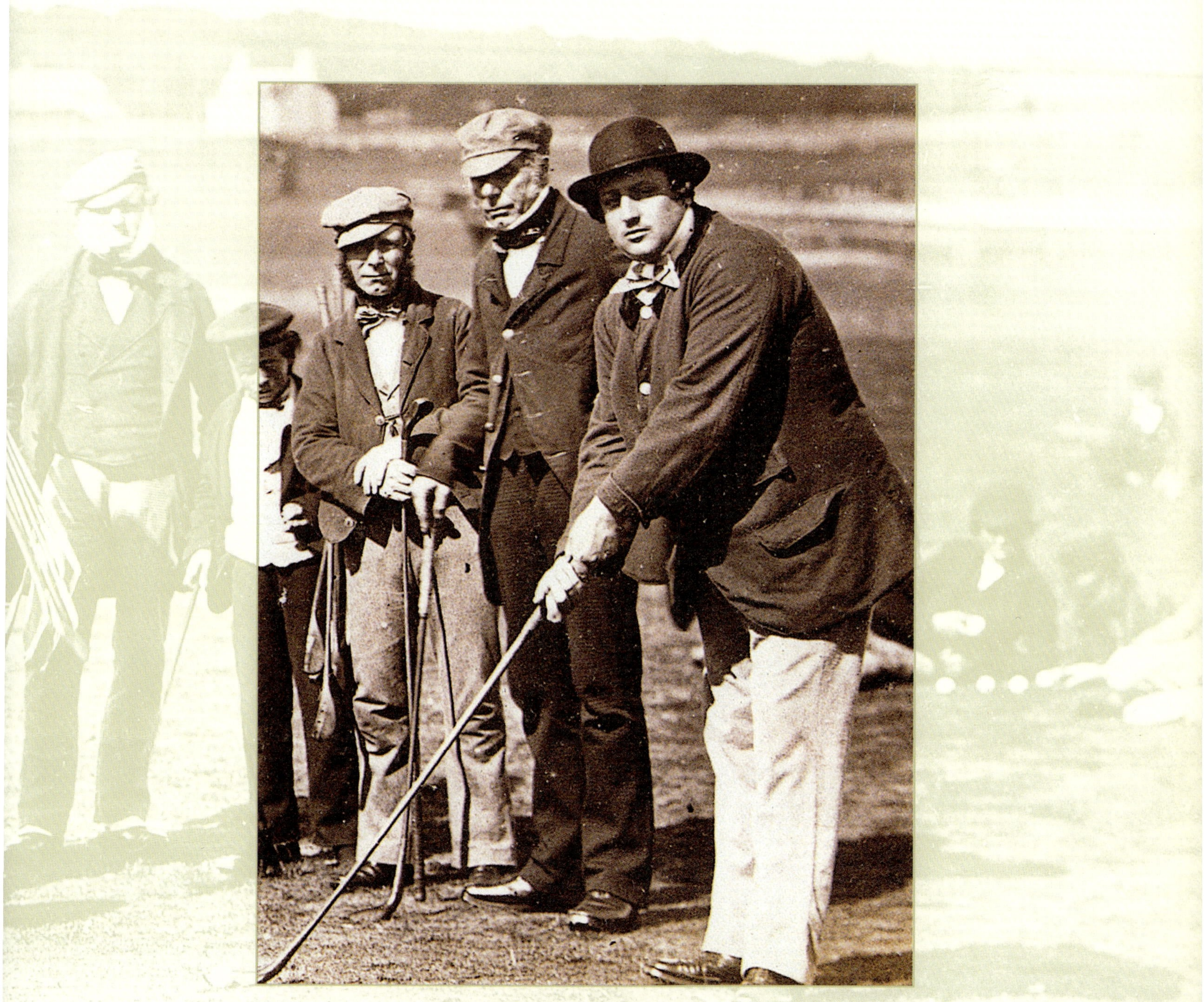

Ghostly Images of Golf

The following pages, including this one, contain photographs exactly as they were extracted from Hodge's tattered and crumbling albums rescued by his granddaughter Norah Sheward. They are all fairly well known, and pristine examples have been used in countless modern golf history books and as the basis of new paintings and prints. The ones here have become faded, yellowed and stained by time and carelessness in the 100 to 140 years since they were first printed. In many ways this has failed to diminish the pictures. Rather, it has given them a curious antiquity.

If you can sense the past, here it is, the actors on golf's most famous stage peering faintly into the next millennium from another age. The first photograph shows Old Tom Morris and his son Young Tom, not long before catastrophe enveloped the family with the death of Young Tom's wife and baby, then Young Tom's death as well. No Thomas Hodge paintings of Young Tom Morris have been discovered to date. The deep sense of loss which engulfed St. Andrews may have been too much to bear for the Hodge family as well.

Right: a clipping from a newspaper covering the match that killed Young Tom Morris in 1875.

Far right: Old Tom Morris and his son Young Tom.

GOLF.

MATCH AT ST. ANDREWS.

The match, for £50 a side, between Mr Arthur Molesworth of Westward Ho! and Tom Morris, jun, of St Andrews, which commenced last week, was continued on the St Andrews Links on Saturday, when the seventh and eighth rounds were played. The weather was exceedingly stormy, and during the forenoon heavy showers of snow fell at intervals, covering the green with a considerable coating, necessitating the sweeping of the putting green and the use of red balls. Under such circumstances it might be supposed that the play would be bad, but the scores made were very fair. In the first turn Mr Molesworth had the pull, and came in 2 holes up. He also secured the afternoon round by 1 hole, making him 3 holes and 2 rounds ahead on the day's play. Six rounds, or 108 holes, had now been played, Young Tom having the lead of 9 in holes and 2 in rounds. The approximated scores were :—Seventh Round : Mr Molesworth, out 50, in 50—total, 100. Young Tom, out 48, in 48—total 96. Eighth round : Mr Molesworth, out 47, in 50—total, 97. Young Tom, out 47, in 44—total, 91. The match was resumed on Monday, and the green was several inches deep with snow, while heavy showers fell at intervals, accompanied by a strong breeze from the sea. Morris was disinclined to proceed, and the umpire (Mr Oliphant of Rossie) was also of opinion that it was not weather for golf, but Mr Molesworth and his father, Captain Molesworth, stated that it would inconvenience them to delay, and a start was at once made, despite the unfavourable aspect of affairs, a goodly number of spectators accompanying the golfers round the holes. The game at start stood—Morris, 9 up in holes and 2 in rounds. The first hole fell to Morris, while the second was gained by his opponent. They continued thus to give and take, and the round terminated in favour of Mr Molesworth by 1 hole. Morris, however, in the afternoon had decidedly the best of the game, and won the round by 5 holes, making him 4 up on the day's play. The players experienced considerable difficulty, their balls repeatedly being buried in a wreath of snow, while on the green putting was almost an impossibility, and the balls had invariably to be lifted into the hole. The scores were thus necessarily high, the approximation being—Ninth round, Tom Morris 112, Mr Molesworth 115 ; tenth round, Tom Morris 100, Mr Molesworth 118.

Tuesday was the sixth and concluding day, and with a double issue, one half of the stakes depending on the winning of most holes, the other half for the winning of most rounds, Mr Molesworth getting a third. The first five days' play, or 10 rounds, left the game in favour of young Tom by 13 holes and two in rounds, and in the last two rounds played to-day this result has been almost unaltered. The eleventh round was halved. In the last young Tom won the match by 11 up, with 10 to play. He also has the pull by two in rounds, and is thus victor in both issues. Owing to the snow, the play during the last two days was attended with considerable difficulty, and the scores made were necessarily high all through the match. Mr Molesworth has displayed considerable pluck, and played an excellent game, especially in driving, but being a stranger to the St Andrews Links, and unacquainted with such a diversified course, his odds of a third scarcely put him on an equality with his professional antagonist. During the progress of the match large crowds accompanied the players, and a considerable amount of interest has also been manifested by golfers in all parts of the country.

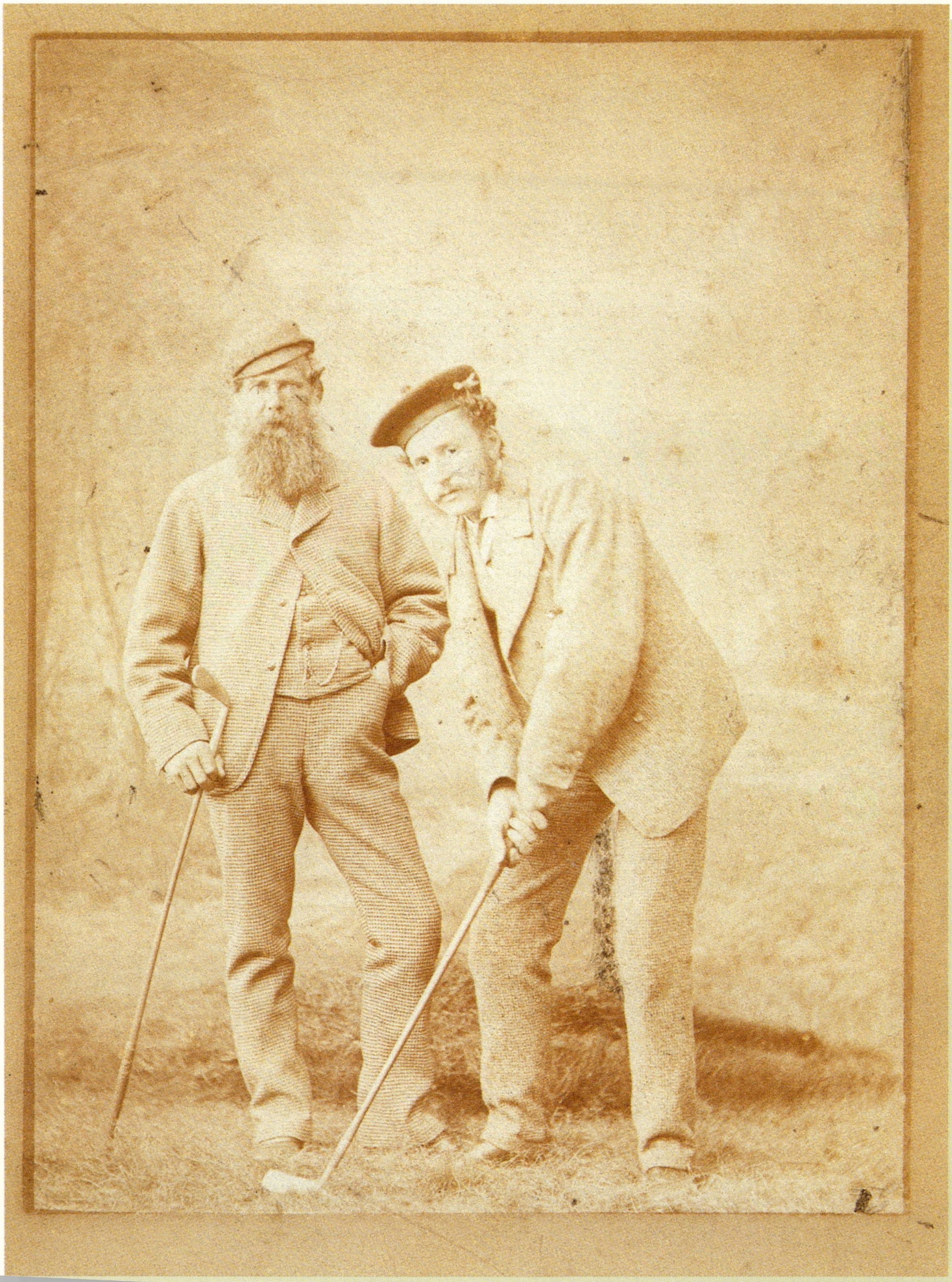

Seven men stand at the first hole at St. Andrews in this group taken by the esteemed local photographer, Thomas Rodger. They include the protagonists in the greatest golf match never played, Allan Robertson and Old Tom Morris versus Willie Dunn and Willie Park. Left to right are the club maker James Wilson and Bob Andrew ("The Rook"), caddying for Willie Dunn who is addressing the ball, and Willie Park. In front, club over his shoulder, and with the beginnings of his pawky smile on his comedian's mouth, is Allan Robertson, then Daw Anderson (caddie) and finally Tom Morris ("Old Tom").

Alongside Tom, but torn off this print, was Bob Kirk, also caddying for the St. Andrews giants; that is, he would have done if the match could have been arranged. Such a clash cost a great deal of money; £400 was at stake when the Robertson-Morris pair defeated the brothers Dunn in 1849, a breathtaking figure in real terms of the day. This takes no account of the heavy betting which stimulated golf as it did other sporting combats of the period like pugilism, pedestrianism, cricket and horse racing.

The principals in this picture are nattily dressed and exude self-possession. They knew their worth, Dunn in his black velvet cap and sharp check suit, Robertson in his favourite red jacket which enhanced his trimly powerful figure. Both Allan and Tom Morris were then close to being pocket Hercules, practically twins except for the marginally more cocky and aggressive demeanour of Robertson. Not a man to cross, as Old Tom found when they quarrelled over the new gutty ball which threatened Robertson's living as a feathery ball manufacturer.

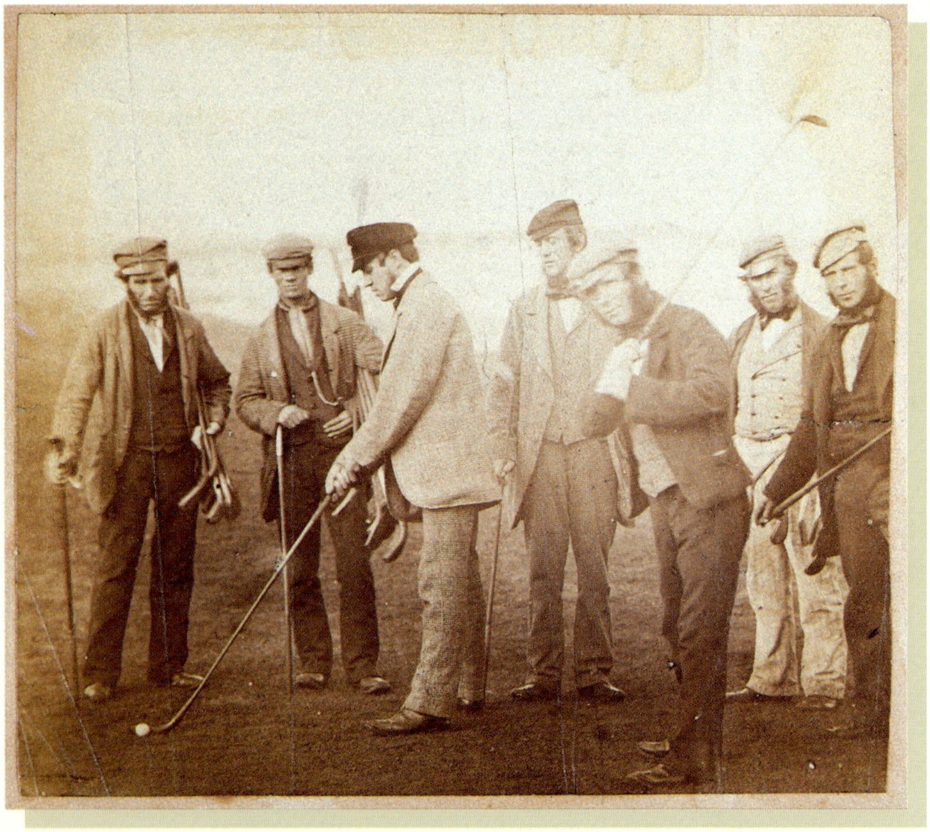

Left: Thomas Rodger's photograph of possibly the greatest golf match never played at St. Andrews.

Entitled "Professional Golfers No.1" in Thomas Hodge's neat lettering, this group was used by the artist to create one of golf's better-known paintings, of Allan Robertson and Old Tom Morris together. Hodge took the pairing exactly as it is seen within this photograph and used it as an illustration in the *Badminton Golf* volume of 1890. This sketch in its turn was plagiarised endlessly, becoming the basis of several modern paintings and prints.

Below, left to right: James Wilson (club maker), Willie Dunn, Bob Andrew ("The Rook"), Willie Park, Tom Morris, Allan Robertson (leaning forward, club in hand), "Daw" Anderson and Bob Kirk. In his own caption, Hodge writes all the names in his usual style except for Robertson, who, as ever, earns the accolade of being described simply as "ALLAN" in capital letters. Robertson's death in 1859 at the age of 44 must have been a great shock for the 32-year-old Hodge, who had lived in St. Andrews for only a few years and had found a hero to worship.

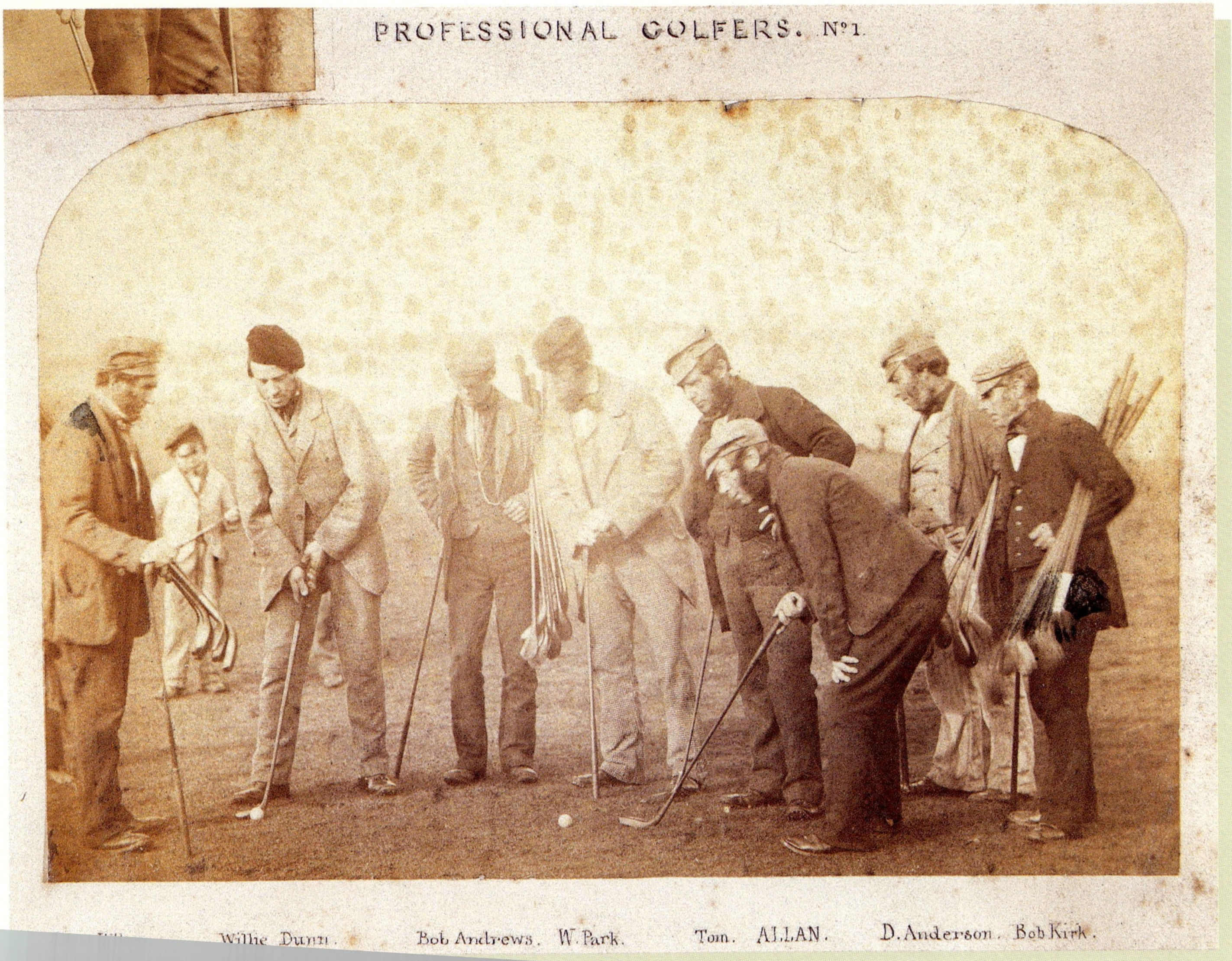

Below: "Professional Golfers No.2" shows the paid players at the 1864 tournament at Perth. Young Tom Morris, then a child prodigy, rests an arm on his father's shoulder. Willie Park is extreme left, Bob Andrew extreme right, says Hodge's caption.

Right: a newspaper clipping marking the match between Tom Morris and Willie Park in 1871.

APRIL **GOLF.—MORRIS v PARK, FOR £200.** 1871

The final contest in this great match, for £100 a side, between W. Park of Musselburgh and Tom Morris of St Andrews, was to have been decided at Musselburgh Green, on Friday last. Play was very evenly balanced until six holes only remained to be decided, and at that stage of the game, the lookers on displaying a considerable amount of animus, the referee (Mr R. Chambers, jun) very properly decided that, to avoid any breach of the peace, which was inevitable, the remainder of the competition should be postponed until the following day. Park, however, persisted in concluding the game as far as he was concerned, and claimed the stakes. On Saturday morning, at eleven a.m., in accordance with the referee's decision, both men appeared on the ground, but Park persisted in his claim to have the stakes, on the ground that he had played out the match on the day fixed by the articles, viz, April 22; that no man had any power to stop the play in the middle of the game; that as Morris had refused to play out the last six holes when called on by him he had done so by himself, and, therefore, won the match. He accordingly refused to play the six holes with Morris unless a new match was made. Mr Chambers, not to be daunted, with a firmness worthy of emulation, thereupon ordered Morris to walk over the course, which he did, holing out the six holes from Mrs Forman's in 4, 4, 5, 5, 6, and 4 strokes respectively. At the conclusion Morris and the referee, as might have been anticipated from the unruly behaviour of a portion of the bystanders on the previous day, were loudly hissed. The referee afterwards handed the stakeholder his decision in writing, which was as follows:—"As referee in the match between Morris and Park on Musselburgh Links, I have to certify that the first 30 holes were played on April 22, and, in terms of my decision, the remaining six holes were played by Morris this day, Park declining to finish the game. I therefore declare Morris to be the winner. (Signed) R. CHAMBERS, JUN.—Musselburgh, April 23, 1870." We understand that Park intends to try his luck in the County Court, and we append a copy of the articles to enable our readers to form their own opinion of his chance of success:—"Musselburgh, March 8, 1870.—We, the undersigned, hereby agree to commence to play our match at golf, for £100 sterling a side, on Tuesday, April 12, and that on St Andrews Links, at twelve o'clock; on Prestwick, April 15; North Berwick, April 19; and on Musselburgh Links, April 22—to play at same hour (twelve o'clock) as at St Andrews. (Signed) TOM MORRIS, WILLIE PARK." Mr R. Dudgeon was stakeholder.

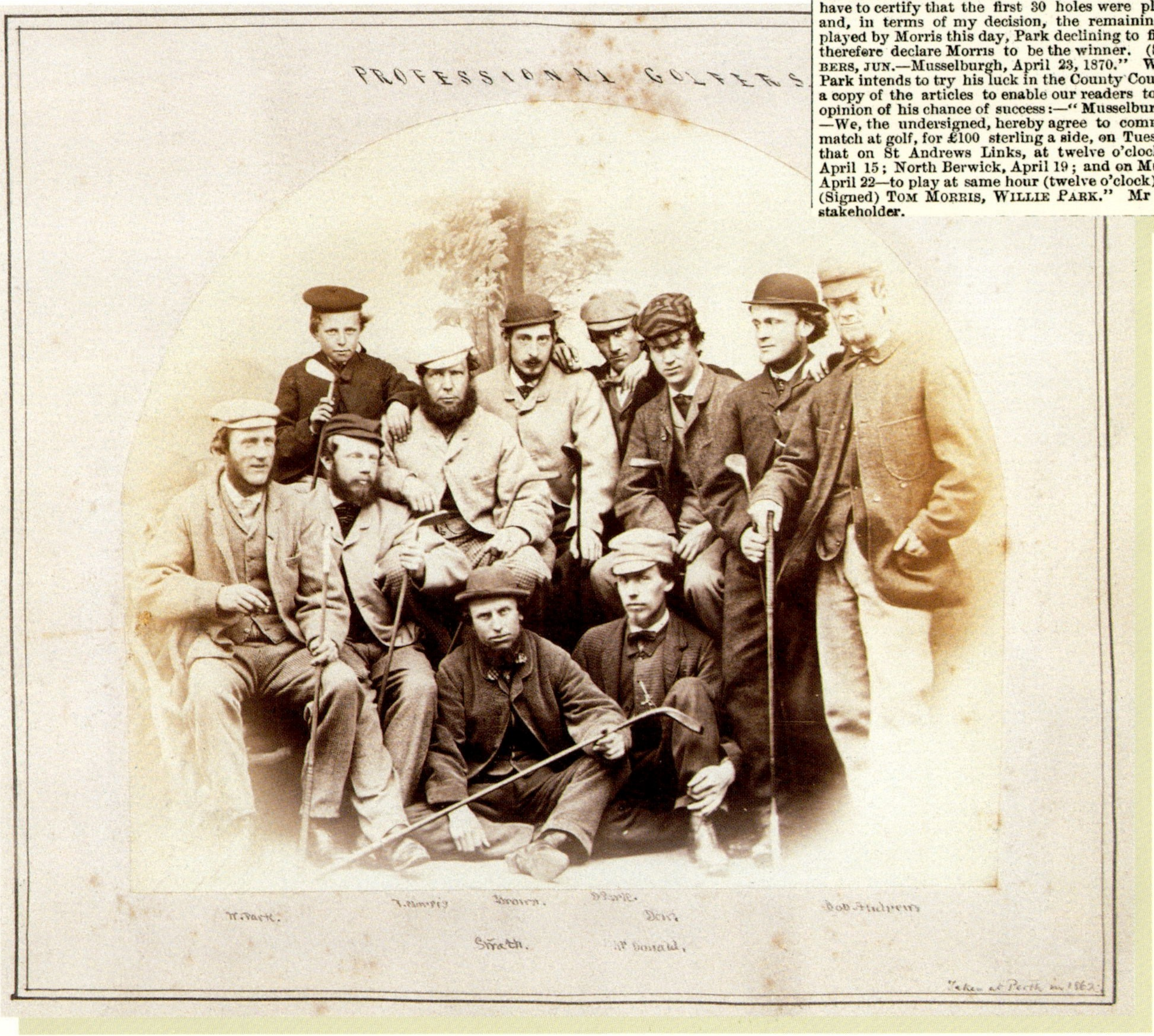

Below: A variation of a well known larger group. Left to right: Mr. George Whyte Melville, Admiral Maitland Dougall, Mr. George Glennie, Col. J. O. Fairlie, Sandy Pirie (caddie). This group was used on page 207 of Everard's history of the R & A.

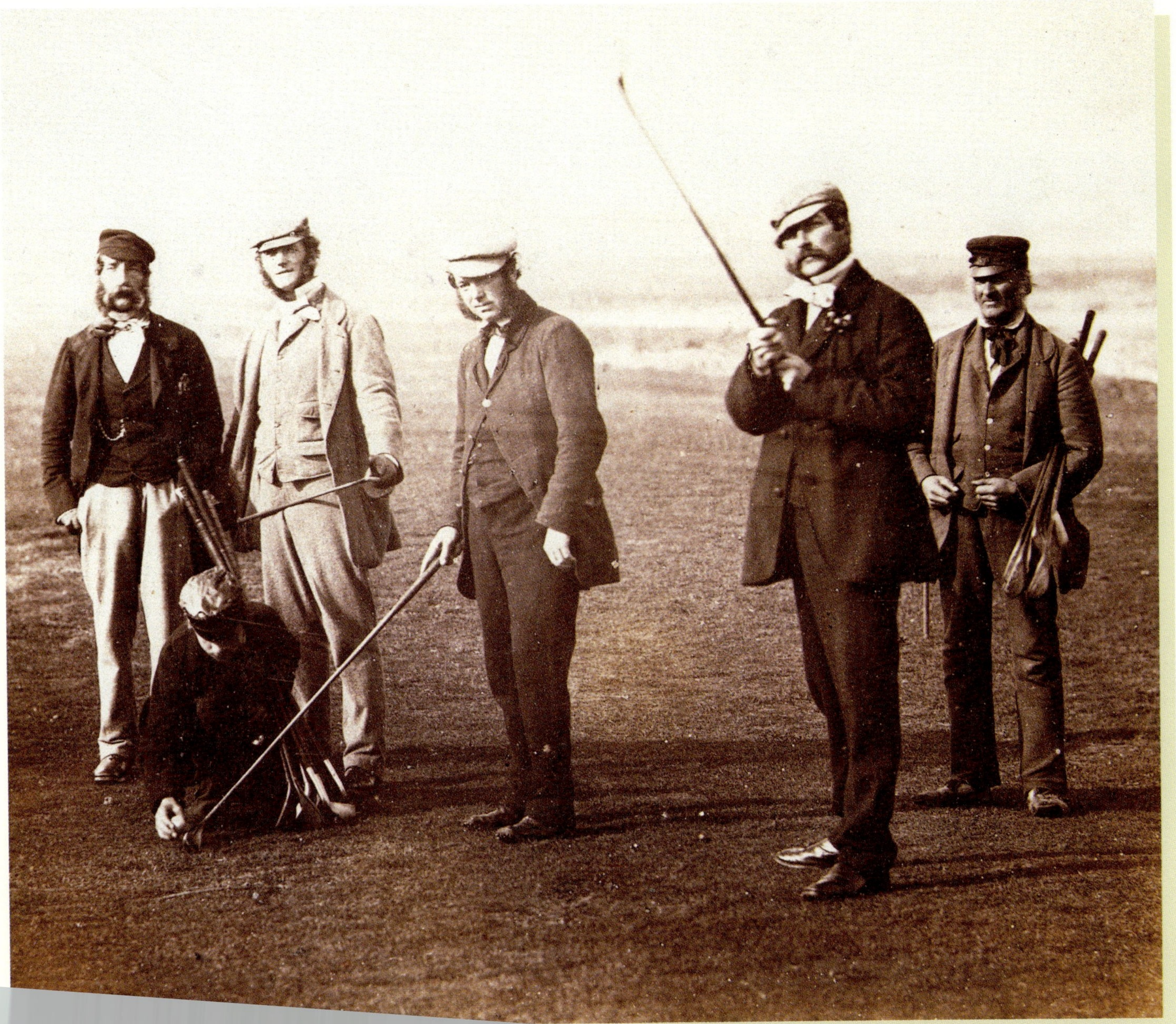

Below: Major Boothby driving off in front of the Royal & Ancient Golf Club watched by amused young caddies. Interesting to note how skeletal Boothby became 15 years after the 1866 photograph of him (p. 38 – seated looking at Hodge's scorecard) at the annual Wimbledon rifle-shooting with his St. Andrews friend and neighbour.

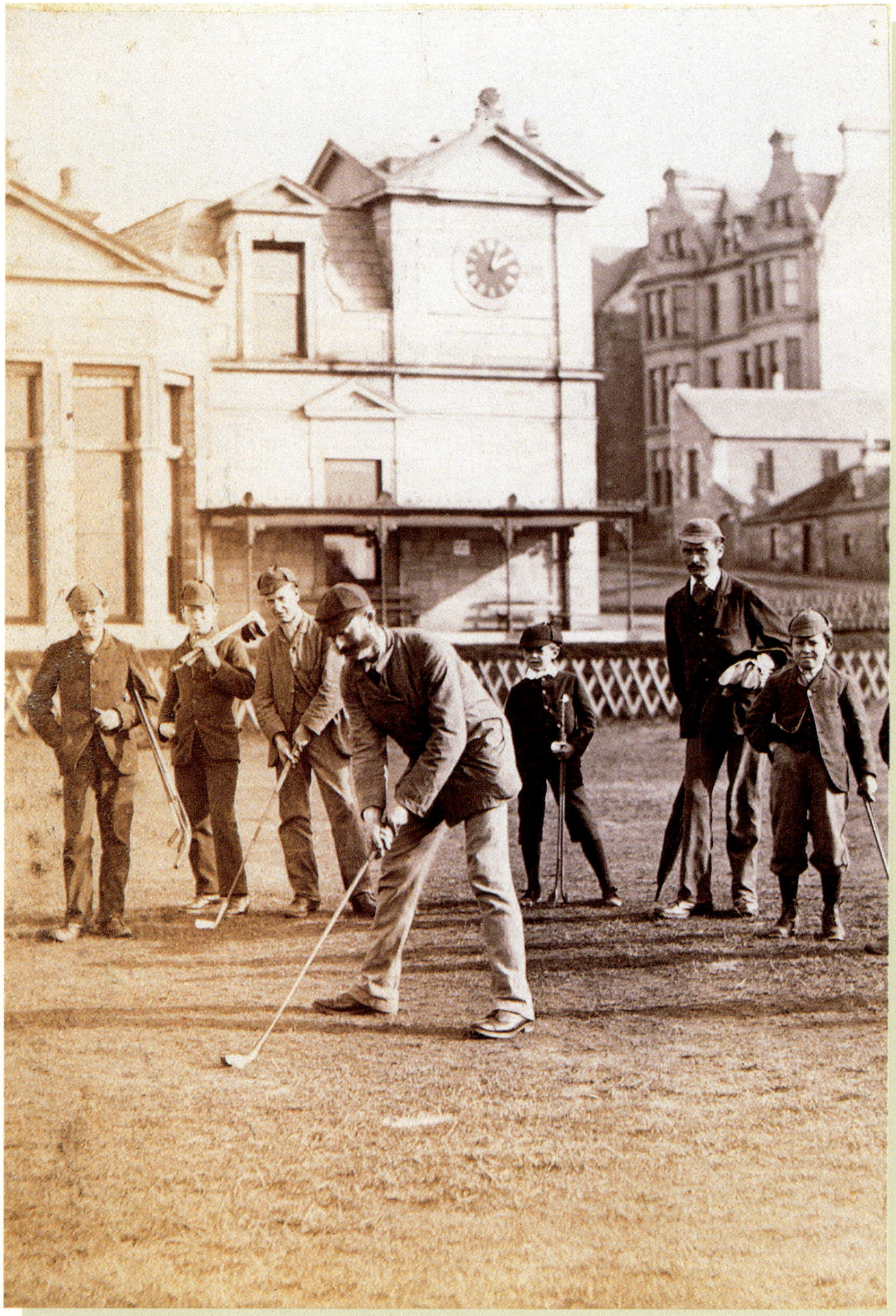

Below: a caption in Harry Everard's history of the Royal & Ancient Golf Club, for the frontispiece, describes this scene as "The finish of the first tournament at St. Andrews". In a rescued album, Hodge entitled his copy of the painstakingly orchestrated scene as "Finish of the tournament in July 1857 won by Chambers; Wallace 2nd". In fact, the first tournament at St. Andrews was won by George Glennie and Captain J.C. Stewart of Fasnacloich for Blackheath in July 1857, Blackheath thereafter describing themselves gleefully as "Champion Golf Club of the World". This picture actually shows the finish of the second tournament, an individual competition indeed won by Robert Chambers with David Wallace second, in July 1858. Curious that Everard and Hodge should fall into the same error. Perhaps the photographic library captioned it wrongly, and time blurred the golfers' memory. Chambers is the golfer putting, with Daw Anderson his caddie. The martyrs' monument can be perceived dimly in the faded background, with the "long, languid and limp" caddie nicknamed "Lang Willie" in his trademark top hat posed on the bench.

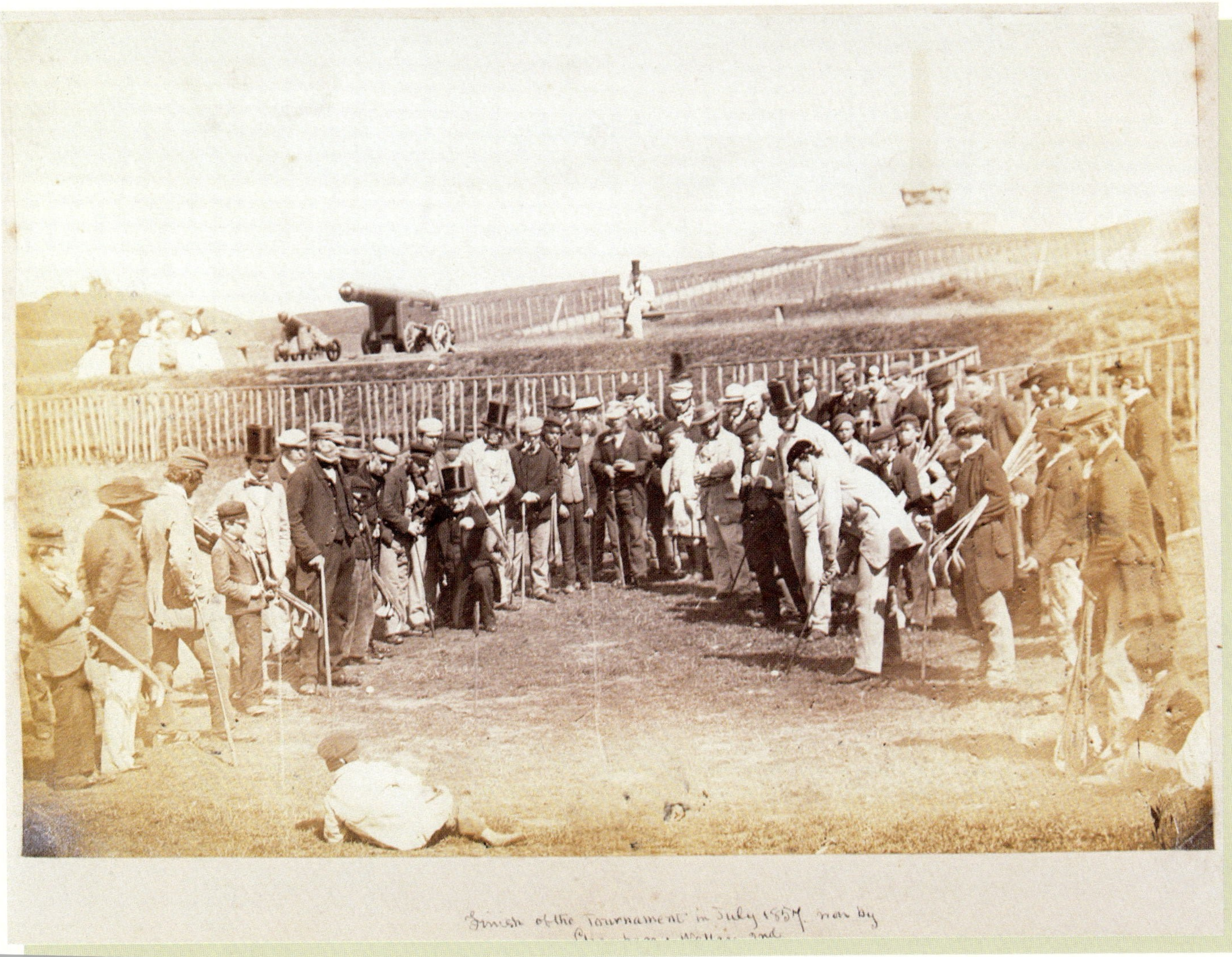

Right: captioned by Hodge in his scrapbook, "Foursome. Tom and Mr. Cathcart against ALLAN and Mr. Weymss". Left to right in the photograph: Pirie (caddie), Tom Morris (behind is an unknown caddie, possibly club maker James Wilson), Robert Cathcart of Pitcairlie, Daw Anderson, elderly man and a boy, unknown, Allan Robertson, Mr. Wallace of Balgrummo, Mr. Hay Weymss.

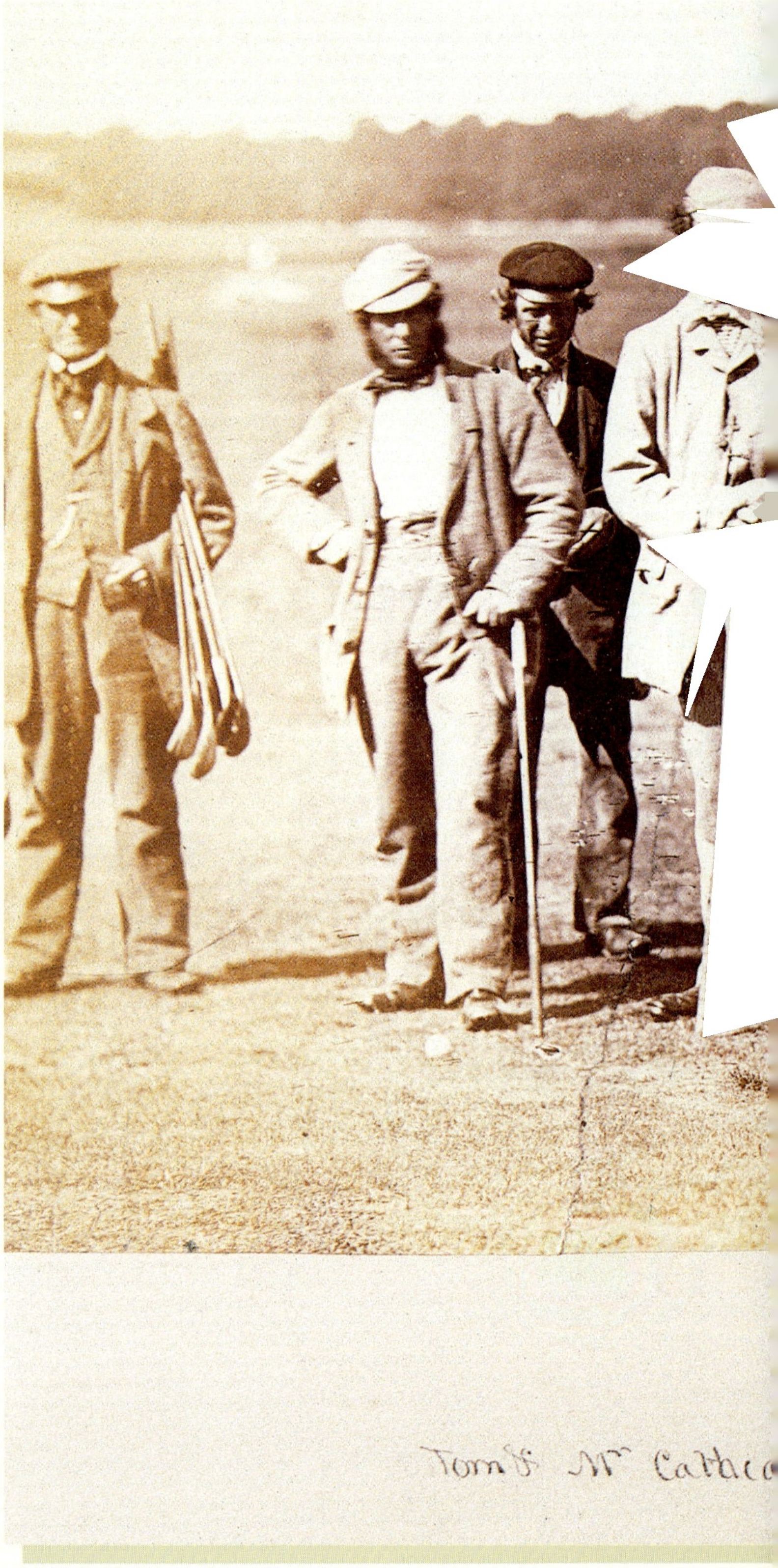

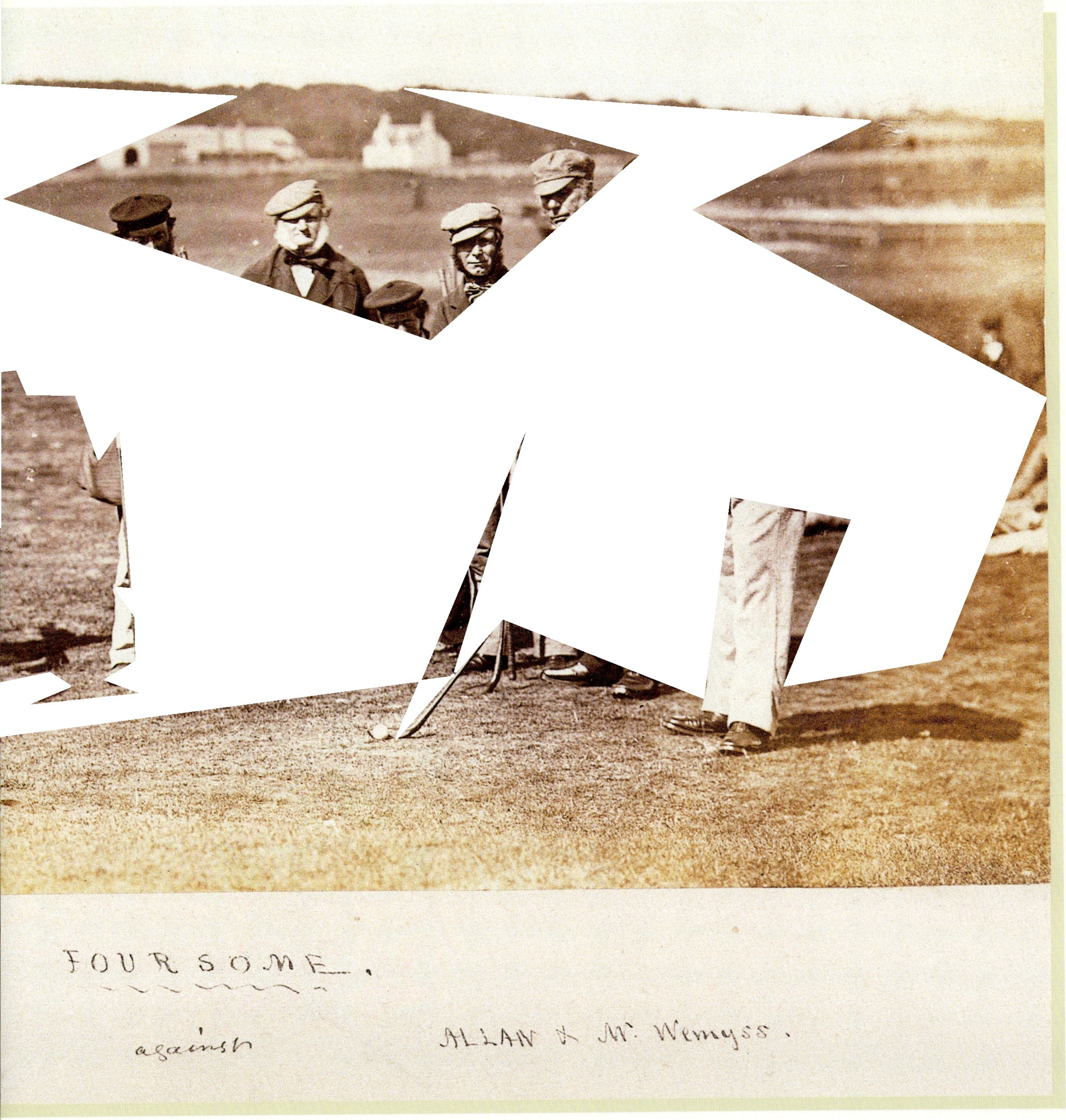
FOUR SOME.
against
ALLAN & Mr. Wemyss.

Links' Conservation

(The great Secret)

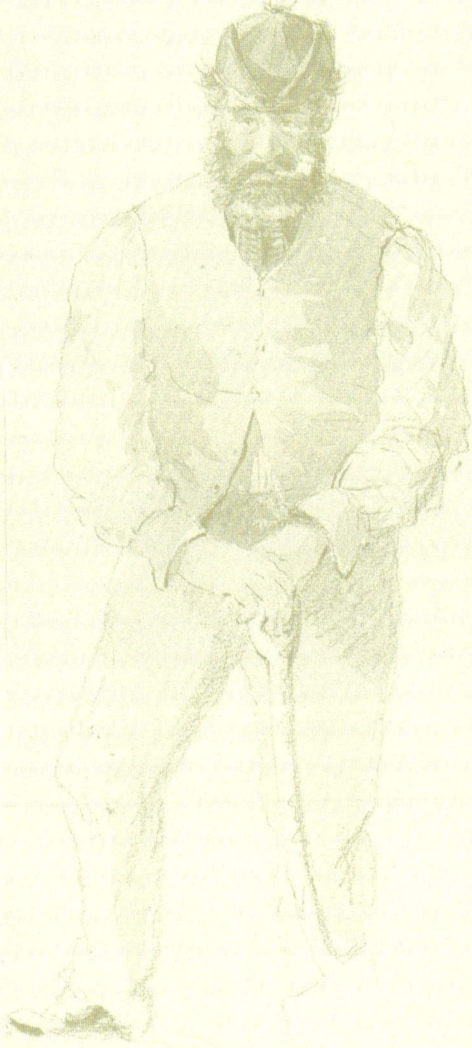

overwrought) "Ou aye! Nae thing bates it,

Links'-conservation

(The great secret)

No- 1

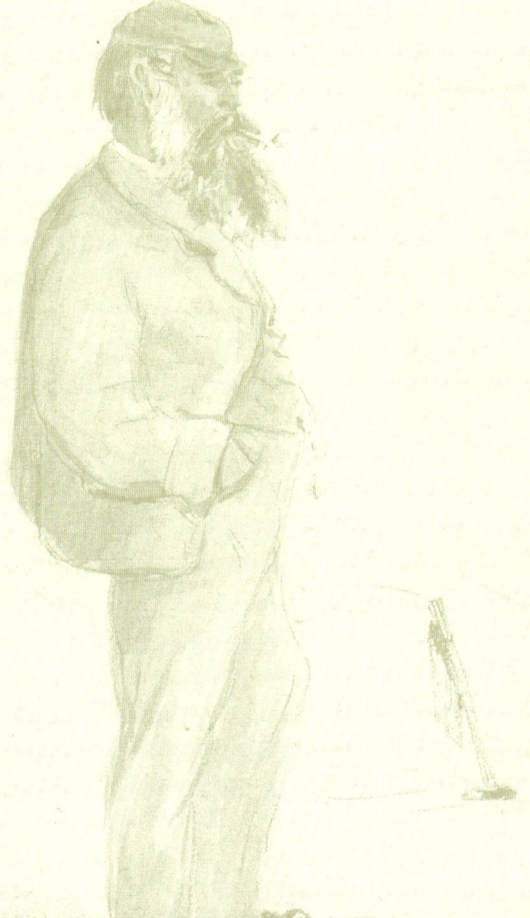

(Hard at work) "Pit on mair Sawn, Honeyman!"

Links Conservation

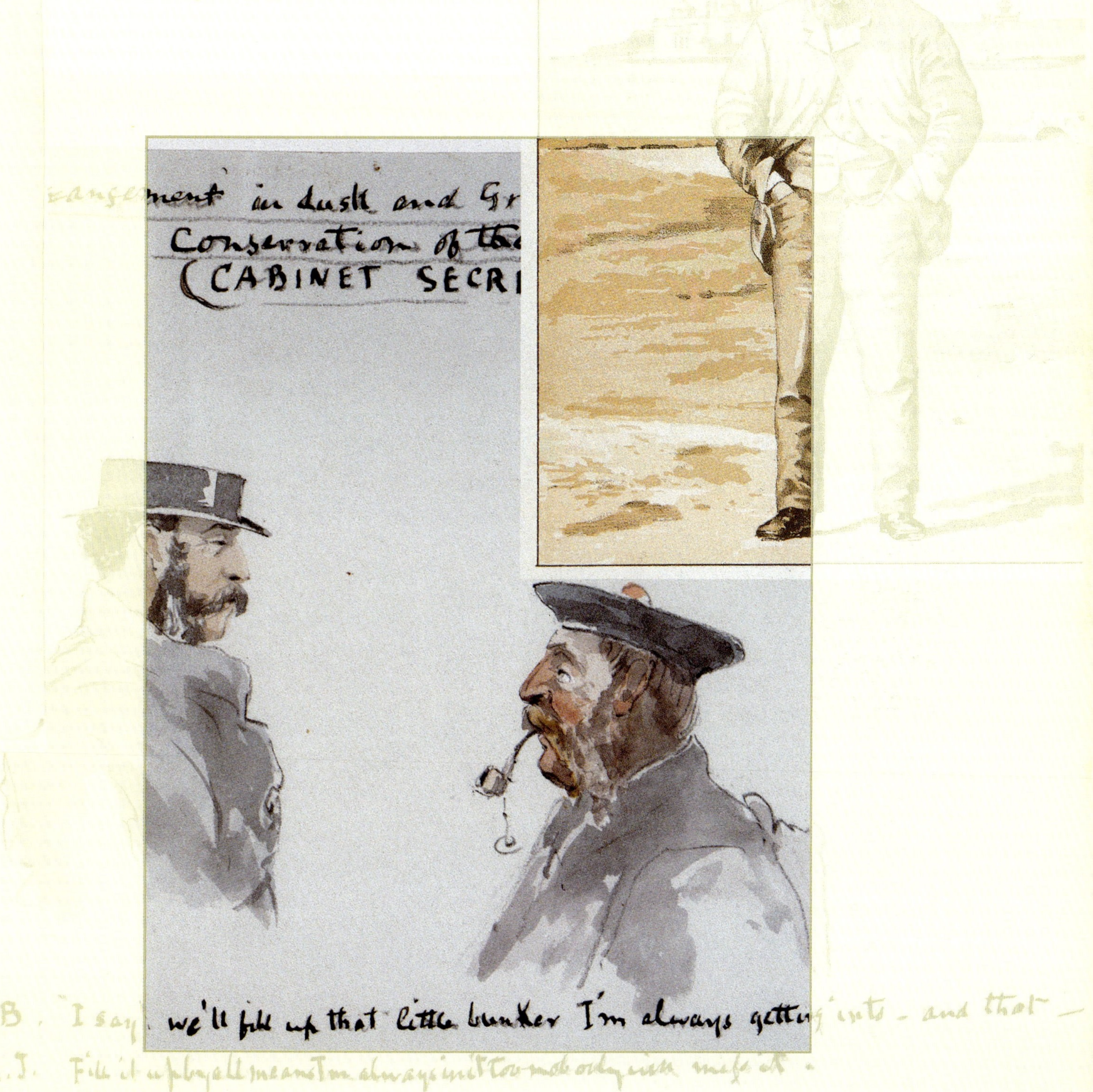

Links Conservation

One of the unfailing topics of conversation in the R & A clubhouse was, and is, the condition of the links. When Thomas Hodge dashed off three not-very-serious drawings on the subject in the mid-1880s, his knowledge of the topic was acute. He had been a member of the links committee himself.

LINKS CONSERVATION No.1

(The great secret) – This shows Tom Morris, links custodian, hands in pockets, *"Hard at work"* says Hodge's caption. Tom calls to his assistant William Honeyman, a good golfer who finished well up in several Open Championships: *"Pit on mair sawn, Honeyman!"*. (Translation, if needed: "Put on more sand, Honeyman".)

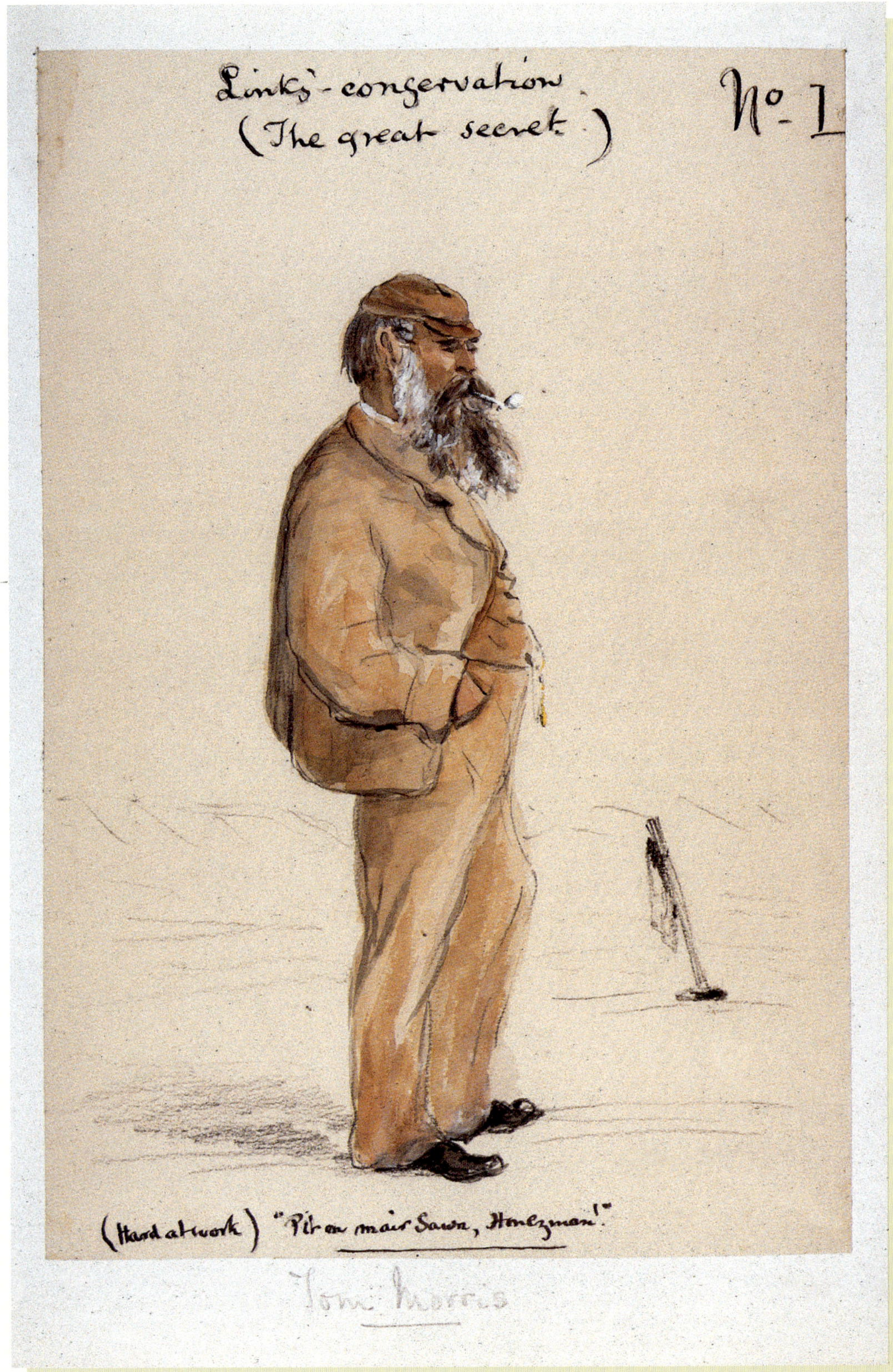

Right: Links conservation No. 1.

LINKS CONSERVATION No. 2

(The great secret) and (also overwrought) – William Honeyman as he leans on his spade, pipe in mouth (says Hodge) replies: "Oh aye! Nae thing beats it, ye ken".

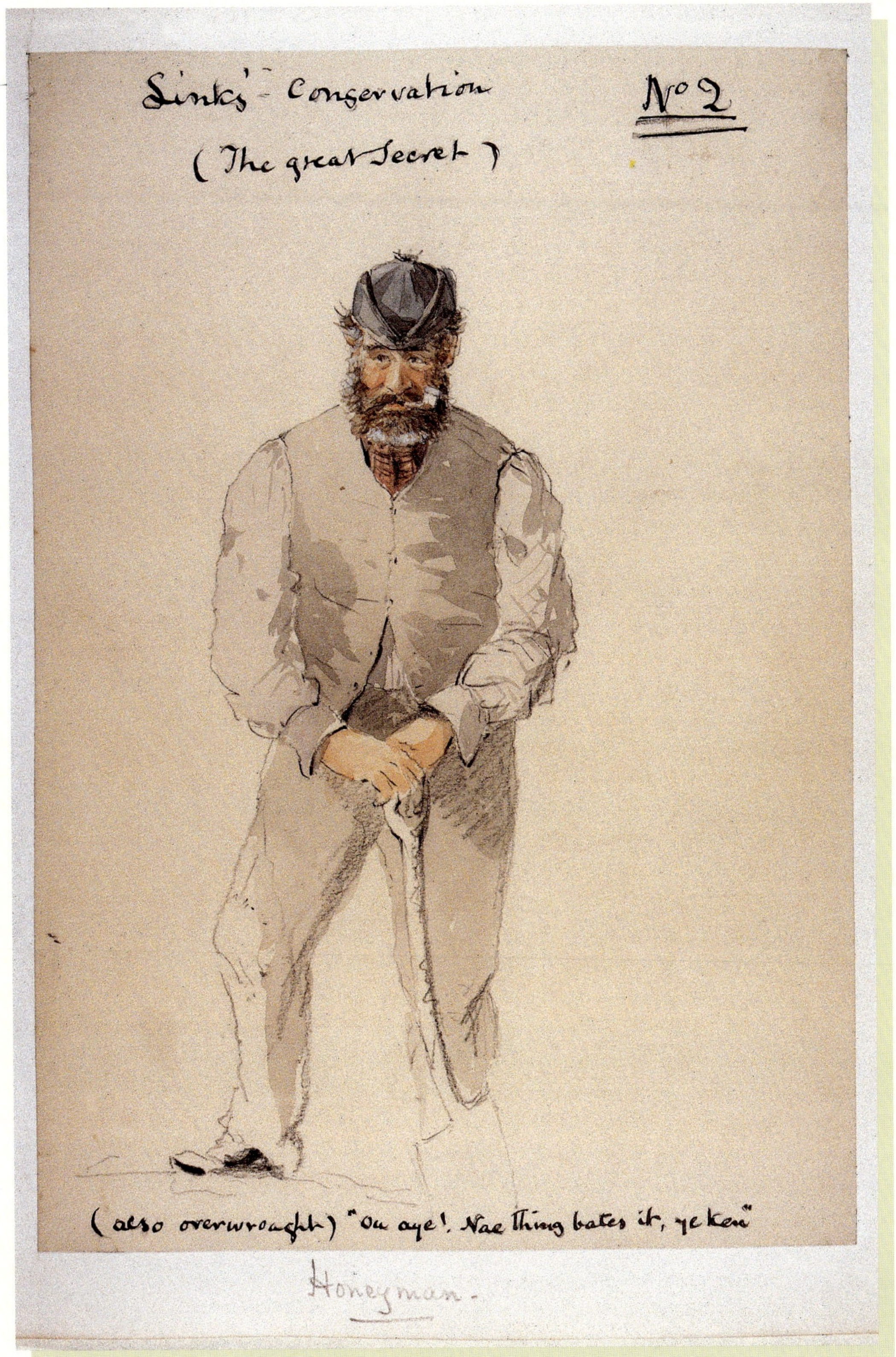

Right: Links conservation No. 2.

ARRANGEMENT IN DUSK AND GREEN

The third anecdote is entitled *"Arrangement in dusk and green (figurative of course). Conservation of the Links. (Cabinet Secret.)"* This shows Robert Boothby (R. I. B.) and Randle Jackson (R. J.), "Conspirators" says a caption handwritten below.

Boothby says to Randle Jackson:

I say we'll fill up that little bunker I'm always getting into – and that –.

R. J. replies:

Fill it up by all means. I'm always in it too; nobody will notice.

A small marvel in this club jest is the way Hodge has trapped the knowing look of Honeyman, a notorious old-soldier (see previous page).

Joking apart, in his lifetime Old Tom Morris improved the course dramatically. He was appointed "servant of the club in charge of the entire course" in 1863, salary £50 a year plus £20 for upkeep of the course.

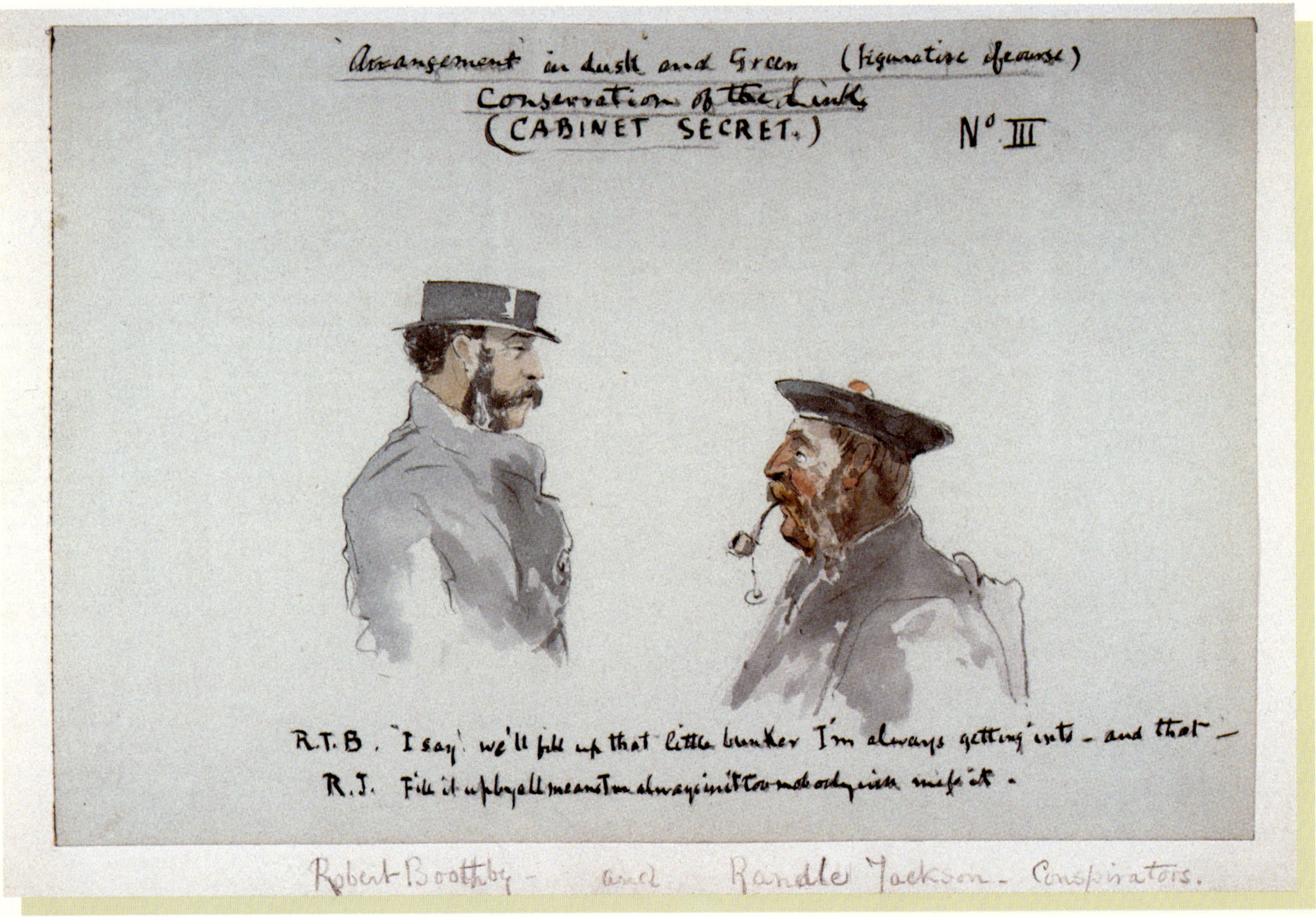

Above: "Arrangement in Dusk and Green".

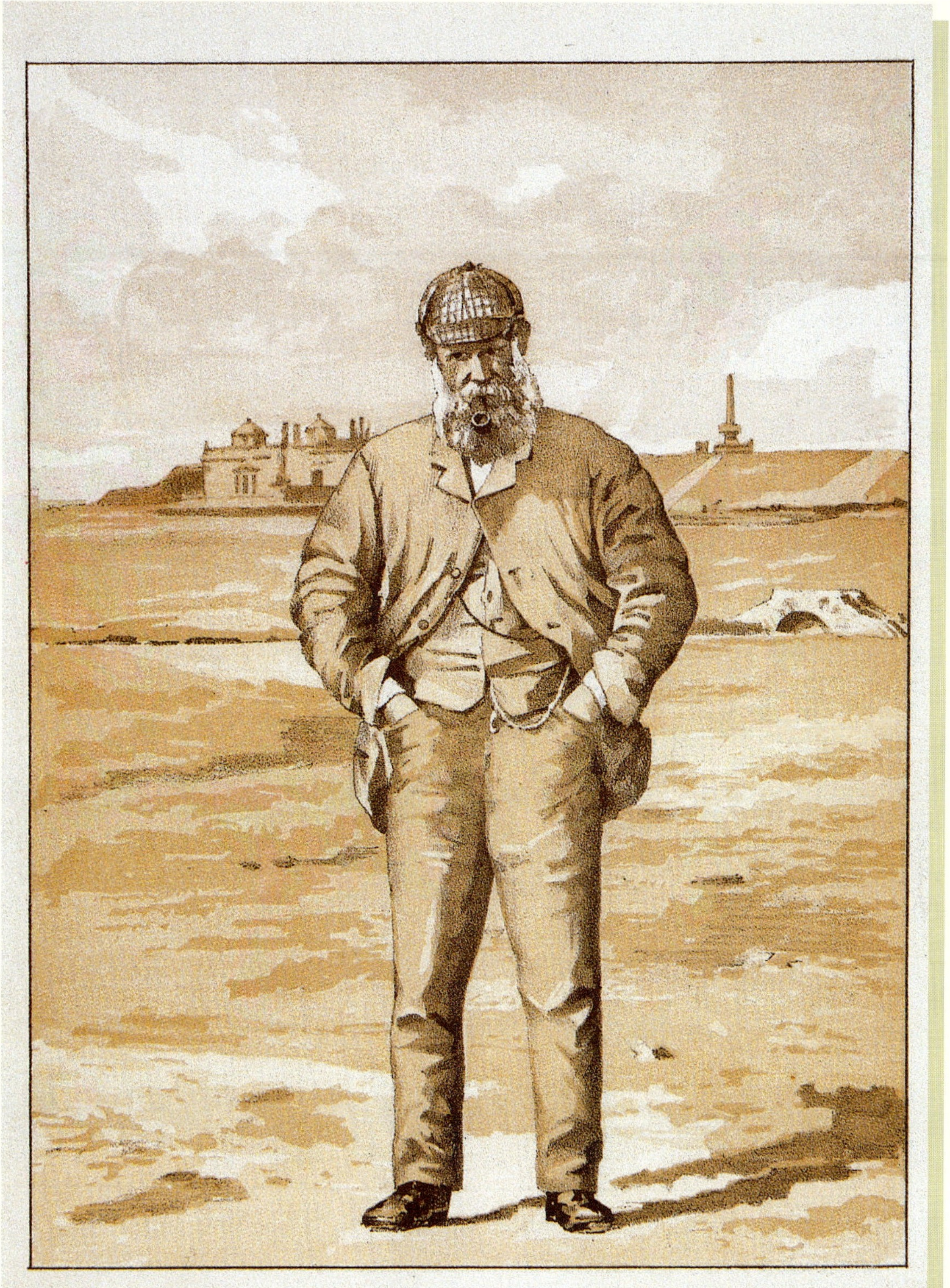

Right: Old Tom in his heyday as custodian of the world's most precious golfing acres. An extremely rare Hodge lithographic print published by Huth of Edinburgh in the 1880s.

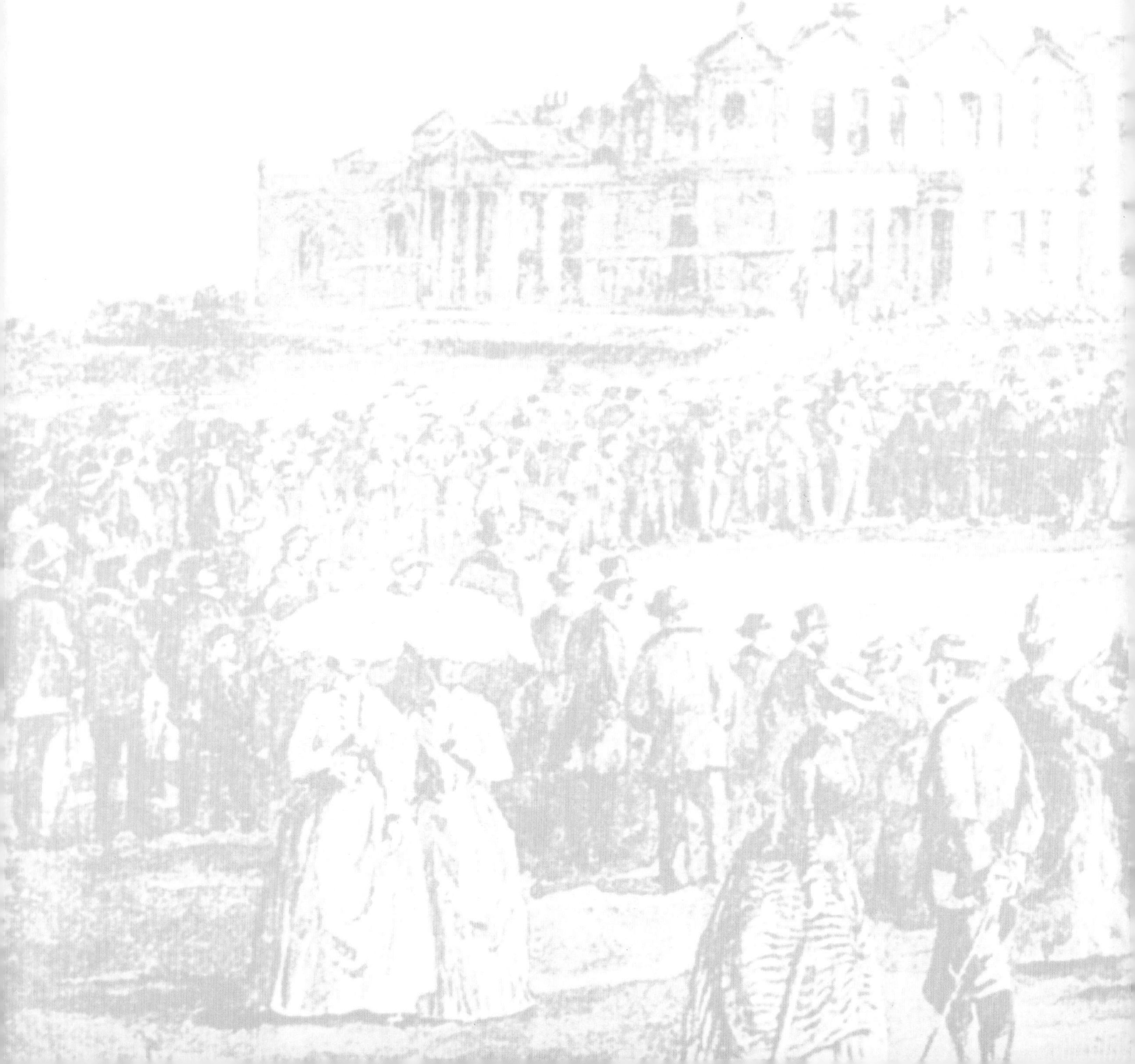

Badminton Golf, The Big Book

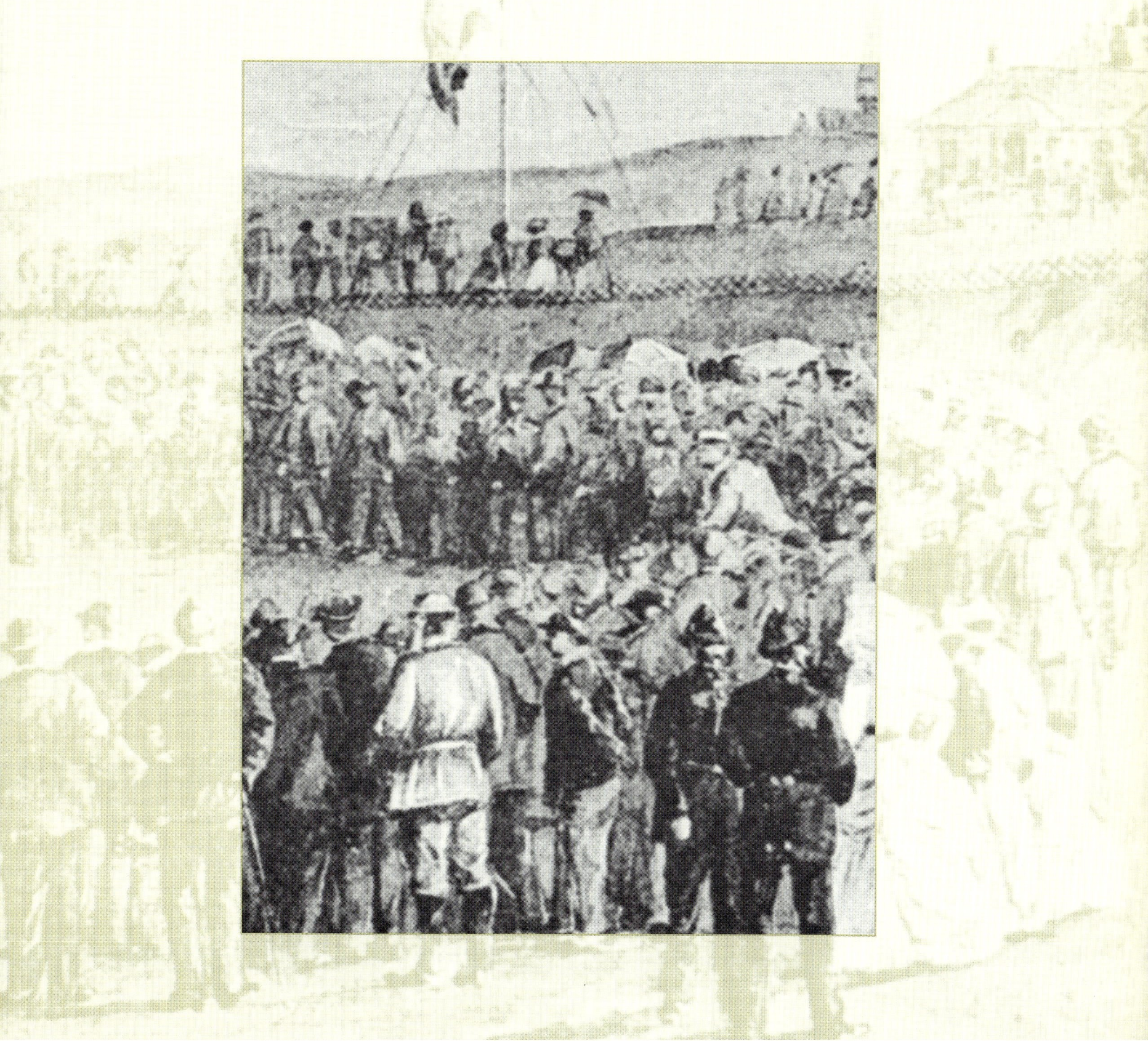

Badminton Golf, The Big Book

Golf books have become a giant industry with the spread of the game. But when Thomas Hodge was invited to help illustrate the *Golf* volume of the famous *Badminton* series in 1890, it was something of a dubious honour. There was then considerable doubt whether enough material and enough public interest existed to support a complete book on the esoteric topic. It is as well to remember this when recognising the hallowed place *The Badminton* now holds as one of the early bibles of the game.

In fact, it doesn't seem five minutes since the entire library of Badminton sports books was among the most despised shelf-fillers in second-hand bookshops.

Hodge's contribution of portraits of famous Victorian golfers and golfing anecdotes was praised, then after a couple of decades forgotten, as was the entire series. Its several yards of brown boarded volumes on cricket, athletics and football, hunting, shooting and fishing, horse-racing, skating and cycling, and several other sporting subjects, including poetry (!), lurked everywhere in British junk shops, dusty, dirty and often damp-stained. Thousands must have been thrown away. Not now.

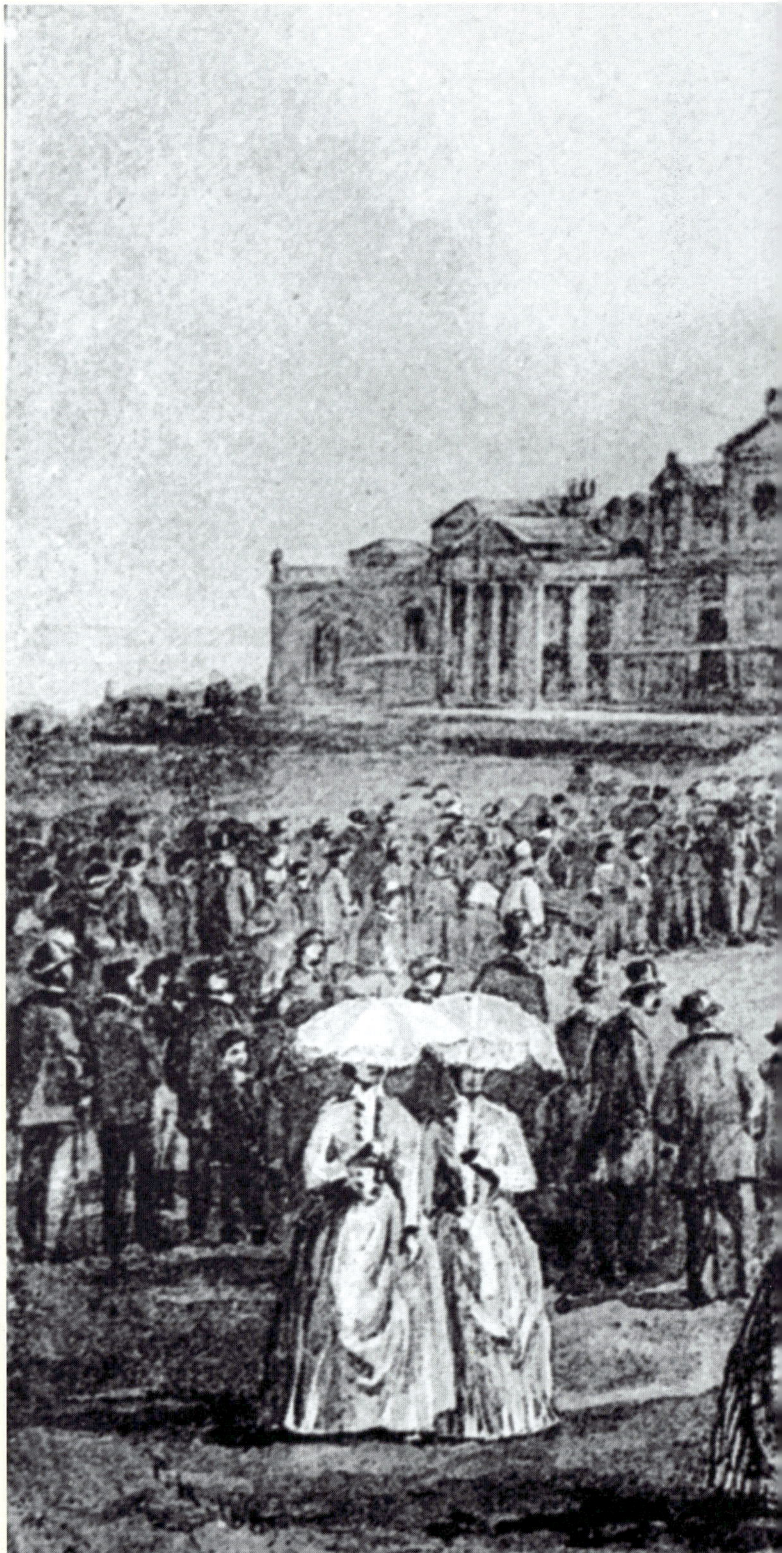

Right: Hodge produced another busy medal-day scene at St. Andrews for the Badminton volume. Again, because of the hazy reproduction of Hodge's original (whereabouts unknown), the quality is sadly diminished. However, what is clear is that between 1862 and 1890 the size of the golfing crowd has trebled.

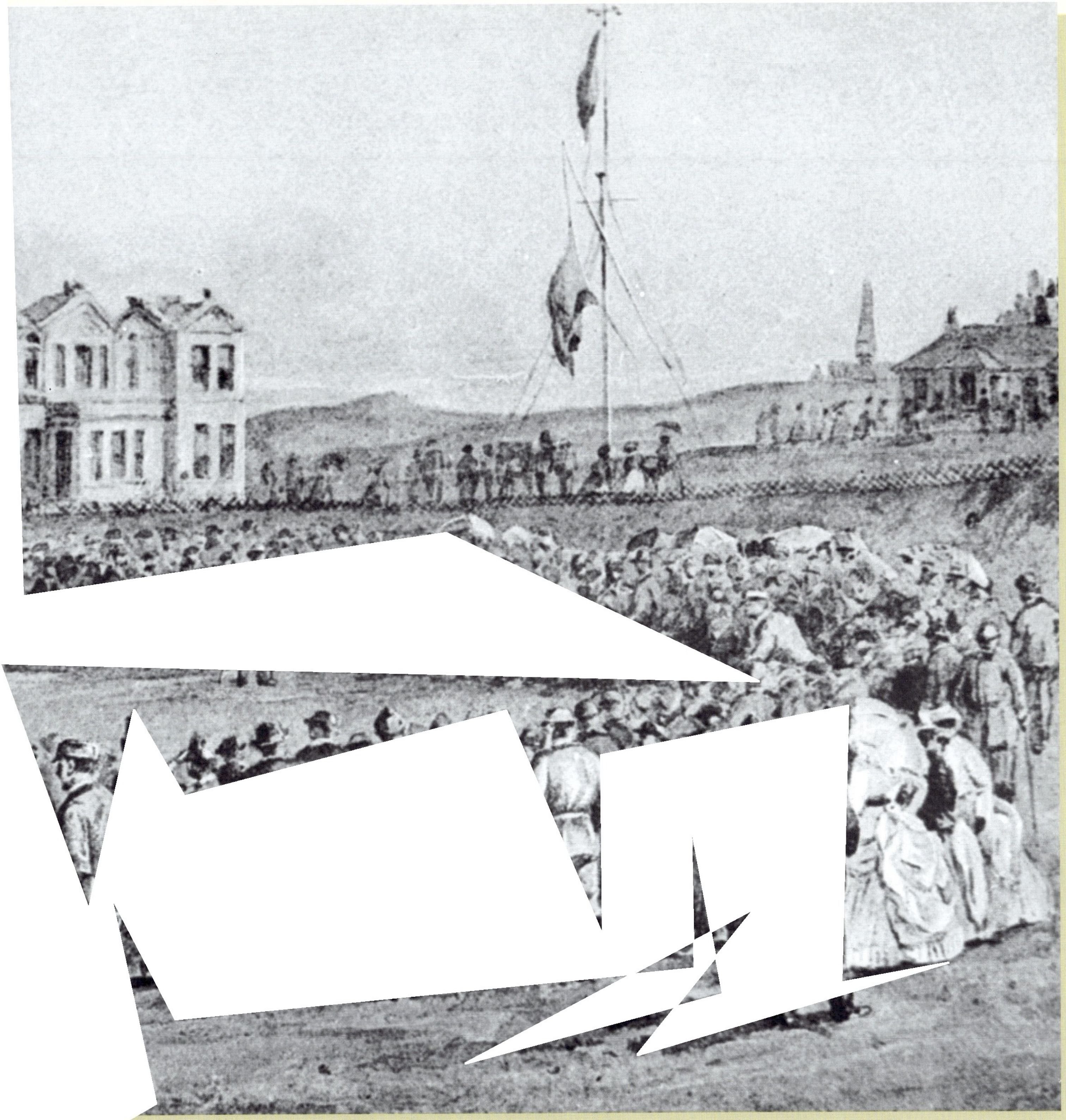

Until 1983, any slight reference to Thomas Hodge usually stemmed from his work as joint illustrator of the classic *Badminton Golf* volume first published nearly a century earlier. Often the comment was derogatory as these particular pale drawings of famous golfers clearly owed a great deal to photographic references. In the late 1990s the use of photographs and optical devices by famous artists, old masters indeed, has been "revealed". So Hodge has been in good company all along. Furthermore, it is impossible to imagine how he could have recalled the minutiae of the golfing fraternity's looks and styles without the images preserved over 30 years by the camera.

APPROACHING THE LAST HOLE

Hodge's skill at sketching with brush and in monotone is emphasised in this portrait of a Royal & Ancient character called James Wolfe Murray whose privilege in old age was to ride round the course on his pony. Wolfe Murray, of aristocratic Scottish blood, is mentioned in the writings of George Fullerton Carnegie in 1842 and appears in Charles Lees' painting *The Golfers* of 1847. Bud Dufner, of the modern tract *Golfiana*, tells that Wolfe Murray once challenged Young Tom Morris to a match, using a bow and arrows against Morris's clubs and ball. Murray lost narrowly.

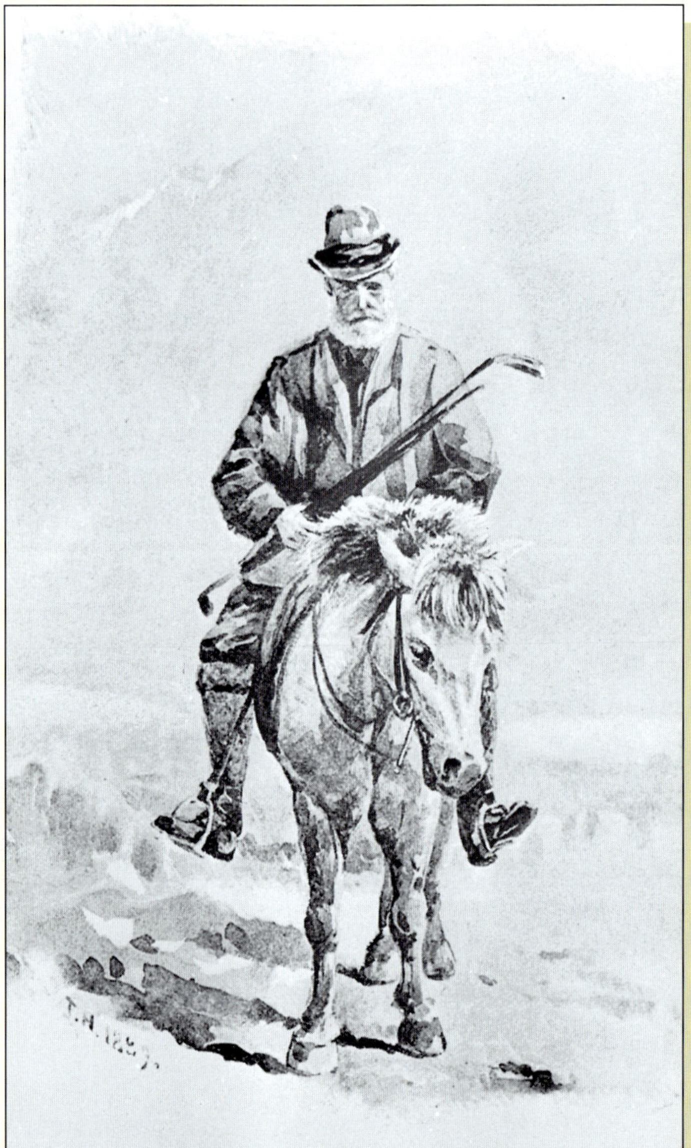
'APPROACHING THE LAST HOLE'

Above: "Approaching the Last Hole", Hodge's portrait of James Wolfe Murray on his pony.

ILLUMINATED LETTER "G"

Here Hodge records an incident in November 1880 during a foursomes at St. Andrews. At the last hole out, a good drive from the tee had just stopped rolling when a common crow alighted beside the ball, looked at it for a moment, then picked it up and flew off. The shouts and laughter of the golfers scared the bird, which dropped the ball 150 yards away. The incident was treated as a "rub of the green", and the ball played from where the bird dropped it.

ILLUMINATED LETTER "A"

The boy whose cricket bats and club form the illustrated letter "A" is Guy Campbell, later Sir Guy Campbell and a noted player and collector. An unfinished manuscript of his of life at St. Andrews in the early part of the 20th century was sold in 1999 at auction in London for £2,000.

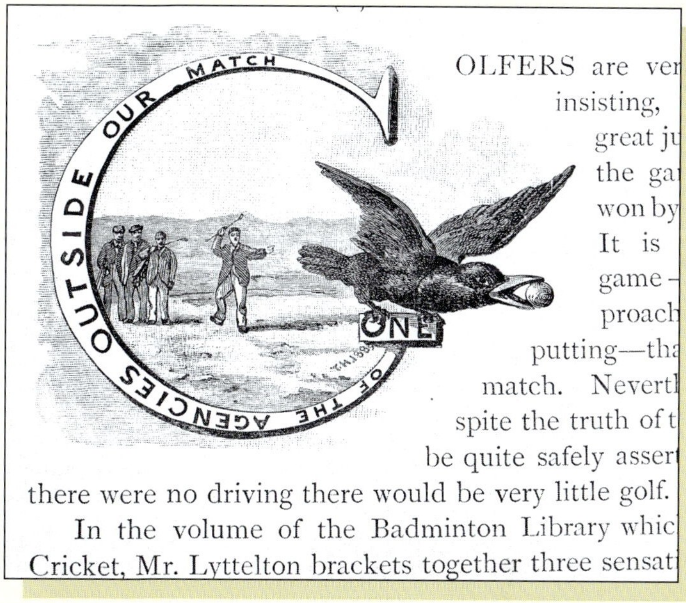

OLFERS are ver
insisting,
great ju
the ga
won by
It is
game -
proach
putting—tha
match. Nevert
spite the truth of t
be quite safely asser
there were no driving there would be very little golf.
In the volume of the Badminton Library whic
Cricket, Mr. Lyttelton brackets together three sensat

Above right: illuminated letter "G" records an unusual incident.

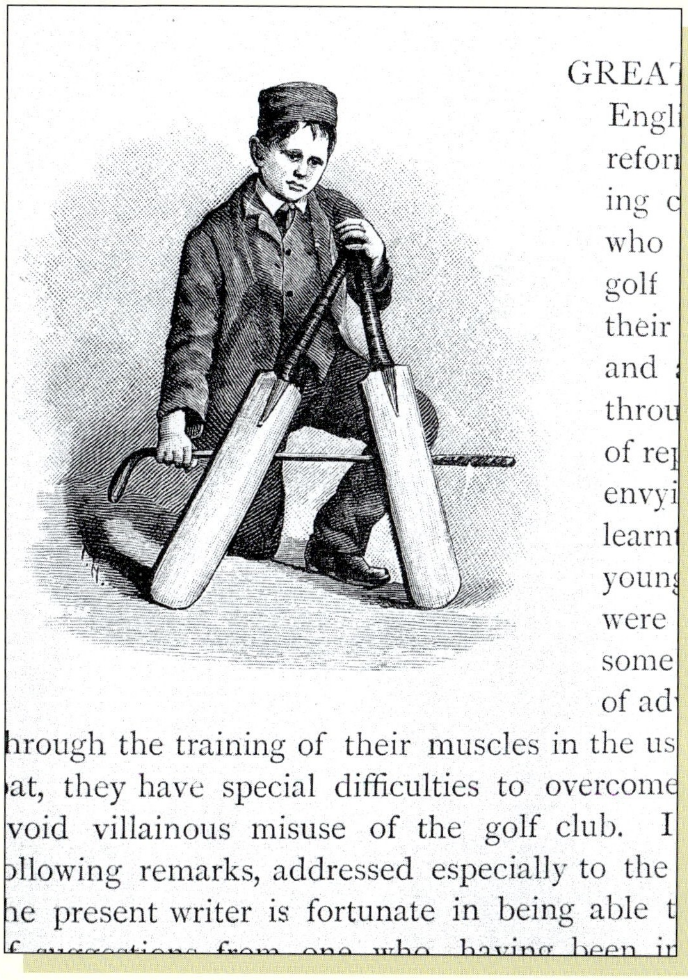
GREAT
Engl
refor
ing c
who
golf
their
and
throu
of re
envyi
learn
youn
were
some
of ad
hrough the training of their muscles in the us
at, they have special difficulties to overcome
void villainous misuse of the golf club. I
ollowing remarks, addressed especially to the
he present writer is fortunate in being able t

Right: Guy Campbell is Hodge's subject for his illuminated letter "A".

MR. A. F. MACFIE

Allan Fullerton Macfie was the winner of the first Amateur Championship held in 1885, but this feat was not recognised officially until 1920 when the Royal & Ancient began to control the event. Until this point there had always been squabbles about the restricted entry of competitors in 1885 and for 35 years 1886 was recognised as the starting point.

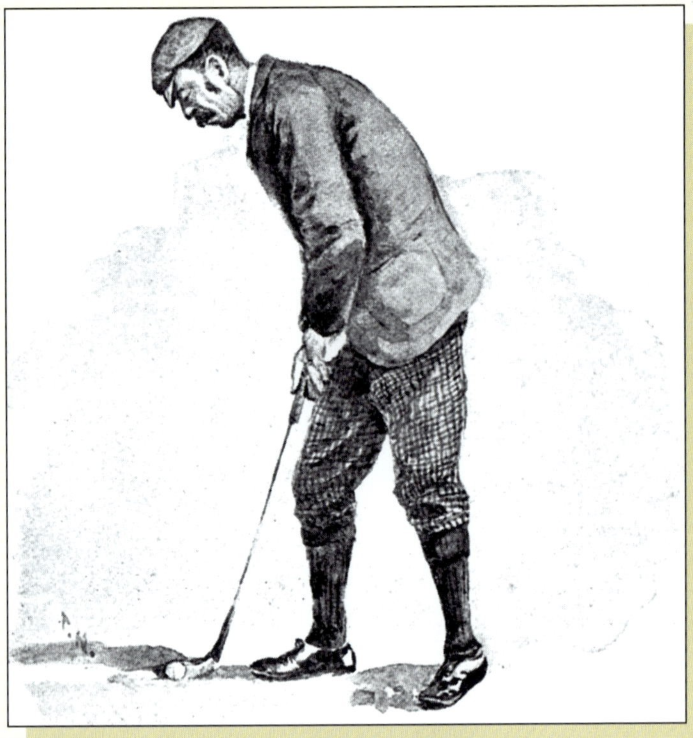

Right: Mr. A. F. Macfie.

WILLIE FERNIE

Willie Fernie of Dumfries, and sundry other clubs during his career, won the Open Championship at Musselburgh in 1883 after a play-off against Bob Ferguson. Fernie finished high up in several Opens and was second to Ferguson at St. Andrews in 1882.

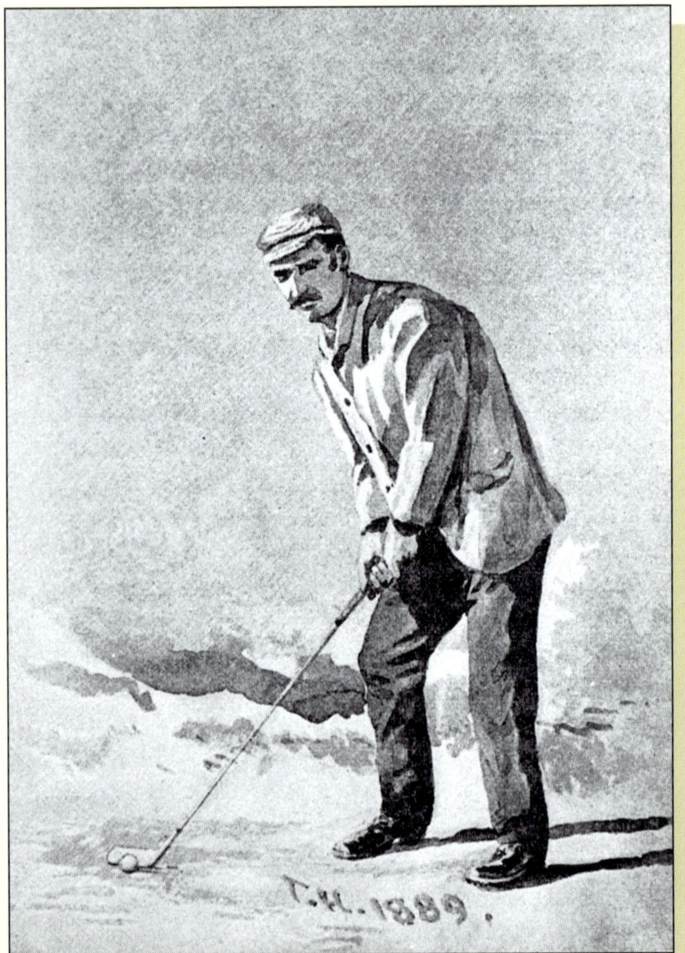

Left: Willie Fernie.

WILLIE CAMPBELL

Willie Campbell, another itinerant golf professional originally of Musselburgh, finished second to David Brown in the 1886 Open, then third, fourth and sixth in the next three years.

Right: Willie Campbell.

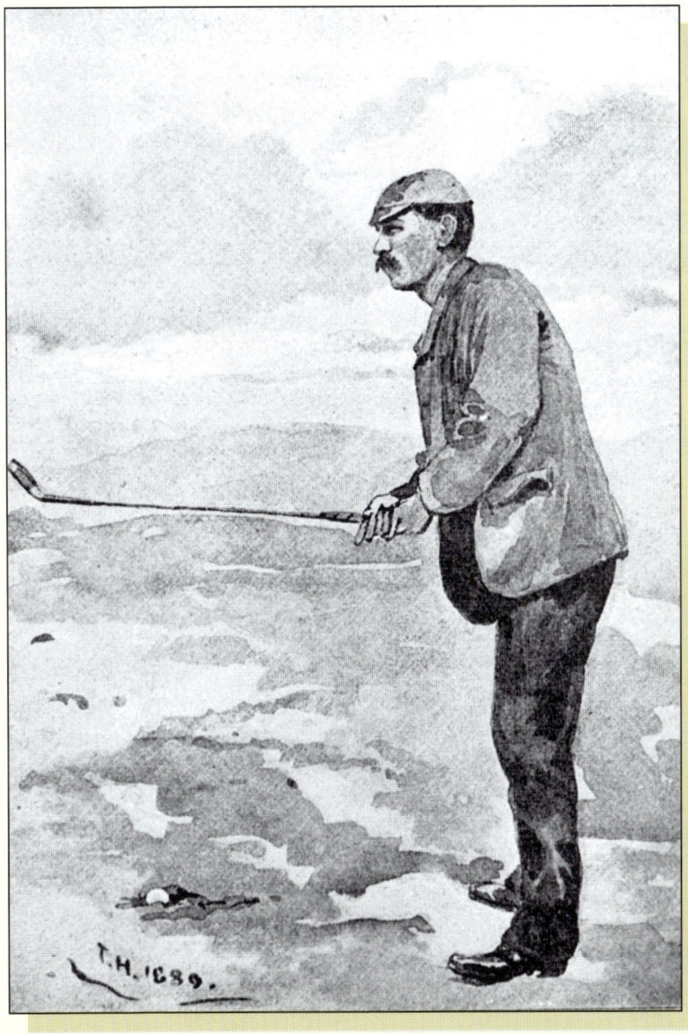

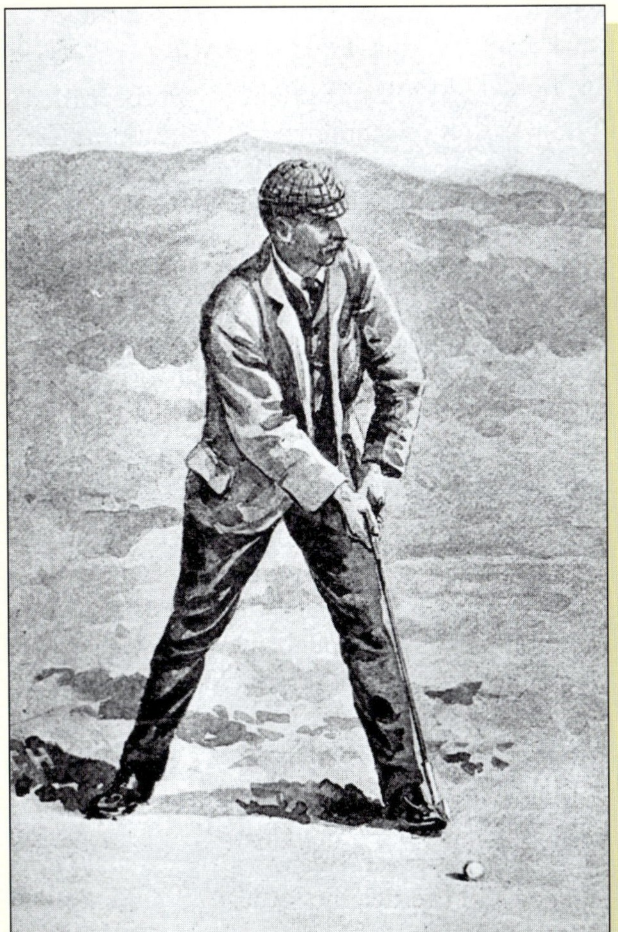

OFF THE LEFT LEG

Johnnie Laidlay, a study very similar to the one of this famous R & A member discovered in the 1980s pictured with George Glennie.

Left: Johnnie Laidlay.

MR. GEORGE GLENNIE

George Glennie's portrait, as with the Laidlay study, is very similar to the ones of these famous R & A members discovered in the 1980s. Glennie's portrait struck a powerful chord at the Royal & Ancient and at Blackheath, where it was used as an engraved decoration on various medals.

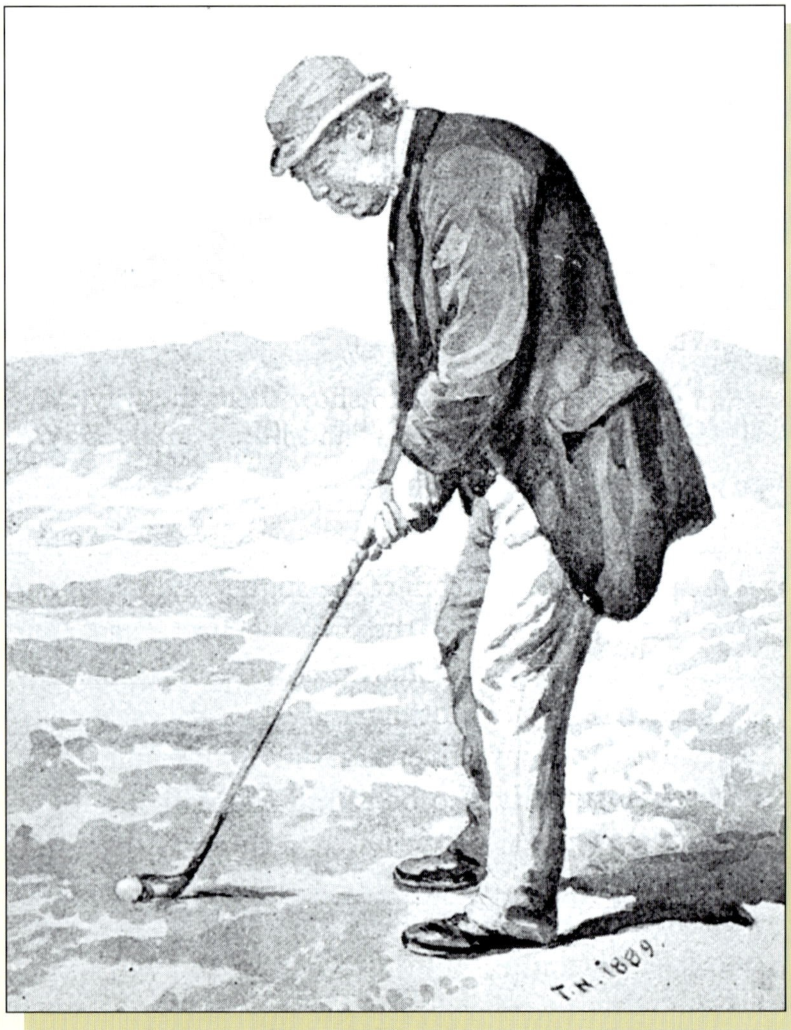

Right: George Glennie.

MR. ROBERT CLARK

Robert Clark was a rugged strongman on the golf course, and Hodge's portraits always make it plain that this was one Scot not to trifle with off it either.

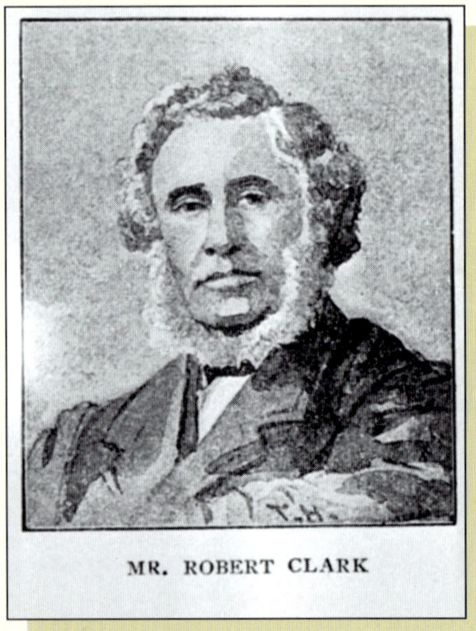

Left: Robert Clark.

HE LOOKS AT THE HOLE FROM THE BALL

Thomas Hodge was not shy in using his own image to illustrate golfing points. Here he sizes up a putt, but the underlying dig here may be that putting was his notorious failing.

Right: Thomas Hodge.

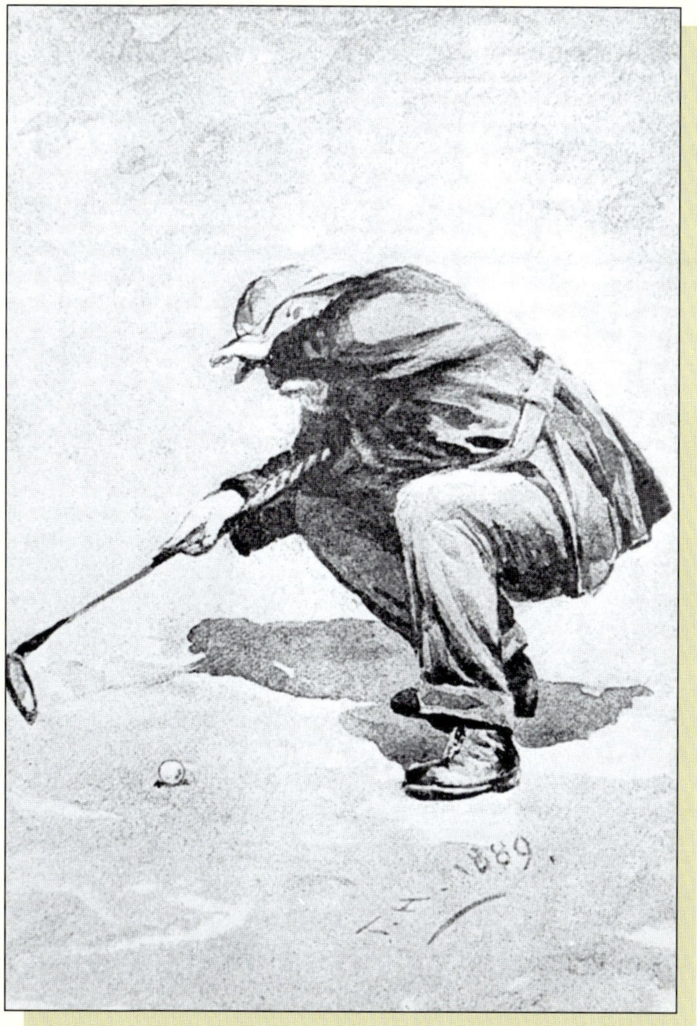

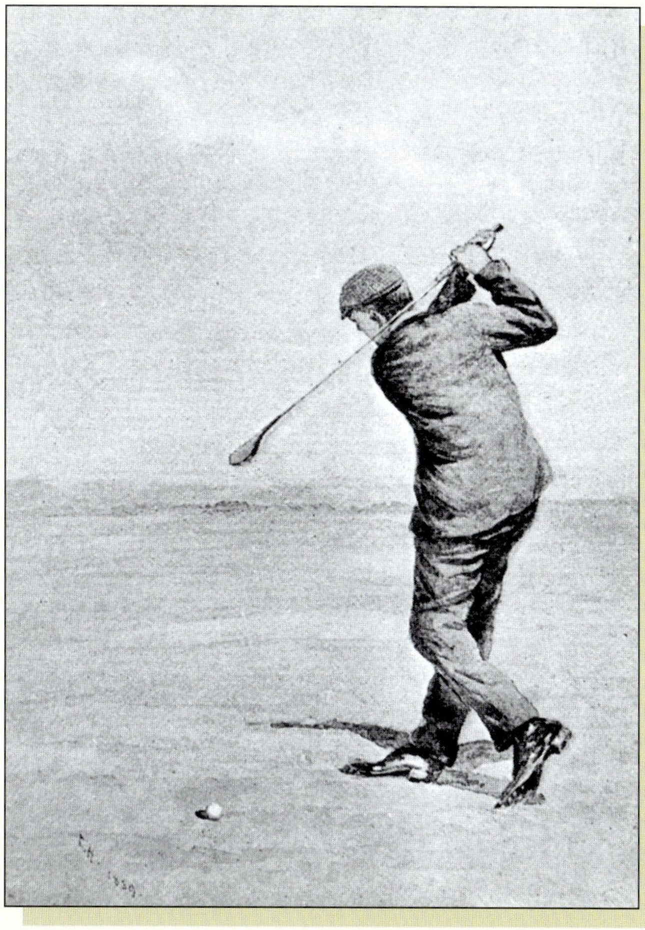

THE ST. ANDREWS SWING

"The St. Andrews Swing" is performed here by Hugh Kirkaldy, brother of the legendary Andra Kirkaldy, and Open Champion in 1891, the year after this image was published.

Left: Hugh Kirkaldy.

THE MAN TO BACK

"The Man to Back" is W. McKinnon, a hearty scene emphasising that Hodge and his family thought serious trenching was essential to fortify body and spirit.

Right: W. McKinnon.

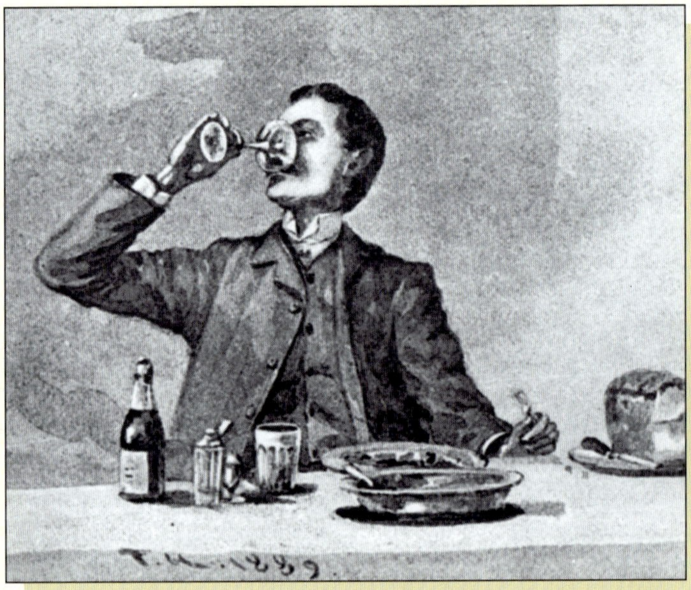

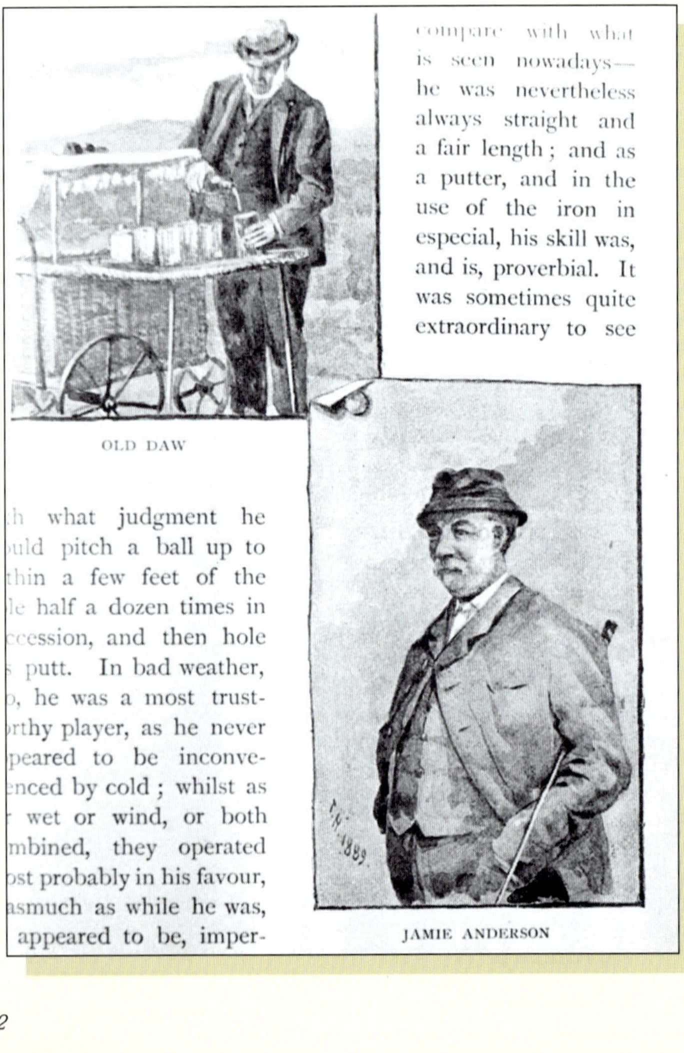

compare with what is seen nowadays— he was nevertheless always straight and a fair length; and as a putter, and in the use of the iron in especial, his skill was, and is, proverbial. It was sometimes quite extraordinary to see

OLD DAW

h what judgment he
ould pitch a ball up to
thin a few feet of the
le half a dozen times in
ccession, and then hole
putt. In bad weather,
, he was a most trust-
rthy player, as he never
peared to be inconve-
nced by cold; whilst as
wet or wind, or both
mbined, they operated
st probably in his favour,
asmuch as while he was,
appeared to be, imper-

JAMIE ANDERSON

OLD DAW AND JAMIE ANDERSON

The Andersons. Old Daw and his ginger beer cart on the St. Andrews links. Below is his son Jamie at the height of his fame, still well fed and prosperous on the strength of his triple Open Championships in 1877, 1878 and 1879.

ALLAN ROBERTSON AND TOM MORRIS

Allan Robertson (crouching) and Old Tom Morris together on the green. This became Thomas Hodge's most famous image. During the 20th century, countless prints and paintings were based on Hodge's original perceptive extraction of this anecdote from the 1850s group photograph on St. Andrews' links by Thomas Rodger.

Left: Old Daw and his son Jamie.

Right: Allan Robertson and Tom Morris.

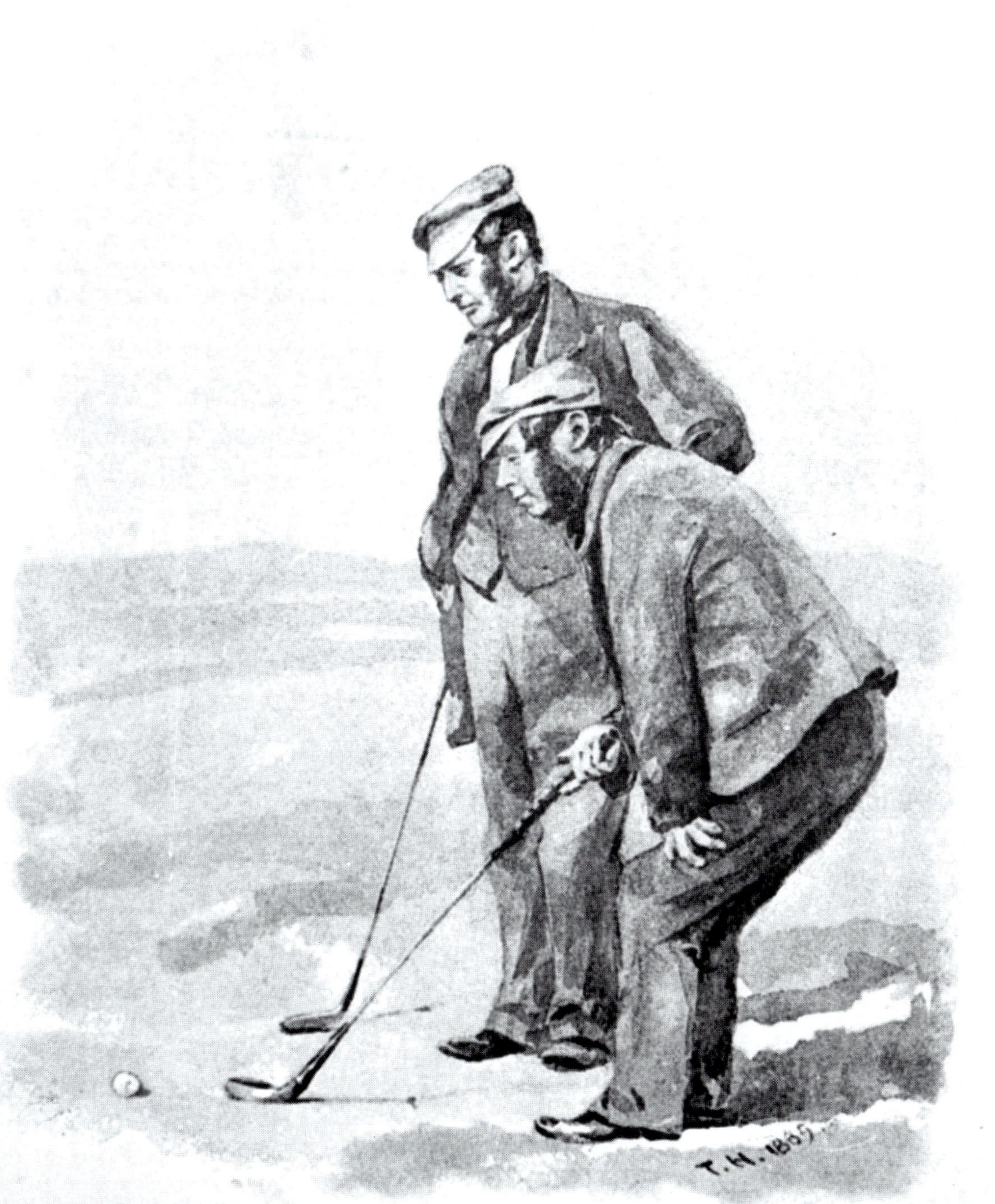

ALLAN ROBERTSON AND TOM MORRIS

ILLUMINATED LETTER "T"

Another illustrated letter, this time a "T" formed by a man in a long apron holding two bags of golf balls in out-stretched hands. This is the well known professional and equipment maker, Bob Martin, twice winner of the Open Championship in 1876 and 1885, both times at St. Andrews. He was also highly placed in several other Open Championships of the 1870s and 1880s. He was awarded the title in 1876 after a tie with David Strath of North Berwick of 176 for the two rounds. Strath refused to play off after he was accused of breaking the rule about not playing his shot while other competitors were still on the final green.

Right: Bob Martin.

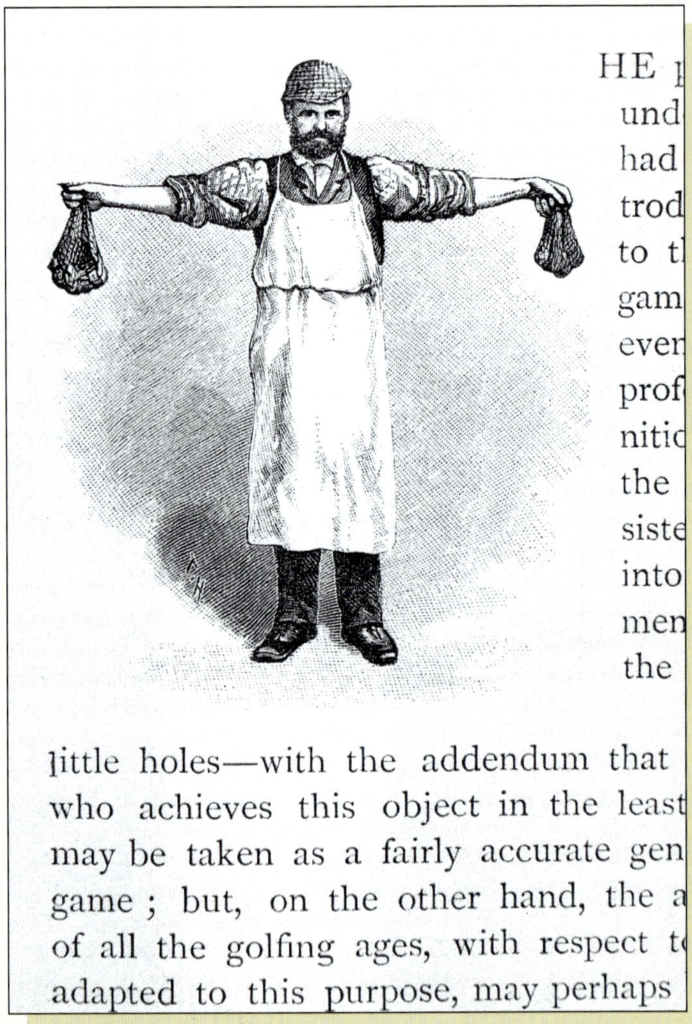
HE p
und
had
trod
to t
gam
even
prof
nitic
the
siste
into
men
the

little holes—with the addendum that
who achieves this object in the least
may be taken as a fairly accurate gen
game ; but, on the other hand, the a
of all the golfing ages, with respect t
adapted to this purpose, may perhaps

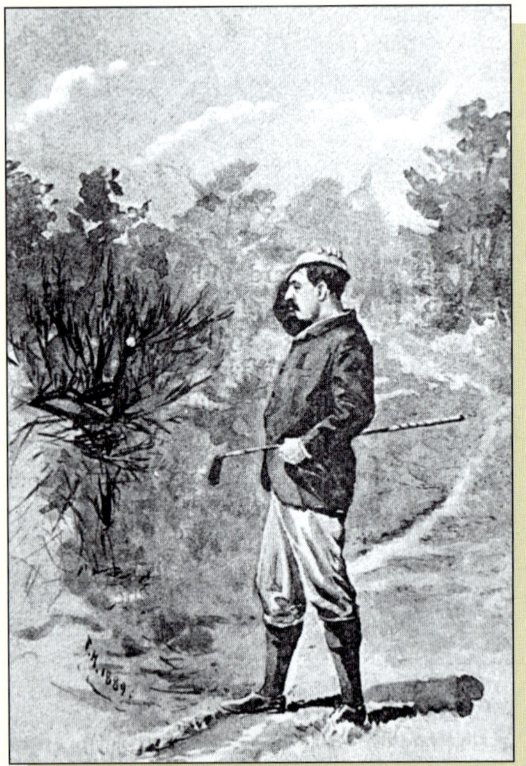

A CHAMPION IN DIFFICULTIES

Whether Hodge invented this conundrum, or it actually happened during a match, is not known.

Left: "A champion in difficulties".

SIR ROBERT HAY, BART.

Another fine portrait of Sir Robert Hay, a senior golf statesman of the 19th century.

AGRICULTURE

Freddie Tait is Hodge's golfer hacking his way out of trouble with earth flying.

Right: Sir Robert Hay.

Below: Freddie Tait.

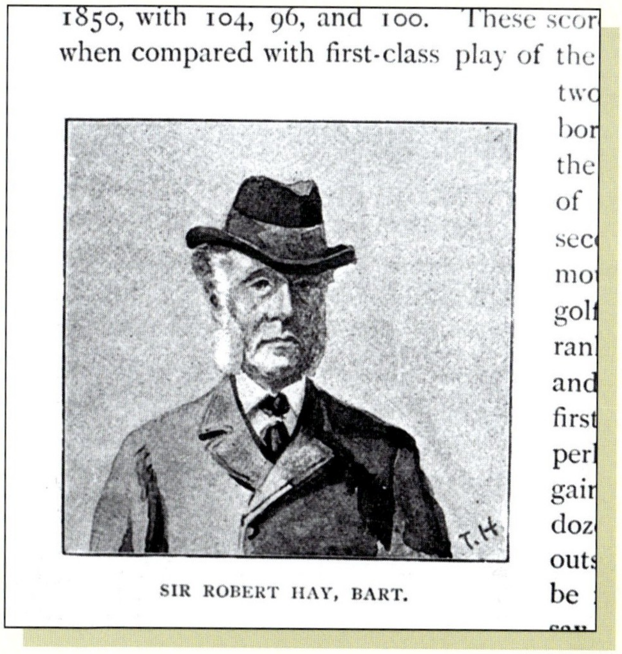
1850, with 104, 96, and 100. These scor
when compared with first-class play of the
twc
bor
the
of
sec
mo
gol
ran
and
first
per
gair
doz
outs
be

SIR ROBERT HAY, BART.

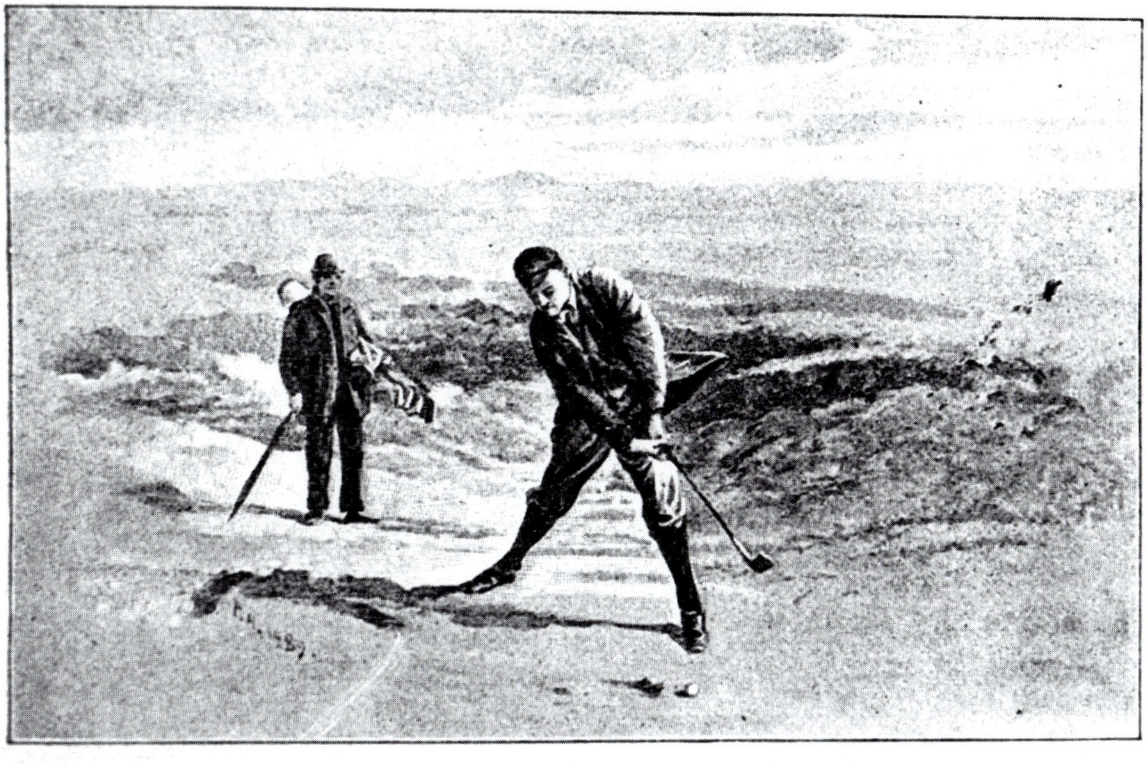

AGRICULTURE

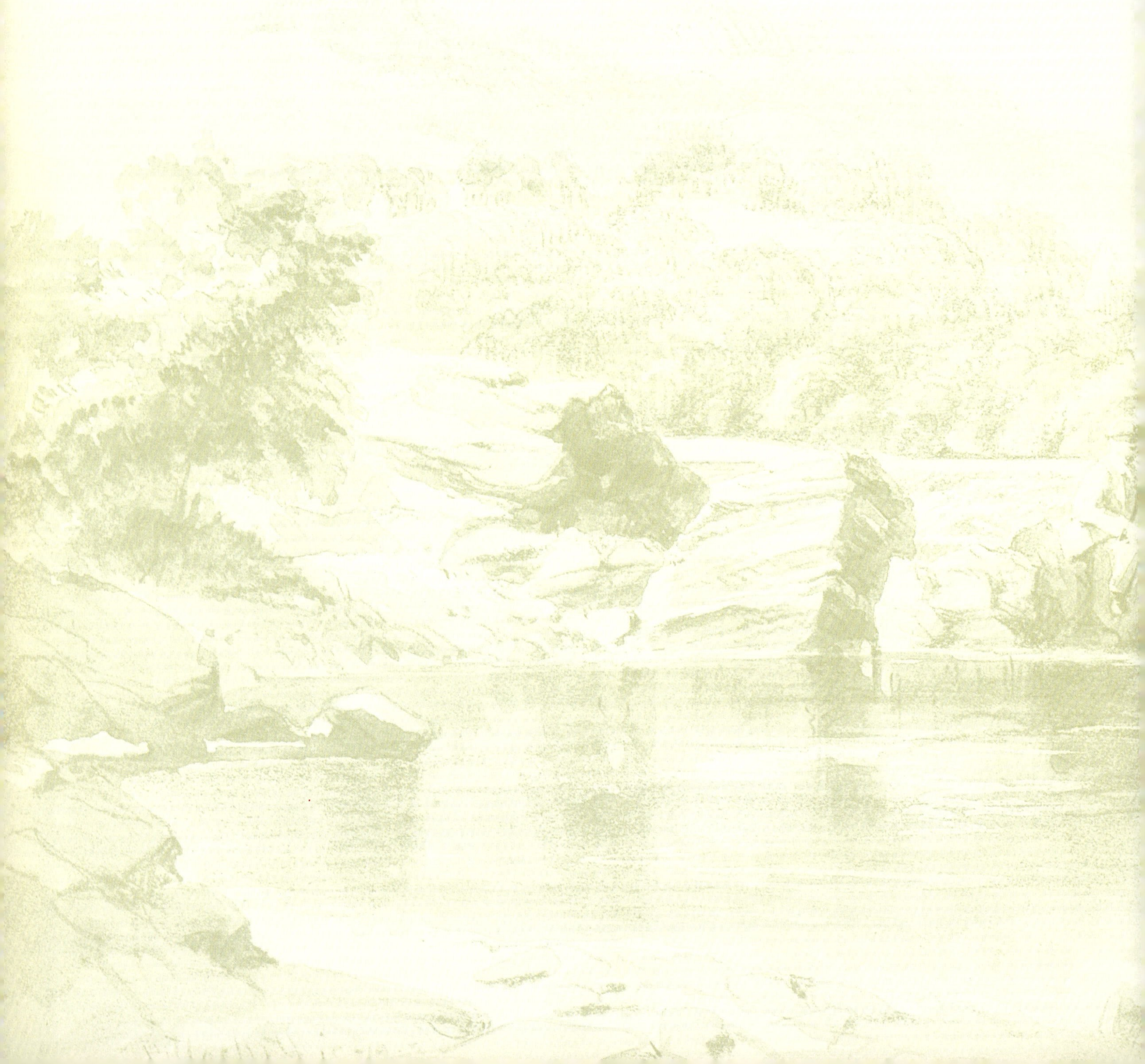

Thomas Hodge on Holiday

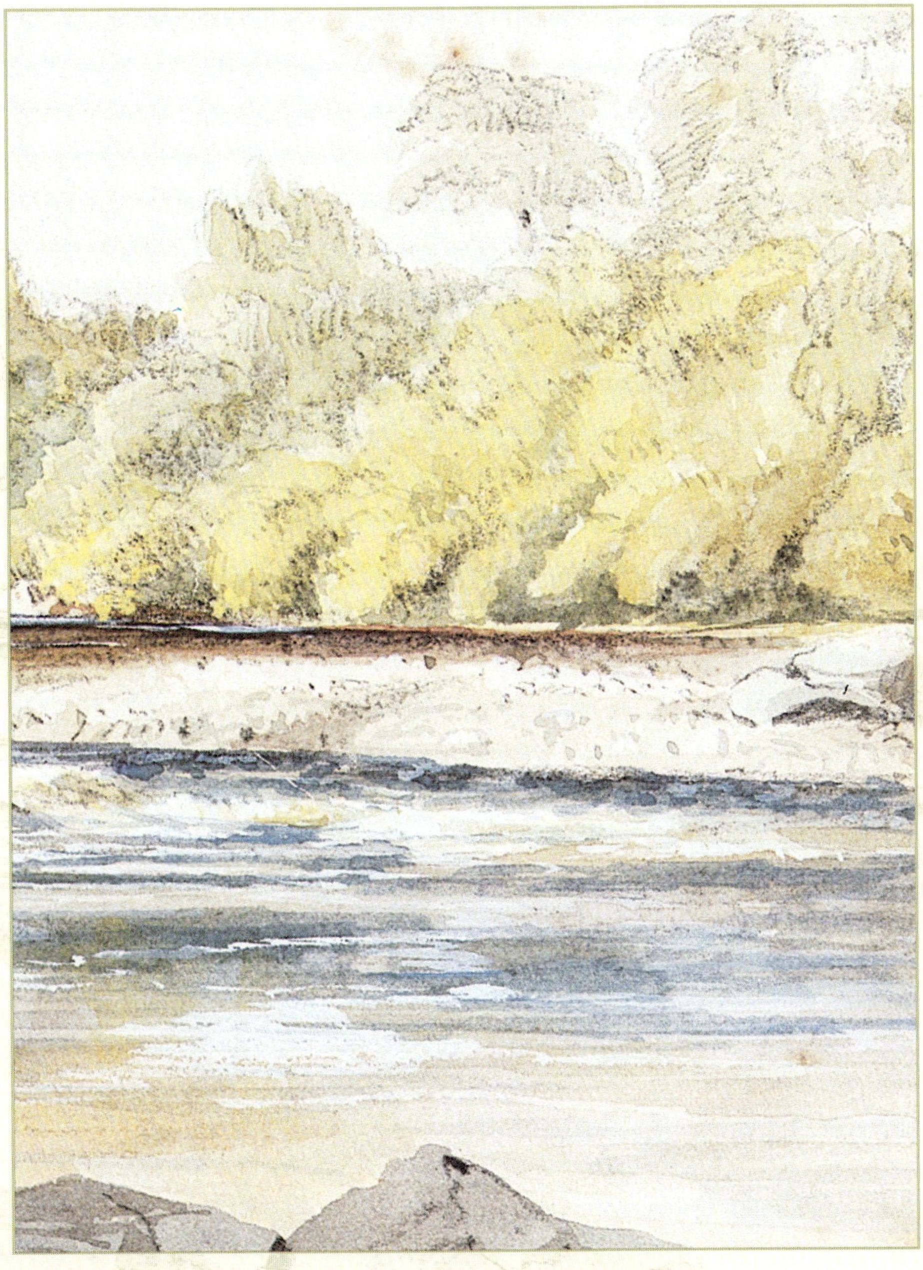

Thomas Hodge on Holiday

Thomas Hodge ventured abroad for his bachelor holidays. He wrote long descriptions of his travels to his sisters which reveal something not always pleasant about the Victorian Briton's attitudes abroad. Although shown to be absurdly chauvinistic and racist by the standards of a century later, Hodge surely must be measured by the confines of the era in which he lived. He was a fairly typical 19th-century English patriot away from the island, thirsting for knowledge in many ways though chronically blinkered in his view of that deeply inferior fellow, the foreigner.

When he started to write the following (edited) sagas in the 1860s, he was a single man of 39, bald on top but heavily muttonchop-whiskered, prone to his own brand of humour and to headmasterish pomposity. It is all too painfully obvious that some of his yarns eventually rebounded wickedly on the nation Hodge and the majority of his kind felt to be so superior.

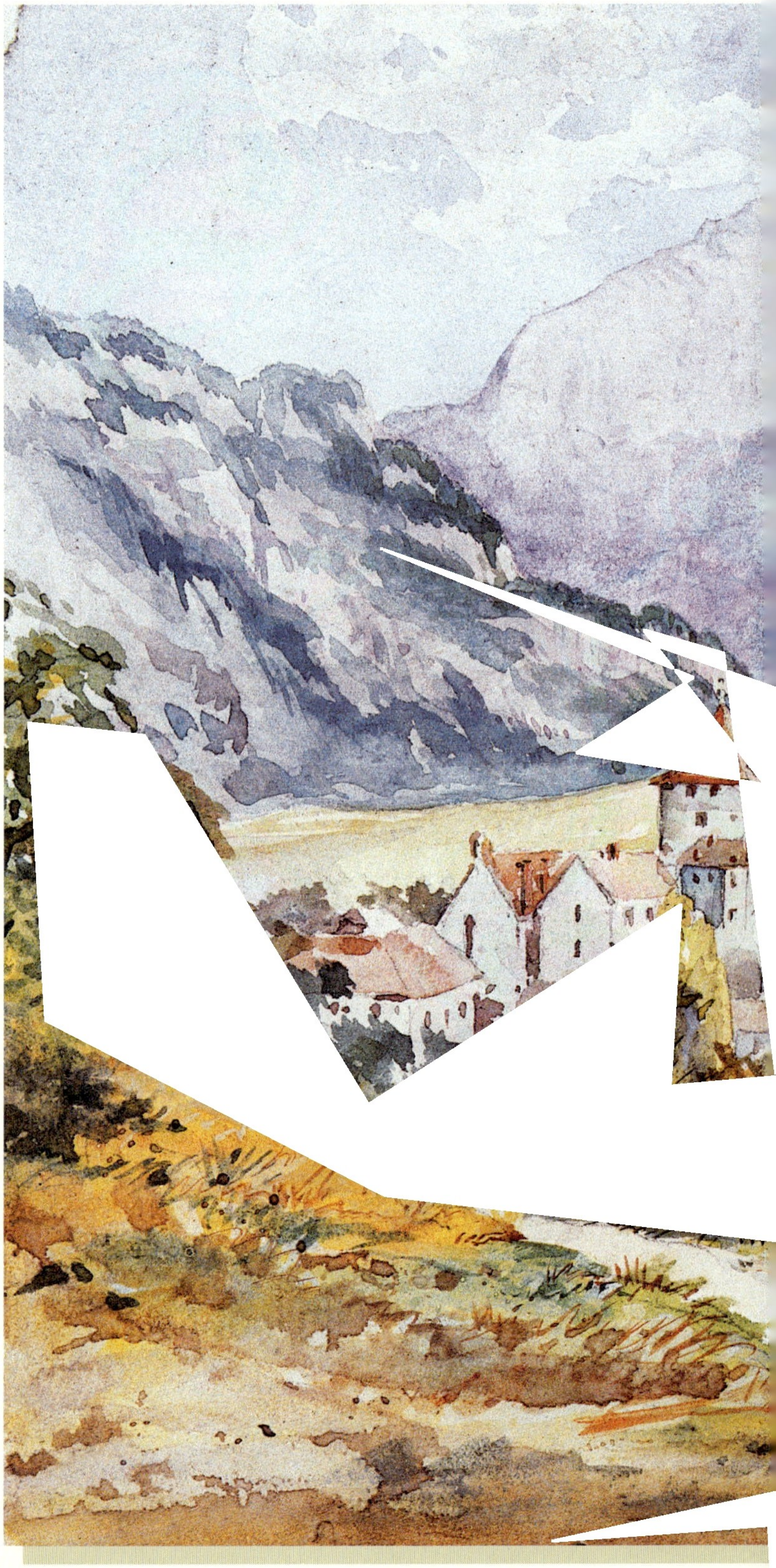

Right: wherever he travelled on holiday, Hodge always had his paints handy. His Alpine views were sometimes slapdash, sometimes quite fine.

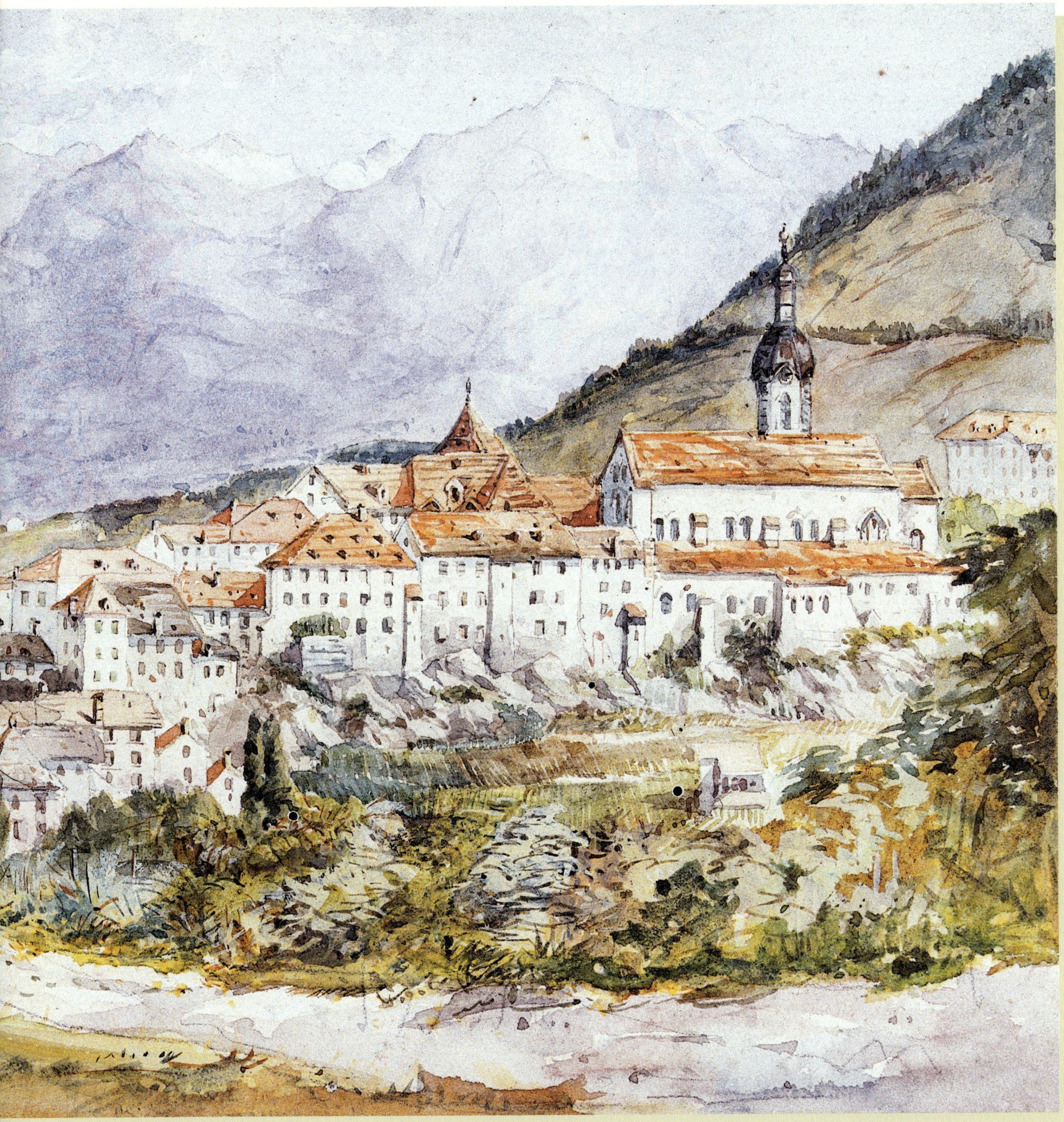

Hodge's 1866 Tour

Letter to a sister from the Hotel de Lille et d'Albion
Rue St. Honoré, Paris, July 22, 1866

"You have seen Boothby before this arrives and he has told what happened to us at Wimbledon. Suffice here to say that I enjoyed my camp life for the short week and was weary of it when I left.

From Wimbledon to Charing X, where they kept me longer than I intended by refusing to cash a circular note, and I was obliged to wait to change it at the Bank the next day. In the interval I went to Woolwich to see Fred Wyton. Thence to Dover where I put up at the "Lord Warden", a large and well appointed hotel. Next across the Channel to Callais.

(Note: Boothby was a friend and golfing partner. When Hodge refers to Wimbledon it was an occasion when he went rifle shooting with the volunteers).

You feel at the moment of landing you are in another quarter of the globe. The manners, costumes, language, all testify to a different race which no amount of steam will ever modify. Compared with us they are quite third rate and inferior in every way.

Their childish, hilarious reception of trifles marks a lower phase of manliness, and, contrasted with the solemn heroes of Wimbledon, their cockhatted, bearded officials in giggling idiotry were at a decided disadvantage.

The women I can't make out distinctly, but if they take pride in the remotest degree in their He's provided for them, why I feel for them unmitigated pity.

On by a fast train through cut and uncut cornfields to Paris. They won't think of harvest in England for a month or six weeks at least. That 21 miles of Dover straits is, for the distance, the greatest barrier this world can show.

There are a great many English people at this hotel, which is very large – my number is 109 and they make up 400 beds.

This place is so constructed that the rooms are in full view of opposite neighbours. Being very warm, with the windows thrown open, while dressing you have the advantage of seeing and being seen. One of my fair friends – French by the look of her – first dons stockings and slippers, then washes very partially in her nightdress. She lets me in very completely for all the mysteries of her toilette, which I will not more particularly describe here, and finishes up by sitting radiant in her balcony. I notice her at times looking my way with much composure, but if she is now edifying her friends with what she saw from my open window her narrative will be very different from mine.

I find some difficulty in talking French and don't attempt it often. I confound the êtres and avoirs, genders and tenses, with delightful nonchalance. The women, dressed to perfection, are not always goodlooking, but always goodtempered and smiling, inviting an address. They walk badly with a jerk – the contrary of sailing majestically."

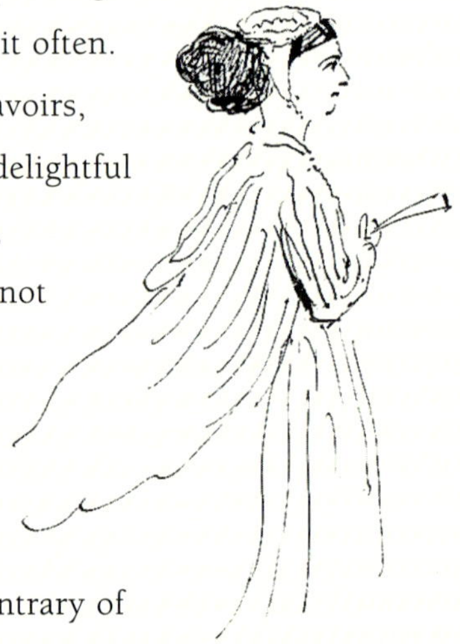

French & don't attempt it often – Confound the être, & avoir, genders & tenses, with delightful nonchalance – The women dress to perfection, are not always good looking, but always good tempered & smiling inviting an address – walk badly with a jerk – the contrary of sailing majestically – This is a faint attempt. the skirt of the dress is very long – vertical stripes chiefly worn – not so much red hair as I expected. & carry a fan or stick in their hand.

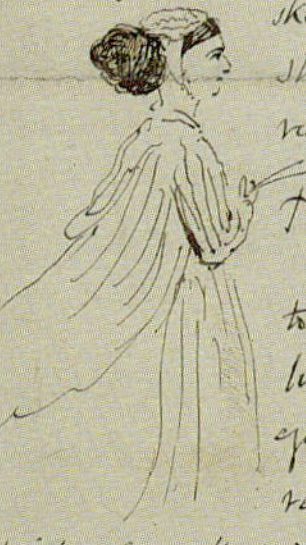

I shall probably go to ~~Pisa~~ Switzerland tonight. It is a long journey of 14 hours to Geneva. Perhaps I shan't go there at all – but shall certainly return by way of Paris & put up at this hotel so that if you have anything particular to write about address me here & I shall get it on my return. Do the hospitable towards Mr. Birch. This portmanteau you were so sure of being mine has a brass plate on it with Ewing's name, now who's right! Tell the Hebdens to be good boys

Veuillez, ma cousine, bien sincèrement votre frère bien affectionné

Thomas –

Rue St Honoré.

Hôtel de Lille et d'Albion.
Paris
July 22. 1866

Are you there Miss?

You have seen Brotherby before this arrives & he has told what happened to us at Wimbledon. Suffice here to say that I enjoyed my camp life for the short week, and was weary of it when I left. Took Reynolds down one day: as I thought, it was an amusing day's outing for him as he protested with many expressions of obligation. Bolt was there too, two or three days consecutively: I was soon tired of that gentleman and only encouraged him to – go away! From Wimbledon to Charing X where they kept me longer than I intended by refusing to cash a circular note, and I was obliged to wait to change it at the Bank next day: in the interval I went to Woolwich to see Fred Weston. Thence to Dover where I put up at the "Lord Warden" a large & well appointed Hotel. Next day across the Channel to Calais. You feel at the moment of landing you

are in another quarter of the globe – The manners, costumes, language, all testify to a different race which no amount of steam will ever modify. Compared with us they are quite third rate and inferior in every way: their childish hilarious reception of trifles marks a lower phase of manliness – & contrasted with the solemn heroes of Wimbledon, their cocked hatted bearded officials, in jiggling idiotcy, were at a decided disadvantage – The women I can't make out distinctly, but if they take pride in the smallest degree in the WC's provided for them, why I feel for them unmitigated pity. On by a fast train through cut and uncut cornfields to Paris. They won't think of harvest in England for a ~~week~~ month or 6 weeks at least – that 21 miles of Dover Straits is for the distance the greatest barrier this world can show. There are a great many English people at this Hotel which is very large – my number is 109 and they make up 400 beds – My luck is always to find myself at the top of every Hotel I go to whether Charing X, Lord Warden, or this: such an everlasting climbing – This place is so constructed that the rooms are in full view of opposite neighbours; being very warm with the windows thrown open, while dressing you have the advantage of seeing & being seen. One

of my fair friends – French by the look of her – first dons stockings & slippers, then washes very partially in her night dress – She lets me in very completely for all the mysteries of her toilette which I will not more particularly describe here, and finishes up by sitting radiant in her balcony. I notice her at times looking my way with much composure, but if she is now edifying her friends with what she saw through my open window, her narrative will be very different from mine – Went to morning service at Notre Dame this morning – put a franc by mistake into the Holy Water which I mistook for an alms box, kissed my hand sweetly to the old priest who held out something or other for me to touch, gave another franc to an old woman who greeted me with "[illegible]", and then seated myself with other worshippers on a rush bottomed chair. Saint-Sacrament going on – good music, magnificent singers. much marching about of golden vestured priests. Lighted candles in most places – Presently some bread lighted up & borne on the shoulders of two small boys preceded by a man with Cocked Hat & silver headed stick – This I feel to be the consummation of absurdity. Get up walk about & look at the statuary, one example of a dying Archbishop the one shot in late years, being remarkably fine. I find some difficulty in talking

Thomas Hodge on Holiday

Belle Vue Hotel.

Neuchatel, Switzerland, July 24, 1866

"To this from Paris in two days, breaking the journey at Dijon. On Sabbath afternoon walked on the Champs Elyses – that emporium of fun for children – all sorts of amusements. Hundreds gather round a French Punchinello who finally died the same death as the one of our young days. Merry-go-rounds filled with pleasure-seeking six-year-olds. Some drove four-in hand goat carriages and others sailed their little boats in the fish ponds. Many played football and other games. There is no such sight in Europe as is seen under the leafy shade of the Champs Elyses.

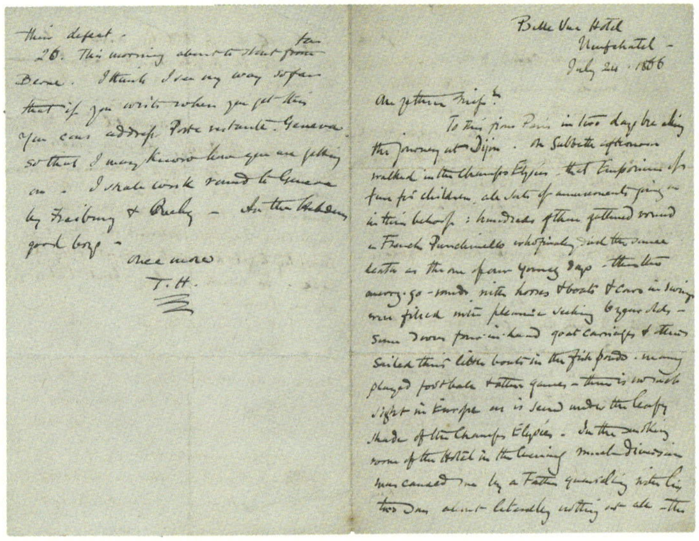
their defeat. —
26. This morning about to start from Berne. I think I see my way so far that if you write when you get this you can address Poste restante. Geneva. so that I may know how you are getting on. I shall work round to Geneva by Freiburg & [illegible] — [illegible] good boys —
Once more
T.H.

Belle Vue Hotel
Neufchatel –
July 24 · 1866

[illegible]
To this from Paris in two days breaking the journey at Dijon. On Sabbath afternoon walked in the Champs Elysees – that emporium of fun for children, all sorts of amusements going on in their behalf: hundreds of them gathered round a French Punchinello who finally died the same death as the one of our young days – then the merry-go-rounds with horses & boats & cars in swings were filled with pleasure seeking 6 year olds – some drove four-in-hand goat carriages & others sailed their little boats in the fish ponds. many played football & other games – there is no such sight in Europe as is seen under the leafy shade of the Champs Elysees. In the smoking room of the Hotel in the evening much diversion was caused me by a Father quarrelling with his two sons about [illegible] nothing at all – the

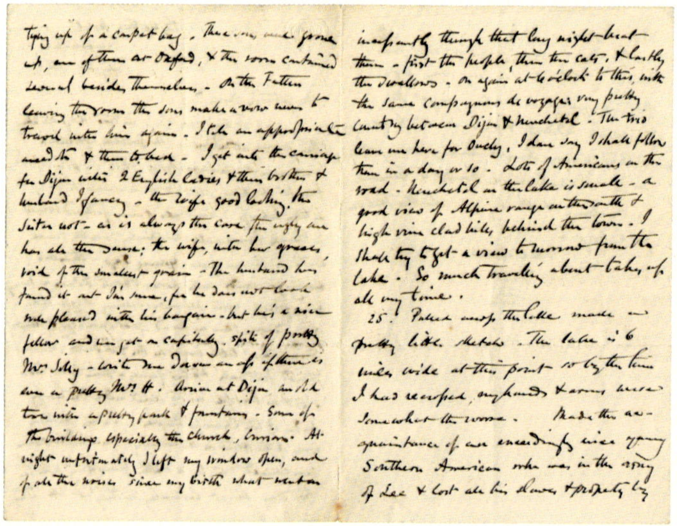
tying up of a carpet bag. These are grown up, one of them at Oxford, & the room contained several besides themselves. On the Father leaving the room the sons make a vow never to travel with him again. I take an opportunity [illegible] & then to bed. I get into the carriage for Dijon with 2 English ladies & their brother & husband I fancy – the wife good looking, the sister not – as is always the case the ugly one has all the sense; the wife, with her graces, void of the smallest grain. The husband has found it out I'm sure, for he does not look well pleased with his bargain – but he's a nice fellow and we get on capitally. 'spite of pretty Mrs Silly – write me down an ass if there is ever a pretty Mrs H. Arrive at Dijon an old town with a pretty park & fountains. Some of the buildings especially the church, curious. At night unfortunately I left my window open, and of all the noises since my birth what with

incessantly through that long night beat them – first the people, then the cats, & lastly the swallows. On again at 6 o'clock to this, with the same compagnons de voyage. Very pretty country between Dijon & Neuchatel. The trio leave me here for Ouchy, I dare say I shall follow them in a day or 10. Lots of Americans on the road. Neuchatel on the lake is small – a good view of Alpine range on the south & high vine clad hills behind the town. I shall try to get a view tomorrow from the lake. So much travelling about takes up all my time.
25. Pulled across the lake made a pretty little sketch. The lake is 6 miles wide at this point so by the time I had recrossed, my hands & arms were somewhat the worse. Made the acquaintance of an exceedingly nice young Southern American who was in the army of Lee & lost all his slaves & property by

I get into the carriage for Dijon with two English ladies and their brother and husband I fancy – the wife good-looking, the sister not. As is always the case, the ugly one has all the sense, the wife, with her graces, void of the smallest grain. The husband has found it out I'm sure, for he does not look well pleased with his bargain. But he's a nice fellow and we get on capitally, 'spite of pretty Mrs. Silly. Write me down as an ass if there is ever a pretty Mrs. H.

July 25

Pulled across the lake at Neuchatel and made a pretty little sketch. The lake is six miles wide at this point, so by the time I had recrossed my hands and arms were somewhat the worse. Made the acquaintance of an exceedingly nice young Southern American who was in the army of Lee and lost all his slaves and property by their defeat."

Berne, July 26, 1866

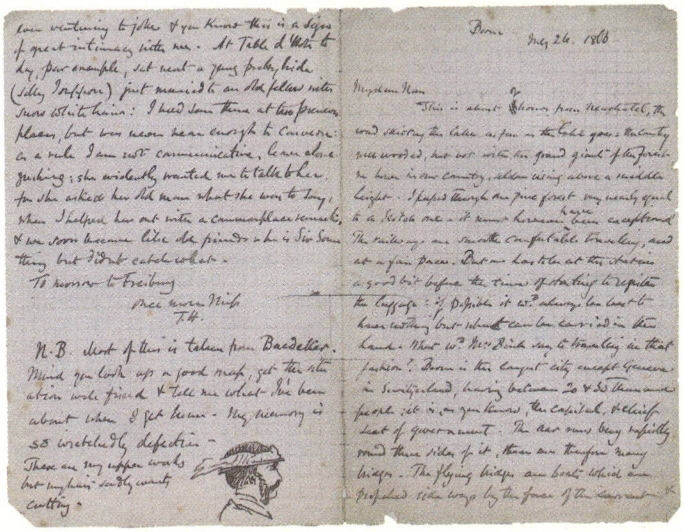

"Today I went into a badhouse; and the greatest publicity is given to them by signboards. You know of course that bad means bath. Parts of the river are staked off and the course of the stream modified, and over it is built a wooden house to ensure secrecy to those who make use of the badhouses.

The greatest attraction of Berne is the view it commands of the snowy peaks of the Bernese Oberland, alps which in clear weather like today may be seen from every open space. Nothing can exceed the sublimity of these mountains. Today was very favourable and we saw what is called Alpgluhen (Glow of the Alps). Long after the shades of evening, the mountains begin to glow from their base upwards as if illuminated by a bright internal fire.

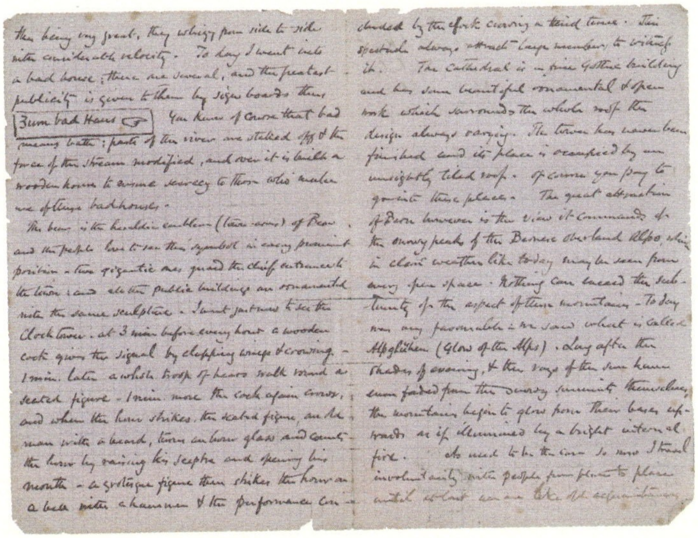

I travel involuntarily with people from place to place until at last we are like old acquaintances, even venturing to joke, and you know this is a sign of great intimacy with me. At Table d'Hôte today, par example, sat next a young pretty bride (silly, I suppose) just married to an old fellow with snow-white hair. As a rule I am not communicative, leave alone gushing. She evidently wanted me to talk to her for she asked her old man what she was to say, when I helped her out by a commonplaçe remark and we soon became like old friends. He is Sir Something, but I didn't catch what.

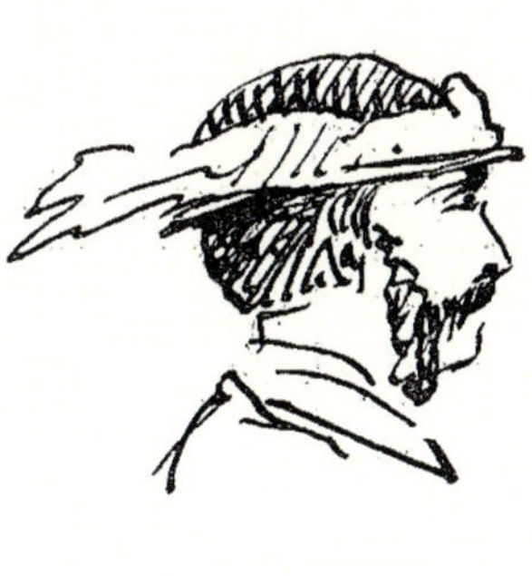

N.B. Most of this is taken from Baedeker. These are my upper works but my hair sadly wants cutting."

Freiburg. Friday, July 27, 1866

"This morning at Berne I got up early and took a sketch from near the river of the Town. I think it will turn out well. On to Freiburg with some lady tourists. Cooks excursionists; seemed nice people, but as a rule excursion ticket people are not first chop.

Freiburg is situated very much like Berne on the steep slopes of a river (Saane). The town is the most remarkable and picturesque in my experience, but the LION is the Church of St. Nichols on account of the organ and the organist Karl Vogt. The organ is the finest in Europe and the organist (I should say) the best in the world. The Hotels issue tickets at a franc apiece, and tonight I toddled in not thinking much about it. But by George, Miss, he woke me up.

I never heard music before. Now 'twas a full brass band, and now a chorus of voices gently stealing from 50 miles

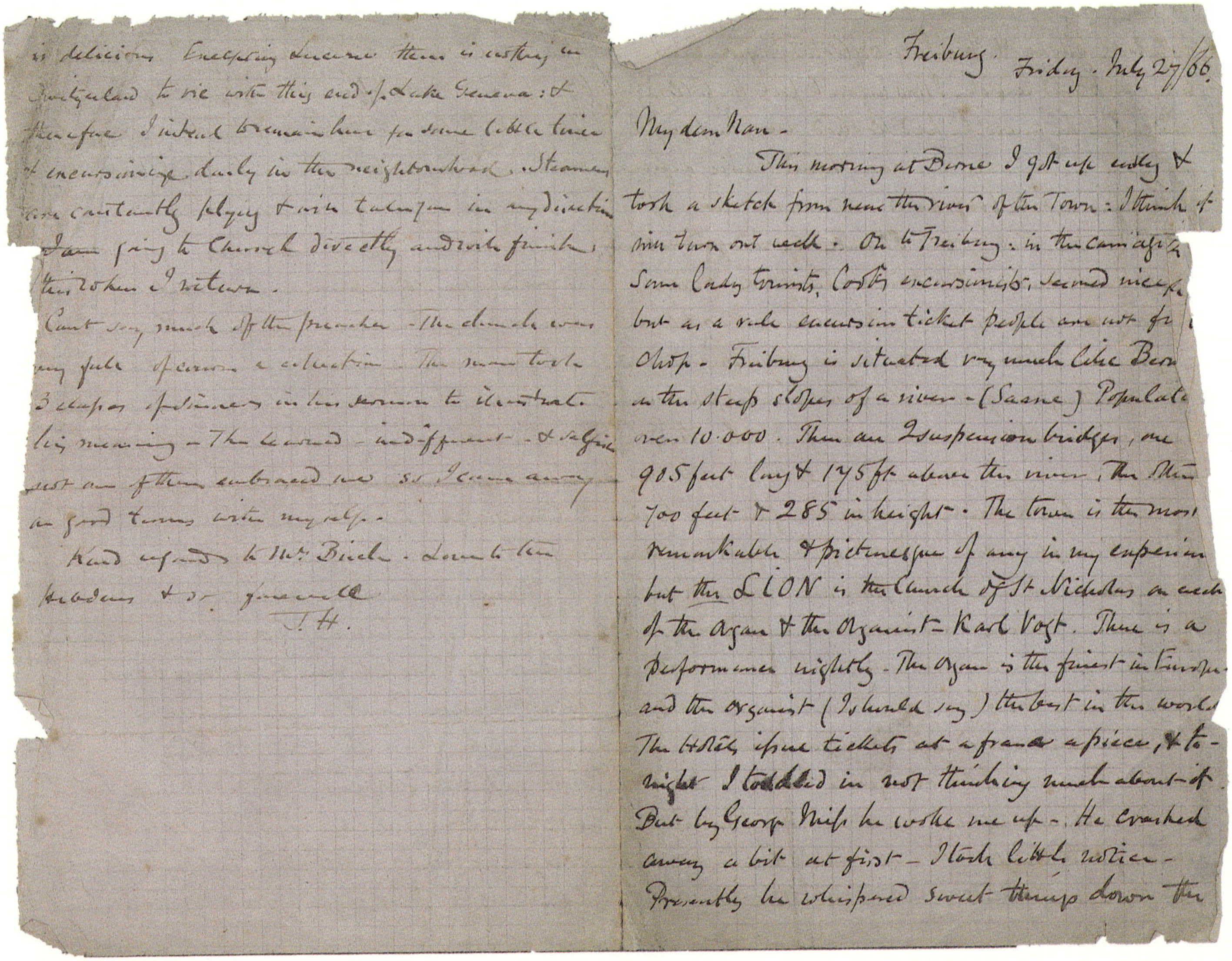
is delicious. Everything because there is nothing in Switzerland to vie with this end of Lake Geneva: & therefore I intend to remain here for some little time & excursionize daily in the neighbourhood. Steamers are constantly plying & rail taking one in any direction. I am going to Church directly and will finish this when I return.
Can't say much of the preacher. The church was very full of course a collection. The man took 3 classes of sinners in his sermon to illustrate his meaning — The learned — indifferent — & religious not one of them embraced me so I came away on good terms with myself.
Kind regards to Mr Birch. Love to the Readers & c. farewell
T.H.

Freiburg. Friday. July 27/66.
My dear Nan —
This morning at Berne I got up early & took a sketch from near the river of the Town. I think it will turn out well. On to Freiburg in the carriage some lady tourists, Cooks excursionists, seemed nice people but as a rule excursion ticket people are not first chop. Freiburg is situated very much like Berne on the steep slopes of a river — (Saane) Population over 10.000. There are 2 suspension bridges, one 905 feet long & 175 ft above the river, the other 700 feet & 285 in height. The town is the most remarkable & picturesque of any in my experience but the LION is the Church of St Nicholas on account of the Organ & the Organist — Karl Vogt. There is a performance nightly. The Organ is the finest in Europe and the Organist (I should say) the best in the world. The Hotels issue tickets at a franc apiece, & to-night I toddled in not thinking much about it. But by George Miss he woke me up. He crashed away a bit at first — I took little notice — Presently he whispered sweet things down the

off to within a yard of me – voices mind you, not imitation, there was no doubt in my mind. Then the earth began to quake, and when this culminated into a thousand harmonious thunderstorms I shrank aside for support against a dark pillar and wept freely. Most of the audience were affected. A man not far from me had wriggled his legs right over the bench in front of him with his head near the floor. He's there now, I dare say. A woman was carried out in a faint and then affected others who felt obliged to leave. He played continuously for one hour, two English airs among the rest. Home Sweet Home was one – but throughout that whole hour there was no harsh, false sound. Baedeker says: 'The organ has 67 stops and 7,800 pipes, some of them 32 feet long'. I say: 'The distance is short and the fare cheap to Freiburg, to listen for an hour to Karl Vogt on the St. Nicholas organ'."

Ouchy, near Lausanne, Sunday

"I got up at six o'clock yesterday morning for a sketch of Freiburg. So much time is consumed in the railway, little is left for anything else. Getting up betimes is the only way of obviating this loss. Where are all the young women in Switzerland? I see nothing but old – and oh! so ugly – women and children.

Ouchy is but a large Hotel (Beau Rivage). At present there are a great many Americans, a few English, scarcely any French or German. Spend much of my time drawing and writing in my room. Last night they had a ball in the large hall – but not many joined in (the beaus and the keen American girls). Altogether the tone of society here is not of the highest. The scenery is delicious. Excepting Lucerne there is nothing to vie with this end of Lake Geneva."

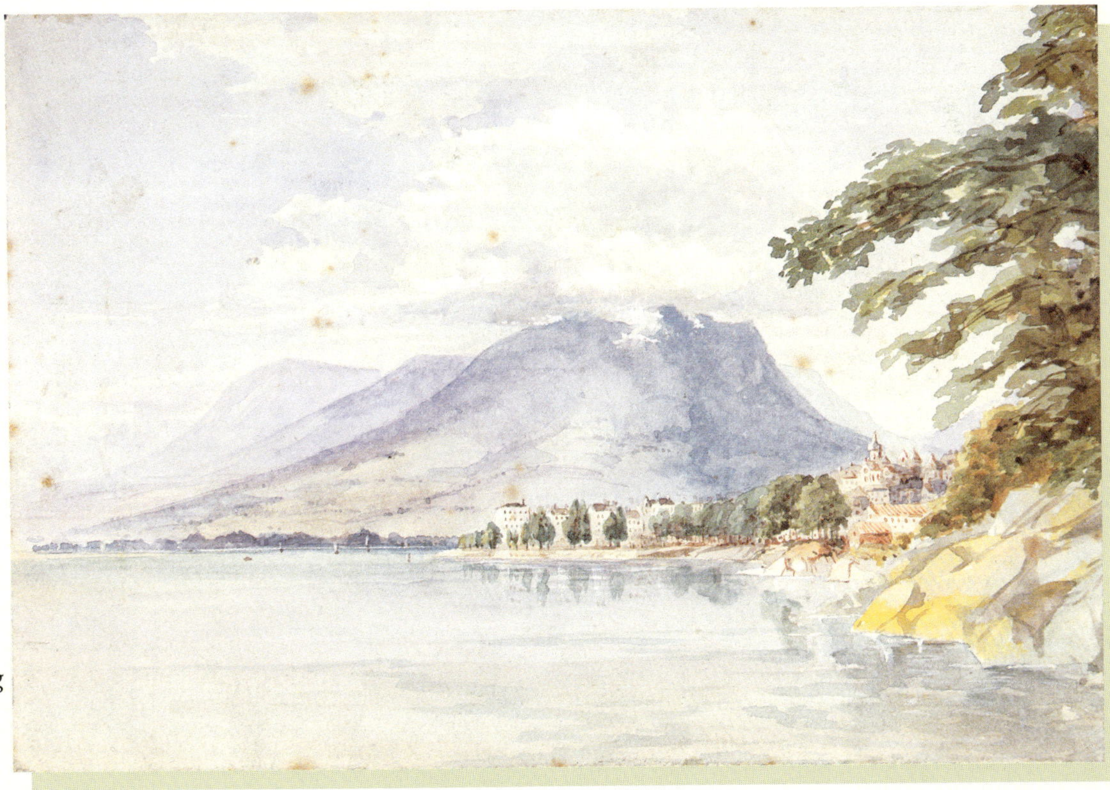

Right: another Swiss-Italian lake scene by Hodge, whose pleasure was to stay by the water whenever possible to enjoy some energetic rowing as well as views.

Thomas Hodge on Holiday

Ouchy, July 31

"We get the Times here the day after publication, three hours only later than we get it at St. Andrews.

The American women are excessively smart, not in the American sense, but as to dress.

My new friend is an Irishman, lately in, tolerably high up and well-to-do I fancy. Unlike most Irishmen, he is of few words. He is just the sort of man I like – we nod at one another of a morning, converse or not as seemeth best; he goes one way, I another. At night we smoke a cigar together and talk a bit – another nod and the thing is done. I hate your obtrusive beggars."

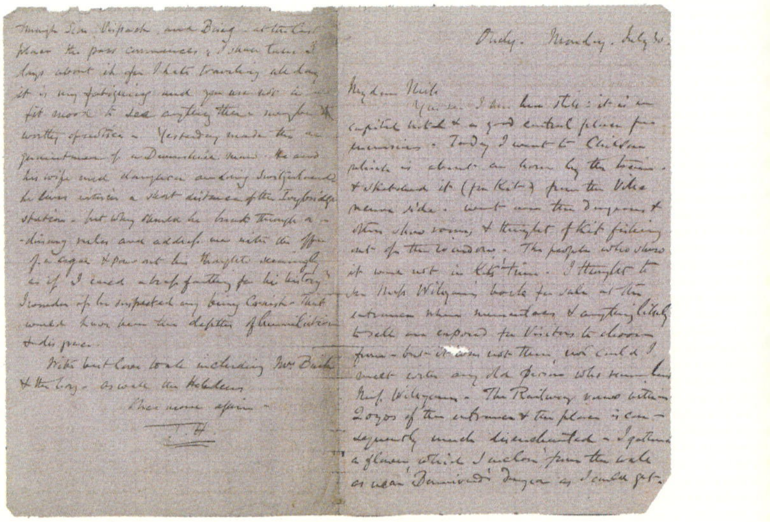

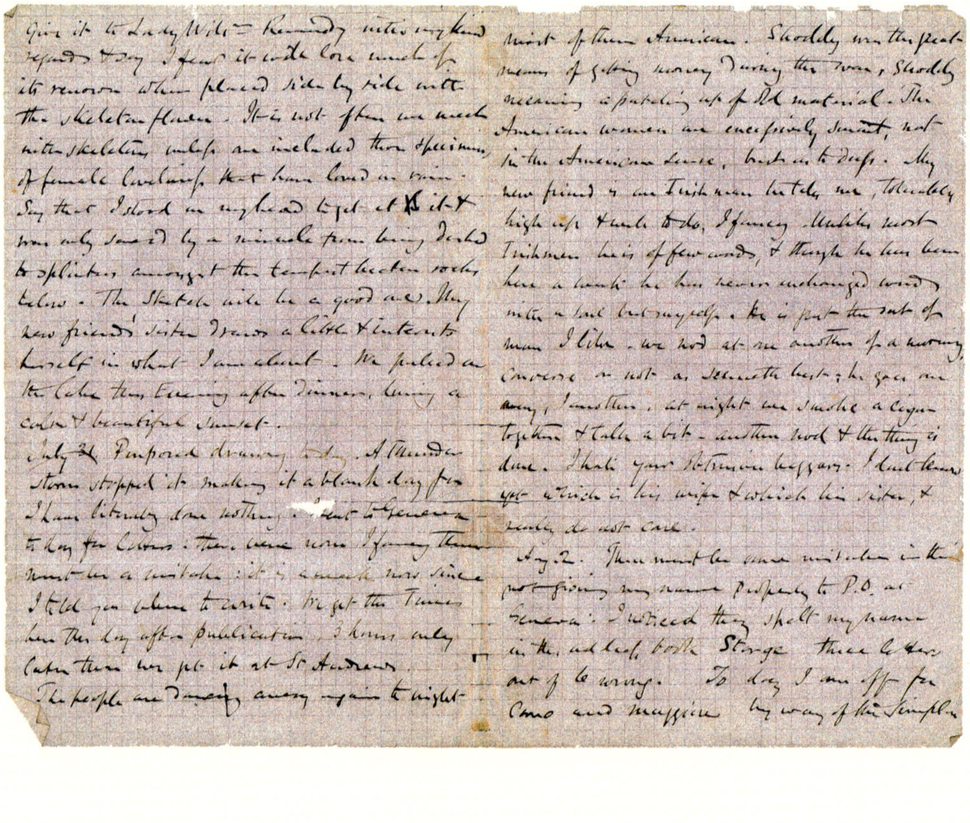

Stresa, nr. Lago Maggiore
Sunday, August 5, 1866

"In Italy at last. Four days ago I left Ouchy – steamed up to the head of the lake to the terminus of "Chemin de Fer" and on to Martigny and Sion, both of which I have previously visited. There is about the Rhone Valley so strong a feeling of desolation and exclusion that, combined with the miserable look of the goitered population, I have much to do to keep myself from a special fit of the blues.

Slept at Sion and caught my first – and trust last – flea. Chatted with an Alpine Club man, who, with an axe and a look of fierce daring, seemed bent on virgin summits. He did not succeed in inducing me to join him – the contour of my calves, probably striking some chord of ascent about him. At Sion I got into the diligence with a Yankee and his courier. I fought with him again the battle of the South from Sion to Brieg, where we slept the night. Next day commenced the Simplon Pass in the same society. The weather was propitious, the Yankee (a bilious man) in extasies. The rugged grandeur and beauty of the descent of this pass into Italy I can never hope to describe without a suspicion of exaggeration. In Switzerland no grapes, no peaches and the time of figs not yet. In Italy in the space of a few hours by the slow diligence, we lunch off all these fruits and most delicious at Domo Dossola. Then on without much variety but always beautiful scenery to Stresa, the point on Lago Maggiore for the finest views. A large, comfortable Hotel. From my window I have a delightful view of islands ornate with palaces and gardens, overdone to the English taste but suited to the Italian.

Monday. Sketch a little daily, and where I have no time for this, pick up photographs. This is the spot for artists, who ought to be here in shoals. As yet I have not met with one. Americans block up the views and the blue hills echo faintly but eternally with their 'guessing' or 'I tell you stranger'. They reduce everything to the standard of bigness – the lakes are ponds and the mountains 'pretty'. they are jealous of nothing belonging to us but our objects of art and old baronial residences. They 'cave in' to London beating New York, but 'in fifteen years, I guess, New York will be so big London would be lost in it and you, stranger, will feel like a silicion unit of the sea shore'."

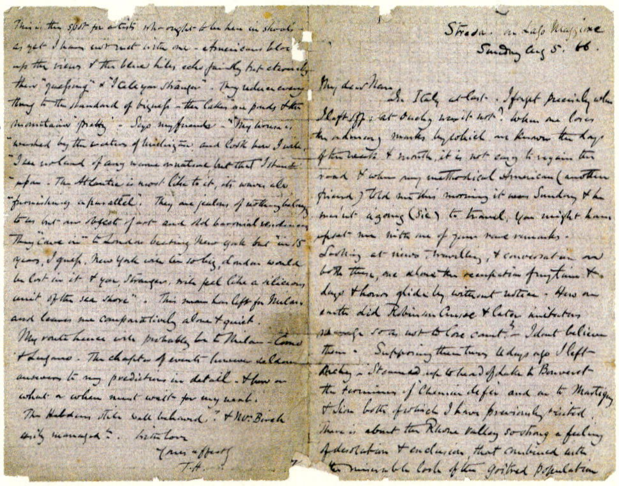

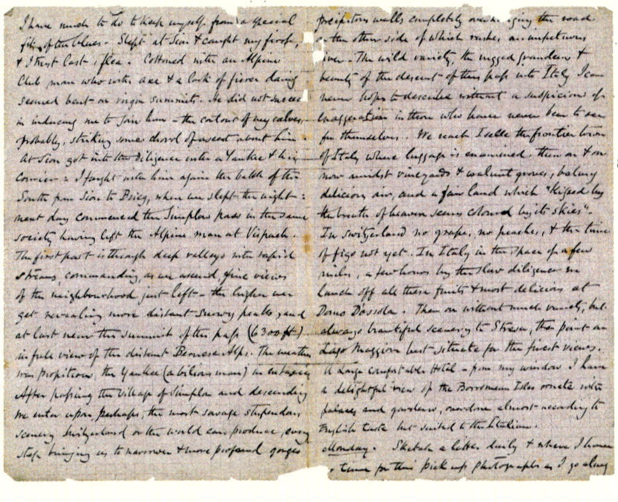

Thomas Hodge on Holiday

Bellagio, Lake Como, August 10, 1866

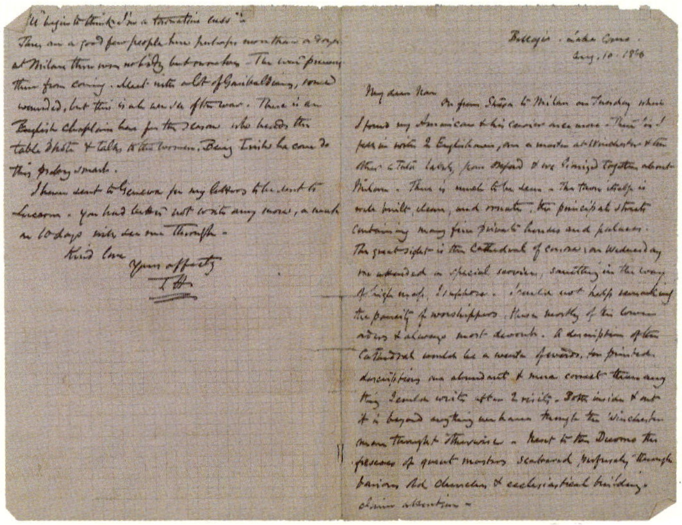

"On from Stresa to Milan on Tuesday, where I found my American and his courier once more. There too I fell in with two Englishmen, one a master at Winchester and the other a tutor lately from Oxford, and we lionised together about Milan. There is much to be seen."

Saturday

"One of the churches, S. Maria delle Grazie, contains Leonardo da Vinci's celebrated Last Supper painted on the wall and consequently in a bad state of preservation. But how wonderful it is! To say that it is the finest painting in the world is only what everybody who knows what art is says. We worshipped there for an hour and a half.

Como itself – the town – I was disappointed in. What we saw of it was dirty and the people a match for it. As we steamed away we were struck with its lovely situation amongst the green hills almost aspiring to be mountains, the town itself very picturesque.

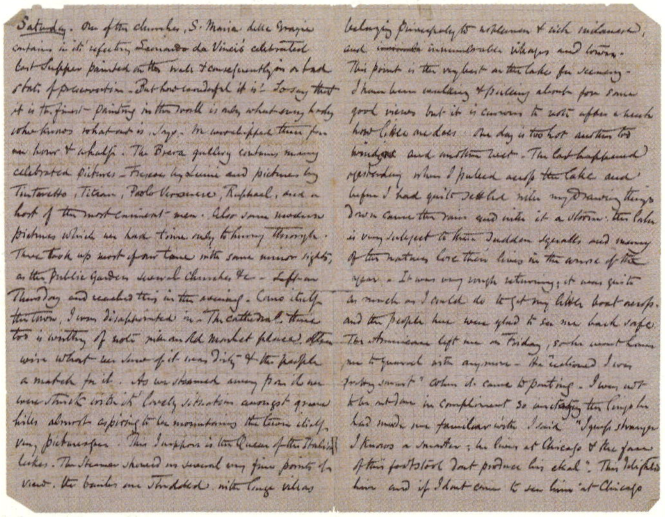

Yesterday when I pulled across the lake, and, before I had quite settled with my drawing things, down came the rain and with it a storm. This lake is very subject to these sudden squalls and many of the natives lose their lives in the course of the year. It was very rough returning. It was quite as much as I could do to get my little boat across, and the people here were glad to see me back safe. The American left on Friday so he won't have me to quarrel with anymore. He reckoned I was 'pretty smart' when it came to painting and if I don't come to see him at Chicago he'll begin to think I'm a 'tarnation cuss'.

Meet with a lot of Garibaldians, some wounded, but that is all we see of the war."

August 22, Leamington

"At Lugano, where I last wrote, I ascended a high point and obtained a lovely panorama. Came thence over the St. Gothard Pass, reach Bale and Paris in twelve hours, had a night's rest there and on to London the next morning, to Leamington next day, where I am now. This trip on the whole I have enjoyed more than my previous one, dependant on the following maxims, which, if recorded, may be valuable to others as well as myself:

1. Never travel with a party. I have scarcely met with a family, or a friendly few, who were not at loggerheads amongst themselves and welcomed me as a relief to the tedium of their verbal intercourse. What a bore married life is!

2. Travel 1st class and go to the best hotels. It is cheapest in the end, for what can repay one for the worry of hard, uncomfortable seats, crowded carriages, and unwholesome meals and beds with B's in them.

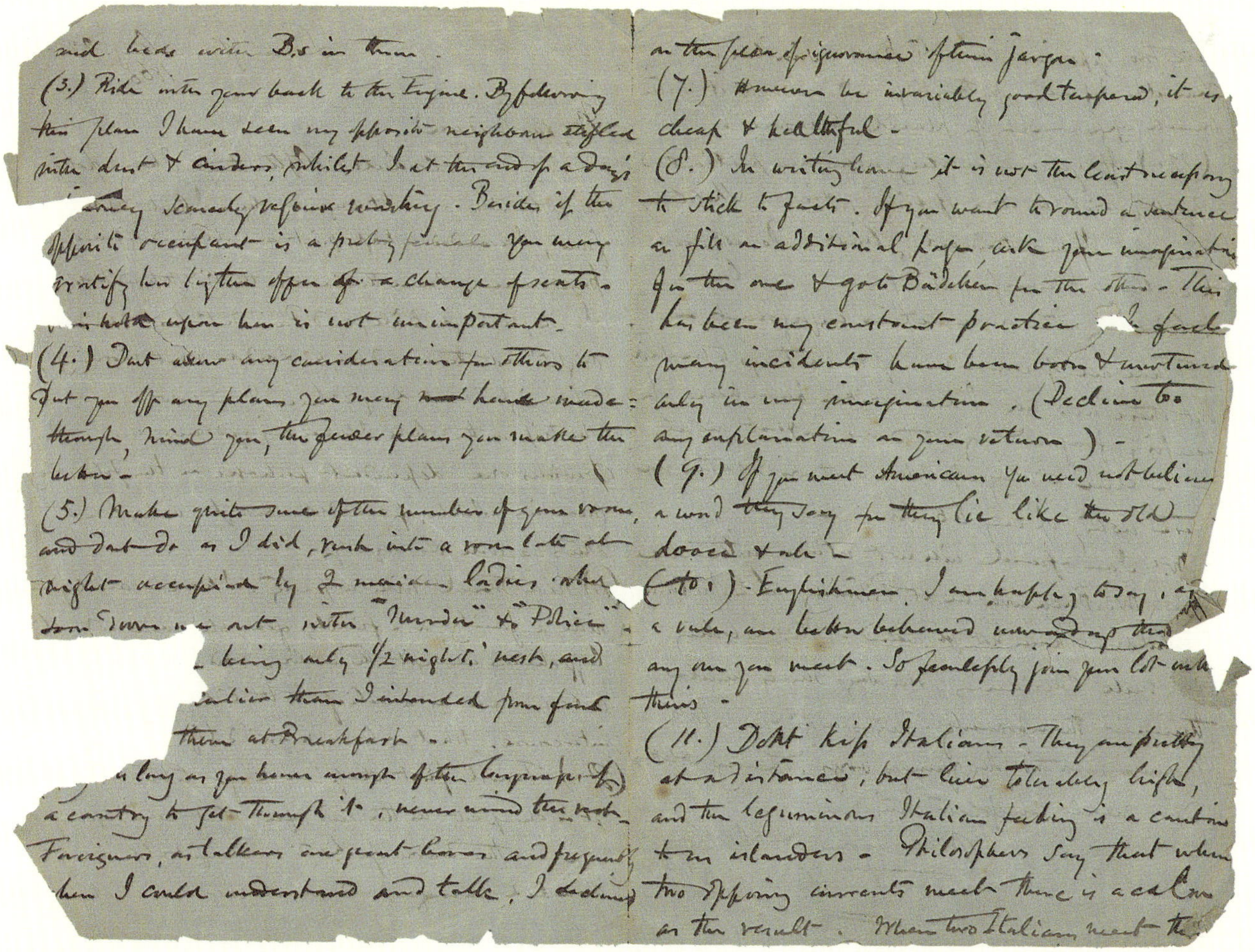

and beds with B's in them.
(3.) Ride with your back to the Engine. By following this plan I have seen my opposite neighbour stifled with dust & cinders, whilst I at the end of a day's [illegible] scarcely require washing. Besides if the opposite occupant is a pretty female you may gratify her by the offer of a change of seats. [illegible] upon her is not unimportant.
(4.) Don't allow any considerations for others to put you off any plans you may have made: though, mind you, the fewer plans you make the better.
(5.) Make quite sure of the number of your room, and don't do as I did, rush into a room late at night occupied by 2 [illegible] ladies who [illegible] out with "Murder" & "Police" [illegible] being only 1/2 night's rest, and [illegible] earlier than I intended [illegible] them at Breakfast.
[illegible] as long as you have enough of the language [illegible] a country to get through it, never mind the rest. Foreigners, as talkers are great bores and frequently when I could understand and talk, I declined on the plea of ignorance of their jargon.
(7.) Always be invariably good tempered, it is cheap & healthful.
(8.) In writing home it is not the least necessary to stick to facts. If you want to round a sentence or fill an additional page ask your imagination for the one & go to Bädeker for the other. This has been my constant practice. [illegible] fact many incidents have been born & nurtured only in my imagination. (Decline too any explanation on your return.)
(9.) If you meet Americans you need not believe a word ~~they say~~ for they lie like the old [illegible] doose & all.
(10.) Englishmen, I am happy to say, as a rule, are better behaved [illegible] than any one you meet. So [illegible] join your lot with theirs.
(11.) Don't kiss Italians. They are pretty at a distance, but live tolerably high, and the leguminous Italian feeding is a caution to us islanders. Philosophers say that when two opposing currents meet there is a calm as the result. When two Italians meet the

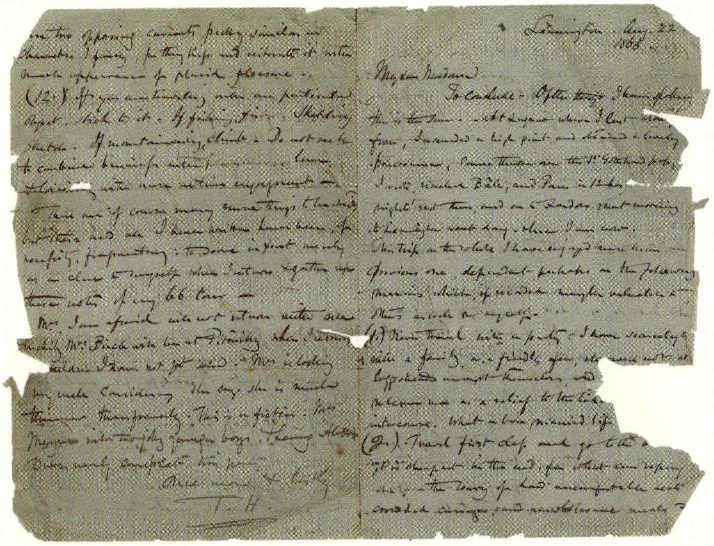
Leamington. Aug. 22. 1868.

My dear Madam

T. H.

3. Ride with your back to the engine. By following this plan I have seen my opposite neighbour stifled with dust and cinders, whilst I at the end of the day's journey scarcely required washing. Besides, if the opposite occupant is a pretty female you may gratify her by the offer of a change of seats. This hold upon her is not unimportant.

4. Don't allow any consideration for others to put you off any plans you may have made, though, mind you, the fewer plans you make the better.

5. Make quite sure of the number of your room and don't do as I did, rush into a room late at night occupied by 2 maiden ladies who soon threw me out with (cries of) 'murder' to 'Police'. The result being only half night's rest and getting up earlier than I intended from fear of seeing them at breakfast.

6. As long as you have enough of the language of a country to get through it, never mind the rest. Foreigners, as talkers, are great bores and frequently when I could understand and talk I didn't on the fear of ignorance, of times jargon.

7. However, be invariably goodtempered. It is cheap and healthful.

8. In writing home it is not the least necessary to stick to facts. If you want to round a sentence or fill an additional page, ask your imagination for the one and go to Baedeker for the other. This has been my constant practice. In fact many incidents have been born and nurtured only in my imagination. (Decline, too, any explanation on your return.)

9. If you meet Americans you need not believe a word they say, for they lie like the old dooce and all.

10. Englishmen, I am happy to say, as a rule, are better behaved nowadays than anyone you meet. So fearlessly join your lot unto theirs.

11. Don't kiss Italians. They are pretty at a distance, but live tolerably high, and leguminous Italian feeding is a caution to us Islanders.

12. If you are travelling with one particular object, stick to it. If fishing, fish. Sketching, sketch. If mountaineering, climb. Do not seek to combine business with pleasure, lone and loitering with some native enjoyment."

1867 Tour

Rotterdam, July 28, 1867

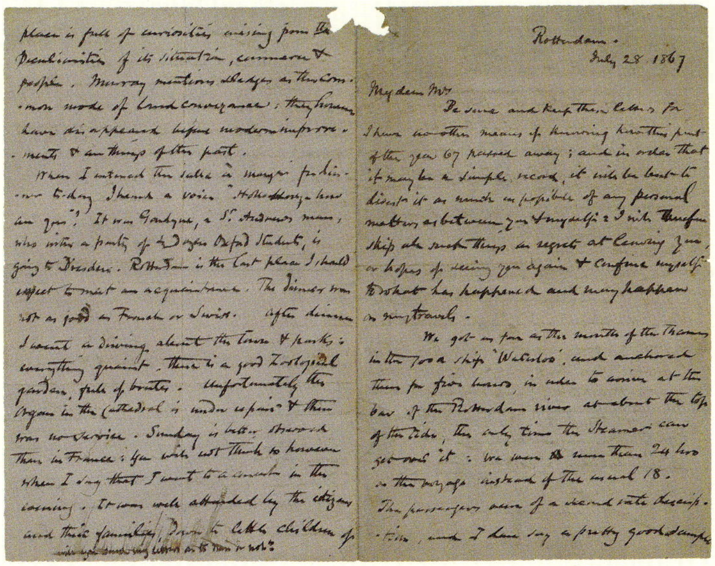

Rotterdam.
July 28 1867

My dear Mr

Be sure and keep these letters for I have no other means of knowing how this part of the year 67 passed away; and in order that it may be a simple record, it will be best to divest it as much as possible of any personal matters as between you & myself: I will therefore skip all such things as regrets at leaving you, or hopes of seeing you again & confine myself to what has happened and may happen on my travels.

We got as far as the mouth of the Thames in the good ship 'Waterloo', and anchored there for five hours, in order to arrive at the bar of the Rotterdam river at about the top of the tide, the only time the Steamer can get over it: we were more than 24 hours on the voyage instead of the usual 18. The passengers were of a second rate description, and I dare say a pretty good sample

place is full of curiosities arising from the peculiarities of its situation, commerce & people. Murray mentions sledges as the common mode of land conveyance; they however have disappeared before modern improvements & are things of the past.

When I entered the salle à manger for dinner today I heard a voice "Hollo Stoney how are you"! It was Goodyear, a St Andrews man, who with a party of 2 dozen Oxford Students, is going to Dresden. Rotterdam is the last place I should expect to meet an acquaintance. The dinner was not as good as French or Swiss. After dinner I went a driving about the town & parks: everything quaint. There is a good Zoological garden, full of beauties. Unfortunately the Organ in the Cathedral is under repair & there was no service. Sunday is better observed than in France: you will not think so however when I say that I went to a concert in the evening. It was well attended by the citizens and their families, down to little children of [illegible]

"We got as far as the mouth of the Thames in the good ship 'Waterloo' and anchored there for five hours in order to arrive at the bar of the Rotterdam river at the top of the tide, the only time the steamer can get over it. We were more than 24 hours on the voyage instead of the usual 18. The passengers were of a second-rate description – cattle dealers, skippers, a lady or two with daughters for a cheap foreign school, etc. There was also a lady artist, who sketched all the craft down the Thames, but I can't say much for her efforts. Agreeable little woman though, and we entertained each other at dinner with talk about the Royal Academy and 'old water colours'.

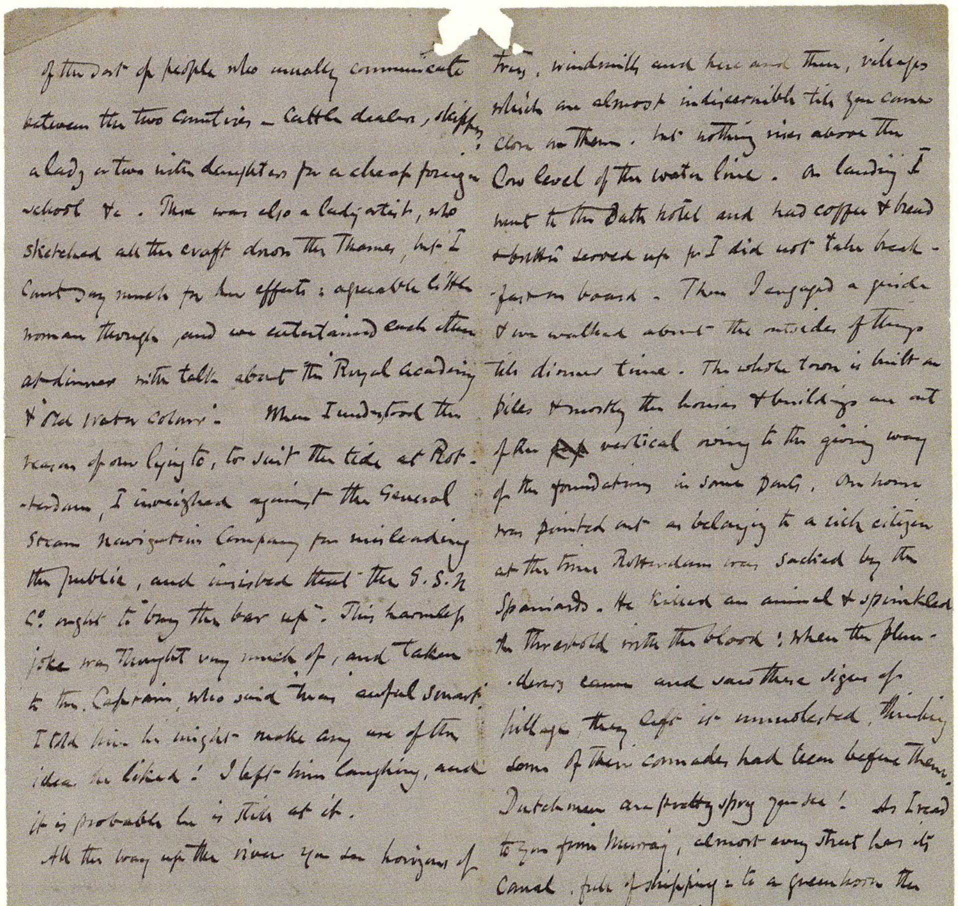

of the sort of people who usually communicate between the two countries – cattle dealers, skippers, a lady or two with daughters for a cheap foreign school &c. There was also a lady artist, who sketched all the craft down the Thames, but I can't say much for her efforts: agreeable little woman though, and we entertained each other at dinner with talk about the 'Royal Academy' & 'old water colours'. When I understood the reason of our lying to, to suit the tide at Rotterdam, I inveighed against the General Steam Navigation Company for misleading the public, and insisted that the G.S.N. Co. ought to "bring the bar up". This harmless joke was thought very much of, and taken to the Captain, who said 'twas "awful smart". I told him he might make any use of the idea he liked! I left him laughing, and it is probable he is still at it.

All the way up the river you see horizons of trees, windmills and here and there, villages which are almost indiscernible till you come close to them. but nothing rises above the low level of the water line. On landing I went to the Bath hotel and had coffee & bread & butter served up for I did not take breakfast on board. Then I engaged a guide & we walked about the outside of things till dinner time. The whole town is built on piles & mostly the houses & buildings are out of the vertical owing to the giving way of the foundations in some parts. One house was pointed out as belonging to a rich citizen at the time Rotterdam was sacked by the Spaniards. He killed an animal & sprinkled the threshold with the blood; when the plunderers came and saw these signs of pillage, they left it unmolested, thinking some of their comrades had been before them. Dutchmen are pretty spry you see! As I read to you from Murray, almost every street has its Canal, full of shipping: to a greenhorn the

Sunday is better observed here than in France. You will not think so however when I say that I went to a concert in the evening. It was well attended by the citizens and their families, down to little children of four or five years of age. Boys of eight take their cigars and liquor just like their elders. Is this to be condemned? Those who can receive it may?

Thomas Hodge on Holiday

The Dutch, male and female, are ill-looking and ungainly, but impress you certainly with a strong idea of their simplicity and honesty. For almost the first time I feel myself handsome, with small feet and hands. The feeding is not at all good at the Hotel. The luxurious Inns of Switzerland are the growth of the requirements of the fastidious English. Until the English make this a highroad and frequent it constantly, the Dutch people will be satisfied with their poor fare."

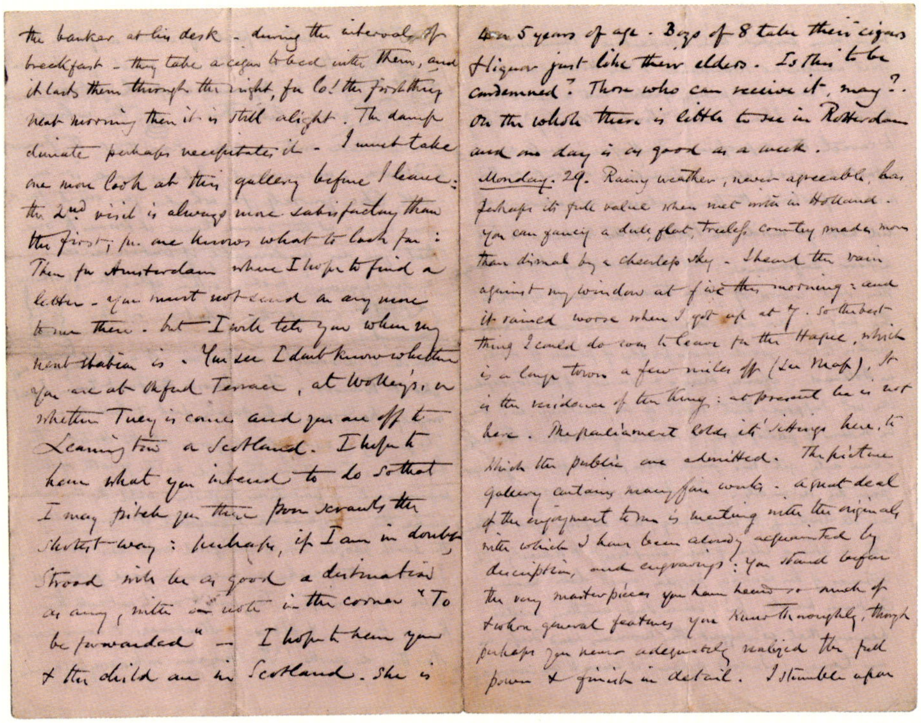

the banker at his desk – during the intervals of breakfast – they take a cigar to bed with them, and it lasts them through the night, for lo! the first thing next morning then it is still alight. The damp climate perhaps necessitates it – I must take one more look at this gallery before I leave: the 2nd visit is always more satisfactory than the first, for one knows what to look for: Then for Amsterdam where I hope to find a letter – you must not send any more to me there – but I will tell you where my next station is. You see I don't know whether you are at Oxford Terrace, at Wolley's, or whether Tuey is come and you are off to Leamington or Scotland. I hope to hear what you intend to do so that I may pitch you there from towards the shortest way: perhaps, if I am in doubt Strood will be as good a destination as any, with a note in the corner "To be forwarded" – I hope to hear you & the child are in Scotland. She is

two 5 years of age. Boys of 8 take their cigars Higuor just like their elders. Is this to be condemned? Those who can receive it, may?. On the whole there is little to see in Rotterdam and one day is as good as a week.

Monday 29. Rainy weather, never agreeable, but perhaps its full value when met with in Holland. You can fancy a dull flat, treeless country made more than dismal by a cheerless sky. I heard the rain against my window at five this morning & and it rained worse when I got up at 7. So the best thing I could do was to leave for the Hague, which is a large town a few miles off (see map). It is the residence of the King: at present he is not here. The parliament hold its sittings here, to which the public are admitted. The picture gallery contains many fine works – a great deal of the enjoyment to me is meeting with the originals with which I have been already acquainted by description, and engravings: you stand before the very masterpieces you have heard so much of & whose general features you know thoroughly, though perhaps you never adequately realized the full power & finish in detail. I stumble upon

Tuesday 30, Amsterdam

"This is more of a place in every way than Rotterdam. The houses and buildings are quite as grand and the shops as good as any town, barring London and Paris, that I have seen. There are 35,000 Jews in the town and though they number so many they keep their race quite distinct. You never meet with any mixture. There is the unmistakable Dutchman and the irrepressible Jew, and every man is one or the other. The Jews are mostly engaged in diamond cutting.

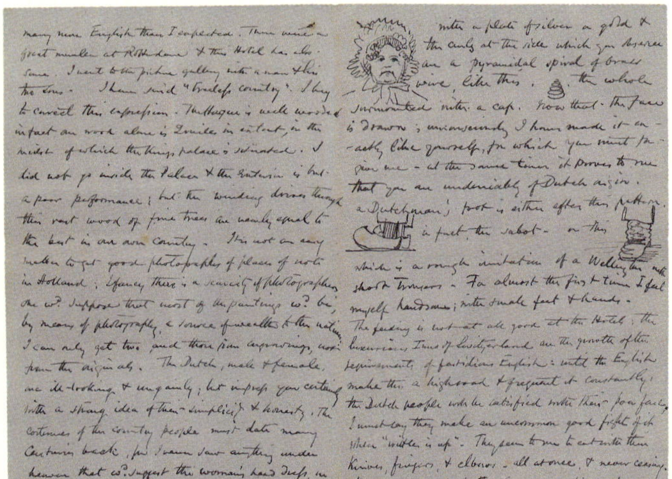

many more English than I expected. There were a great number at Rotterdam & the Hotel has also some. I went to the picture gallery with a man & his two sons. I have said "treeless country". I beg to correct this expression. The Hague is well wooded in fact one wood alone is 2 miles in extent, in the midst of which the King's palace is situated. I did not go inside the Palace & the Exterior is but a poor performance; but the winding drives through this vast wood of fine trees are nearly equal to the best in our own country. It is not an easy matter to get good photographs of places of note in Holland; I fancy there is a scarcity of photographers. One w^d^ suppose that most of the paintings w^d^ be, by means of photography, a source of wealth to the nation. I can only get two, and those from engravings, not from the originals. The Dutch, male & female, are ill-looking & ungainly; but impress you certainly with a strong idea of their simplicity & honesty. The costumes of the country people must date many centuries back, for I never saw anything under heaven that w^d^ suggest the woman's head dress, in our times. Instead of hair it seems to be covered

with a plate of silver or gold & the curls at the side which you observe are a pyramidal spiral of brass wire, like this, the whole surmounted with a cap. Now that the face is drawn, unconsciously I have made it exactly like yourself, for which you must forgive me – at the same time it proves to me that you are undeniably of Dutch origin. A Dutchman's foot is either after this pattern, in fact, the sabot – or this which is a rough imitation of a Wellington with short trousers. For almost the first time I feel myself handsome; with small feet & hands. The feeding is not at all good at the Hotel; the luxurious Inns of Switzerland are the growth of the requirements of fastidious English: until the English make this a highroad & frequent it constantly, the Dutch people will be satisfied with their poor fare, I must say they make an uncommon good fight of it when "vittle is up". They seem to me to eat with their knives, fingers, & elbows – all at once, & never ceasing. How they do smoke! The clergyman on his way to church

I fell in with two men in the mercantile line. They are well informed, scientific, unrefined but honest Englishmen, and after all, they are the finest race on earth, I think. In the evening we went to some gardens when there was open-air amusements, theatrical and others. The plays were in French, the songs German with one or two exceptions which were Dutch. They, of course, caricatured the Englishman, 'Anglais au bal', and made him out a disagreeable, drunken, noisy brute. It was so unlike that we laughed more than anyone else. If there had been any truth in the representation we should have felt more shame than mirth, ne'est ce pas?"

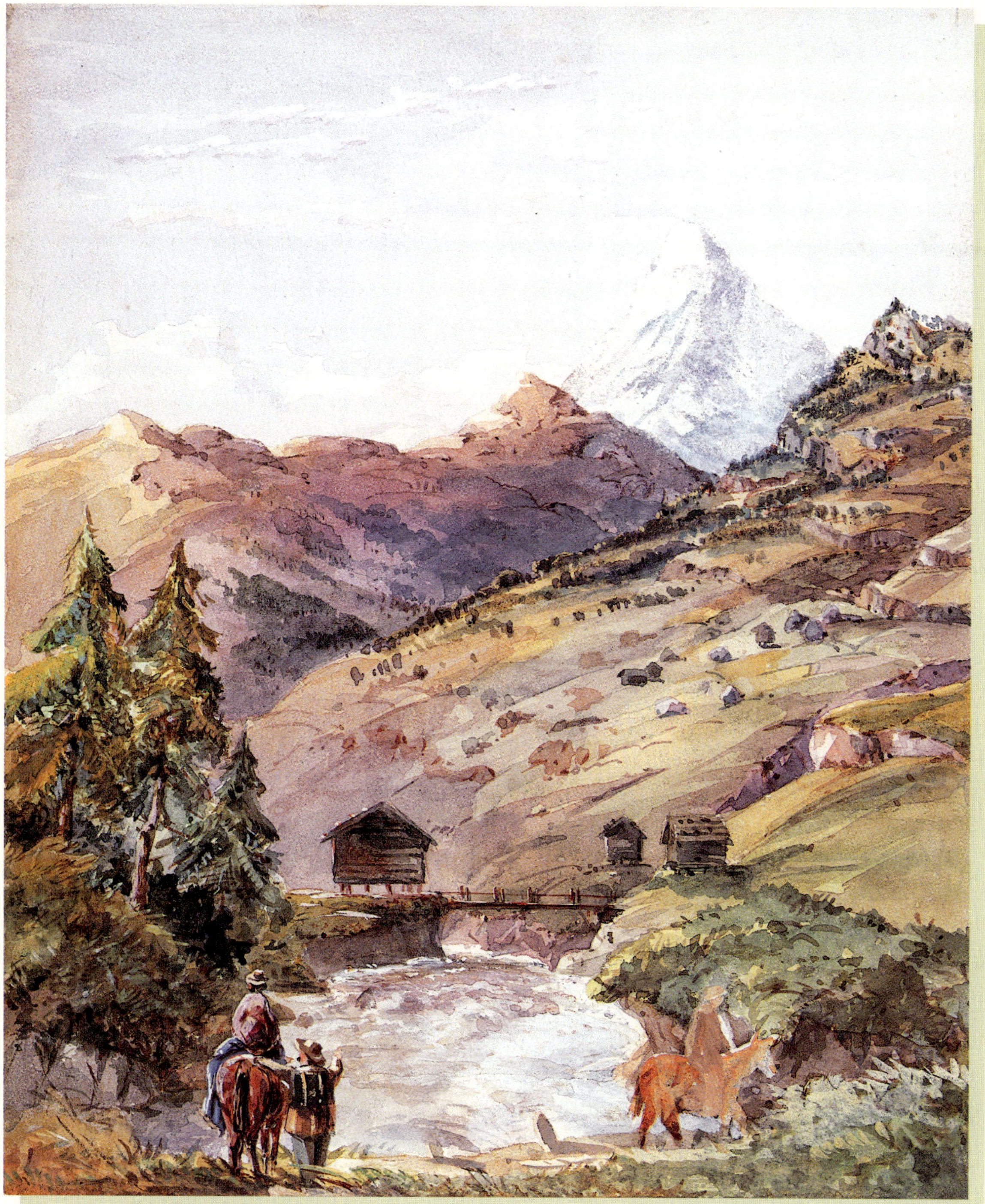

Above: a distant view of the Matterhorn captured by Hodge from the valley below. The painting is unfinished. Hodge was obviously on holiday abroad in 1863 as a pencilled inscription under this painting indicates.

Thomas Hodge on Holiday

Wednesday, July 31, Amsterdam

"If the picture gallery here were joined with that of The Hague, the collection would be perhaps the finest in Europe. As it is they are out of sight the best of the Dutch school, which as you know in their day was the most eminent.

The American travellers are thickening now. Gradually I hear more nasal noises at meals and catch phrases which remind me of that 'tarnation cute country service'."

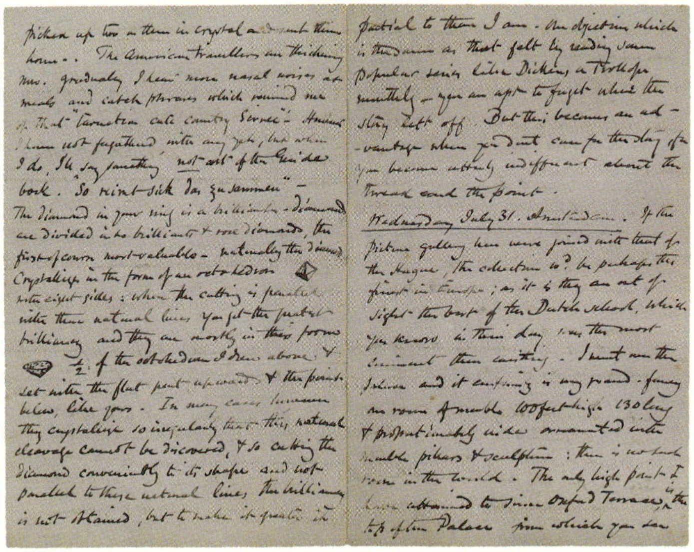

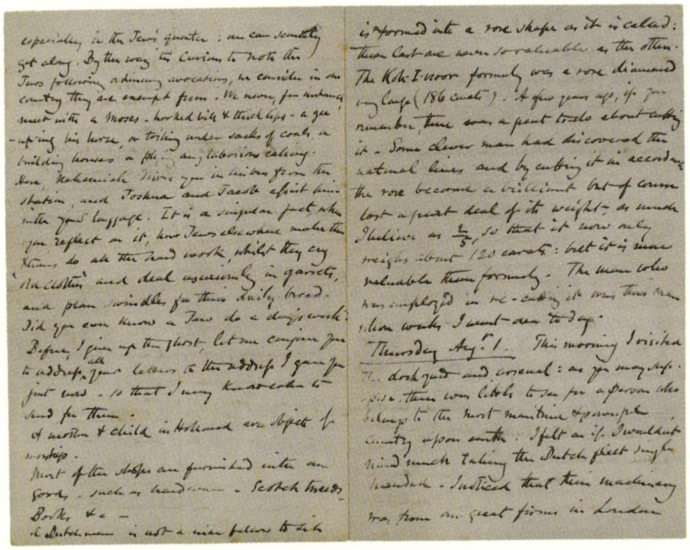

Thursday, August 1

"This morning I visited the dockyard and arsenal. As you may suppose there was little to see for a person who belongs to the most maritime and powerful country upon earth. I felt as if I wouldn't mind much taking the Dutch Fleet single handed. I noticed that their machinery was from our great firms in London and Manchester. Saw more galleries of paintings, and what astonished me most, some beautiful watercolours of modern Dutch artists and a few of our own, though they are not well represented. There is no country like our own for watercolours. The Old Society this year had one painting valued at £1,000. This is the largest price ever asked for a watercolour and marks more than by any other proof what a stride watercolours have made in the present day.

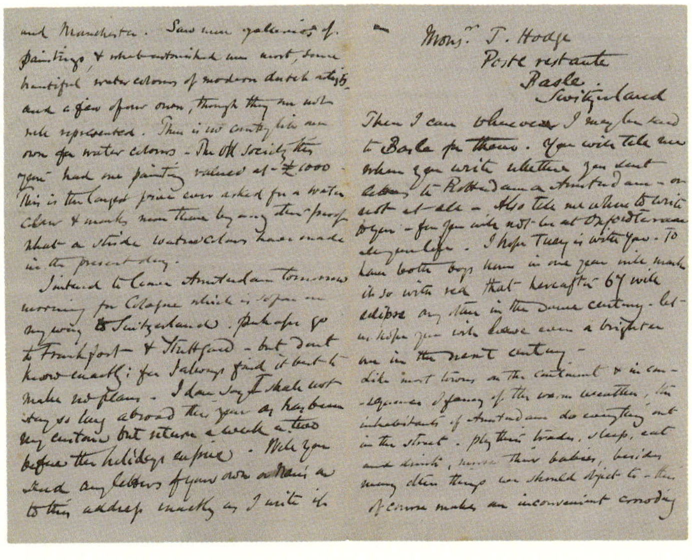

The inhabitants of Amsterdam do everything out in the street – ply their trades, sleep, eat and drink, nurse their babies, besides many other things we should object to. This, of course, makes an inconvenient crowding, especially in the Jews' quarter; one can scarcely get along. 'Tis curious to note the Jews following ordinary avocations we consider in our country they are exempt from. We never, for instance, meet with a Moses a geeing-up his horse or toiling under sacks of coals, a-building houses or plying any laborious calling. Here, Nehemiah drives you in his van from the station and Joskna and Jacob assist him with your luggage. It is a singular fact, when you reflect on it, how Jews elsewhere make the Xtians do all the hard work."

Saturday, August 3, 1867, Coblenz

"The Moselle joins the Rhine here – the blue Moselle, sparkling Moselle. By the same token I had some for dinner just now, not nearly so good as we get at home. An Englishman went up to the waiter on board the boat just now and I overheard this: 'I say, do you understand English?' 'Yas saire! A leettle.' 'Just now you brushed by this lady and struck her on the bonnet and moved off without apology. I have two minds about knocking your d..... head off as it is. Don't let anything like it happen again or I'll pitch you into the Rhine or the engineroom.' Aye! and he would too. Considering the waiter was the biggest man

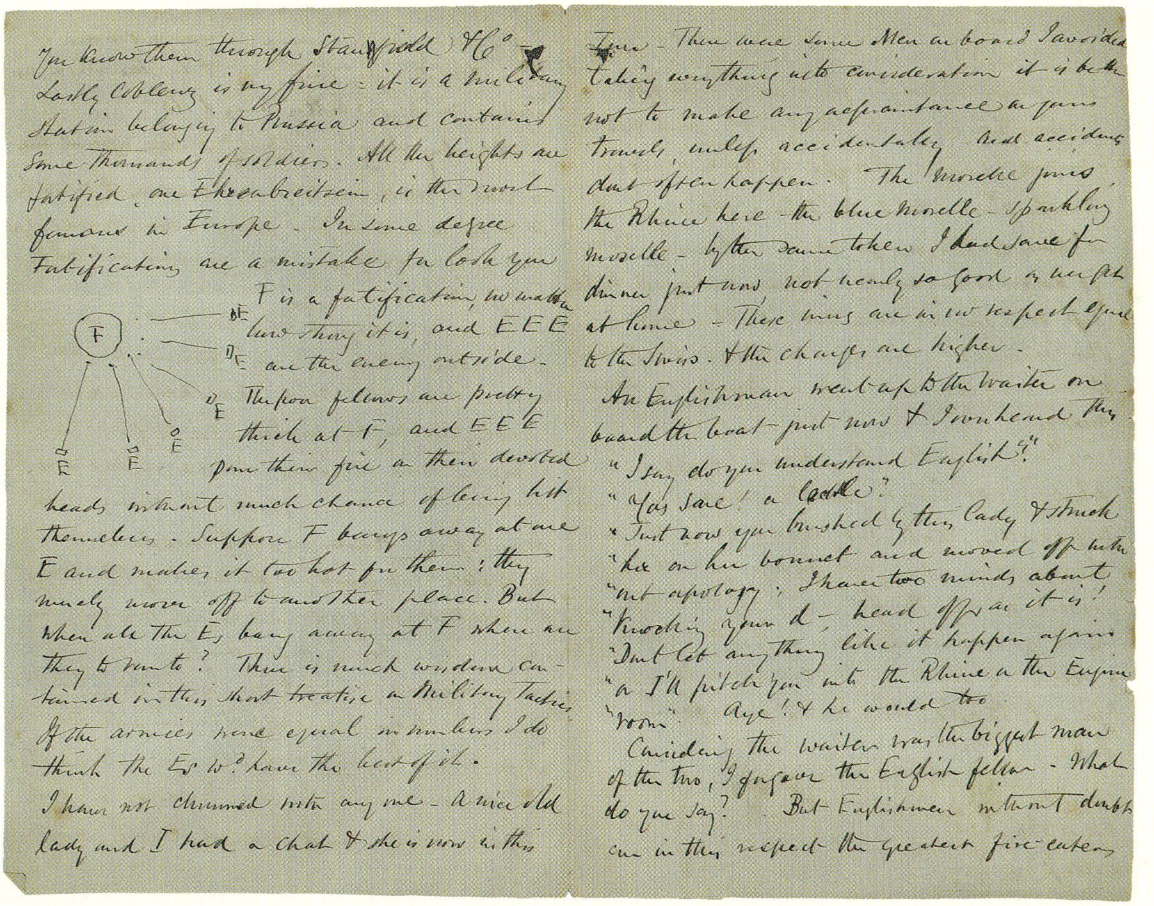

You know them through Stansfield & Co.
Lastly Coblenz is [illegible]: it is a military
Station belonging to Prussia and contains
some thousands of soldiers. All the heights are
fortified, one Ehrenbreitstein, is the most
famous in Europe. In some degree
Fortifications are a mistake for look you
F is a fortification, no matter
how strong it is, and EEE
are the enemy outside.
The poor fellows are pretty
thick at F, and EEE
pour their fire on their devoted
heads without much chance of being hit
themselves. Suppose F bangs away at one
E and makes it too hot for them: they
merely move off to another place. But
when all the Es bang away at F where are
they to run to? There is much wisdom con-
tained in this short treatise on Military Tactics.
If the armies were equal in numbers I do
think the Es wd. have the best of it.
I have not chummed with any one – a nice old
lady and I had a chat & she is now in this

Tour – There were some men on board I avoided
taking everything into consideration it is better
not to make any acquaintance on your
travels, unless accidentally. And accidents
don't often happen. The Moselle joins
the Rhine here – the blue Moselle – sparkling
Moselle – by the same token I had some for
dinner just now, not nearly so good as we get
at home – These wines are in no respect equal
to the Swiss. & the charges are higher.
An Englishman went up to the waiter on
board the boat just now & I overheard this
"I say do you understand English?"
"Yas saire! a leettle"
"Just now you brushed by this lady & struck
"her on her bonnet and moved off with-
"out apology; I have two minds about
"knocking your d— head off as it is!
"Don't let anything like it happen again
"or I'll pitch you into the Rhine or the Engine
"room" Aye! & he would too.
Considering the waiter was the biggest man
of the two, I forgave the English fellow – What
do you say? But Englishmen without doubt
are in this respect the greatest fire-eaters

of the two, I forgave the English fellow – what do you say? But Englishmen without doubt are in this respect the greatest fire-eaters, not braggarts, of any hemisphere. I admire it in others, although for myself I do not practice it the least, being rather of a submissive turn. This is the kind of bed I sleep in.

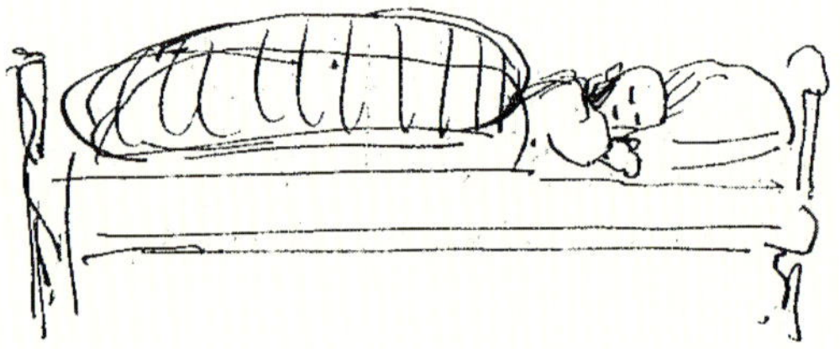

Monday, August 5, Mayence

"I was so annoyed yesterday, losing my portmanteau through the carelessness of the sailors, that I wasted all my time fuming until it turned up which it did late in the evening."

August 6, Mayence

"Yesterday was the pleasantest of all, the weather very fair, the scenery too, and the company agreeable. There were a father, mother, two girls and a son, English people; we fraternised until they left at some place to drink the waters. It is the favourite excuse now for the women to get abroad – bribe their doctors to recommend Weisbaden or Kissinger, and off they go.

The market place this morning early was filled with country people, principally women selling fruit, shoes and whatever the country produces.

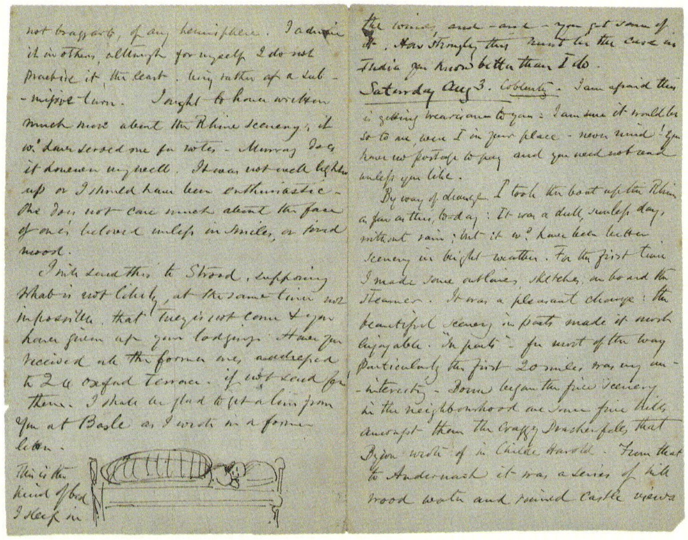

I wish to passion I had left my nose at home. The garlic and oil mixed is positively beastly. Crowds of people whose delight and daily food is this mixture emit a stench that it's no exaggeration to say has no parallel and would knock you down if you weren't in some degree prepared for it. It is a great drawback and there is no help except in saturating yourself in the same muck and acting on the offensive. Their

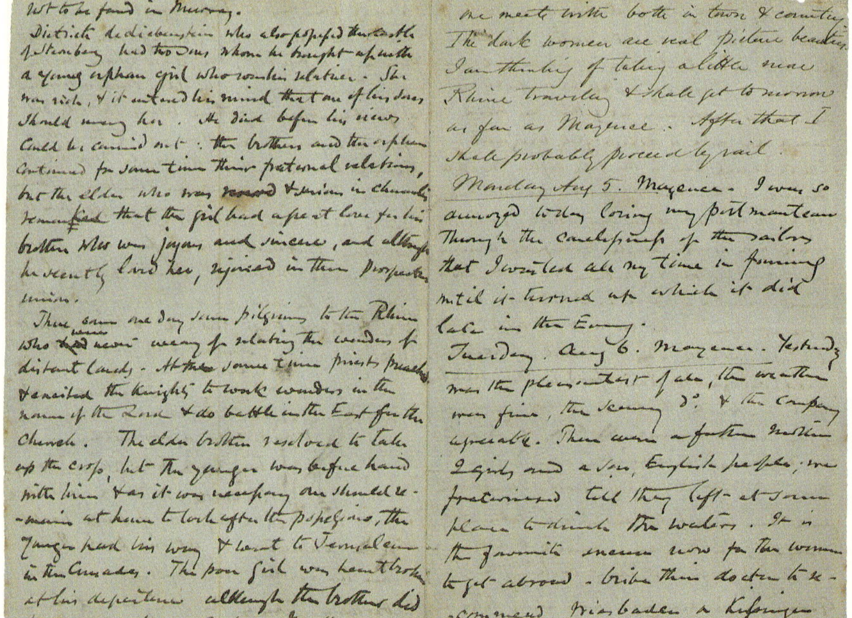

cooking in Germany is nasty; I shall never like it. I went from Frankfurt. The only difference I perceived between Frankfurt and the other German towns is that people dress a l'Anglais; they are our fashions run mad. There are a great many English here, but it is by no means confined to the English this extra-fashionable outburst. Here's a young lady (illustration), and the men are even worse than this – tight bags, low hats and a horsey smell. How everybody smokes, and in this climate nobody works."

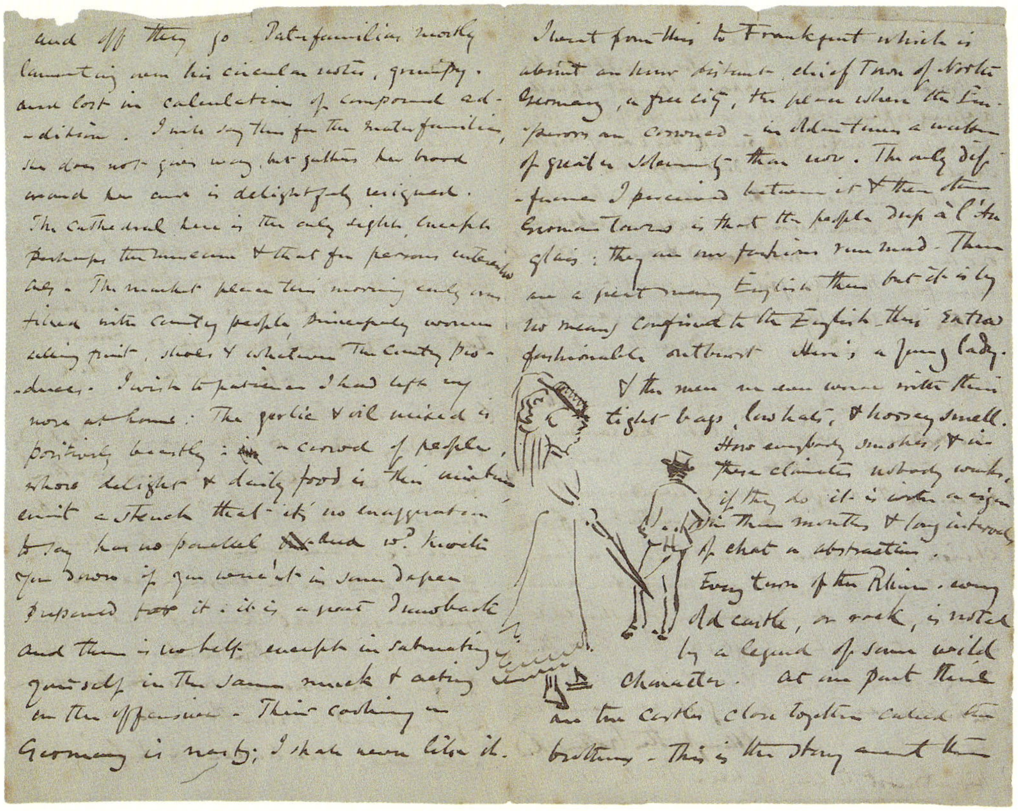

Friday, August 9, 1867, Schffhausen Falls

"I hear there is cholera in many parts of Switzerland, which is causing a little uneasiness to families who are travelling. At Zurich especially it is said to be raging."

Sunday, August 11, Chur

"We went to church today. A dark man, a cross between a Negro and a Jew, preached; it was not satisfactory. I went with two parsons who criticised him very severely and questioned the system of subjecting the Upper Classes of English church people to such ministration."

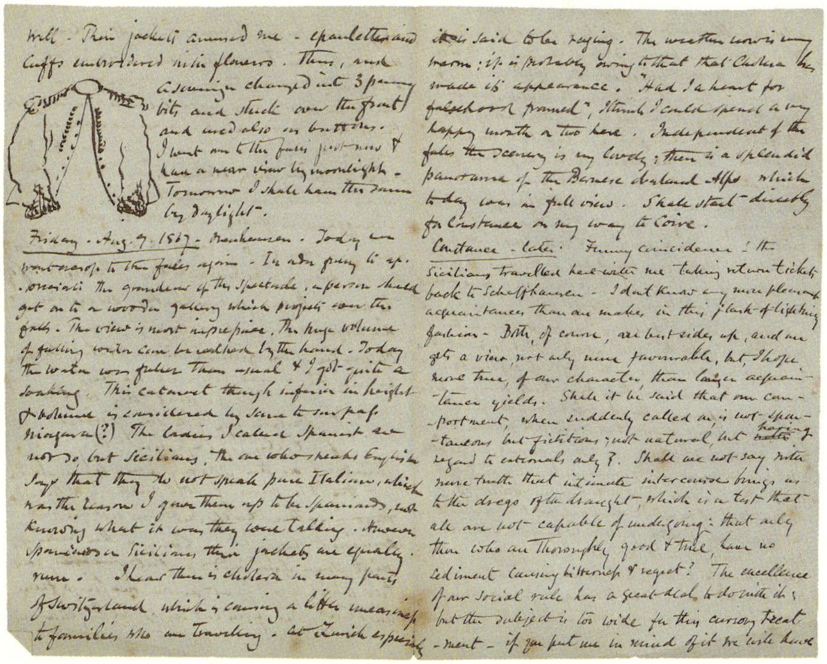

Thomas Hodge on Holiday

Monday 12

"Grouseshooting begins. Cheers! Have you the same hot weather we are suffering under? I can only go out under an umbrella, and am all over heat bumps. The scratching of them is some compensation for the annoyance. The proportion here is: 5 Americans, 3 German, 2 English, occasionally a French or Italian, but rare."

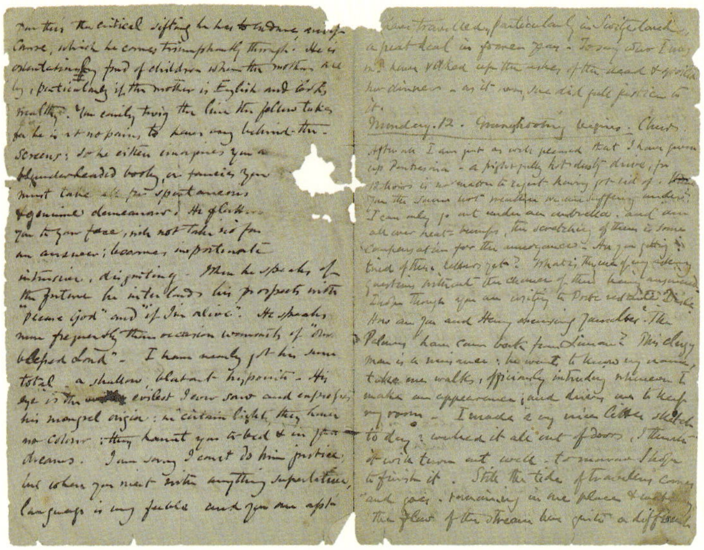

Tuesday 13, Coine

"The fruit looks tempting as you walk along the rich hill slopes, but like some of our acquaintances it is best to keep them at a distance. I shall now work gradually homewards. I do think if it were not for the Black Clergyman I should have remained here a day or two longer. He is a frightful toady, talks of all the great people he has met, and who, when he was in England, were of his congregation. The people of this country are a degraded race. The whole of this valley is full of cretinism and every person is more or less affected. Still there are degrees of badness, and the Rhine valley is not equal to the Rhone or Aosta valleys."

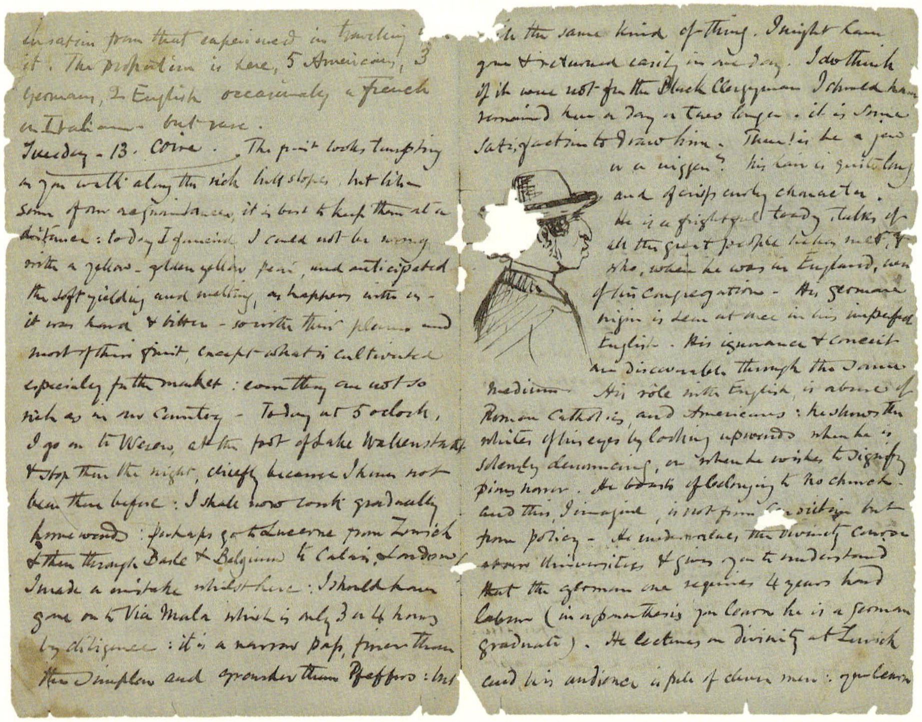

Wiren, Tuesday

"A place little known and visited, but I must say remarkably worth a visit. I find here none of the noble, none of the mighty; a few German fraus and their old men, a few German brides and their gudemen; but not an Englishman, not a Frenchman – no crinolines, no knickerbockers. Not a word of English is of any use here. The inn is primitive and not unlike the Swiss doll's houses we are acquainted with. A glorious moonlight; I am looking out now

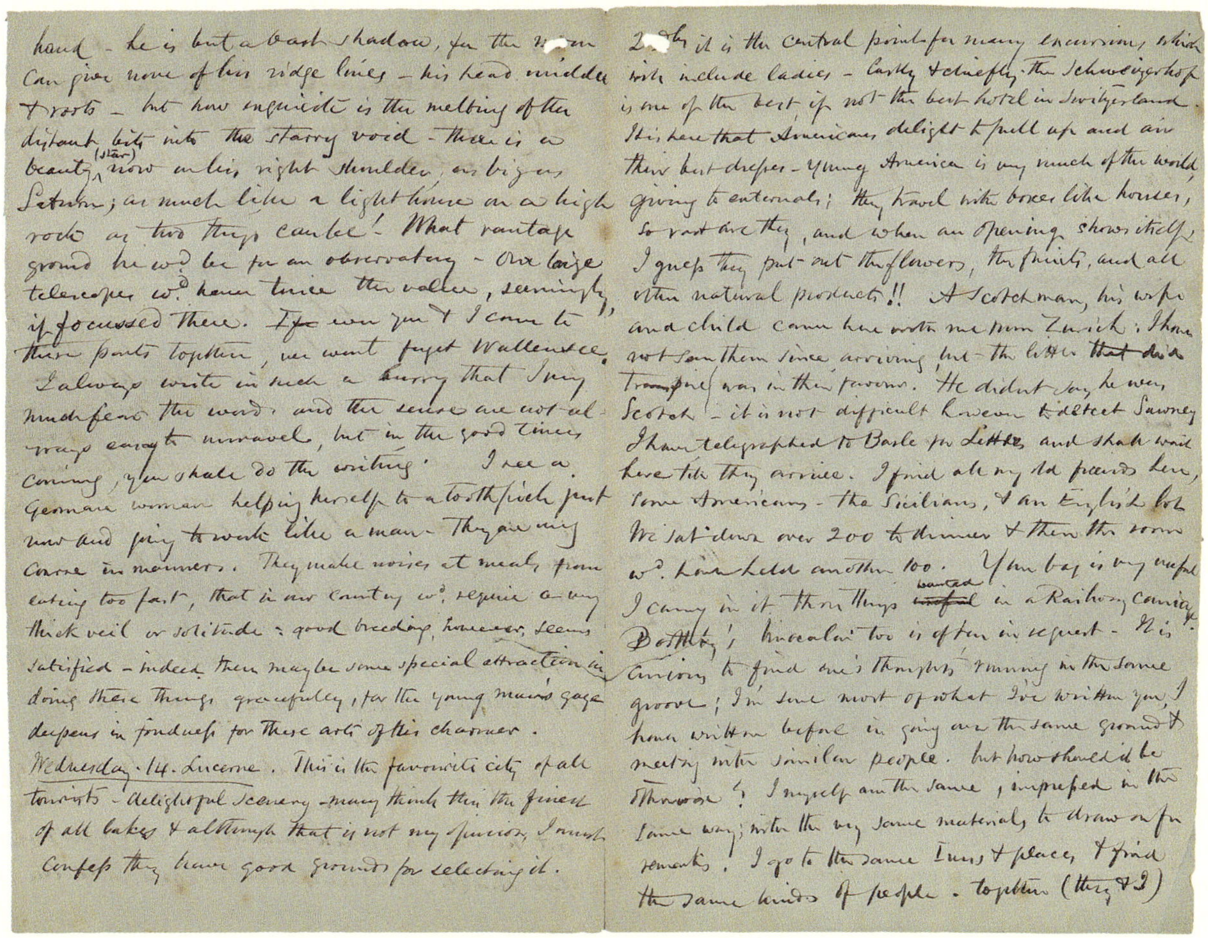

hand – he is but a vast shadow, for the moon can give none of his ridge lines – his head middle & roots – but how exquisite is the melting of the distant bits into the starry void – there is a beauty (star) now on his right shoulder, as big as Saturn; as much like a lighthouse on a high rock as two things can be! What vantage ground he w^d be for an observatory – One large telescope w^d. have twice the value, seemingly, if focussed there. If ever you & I come to these parts together, we won't forget Wallensee. I always write in such a hurry that I very much fear the words and the sense are not always easy to unravel, but in the good times coming, you shall do the writing. I see a German woman helping herself to a toothpick just now and going to work like a man. They are very coarse in manners. They make noises at meals from eating too fast, that in our country w^d. require a very thick veil or solitude: good breeding, however, seems satisfied – indeed there may be some special attraction in doing these things gracefully, for the young man's gaze deepens in fondness for these arts of his charmer.
Wednesday 14. Lucerne. This is the favourite city of all tourists – delightful scenery – many think this the finest of all lakes & although that is not my opinion, I must confess they have good grounds for selecting it.

2ndly it is the central point for many excursions, which will include ladies – Lastly & chiefly, the Schweizerhof is one of the best if not the best hotel in Switzerland. It is here that Americans delight to pull up and air their best dresses – Young America is very much of the world giving to externals; they travel with boxes like houses, so vast are they, and when an opening shows itself, I guess they put out the flowers, the fruits, and all other natural products!! A Scotchman, his wife and child came here with me from Zurich: I have not seen them since arriving but the letter ~~that did~~ transpired was in their favour. He didn't say he was Scotch – it is not difficult however to detect Sawney. I have telegraphed to Basle for Letters and shall wait here till they arrive. I find all my old friends here, some Americans – the Sicilians, & an English lady. We sat down over 200 to dinner & then the room w^d. have held another 100. Your bag is very useful I carry in it those things ~~useful~~ wanted in a Railway Carriage [illegible]; knowledge too is often in request – It is curious to find one's thoughts running in the same groove; I'm sure most of what I've written you, I have written before in going over the same ground & meeting with similar people. but how should it be otherwise? I myself am the same, impressed in the same way; with the very same materials to draw on for remarks! I go to the same Inns & places, & find the same kinds of people – together (they & I)

on a grand mountain of 10,000 feet, close enough meseems to be touched with the hand. I see a German woman helping herself to a toothpick just now and going to work like a man. They are very coarse in manners. They make noises at meals from eating too fast that in our country would require a very thick veil or solitude. Good breeding however seems satisfied – indeed there may be some special attraction in doing these things gracefully, for the young man's gaze deepens in fondness for these arts of his charmer."

Wednesday 14, Lucerne

"This is the favourite city of all tourists – delightful scenery, many think the finest of all lakes. Firstly it is the central point for many excursions which will include ladies. Lastly and chiefly, the Schweizerhof is one of the best, if not the best, hotels in Switzerland. It is here that Americans delight to pull up and air their best dresses. Young America is very much of the world, giving to externals. They travel with boxes like houses so vast are they, and when an opening shows itself, I guess they put out the flowers, the fruits and all the natural products!"

Thomas Hodge on Holiday

Thursday 15, Lucerne

"Whenever I have the chance, I take boat and saunter. This hot, blazing hot, day found me early with most of my garments doffed and a good deal of skin showing, paddling to and fro, watching the bathers, making a sketch, or thinking of nothing – all of which luxuries cost but 5d an hour. True relaxation consists more in doing nothing in a far-niente fashion than in amusements which very frequently (in hot weather especially) partake of the nature of hard work. By way of getting into a cool place, I went into the principal church just now and sat down in a corner, prepared to do a little worship if the spirit moved me. But the organ began to play and the choir to chant and I went off into the land of nod, quite overcome by the morning's pull on the lake. I am writing this in the reading room which is now pretty full of rank and fashion (American) waiting for dinner. The American men are the conventional type, mostly – having Abe Lincoln's head on their shoulders (illustration). I have not seen pret

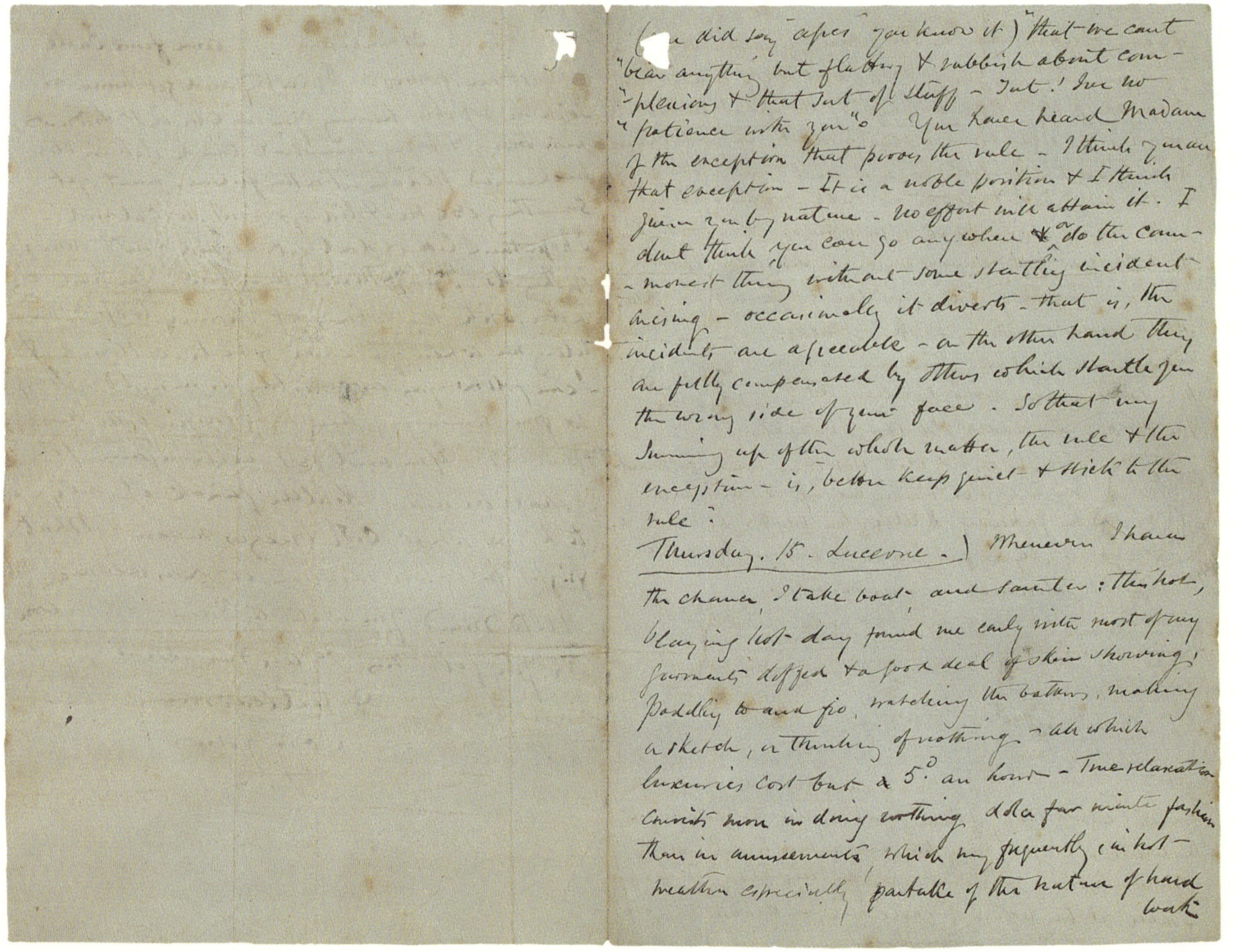

(... did say "after" you know it) "that we cant
"bear anything but flattery & rubbish about com-
"plexions & that sort of stuff – Tut! I've no
"patience with you". You have heard Madam
of the exception that proves the rule – I think you are
that exception – It is a noble position & I think
given you by nature – no effort will attain it. I
don't think you can go anywhere & or do the com-
-monest thing without some startling incident
arising – occasionally it diverts – that is, the
incidents are agreeable – on the other hand they
are fully compensated by others which startle you
the wrong side of your face. So that my
summing up of the whole matter, the rule & the
exception – is, better keep quiet & stick to the
rule.

Thursday. 15. Lucerne.) Whenever I have
the chance, I take boat and saunter: this hot,
blazing hot day found me early with most of my
garments doffed & a good deal of skin showing;
paddling to and fro, watching the bathers, making
a sketch, or thinking of nothing – all which
luxuries cost but a 5d an hour – True relaxation
consists more in doing nothing à la far niente fashion
than in amusements which very frequently (in hot
weather especially) partake of the nature of hard
work

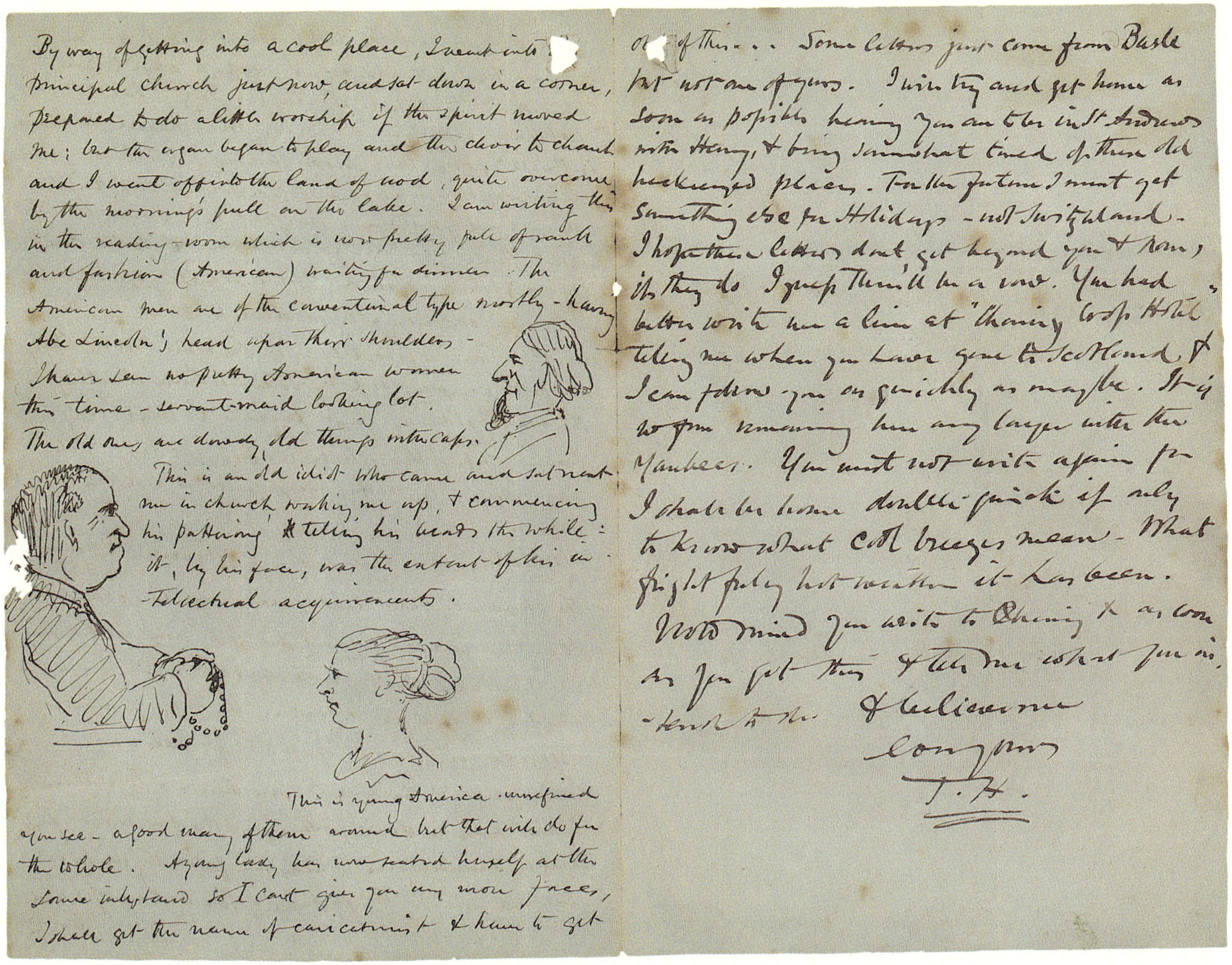

By way of getting into a cool place, I went into the principal church just now, and sat down in a corner, prepared to do a little worship if the spirit moved me; but the organ began to play and the choir to chant and I went off into the land of nod, quite overcome by the morning's pull on the lake. I am writing this in the reading-room which is now pretty full of rank and fashion (American) waiting for dinner. The American men are of the conventional type mostly - having Abe Lincoln's head upon their shoulders -
I have seen no pretty American women this time - servant-maid looking lot.
The old ones are dowdy old things with caps.

This is an old idiot who came and sat next me in church waking me up, & commencing his pattering & telling his beads the while: it, by his face, was the extent of his intellectual acquirements.

This is young America unrefined you see - a good many of them around but that will do for the whole. A young lady has now seated herself at the same inkstand so I can't give you any more faces, I shall get the name of caricaturist & have to get out of this... Some letters just come from Basle but not one of yours. I will try and get home as soon as possible hearing you are to be in St Andrews with Henry, & being somewhat tired of these old hackneyed places. For the future I must get something else for Holidays - not Switzerland - I hope these letters don't get beyond you & Tom; if they do I guess there'll be a row. You had better write me a line at "Charing Cross Hotel" telling me when you leave for Scotland & I can follow you as quickly as may be. It is no fun remaining here any longer with the Yankees. You must not write again for I shall be home double quick if only to know what cool breezes mean - What frightfully hot weather it has been.

Never mind you write to Charing X as soon as you get this & tell me what you do.
- [illegible] & believe me
Ever yours
T. H.

ty American women this time – a servant-maid looking lot. The old ones are dowdy old things with caps. This is young America (illustration of girl) – unrefined you see, a good many of them around, but that will do for the whole. A young lady has now seated herself at the same inkstand so I can't give you any more faces. I shall get the name of caricaturist.

I will try and get home as soon as possible, hearing that you are to be in St. Andrews and being somewhat tired of these old, hackneyed places. I must find something else for holidays – not Switzerland. I hope these letters don't get beyond you. If they do, I guess there'll be a row. It's no fun remaining here any longer with the Yankees. I shall be home double quick if only to know what cool breezes mean. What frightfully hot weather it has been."

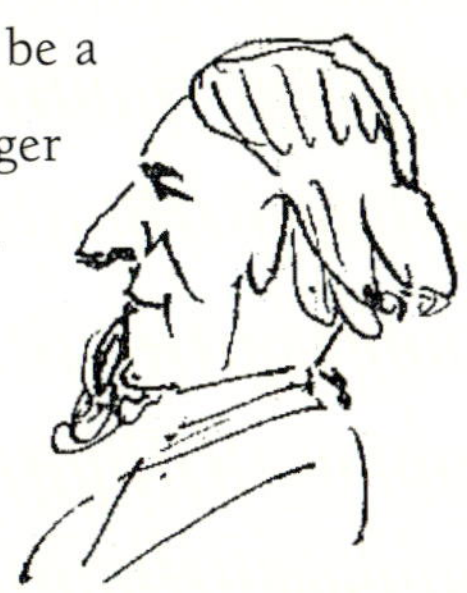

Thomas Hodge on Holiday

Thomas Hodge did not neglect his native British land in taking his vigorous holidays. Even his honeymoon was spent rowing in any handy lake. Here he and his young bride push away from the edge of Lake Windermere, a faded circular watercolour inspired by the accompanying photograph.

Right: Thomas Hodge on his honeymoon, rowing in the Lake District on Lake Windermere.

Below: the inspiration behind the circular honeymoon painting, a faded photograph of the honeymooners.

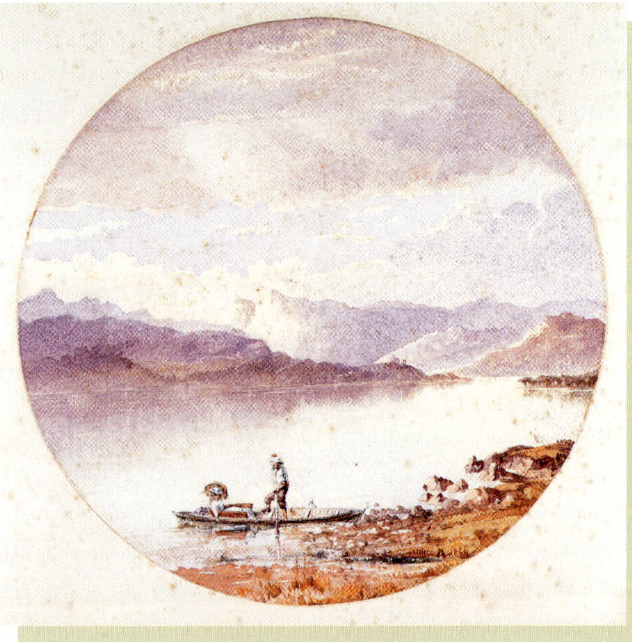

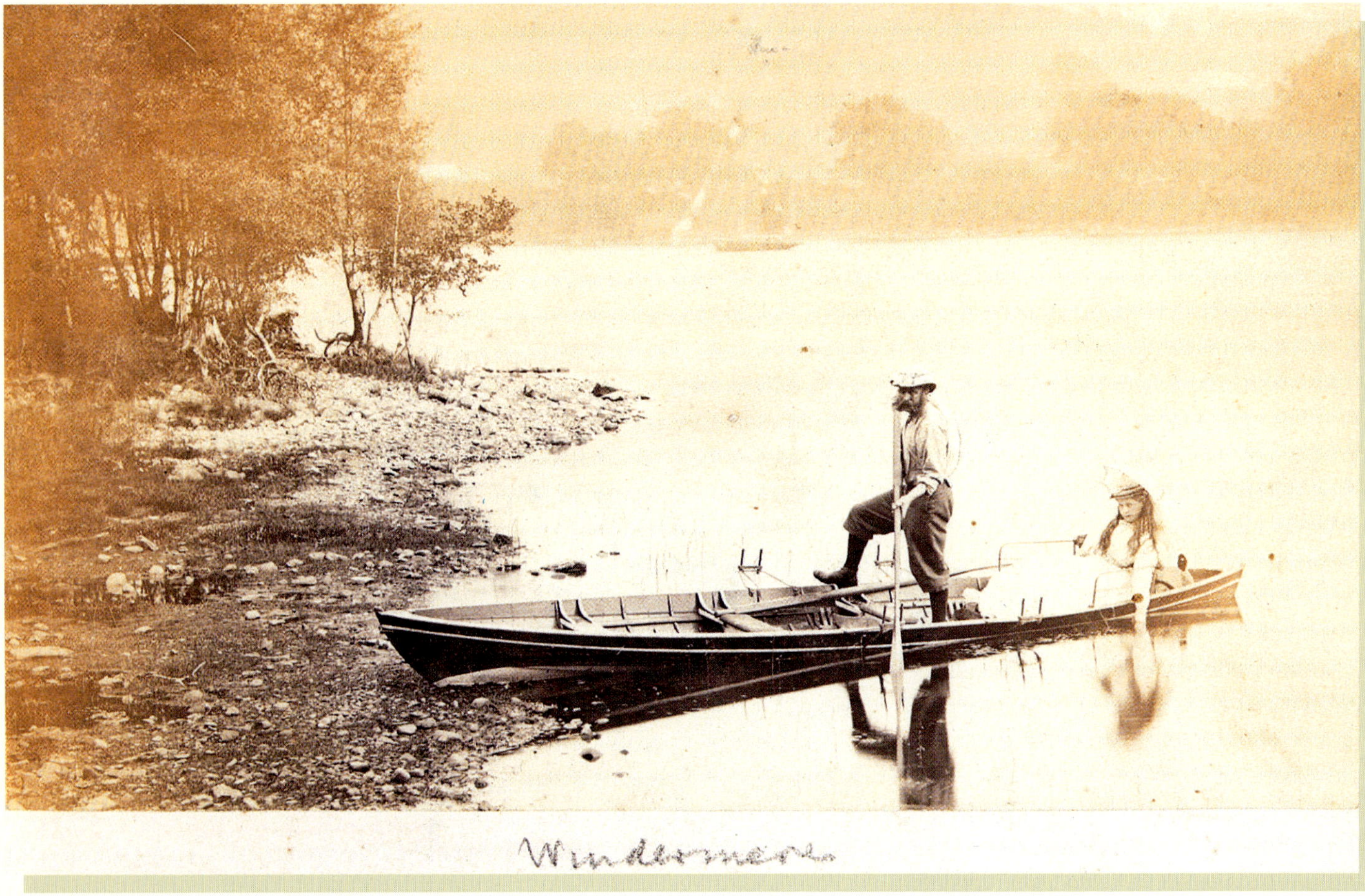

Dramatic and peaceful scenes caught the artist's eye as he strode through the Scottish glens. From powerful rock arrangements by roaring waterfalls to curious and venerable bridges – all were there to be painted.

Below: a dramatic sketch of a rock formation.

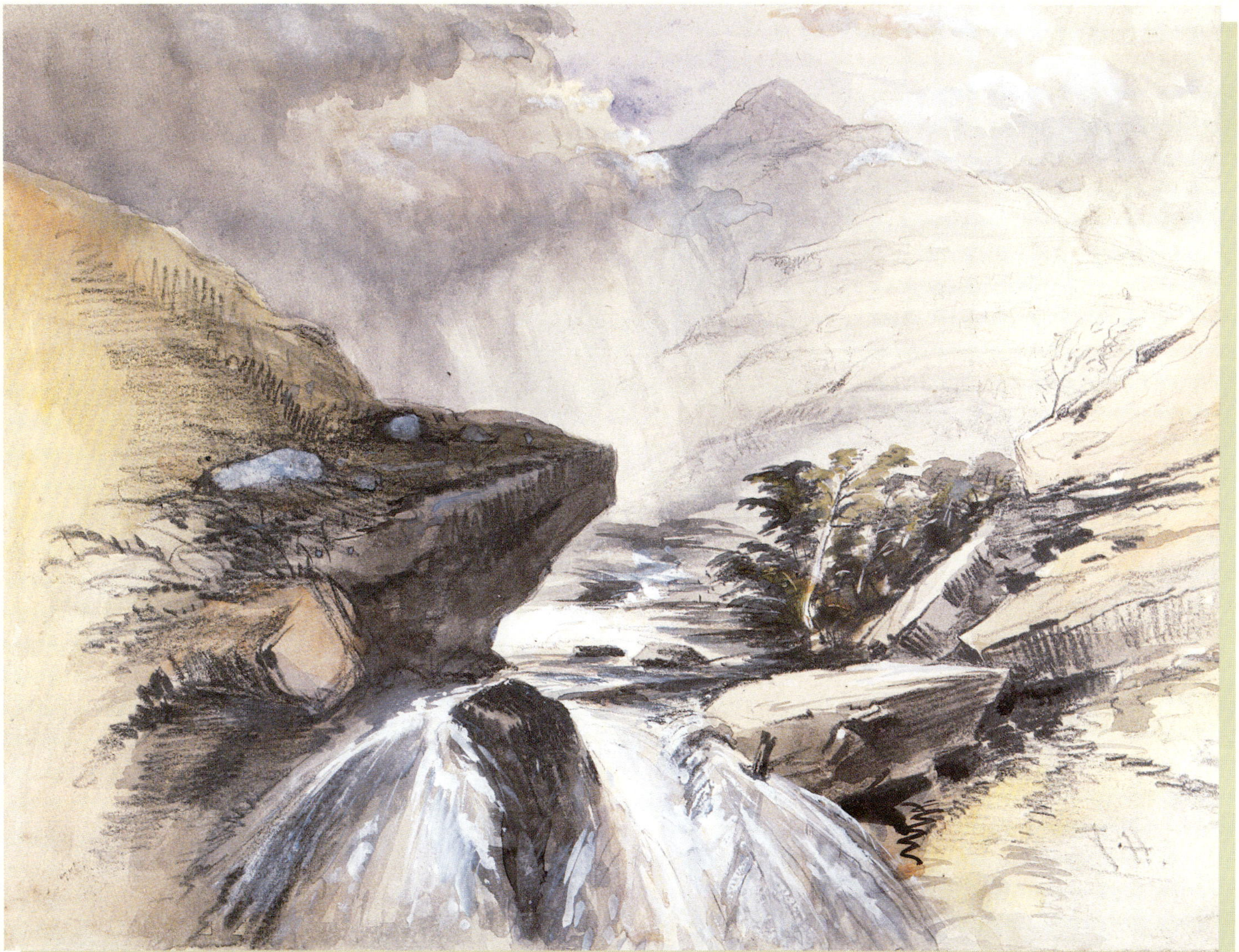

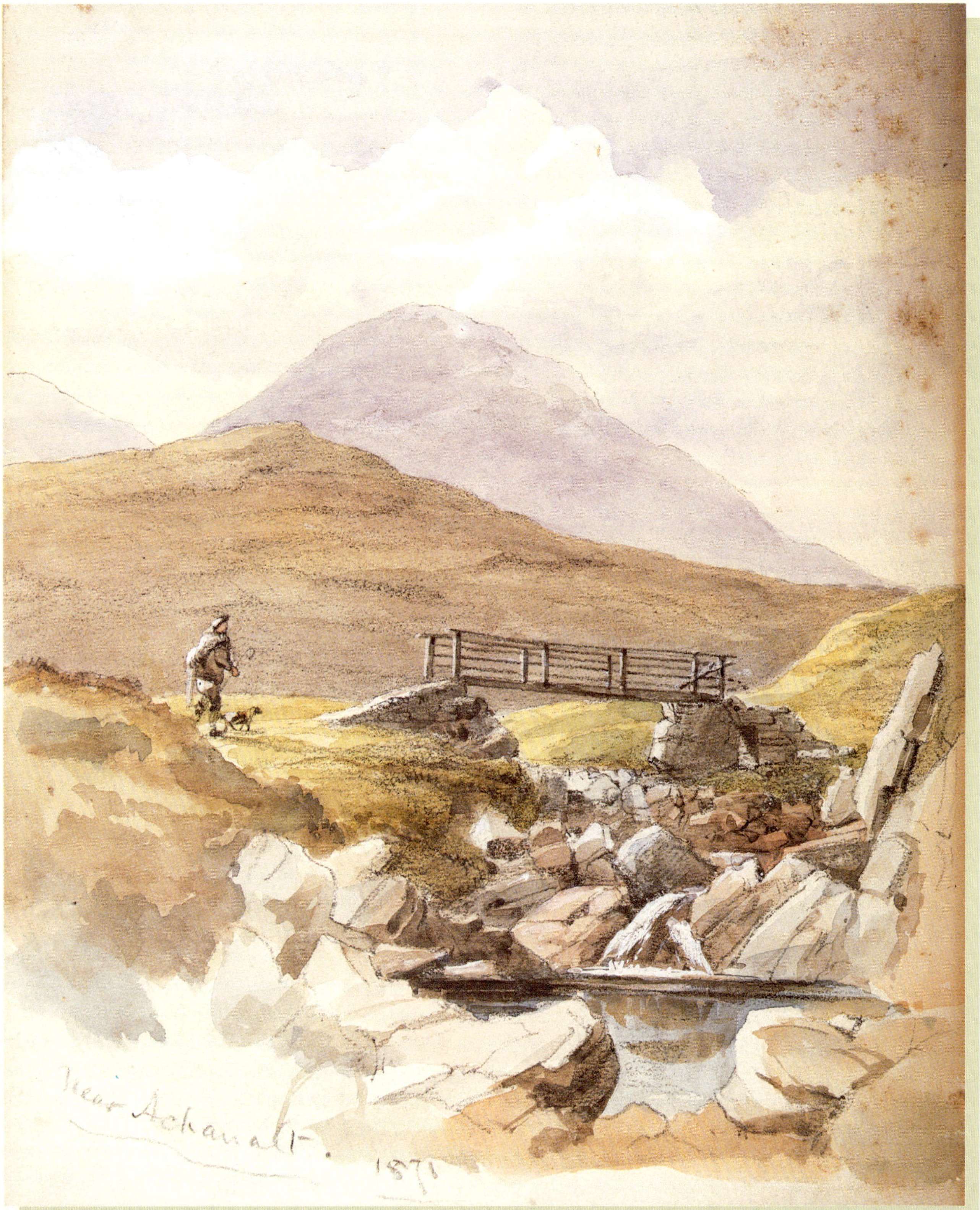
near Achanalt. 1871

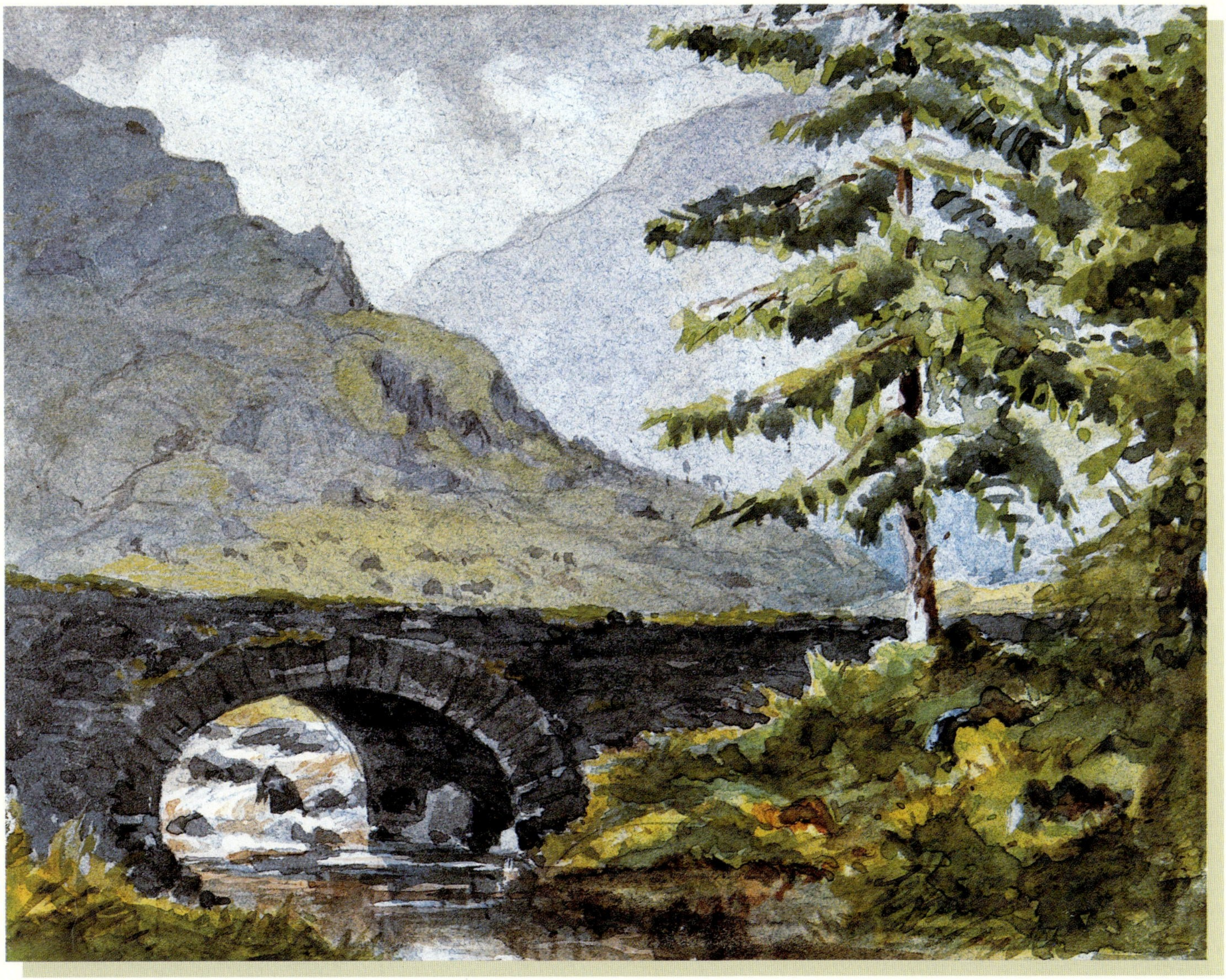

Left and above: Hodge's travelling was restricted as a married man in the 1870s. Fewer jaunts abroad, but renewed interest in the mountains and glens of Scotland. Ancient bridges were focal points in these surviving sketches rescued by his granddaughter, Norah Sheward.

Thomas Hodge on Holiday

Below and right: Thomas Hodge was also a noted angler and he recorded here two of his fishing trips to waters both foaming and still.

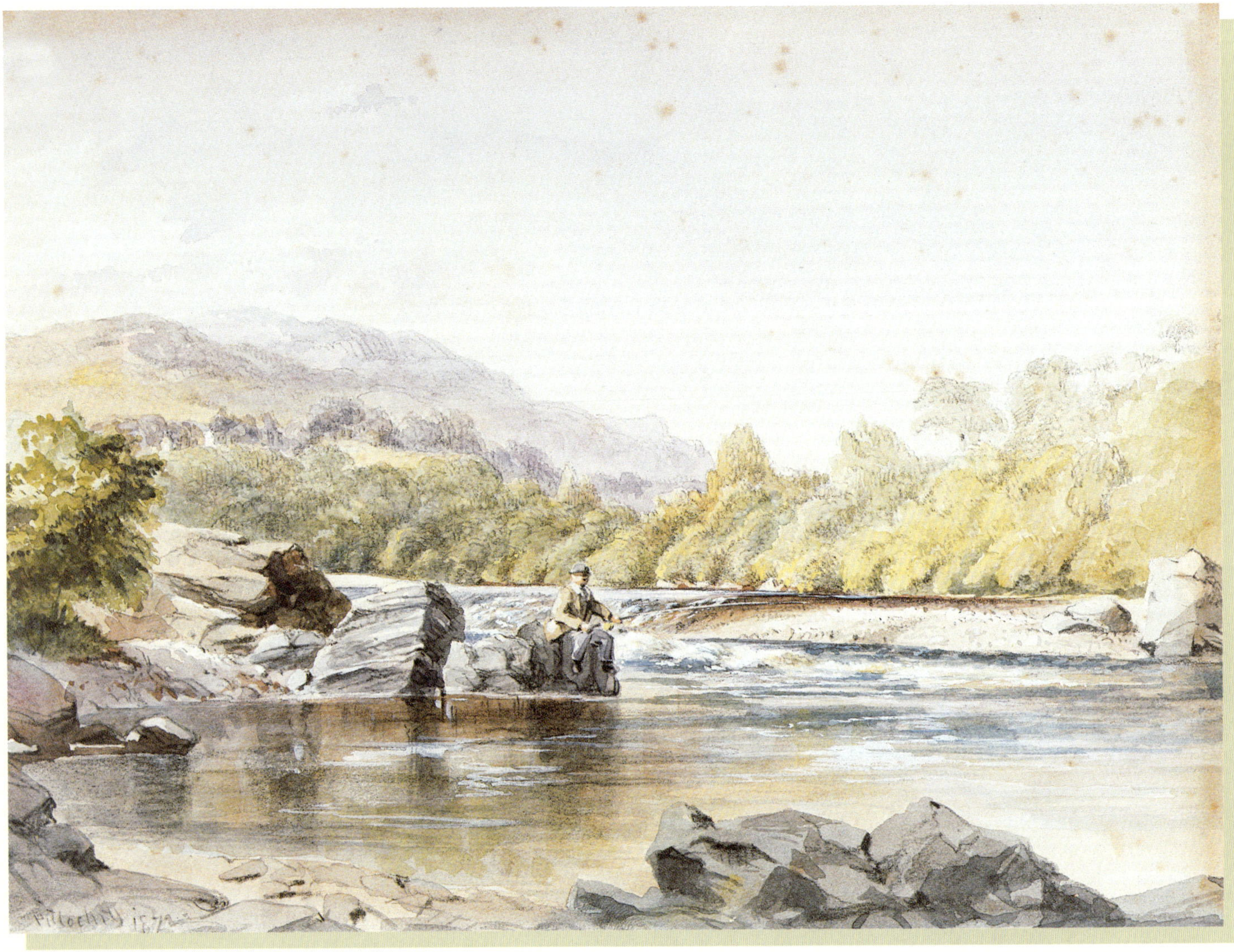

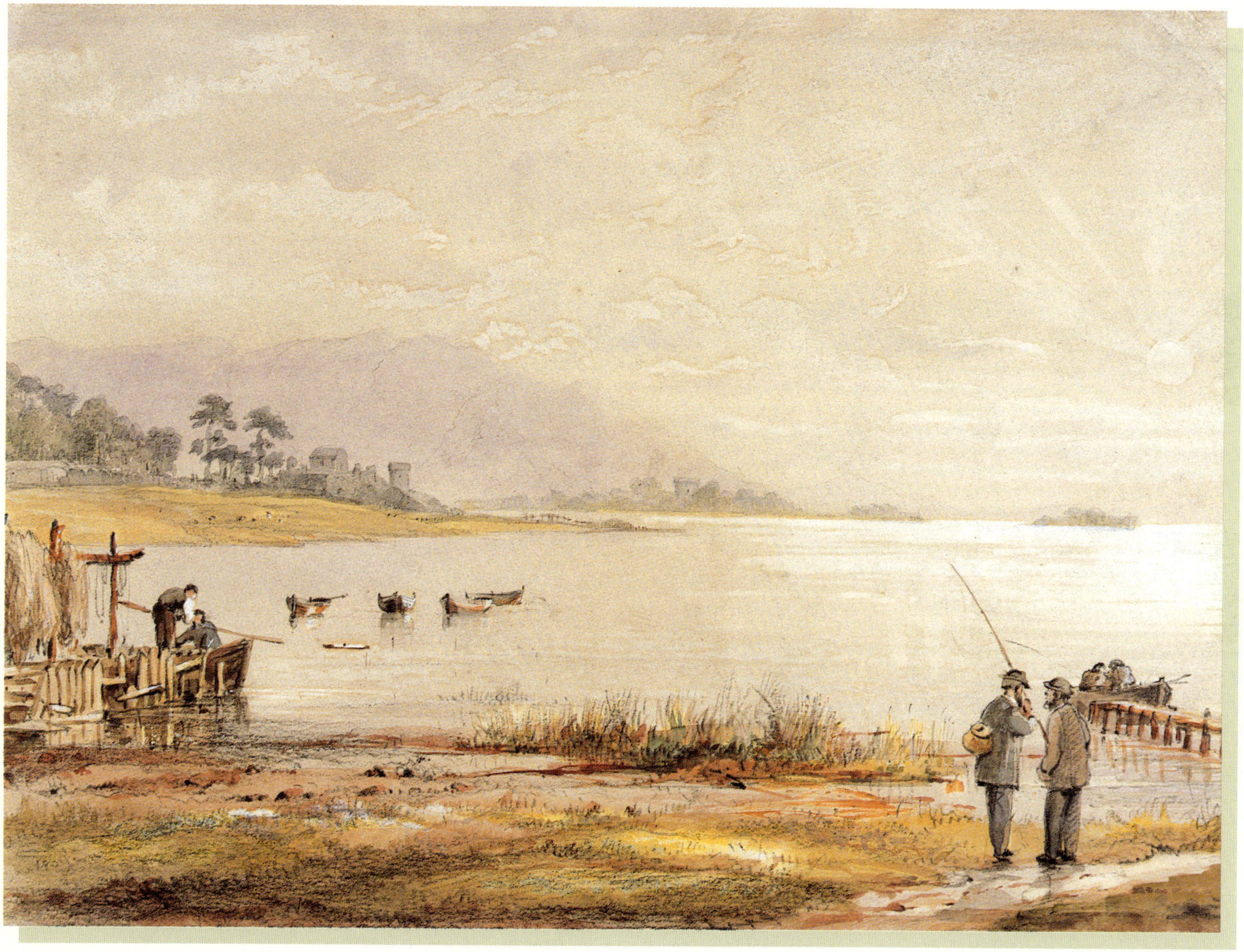

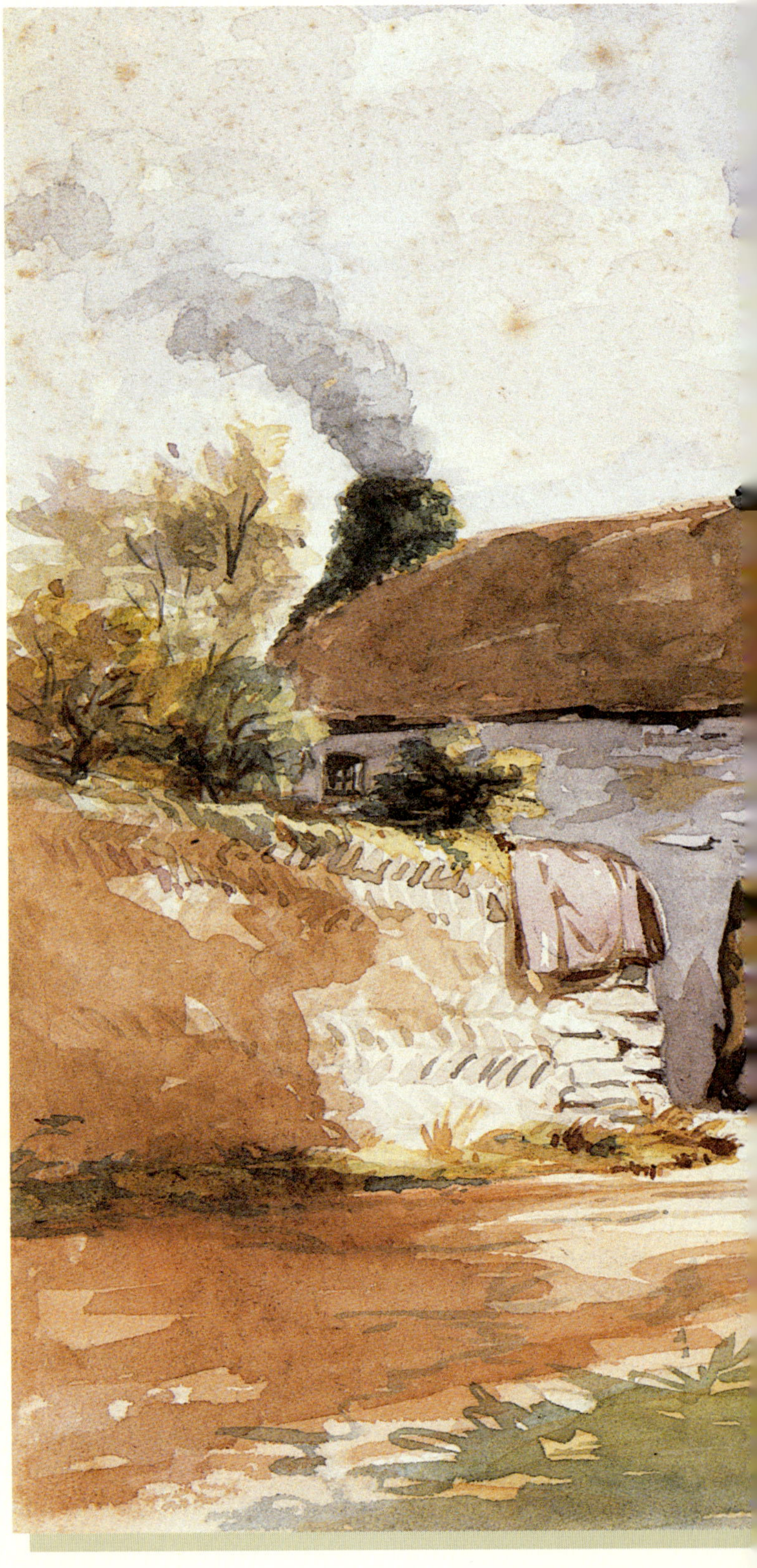

Right: a trip back home to Cornwall produced this anecdote of a sleepy hamlet with a farmer and his boy watching life go by in their traditional linen smocks.

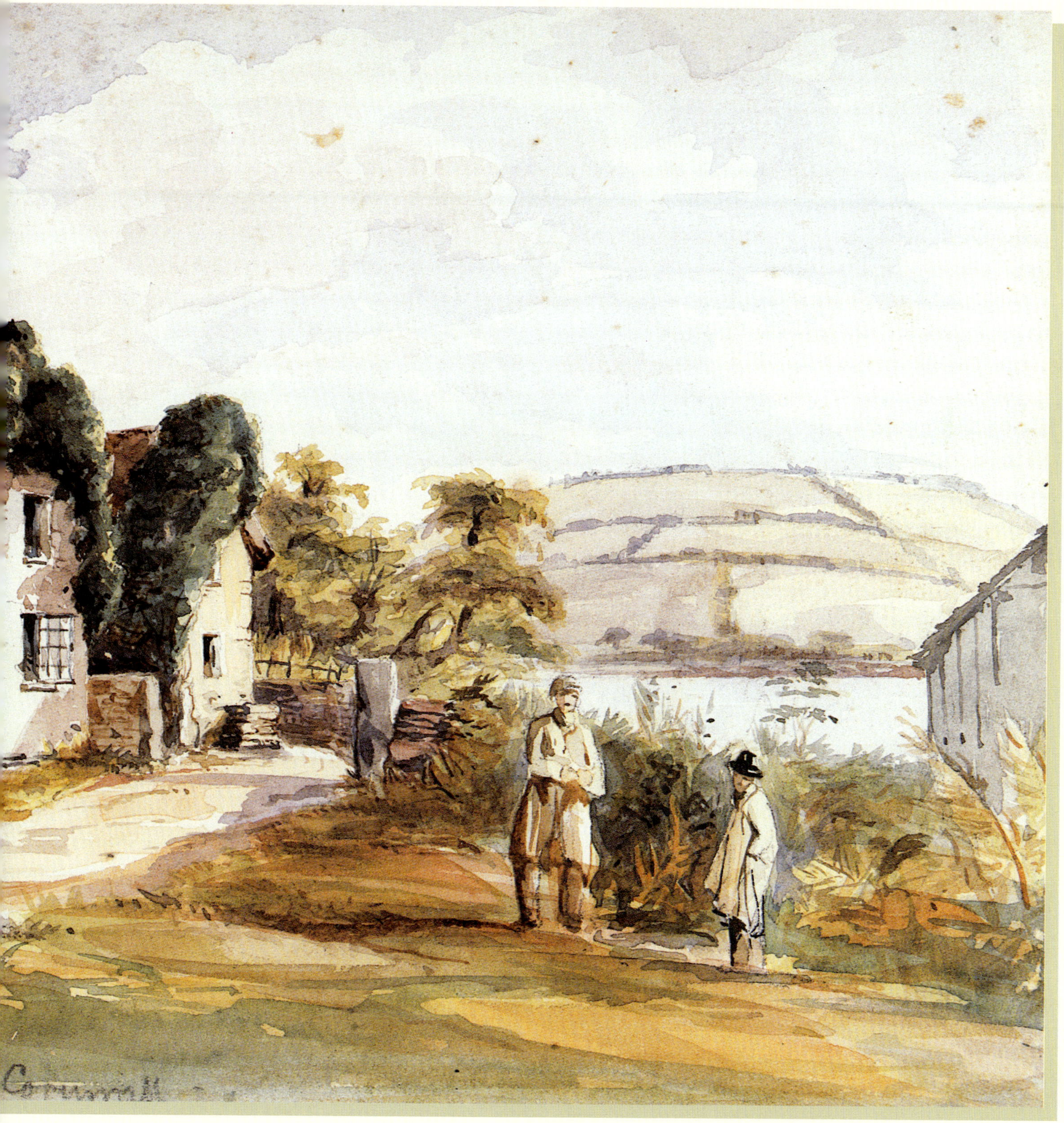
Cornwall

Bibliography, Acknowledgments, Index and the Author

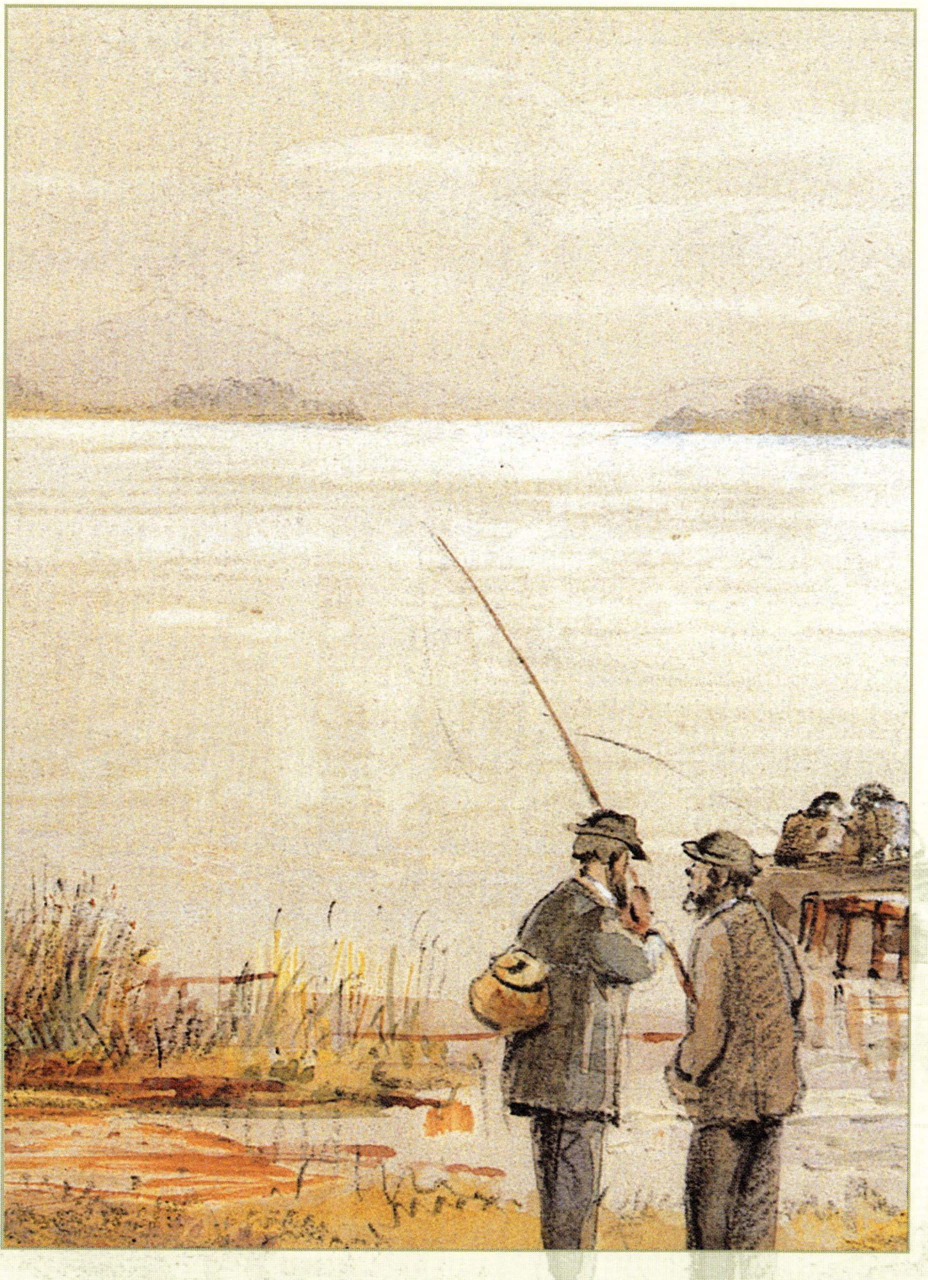

Bibliography

Golf, a Royal and Ancient Game
R and R Clark, Edinburgh 1875

A History of the Royal and Ancient Golf Club, St. Andrews 1754-1900.
Author: H. S. C. Everard
William Blackwood and Sons 1907

Badminton Library Golf
Author: Horace G. Hutchinson and other contributors, including illustrations by Thomas Hodge Longmans Green and Co., London, 1890

Famous Golf Links
Illustrations: Thomas Hodge and others
Longmans Green and Co., London, 1891

The Golf Book of East Lothian
Author: The Rev. John Kerr
Edinburgh 1896.

St. Andrews,
Author: Andrew Lang
Illustrations: Thomas Hodge
Longmans, London 1893

Golf
Author: W. T. Linskill
(part of the All England Series)
George Bell and Sons, London 1889

F. G. Tait, A Record
(his life, letters and golfing diary)
Author: John L. Low
J. Nisbet and Co. Ltd, London 1900

Life and Scientific Work of Peter Guthrie Tait, Cambridge
University Press 1911

Acknowledgments

Picture credits:

University of St. Andrews picture library, pages 12, 21, 76, 158

St. Andrews Preservation Society Museum, pages 35, 159, 141

Mathew Weinreb for Sports Design, pages 2, 11, 13, 14, 17, 18, 19, 26, 28, 29, 30, 32, 36, 37, 38, 39, 44, 45, 49, 50, 51, 55, 57, 59, 61, 64, 68, 69, 70, 71, 75, 78, 82, 83, 84, 85, 86, 87, 88, 89, 90, 91, 92, 93, 94, 95, 96, 97, 98, 99, 100, 101, 102, 103, 104, 105, 106, 107, 108, 109, 110, 111, 112, 113, 114, 115, 117, 118, 119, 121, 122, 123, 132-133, 136, 137 (top), 138, 139, 144, 145, 146, 147, 148, 149, 151, 153, 160, 161, 162, 163, 167, 168, 169, 170, 171, 173, 174-175, 178, 179, 180, 181, 198-199, 205, 213, 222-223, 224, 225, 226, 227, 228-229

Morton Olman and clients, pages 56, 79, 116, 157

Old Course Hotel, page 136

Royal & Ancient pages 53, 131

Badminton, pages 65, 184-185, 186-187, 188-189, 190-191, 192-193, 194-195

Sundry Thomas Hodge portraits: University of St. Andrews picture library and Weinreb for Sports Design.

Index

A

B

C

D

E

F

G

H

I

Index

R

S

T

U

W

The Author – Harry Langton

Harry Langton has been writing about sport since leaving Bridlington School, in East Yorkshire, at the end of the Second World War, aged fifteen. From a local weekly newspaper, he worked his way through provincial evening and daily newspapers to Fleet Street in the mid 1950s. Here he worked on the ***Daily Express*** working on colour productions and as a sports news editor until 1972, when he took early retirement.

The small sum of money which was paid to him on retirement helped to fund a sporting prints business he set up in Islington. At this time the Islington area of London was not noted so much for its famous and important residents and trendy cafes and shops as for violent muggings and vermin infestations. However, there was also a blossoming antiques market which enabled Harry to follow-up a lifetime's interest in the history of popular sport; buying and selling wondrous quantities of antiques and works of art associated with golf, cricket, football games, tennis and horse racing.

This area of the antiques business was very much at its infancy back in the 1970s, and Harry was not commonly regarded as a serious dealer at this time. After five or six years of being the antique world's joke, about half-a-dozen smart young men suddenly realised that his sporting antiques caper was worth copying and the sporting antiquities business began its steady boom. Harry, by this time, was established and had managed to find and buy the cream of sporting antiquities, helping to fill the Wimbledon Lawn Tennis Museum with fantastic items through its original patron, Thomas Todd. He began to see paintings and antiques occasionally bought by him for £1.00 and resold for £25.00, subsequently sold again at auction by others for many thousands of pounds as the sporting antiques market became a thriving international industry.

Harry's strength of character, sharp wit and inability to suffer fools gladly earned him the reputation of being "the rudest goddam shopkeeper in Europe" and as a result was on the unofficial list of London tourist attractions. In 1980, weary of this, he sold his little "gallery" and, for the first time in his rocky commercial career, he made a profit. This encouraged him to continue dealing in sporting antiques with an overwhelming partiality for football games, tennis and golf. Although not a fanatical golf player, he has always had a truffle-dog's nose for sniffing out golf pictures and has become respected for his knowledge in this area. When the first Thomas Hodge cache more or less fell into his lap in 1983, it was a glorious discovery. Unknown to him at the time the emergence of these wonderful works of art was to become the starting point of a relationship between Harry and Thomas Hodge which would last for at least the next 20 years. Possibly through journalistic instinct left over from a previous career Harry was inspired by the faded tiny water-colours to pursue Thomas Hodge and find out all he could on this ghostly character from the past, who we now know played an important roll in recording the most illustrious era of golfing history. The result is ***Thomas Hodge, the Golf Artist of St. Andrews***; undoubtedly an unfinished work as the works of Hodge illustrated in this book are without question the tip of an iceberg still undiscovered.

As well as golf and tennis, Harry hopes to produce another book on football. He wrote the text for the illustrated book of the ***F. I. F. A. Museum Collection*** in 1996, which is about to become the National Football Museum at Preston, for which Harry is the consultant. Since 1988 he and his wife Ann have produced many international exhibitions on the history of football games together with extensive catalogues and publications in Italy, France, Germany, the USA and the UK.

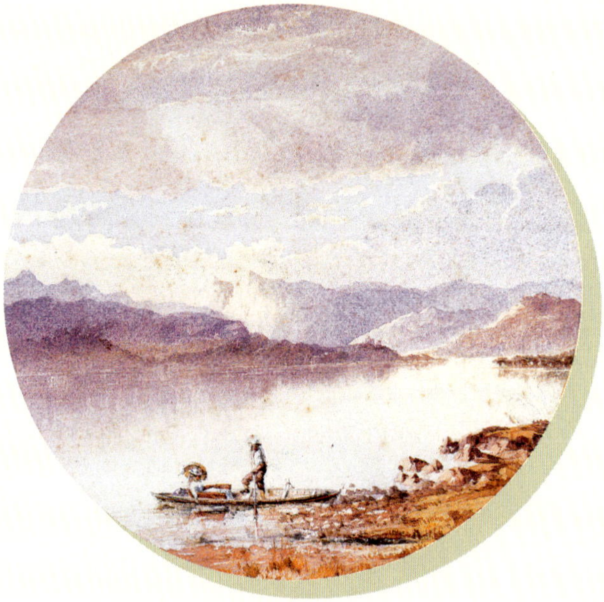

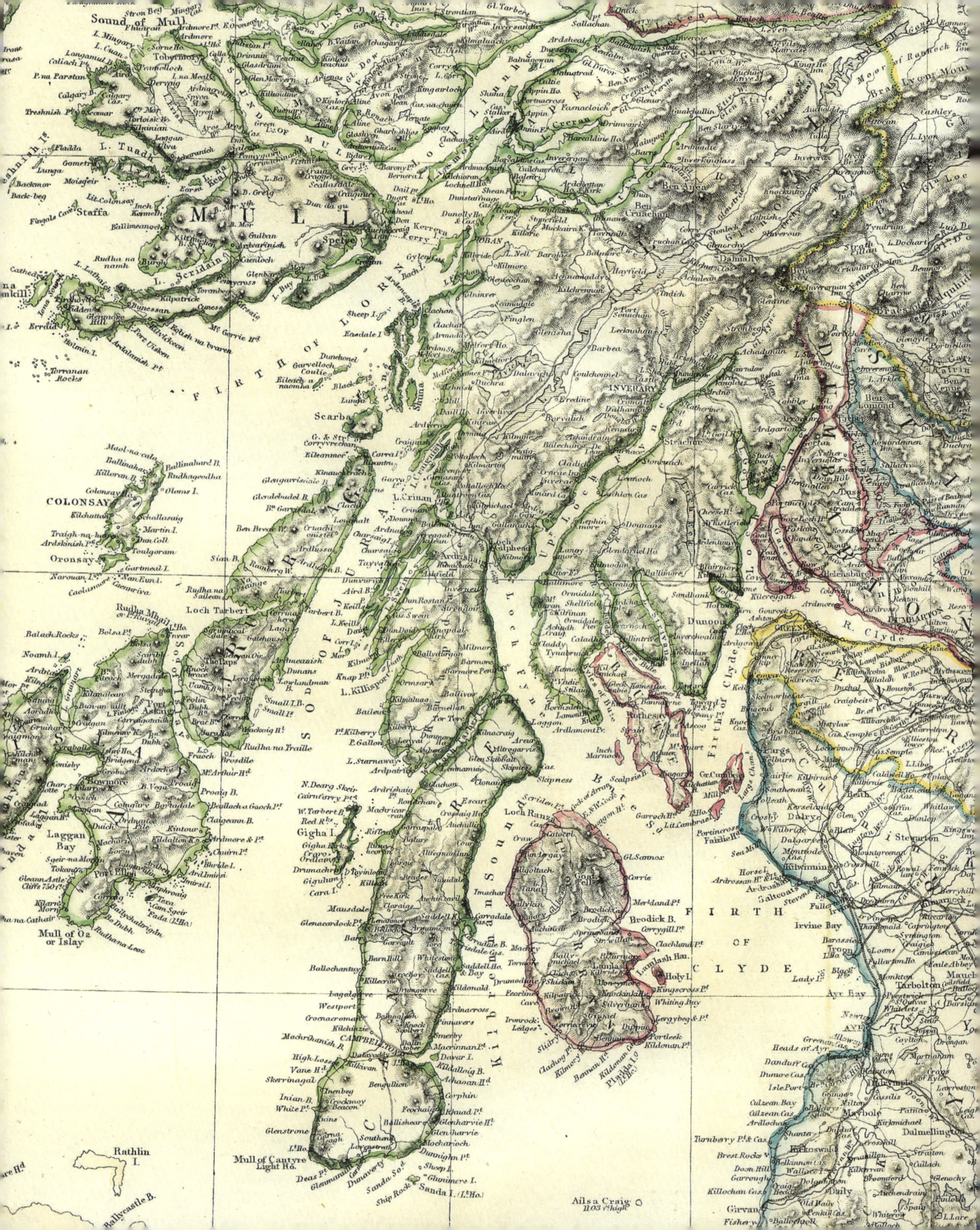

Sound of Mull
Tobermory
Staffa
MULL
L. Scridain
Iona
FIRTH OF LORN
OBAN
Kerrera
Easdale I.
Scarba
Lunga
Shuna
INVERARY
Dalmally
L. Lyon
COLONSAY
Oronsay
Loch Tarbert
Jura
The Paps
Laggan Bay
Bowmore
Port Ellen
Mull of Oa or Islay
Gigha I.
Cara I.
CAMPBELTOWN
Sanda I.
Mull of Cantyre Light Ho.
Rathlin I.
Ballycastle B.
Ailsa Craig 1103 ft. high
Loch Ranza
Brodick B.
Lamlash Har.
Holy I.
Kildonan Pt.
FIRTH OF CLYDE
Rothesay
Dunoon
Helensburgh
Greenock
Dumbarton
R. Clyde
Ben Lomond
Loch Fyne
Loch Crinan
Irvine Bay
Kilwinning
Ayr Bay
Heads of Ayr
Maybole
Girvan
Tarbolton
Kirkoswald
Dalmellington
Stewarton
Saltcoats
Ardrossan
Largs
Ben Cruachan
Ben Nevis
Appin
Lismore
Sallachan
Fingals Cave
Treshnish Pt.
Ulva
Inch Kenneth
Torranan Rocks
Skipness
Tarbert
Ardlamont Pt.
Toward Pt.
Loch Long